Graph Analysis
and Visualization

Graph Analysis *and* Visualization

DISCOVERING BUSINESS OPPORTUNITY IN LINKED DATA

Richard Brath | David Jonker

WILEY

Graph Analysis and Visualization: Discovering Business Opportunity in Linked Data

Published by
John Wiley & Sons, Inc.
10475 Crosspoint Boulevard
Indianapolis, IN 46256
www.wiley.com

Copyright © 2015 by John Wiley & Sons, Inc., Indianapolis, Indiana
Published simultaneously in Canada

ISBN: 978-1-118-84584-4
ISBN: 978-1-118-84569-1 (ebk)
ISBN: 978-1-118-84587-5 (ebk)

For general information on our other products and services please contact our Customer Care Department within the United States at (877) 762-2974, outside the United States at (317) 572-3993 or fax (317) 572-4002.

Wiley publishes in a variety of print and electronic formats and by print-on-demand. Some material included with standard print versions of this book may not be included in e-books or in print-on-demand. If this book refers to media such as a CD or DVD that is not included in the version you purchased, you may download this material at http://booksupport.wiley.com. For more information about Wiley products, visit www.wiley.com.

Library of Congress Control Number: 2014951021

To Bayla, Abe, and Hana, who provide endless support for all my endeavors.

—*Richard Brath*

To Heather, Micah, Avril, and Naomi for their love and sacrifice in the making of this book. To Chris White for his vision and support in striving to put better tools in the hands of those who need them most.

—*David Jonker*

ABOUT THE AUTHORS

Richard Brath is actively involved in the research, design, and development of data visualization and visual analytics for both research and commercial applications. His solutions range from rich interactive visualizations for mobile devices to large multi-touch, multi-screen installations, and web-based analytical visualizations for business applications. Brath's visualizations are used by hundreds of thousands of people every day in applications as diverse as trading, professional sports, and broadcast television.

David Jonker is a co-founder and Senior Partner of Uncharted (formerly Oculus Info Inc). He is a designer and developer of visual analytics tools and platforms for web-based, distributed, and mobile use. His work over the past two decades includes visualization systems and content for the NASDAQ MarketSite real-time broadcast center in Times Square. He is currently a lead on the DARPA XDATA program. Jonker and Brath are business partners and regular presenters and publishers of work in leading industry and research forums.

ABOUT THE TECHNICAL EDITORS

Scott Langevin is a director and research scientist at Uncharted, with more than 12 years of industry and academic experience. He holds a PhD in computer science from the University of South Carolina, and has a background in machine learning, service-oriented computing, and software engineering. Langevin's research interests are in probabilistic graphical modeling, large-scale visual analytics, and adaptive user interfaces.

Peter MacMurchy has been a professional software developer for more than 15 years, focusing on UX, UI, and interactive data-visualization tools. He acquired a keen interest in information visualization from coursework while studying computer graphics for his master of science degree in computer science at the University of Calgary. Since then, he's continued to develop visualization and interactive software for finance, film, energy, and other industries.

CREDITS

Executive Editor
Robert Elliott

Project Editor
Kevin Shafer

Technical Editors
Scott Langevin
Peter MacMurchy

Production Editor
Rebecca Anderson

Copy Editor
Kim Cofer

**Manager of Content Development
and Assembly**
Mary Beth Wakefield

Marketing Director
David Mayhew

Marketing Manager
Carrie Sherrill

**Professional Technology and
Strategy Director**
Barry Pruett

Business Manager
Amy Knies

Associate Publisher
Jim Minatel

Production Manager
Kathleen Wisor

Project Coordinator, Cover
Patrick Redmond

Compositor
Maureen Forys,
Happenstance Type-O-Rama

Proofreader
Kim Wimpsett

Indexer
Johnna VanHoose

Cover Designer
Wiley

Cover Image
Courtesy of David Jonker

CONTENTS

INTRODUCTION

This book is about the application of graph visualization and analysis for business. Graph applications are a unique and valuable resource for discovering actionable insights in data. In recent years, analysts inside some of the world's most innovative companies have been intensively exploring graph-based approaches to a gain deeper understanding of the dynamics of their businesses while discovering opportunities and strategies for improvement.

As the volume, variety, and velocity of available data has grown, so has the need for techniques and technology to make sense of it all. Organizations have become acutely aware of the limitations of simple dashboard-style charts. Dashboards are good at showing metrics and trends. They can inform you when areas of business are underperforming or outperforming others, but they cannot begin to tell you *why*, and understanding why is key to taking effective action.

The function of a graph is to represent links between things, revealing the structure and nature of relationships in data. Relationships are fundamental to the why and the how of things, which is one of the reasons graph analysis and visualization has so much potential for value.

Looking back on 20 years of our personal history designing and building new applications for business and intelligence analysts, the authors realize that graphs have played a role in many of those solutions. Today, several of our most significant research and software development efforts are, in essence, graph-based.

Despite the utility of graphs, however, little has been published about the application of graphs outside of the world of science, and even less has been published about graph design. With recent advancements in the capabilities of open source graph tools and libraries, graphs have become accessible to every business analyst, but access to knowledge of effective principles and techniques for graph analysis and visualization remains relatively limited. Our hope in writing this book is to help change that.

WHO THIS BOOK IS FOR

This book is for data scientists and analysts interested in applying graph analysis to decision-oriented problems. The examples provided are taken from the business world, but the principles and techniques used are highly relevant to government and non-profit problems as well.

No prior knowledge of graph theory or practice is required. A reader who is new to graph analysis should find it useful to read this book from start to finish. More experienced readers may choose to skip ahead to subjects of interest in Part 3, which expands in detail on specific analytic themes.

Some examples in this book include light programming, but the majority of sample applications use point-and-click tools. In both cases, a moderate level of technical aptitude will be required.

HOW THIS BOOK IS STRUCTURED

This book is composed of four parts. The first part represents a broad introduction to the subject of graphs. Subsequent parts are organized into progressively more specialized or advanced topics. Chapters 3 through 10 are written by Richard Brath, and the remaining chapters by David Jonker.

- **Part 1**—In the first part of the book, the authors provide an overview of graph applications in business and introduce various types of graphs, which are covered in more detail in Part 3.

- **Part 2**—The second part provides a comprehensive look at the major steps in the process of graph visualization and analysis.

- **Part 3**—The third part of this book is organized into distinct analytic themes and associated graph types and techniques.

- **Part 4**—The fourth part focuses on advanced topics representing areas of ongoing research, as well as fundamental design principles.

MATERIALS FOR DOWNLOAD

This book includes online data files, source code distributions, and graph visualization files to accompany the examples provided. These Supplemental Materials are organized by chapter. The software required to view or run these files is described in each of the chapter examples. Files for download include the following:

- **Data files**—Most data files are available in a generic format such as text (.txt) or comma-separated values (.csv), which can be read directly into graph software or otherwise used by programs. In some cases, there will be two files, one for nodes and one for edges (that is, the links between nodes). In other cases, graph data files will be provided in a graph-specific file format, such as .gdf or .graphml. These are formats that many graph tools import directly.

- **Excel files**—There are a few Excel spreadsheet examples identified by .xls or .xlsx file extensions. These require Microsoft Excel in order to run.

- **Graph visualization files**—Some examples also include graph visualization files such as .gephi or .cys. These are files associated with specific graph visualization software such as Gephi or Cytoscape, respectively. To view these files, you must first download the free graph visualization software package and install it. See the following section for details.

- **Python code**—Programming examples use the Python language. These programming files are identified by the extension .py. Python examples are done in version Python 3.*x* and require the download and installation of Python. See the following section for details.

- **HTML and JavaScript**—Examples using JavaScript are typically web pages containing JavaScript and identified as .html files. These files will run in a standard modern web browser such as the latest version of Chrome or Firefox.

Source code for the samples is available for download from the following website:

    www.wiley.com/go/GraphAnalysisVisualization

WHAT YOU NEED TO TRY THE EXAMPLES

A variety of tools are used in the book to process data and/or visualize data. In order to use the data files previously identified, the following software may be required:

- **Gephi**—The end-user point-and-click free software product Gephi (`https://gephi.github.io/`) is used for many of the graph visualization examples in the book. Many of the data files can be imported into Gephi for analysis and visualization. Chapter 7 of the book discusses some of Gephi's features, building on the basic graph analysis process described in Chapters 3 through 6.

- **Cytoscape**—Cytoscape (`www.cytoscape.org/index.html`) is another free end-user software tool for graph analysis used in many examples in the book. Many of the data files can also be imported in Cytoscape for analysis and visualization. Chapter 7 discusses some of Cytoscape's features and also outlines some of the differences between Gephi and Cytoscape.

- **yEd**—yEd (`www.yworks.com/en/products/yfiles/yed/`) is an alternative free end-user point-and-click software product made by yWorks for graph analysis and visualization.

- **Excel**—Microsoft Excel (`http://products.office.com/en-us/excel`) spreadsheets are used in several examples. Excel is not free, but most readers will already have a copy, and Microsoft does allow download for time-limited evaluations. Several examples also use the NodeXL plug-in for Excel.

- **NodeXL**—Excel allows developers to create plug-ins that access and enhance Excel's functionality. NodelXL (`http://nodexl.codeplex.com/`) provides graph functionality for social network data retrieval, as well as graph analysis and visualization.

- **Python**—For programmatic manipulation of data, the Python 3 (`https://www.python.org/`) programming language is used in some examples. Python is freely available.

- **A modern browser**—While any modern web browser should be capable of viewing the JavaScript/HTML examples, Chrome (`https://www.google.com/intl/en_us/chrome/browser/`) was the browser used by the authors.

- **D3.js**—D3 (http://d3js.org/) is a JavaScript library used to create a variety of interactive data visualizations in a browser, and used, for example, in Chapter 8.

- **Aperture JS**—Aperture JS (http://aperturejs.com/) is a JavaScript framework library used in some of the examples in the later part of the book, for example, in Chapter 12.

- **Titan**—A Titan (http://thinkaurelius.github.io/titan/) graph database is used for several big data examples found in Chapter 14.

To use these software libraries and tools, you will need to download them yourself and install them, with the exception of the JavaScript libraries, D3.js, and Aperture JS. These are packaged with the examples for download from the companion website specified earlier.

CAVEATS

The chapters in this book use case study examples to illustrate various applications and forms of graphs and how to use them yourself. Illustrations make use of real tools and real data where possible. There are caveats to keep in mind with both of these.

While the authors have used open source tools that are freely available to anyone, many of these tools are still works in progress and, as such, lack some of the polish and robustness you might expect of a finished product. Expect that a little extra patience will, at times, be the price of being an early adopter. Another aspect of documenting work-in-progress tools is that they are more likely to change. Use the tool-related steps in this book as general guidelines to a process. If the user interface does not seem to be exactly as described, find the matching items in the newer interface. If you cannot find them yourself, a quick Internet search is usually enough to find what you're looking for.

The other caveat to keep in mind is about the data being analyzed. A book like this depends on public data sets. While immense strides have been made in recent years in opening up corporate data sets to the public for advancing the art and science of analytics and visualization, private data sets are invariably larger and richer. While the analysis in this book is true to the data used, in many cases the data is only a proxy or sample of what can be found inside a corporate network. Treat the analysis as a template approach that can be reproduced with access to all of your data.

CONVENTIONS

To help you get the most from the text and keep track of what's happening, a number of conventions have been used throughout the book.

> **WARNING**
>
> Warnings hold important, not-to-be-forgotten information that is directly relevant to the surrounding text.

> **NOTE**
>
> Notes indicate notes, tips, hints, tricks, or and asides to the current discussion.

> **TIP**
>
> Tips are hints or tricks to help you master the information being discussed.

As for styles in the text:

- New terms and important words are *highlighted* when introduced.
- Keyboard strokes are shown like this: Ctrl+A.
- Filenames, URLs, and code within the text are shown like so: `persistence.properties`.

Graph Analysis *and* Visualization

## PART 1

Overview

The first part of this book introduces the subject of graphs and provides answers to two essential questions: why are graphs valuable to business analysis, and what kinds of opportunities can they be used to discover? A wide spectrum of techniques and applications are discussed, drawing from history and real-world experience. Case examples are used to illustrate value.

Before proceeding to a discussion of the process of graph analysis in the second part of the book, this overview provides you with a sense of just how many types of graphs there are and how many areas of potential value exist, even within a single business. References serve as a guide to subsequent chapters in the third part of the book, which cover each class of graph in more detail and step through tutorial style applications of graph analysis.

Table P1-1 describes the topics of Chapters 1 and 2.

TABLE P1-1: Overview

TOPIC		DESCRIPTION
Why Graphs? (Chapter 1)	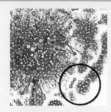	What are graphs, and why are they useful to a business analyst? Chapter 1, "Why Graphs?," introduces the concept of graphs, and defines several key terms used in this book. Select historical and modern anecdotes recount applications of graph analysis and visualization in business, documenting a steady rise to prominence spurred on by today's challenges of vast and complex data. Real-world cases attest to the value of graphs.
A Graph for Every Problem (Chapter 2)		Chapter 2, "A Graph for Every Problem," provides a systematic overview of the wide variety of graph types and the kinds of problems they are useful for solving. The discussion begins with an example contrasting how relationships revealed in other ways can also be expressed using nodes and links. Subsequent topics describe graph techniques for gaining business insights involving hierarchies, communities, flows, and spatial networks. References are included to further detail in subsequent chapters.

WHY GRAPHS?

This book is about graphs and how graphs can be used to help solve business problems. When many people hear the word "graph," they think bar charts or line charts, and rightly so, because those are also sometimes known as bar graphs or line graphs. This book is not about charts. This book is about the node-link diagram kind of graph.

At its essence, a *graph* is a structured representation of connected things and how they are related. As you will discover in the following chapters, graphs are capable of representing complex data in a way that an analyst can make sense of.

Because graphs have a long history in mathematics, discussions about graph analysis and visualization tend to include a lot of confusing esoteric terms such as *edge* and *degree*. This area of study responsible for this is generally known as *graph theory*.

For the discussions in this book, we use more universally accessible and less ambiguous terms where possible. For example, a *link* is a relationship between *nodes* and is typically drawn as a line. Nodes are entities (or essentially "things") that are joined by links. Nodes are often represented visually by a circle.

An edge is another word for a link in graph theory, and the term *degree* becomes a little less opaque if you are familiar with the concept of *six degrees of separation*, popularized by the play and movie of the same name. But only a *little* less opaque, because not only can "degree" mean the minimum number of steps of separation between linked entities, it can also mean the number of link connections that a node has.

In some circles, graphs are still viewed as abstract and difficult-to-understand constructs used mainly by scientists walking around with disheveled hair. Although graphs do have a long-standing tradition in scientific circles, the reality is that, when properly designed and executed, graphs can be one of the most intuitive ways to analyze information. There is a good chance you have used graph representations if you drew things in a notebook or on a whiteboard to think through or explain concepts—which is really a form of visualization.

More importantly, graphs provide a means of gaining highly unique and valuable insight from data. Graph analysis brings complex relationships to light, informing effective decision-making. Visualization is central to that process. Being able to see relationships visually is critical to understanding, whether they be characteristics of the raw data or specific features highlighted by graph analytics.

Information visualization exists for the sole purpose of understanding more, and in less time. Our brains are naturally wired to perceive and comprehend things visually. Reading is a time-consuming, sequential process, requiring the reader to mentally piece together an understanding. Pictures can convey information instantly, revealing complex patterns and outliers in easily digested ways.

There was a time when visualizations were drawn by hand after the painstaking gathering of data. But today, computer systems can harvest vast amounts of data and turn it into pictures in mere milliseconds, enabling analysts to instantly comprehend and act on information. Virtually any business can now benefit from visualization, and, as a result, it has become core to systems across all industries and around the world. Graphs, however, are one of the last forms of visualization to remain underutilized. There was a time, though, when that was true for all information visualization in business.

VISUALIZATION IN BUSINESS

The use of computer-rendered visualization for decision-making in business is a relatively recent phenomenon. Twenty years ago, as recent grads from the University of Waterloo

School of Architecture, we decided to abandon the design of physical landscapes for the lure of an emerging and wide-open new world of virtual landscapes. One of us spent a few years working on three-dimensional (3-D) modeling software before we joined forces with other colleagues to see if similar technology could be applied to the problem of displaying large amounts of abstract information for high-flying decision-makers in finance and other industries. The seeds of that collaborative venture were to grow into an eventual long-term partnership, which included William Wright and another young architect, Thomas Kapler.

In the early days of this venture into business visualization, the value of even primitive charts was not always widely understood or accepted in offices of Fortune 500 companies. Our first pitches to corporate decision-makers started with the most basic of value propositions—that of the value of visualization itself. The pitch started with a slide presenting a small table of numbers and a challenge to the executives in the room to describe patterns. The next slide followed with the same numbers shown in a line chart. Visualized, patterns were immediately clear. In the table, the patterns were clearly not. That basic principle was the foundation for extrapolating how visualization could be even more essential in gaining insights from data that was orders of magnitude bigger and more complex.

At that time, the use of computers for primitive charting was still in its infancy, and beyond that, a product industry for analyzing business data visually was (by and large) yet to be born. What little advanced work that was going on was confined to a handful of corporate research labs and start-ups. Business was uncharted territory, in all senses of the word.

In those early days, one of the obstacles to the adoption of visualization in the business world was the limited graphic capabilities of computer systems at the time. When Edward Tufte's book *Envisioning Information* (Cheshire, CT: Graphics Press, 1990) was published, best-practice examples in the industry were still print-based, and the case studies in his seminal design book were no exception. The average computer was still far behind in quality of display.

When we hit the streets of New York in the early 1990s with novel interactive 3-D demos for financial analysts and traders, they had nearly a hundred pounds of specialized hardware in tow. Powering a single system required a hefty Silicon Graphics Inc. (SGI) computer and monitor. Between wrestling the equipment in and out of taxi trunks, and careening it down city sidewalks on rickety, collapsible hand carts, it didn't take long before a new machine received its first patch of duct tape.

The bigger problem was that pretty much no one on Wall Street (or the rest of the business world, for that matter) had an SGI machine. Interactive visualization software systems were a hard sell when they came with a five-figure price tag per user for a new machine and operating system that didn't run any of their other apps. We generated a lot of buzz making one-off prototypes for a long list of high-profile firms, but progression to wide deployments were hard to come by.

When Microsoft Windows computers finally began to roll out with improved graphics application program interfaces (APIs) and graphics cards, it was a game changer. Access to higher-quality graphics capabilities on most desktops removed the requirement for expensive specialized machines, representing a major step in the democratization of advanced visualization for business use. By the mid to late 1990s, widely deployed high-powered analytics client platforms like the Bloomberg Terminal were running on PCs. Even highly specialized and demanding systems like the NASDAQ MarketSite broadcast wall were run on commodity Windows computers.

As the graphics capabilities of hardware began to mature, awareness of the value of visualization also matured. Timely, accurate, quickly perceived events and trends were critical to making lightning-fast decisions on the trading floor and elsewhere where systems and events needed constant monitoring. In business analysis as well, the value of representing information graphically to aid insight and to support strategic-level decision-making was quickly gaining momentum across all industries.

Surrounded by a rapidly growing market, we found our niche at the fresh and exciting edge of uncharted territory. For example, when the NASDAQ MarketSite began its move from the private confines of a downtown office to a public studio on Times Square, rebuilding its software infrastructure in the process, we were granted the task of designing and building the visualization systems and content. To open on the eve of the Millennium, the new studio would be composed of a 40-foot-long broadcast wall made up of roughly a hundred displays, and an electronic display wrapping the seven-story exterior tower. More than 6,000 stocks and indices would be displayed visually on demand in real time for reporters and the general public.

Before and since then, we have found ourselves with the privilege of working behind the scenes to help many of the world's most innovative companies and organizations solve their toughest information problems visually, through design and technology development. In doing so, we have had an opportunity to witness how the industry has evolved inside the walls of almost a hundred businesses, spanning the most data-intensive of industries. As time has progressed, the volume of available data has only increased, and so has the latent potential of information that can be gained from it. Data is now literally everywhere, waiting to be tapped for actionable insights.

As the realization that visualization is needed to make sense of it all has grown, so has the realization that visualization systems must be highly interactive. It is not sufficient simply to plot data and view it, just as it is not sufficient to simply compute an answer and present it. *Analysis* is an interactive process of rapid query, answer, and exploration, involving computational processes, visual display, and visual manipulation. In the early 2000s, dissatisfaction with the perception of visualization as simply an output channel led the research community to coin the term *visual analytics* to better represent and promote the interactive sense-making aspects of analysis.

Another awareness that has grown with the increasing size and complexity of information problems in business is that a basic palette of line, bar, and pie charts is rarely enough to express all of the valuable information available, and to leverage it for decision-making. Richer forms and combinations of forms are needed. Graphs, as it so happens, are one of the most valuable.

GRAPHS IN BUSINESS

We have been helping organizations visualize and analyze graphs for almost 25 years. Graphs have been around much longer. One of the first graph problems was a deceptively simple question by Leonhard Euler: Was there a route so that each of the seven bridges in Königsberg, Prussia (now known as Kaliningrad, Russia), would be crossed only once, as shown on the left of Figure 1-1. Euler simplified the question into a graph, as shown on the right of Figure 1-1.

Since then, obviously many more problems have been analyzed as graphs, in business as well as science. Many such problems are geographic, just like Euler's.

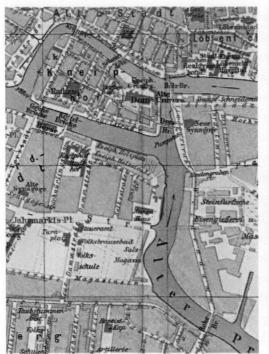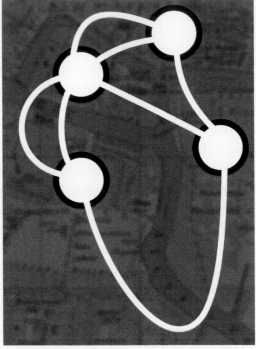

FIGURE 1-1: In the seven bridges of Königsberg problem, Leonhard Euler explored whether each bridge could be crossed only once. On the left is a map showing the seven bridges, and on the right is the graph equivalent.

One of the first graph visualizations we produced was a geographic graph problem as well. In supply chain optimization, the task is to optimize the shipping between factories and warehouses to reduce costs. As shown in Figure 1-2, our visualization depicted the locations of facilities with icons indicating attributes such as type, inventory, capacity, and utilization, as well as major links indicating average costs.

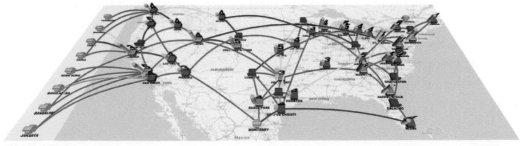

FIGURE 1-2: One of the authors' first visualizations depicted a manufacturing and distribution supply chain network.

Various types of analyses can be done with this kind of supply chain visualization, ranging from inspecting individual routes to rationalizing the overall number of factories and warehouses. One interesting finding was that the costs between two particular factories doubled in March, June, September, and December. On inspection, it was discovered that a particular route was increasing shipping costs heavily at the end of each quarter. Further investigation showed that this route switched from land-based shipping to faster (but more expensive) air-freight shipping. Some questioning revealed that this change was driven by high-level objectives to reach quarterly targets. Because this pattern repeated consistently every quarter, the analysts realized that better planning and coordination between the two factories throughout the quarter could result in a better shipping schedule, and a reduction of shipping costs in the last month of the quarter. Similarly, graph analysis and visualization can be used in the analysis and optimization of other supply chain networks.

NOTE Chapter 9, "Relationships," discusses basic graphs and relationships in more detail.

Finding Anomalies

Spatial graphs are often used to analyze the flow of goods around a company or around the world. One excellent early example of a flow graph is from Joseph Minard in the mid-1800s that, as shown in Figure 1-3, examined emigration around the world. Looking at it, you can easily see the flow of emigrants from the United Kingdom to the colonies, French and Germanic peoples to the United States, Portuguese to Brazil, as well as Africans, Indians, and Chinese to other locations.

Graphs can be made to analyze the movement of people, goods, or money, whether across the world, through processes, or through websites. Another of our early projects was for an airline company that wanted to analyze performance across its route network. Each link in the graph showed a flight route and had metrics such as revenue, passenger counts, efficiency, and profitability.

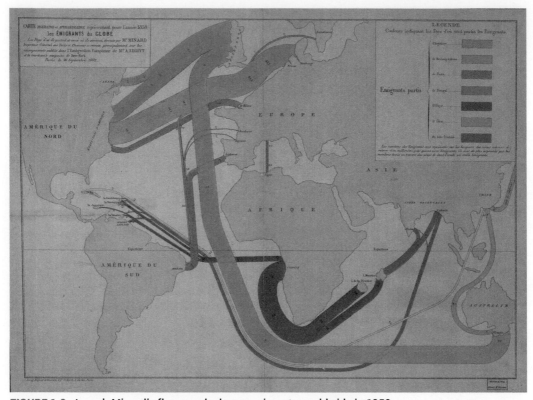

FIGURE 1-3: Joseph Minard's flow graph shows emigrants worldwide in 1858.

> **NOTE** A number of examples in this book look at statistics about movement between locations, specifically in the discussions in Chapter 12, "Flows."

Flow data sets, with an element of time, can quickly become Big Data. In such cases, we have used different strategies for dealing with these dynamic flow graphs, such as clustering. Figure 1-4 shows a recent application for investigating money flow between entities.

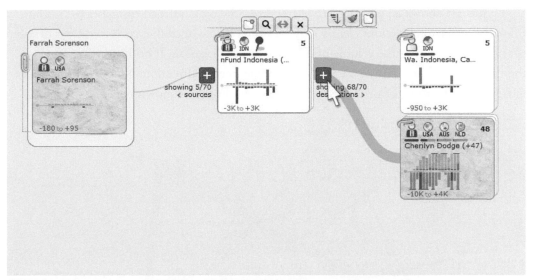

FIGURE 1-4: This flow graph shows money flow over time between different entities.

NOTE

This particular example is discussed in detail in Chapter 15, "Dynamic Graphs."

These graph examples are about finding and understanding anomalies such as unexpected links and unexpected flows. Identifying fraudulent activity and understanding paths through websites are examples of applications of this kind of graph analysis. Finding these anomalies can aid business by improving efficiencies, such as reducing losses or reducing clicks.

Managing Networks and Supply Chains

Pipelines, electrical systems, and railway networks are all large-scale physical networks. They are capital-intensive with large upfront costs that must be recovered through efficient operation. Similarly, large manufacturing and distribution networks have significant investments in plants, transport, warehousing, and other infrastructure. Adjustments must be made as conditions change.

Figure 1-5 shows an old diagram of freight traffic on a railroad from 1912–13. The thickness of various sections clearly indicates the volume of traffic, with two sides of each connection indicating the volume of traffic in either direction. If both sides are equal, then fully loaded box cars are generating revenue in each direction. Note the imbalance in freight traffic to and from Kansas City (top) and Ft. Scott shown here.

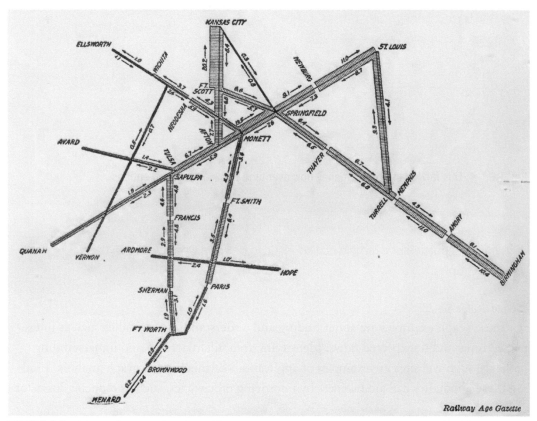

FIGURE 1-5: This graph shows freight traffic density and direction on the St. Louis and San Francisco Railroad in 1912–13.

Image courtesy Prelinger Library (www.prelingerlibrary.org).

Analyzing physical networks is an ongoing requirement for planners. As populations and energy use changes, the electrical grid must be adapted, too. Figure 1-6 shows a portion of the use of electricity on the West Coast of the United States from 2002. It shows only electrical transmission lines that are congested (that is, near capacity), potentially necessitating infrastructure upgrades.

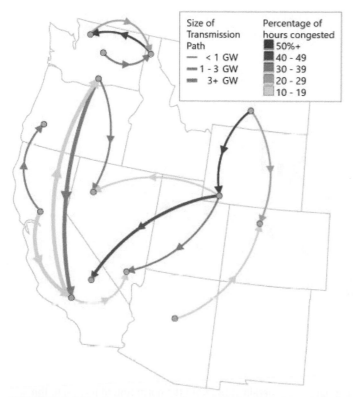

FIGURE 1-6: This shows congested transmission lines in the western United States electrical grid in 2002.

Redrawn based on U.S. Department of Energy National Transmission Grid Study 2002.

Many of these networks being analyzed in long-term planning must also be actively monitored to ensure efficient and trouble-free operation. One such project for us involved real-time data for a natural gas pipeline. In the case of the pipeline, nodes were compressor stations, and links were pipelines between each compressor station. Sensors in the compressor stations collected data such as pressure, flow, how close the compressor is operating to its limits, and alerts (such as a fault in a mechanical compressor). The alert-based system provided one way to easily monitor the system: no alerts equals no problem.

The solution provided was a graph visualization roughly along the lines of the one shown in Figure 1-7. The links were sized based on pipeline capacity, with nodes indicating flow through the station as a 3D bar, colored the node based on the limits (for example, blue for not close to limit and red for close to, or exceeding, limit), and added a significant red flag on top of the node if an alert was triggered.

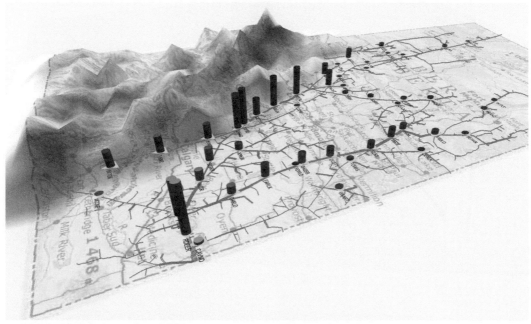

FIGURE 1-7: As shown in this pipeline graph, gas generally flows from the north (top of image) to the south (bottom left).

One interesting incident occurred shortly after we had completed an early version of the visualization. The alert system had no active alarms. But the visualization showed one compressor station operating close to it limits with a high volume going through the station (red in the figure). Inspecting all the node attributes associated with that station via a tooltip indicated no particular problems other than the station was working very hard and close to its limits. Having the whole graph visible meant that the analysts could visually inspect all the neighboring nodes for clues. One of the nodes immediately connected to this node had an extremely low volume (the low blue node immediately to the right).

The operators could easily see that the hard-working node was compensating for the neighbor node—in effect, performing additional work to maintain overall throughput of that portion of the network. This is a good example of where graph visualization is an effective complement to other kinds of graph analytics. The alert system by itself failed to create a message for the problem node, but the visualization provided enough information that the viewer could see the problem and pinpoint its source.

NOTE Geographic graphs are discussed more in this book, particularly in Chapter 13, "Spatial Networks."

Managing networks, regardless of real-time, daily, or monthly analysis, requires understanding multiple variables about both nodes and links in order to assess the overall network health. The graphic depiction of the network and the data acts as an aid to visually navigate hops to assess issues and understand their impact.

Identifying Risk Patterns

Beyond geographic networks, networks can simply be logical connections between things, such as computers or telephones. Figure 1-8 shows an early network drawing of the ARPANET (the forerunner to the Internet). One myth about the early ARPANET was that the network had many paths and decentralized message routing to deter nuclear attacks. However, this decentralization may have been more because of the unreliability of links and nodes in early computing.

Rather than focus on all the logical connections between specific computers, another way to look at the Internet is to examine where the traffic is going from and to. Particularly useful in network security is knowing which computers are targets for potential hackers and attackers, or otherwise performing actions in the network that are anomalous. This is a graph problem that can be drawn to show connections between the source computer (for example, the hacker or the internal thief's computer) and the target computer (for example, the corporate website or the offshore bank account).

Because many different kinds of events can occur (viruses, malware, bots, and so on), there are many different kinds of links. Furthermore, these network events are happening over time. They are transient, appearing and disappearing. There can be many different ways of representing this kind of graph, such as showing all the links, aggregating links by type of event, providing an interface to show links between only a set time period, and so on.

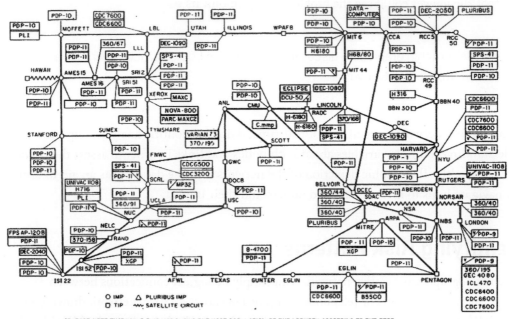

FIGURE 1-8: This early drawing from 1977 shows the ARPANET, the precursor to the Internet.

NOTE

Chapter 9 shows a few examples of graphs representing many links simultaneously.

Figure 1-9 shows a sketch of a graph visualization we constructed that used an interface to show only links over particular time periods. By isolating time periods, the viewer could identify event sequences, potential related events, and potential collaborators—symptomatic of a more organized attack. Also, different kinds of attacks have different visual signatures that stand out when viewing the patterns in a particular time period.

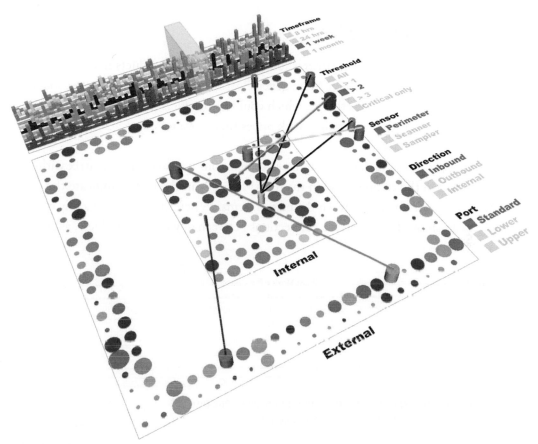

FIGURE 1-9: This graph visualization shows potential anomalies with connections between internal computers (inside) and external computers (around perimeter).

> NOTE Chapter 4, "Stats and Layout," discusses in detail the visual layout of a network.

Visualizing connections and patterns of connections may be useful for spotting risk, such as different types of threats to a physical network as shown here, as well as other types of risk, such as financial counterparty risk. Analyzing risk without graphs may lead to limited conclusions. Graph-based analysis can help reveal how risk exposure may extend to other entities.

Optimizing Asset Mix

The objective of a *market basket analysis* is to understand which products have a strong tendency to be purchased together. More generally, this is a graph where you are looking for strong correlations between things, which could be products purchased together, people who are popular at the same time, stock prices that move together, actors who appear in movies together, and so on.

One old approach to understanding these correlations was to create a matrix with each item listed in the columns and in the rows. The cells in the matrix indicate the strength of the relationship between the pair of items. When there are only a few items, the matrix can show all the possible connections between any pair of products, as shown in Figure 1-10.

Cross-Sell Patterns		First Device Purchased				
		Smart Phone	Music Device	Tablet Computer	Laptop Computer	Desktop Computer
Additional Device Purchased	Smart Phone	-	63%	12%	7%	28%
	Music Device	4%	-	1%	3%	2%
	Tablet Computer	19%	18%	-	18%	19%
	Laptop Computer	11%	6%	11%	-	3%
	Desktop Computer	4%	9%	8%	4%	-

FIGURE 1-10: This adjacency matrix shows how many times one product purchase leads to the purchase of the second product.

> **NOTE** Chapter 7, "Point-and-Click Graph Tools," discusses adjacency matrices in a bit more detail.

As the number of products grows, however, the number of potential connections is exponential. A matrix is less effective when looking at hundreds of items. To address that we have put together visualizations for problems which include analysis of market baskets of products at retail stores, the connections between people via e-mail, and the correlation of stocks.

In one fun example, we took a market basket visualization that we created for a client to compare correlations of financial assets and changed the data to a set of correlations between some of the top Twitter celebrities, as shown in Figure 1-11. The distance between any pair of nodes indicates the strength of the correlation (close nodes have a strong relationship). Because there are many items, we turned off all the links to keep the display clean. Perhaps not surprisingly, there is a strong correlation between celebrities such as Justin Bieber, Lady Gaga, Felicia Day, and Taylor Swift. Inverse correlations are on the flip side in this visualization, and perhaps unsurprisingly, Margaret Atwood and Richard Florida are inversely correlated to the pop stars.

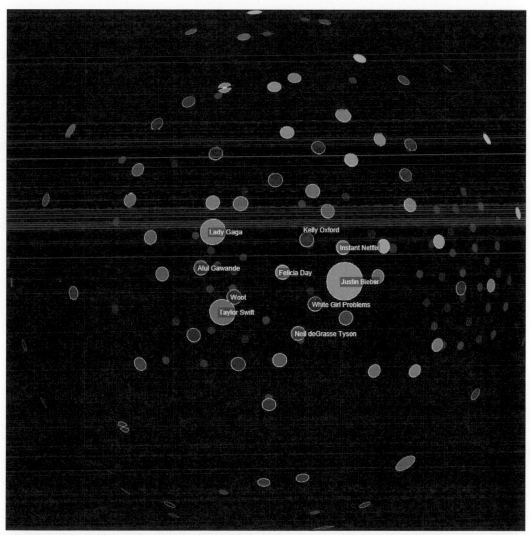

FIGURE 1-11: This shows that the correlations between top Twitter accounts (Justin Bieber, Felicia Day, Lady Gaga, and Taylor Swift) are all close together.

NOTE   Chapter 6, "Explore and Explain," discusses more about market basket analyses.

While an analysis of correlations between celebrities may seem trifling, a similar approach is used to optimize portfolios of other types of assets, such as financial portfolios, pharmaceutical drugs, or oil wells. The proximity of nodes as a result of force-directed layout algorithms (discussed in Chapter 4) provides insights into the asset choices that comprise of a collection of assets, such as close alternatives, isolated singletons, and opposites.

Mapping Social Hierarchies

There is a lot of current interest in social networks. Mapping out social networks goes back hundreds of years.

Figure 1-12 shows the genealogical tree for French royal family from Louis XIV to Louis XVI from the book *A Complete Genealogical, Historical, Chronological, And Geographical Atlas* by M. Lavoisne (Philadelphia: M. Carey and Son, 1820). This wonderful visualization shows direct rulers, spouses, offspring, and branches that merge together again. Nodes are people, with kings shown as crowns, men shown as filled circles, and women shown as transparent diamonds. Links are lines with time proceeding from top to bottom, and horizontal line style differentiates between the children of married spouses (plain line) or mistresses (diamond line).

NOTE   Chapter 5, "Visual Attributes," explores how to use visual attributes such as shape and color. Chapter 16, "Design," discusses related design considerations.

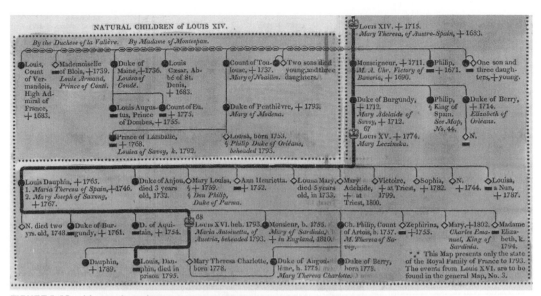

FIGURE 1-12: This portion of a genealogy chart shows the French royal family from Louis XIV to Louis XVI.

Courtesy davidrumsey.com.

In business environments, *organizational charts* (sometimes called *org charts*) are similar to genealogical trees. Although simple org charts work for small hierarchies, other approaches are needed for exploring large hierarchies with thousands of managers or tens of thousands of staff in contact centers. By combining the hierarchical view with time series views, trends and changes in performance can be viewed at any level as a time series, and up and down the hierarchy.

Figure 1-13 shows an early version of a visualization we created for a client showing org charts with time series. Consistent coloring across the nodes and links allows the viewer to track how the positive and negative contributions roll up.

> **NOTE** Chapter 10, "Hierarchies," provides more information about organizational charts.

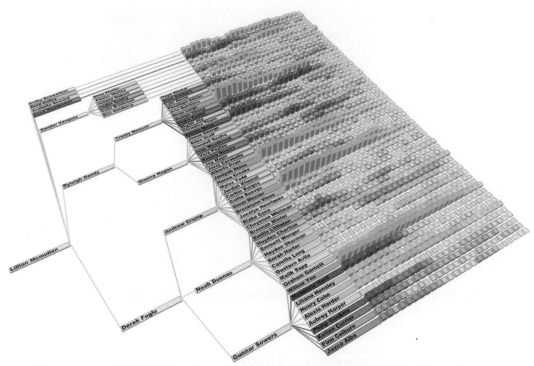

FIGURE 1-13: The left side of this organizational hierarchy uses color to indicate performance through all the levels, with the lowest level expanded on the right side to show performance over time.

Hierarchies are a unique type of graph and can be used to drill down through the organization to assess where the contribution to performance is coming from—for example, based on staff (as shown here) or based on other means such as attribution models. By providing this hierarchical decomposition, management can spot whether issues are localized, within a group or broad-based. Using this insight, they can respond more effectively to these different scenarios.

Detecting Communities

Beyond genealogical charts and the visualization of friend networks, visual analysis of social networks has many other applications. In health care, social networks can be used to analyze relationships and the potential spread of disease. Researchers have mapped out all the "romantic and sexual relationships" in a Midwestern high school (research paper: "Chains of affection: The structure of adolescent romantic and sexual networks" by Bearman, Moody, and Stovel). Out of 832 participating students, 573 were involved in a sexual or romantic relationship. Of those, many (126) were involved with only one partner over the previous 18 months, but there were also larger components where a person may have been involved with more than one other person.

Figure 1-14 (created using Gephi) shows a large component of 288 students linked by sexual relationship. This graph is important because it indicates how approximately 50 percent of sexually involved students could be linked in the diffusion of sexually transmitted diseases (STDs).

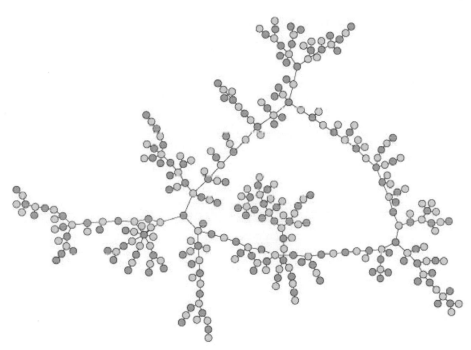

FIGURE 1-14: In this visualization of romantic and sexual relationships at a Midwest high school, you see how a large percentage of students surveyed are connected to each other through long chains of relationships.

The spread of diseases is similar to the spread of viral marketing or the spread of opinions and sentiment. Some firms may have data based on sales referrals or e-mail or extracted from social media such as Twitter.

Analyzing these social networks will often reveal clusters with higher densities of interconnections known in graph terms as *communities*. Identifying these groups of people and how they are connected can help a company identify different customer segments and better understand the dynamics of influence within and between them.

In a large company, social network problems may easily involve millions of nodes. Representing these graphs visually and exploring them for the purposes of extracting meaningful information is exceptionally difficult. Common desktop tools like Gephi (which are limited by in memory processing on a single machine) are not designed for graphs of that size.

We are involved in an ongoing advanced research effort exploring the use of cluster computing for community-detection and graph-drawing techniques to achieve highly scalable zoomable graphs with millions of nodes and tens of millions of links. Figure 1-15 shows an example of one such graph involving referrals. Clusters of medical practitioners seeing the same patients are outlined with circles, indicating communities.

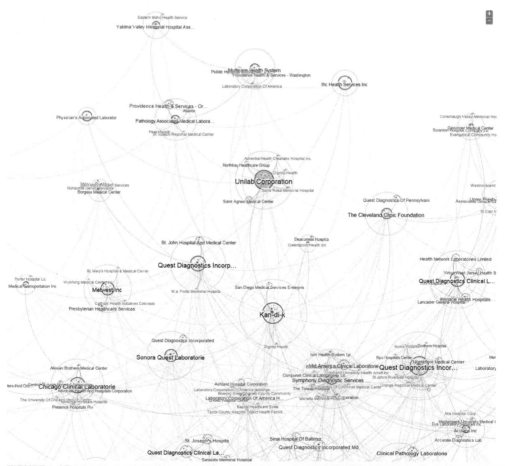

FIGURE 1-15: Use of distributed community-detection techniques and multi-scale graph drawing techniques can reveal community structure in very large graphs. Here, the DocGraph data set is visualized in its entirety, comprising millions of medical practitioner nodes and tens of millions of referral links.

Analysis of social networks can provide insights into clusters of people or organizations and influential connections within and between those clusters. These insights can be used to understand diffusion through a network (such as spread of coupons or a virus) and to understand communities (such as customer segmentation based on connections).

GRAPHS TODAY

In the age of Big Data, many of the world's most data-rich businesses are searching for new ways to make sense of vast streams of complex, irregular, sometimes unverifiable, interconnected data. Graph analysis and visualization is gaining momentum as a tool for helping to do just that. Graphs are particularly good at characterizing complex, compound relationships that are not easily described in black-and-white terms. They are also a natural choice for displaying networks, which are an increasingly integral part of many business data sets.

Desktop tools like Gephi and Cytoscape (which typically originate in scientific communities) have made strides in visual quality and scale for graph visualization and analysis. With their open and extensible nature, these tools can be easily applied to business problems, given the right amount of technical training and determination. With the prospect of cloud-based systems on the horizon, graphs promise to become even more easily accessible to the wider community of business analysts.

The goal of this book is to inspire creative thinking about the potential application of graphs to your own business problems and to share a little of our own domain knowledge in the hopes that you may try it yourself. Step-by-step tool usage and code samples are provided using case examples that demonstrate how graph analysis and visualization can be used to gain insights from data.

SUMMARY

Graph analysis is a powerful tool for discovering valuable information about relationships in complex data, representing significant business opportunity. Graph visualization is essential and, when used properly, can also be extremely intuitive. Information visualization takes advantage of natural perceptive abilities to allow an analyst to see more information, more quickly.

The importance of visualization in business has risen to widespread recognition as the volume of data available continues to increase. During that time, graphs have developed into an instrumental tool, with applicability in areas such as network monitoring, market basket analysis, influence analysis, and optimizing of processes and organizational structures. With the rise of Big Data the importance of techniques suited to dealing with complex relationships has risen with it. Need has fueled technology development, and today graph tools are emerging as a valuable resource available to any business analyst.

Chapter 2 provides a detailed overview of the many kinds of graphs and how they can be used in solving various business problems. The first example provides an illustration of how graphs are effective at intuitively summarizing relationships at a high level, while providing additional levels of detail with further analysis. Additional examples show different forms of graphs, as well as their relative strengths and suitability to answering specific kinds of questions.

2

A GRAPH FOR EVERY PROBLEM

Graphs are one of the most versatile and powerful ways to express complex data—and the least understood. In reality, people use graph techniques in meeting rooms every day, labeling and diagramming relationships to explain their thinking to others. Graphs can express relatively complicated concepts that other visualizations cannot.

When chosen wisely, the right technique can lend the simplest and most intuitive expression of a particular type of information. When chosen poorly (or naively employed), a graph can be painfully abstract and obtuse. One of the primary goals of this chapter is to encourage graph authors to break free of the trap of simple colored nodes and links and to think more creatively about graphs.

This chapter introduces graph solutions and is organized by classes of problems. Later chapters in Part 3 of this book provide in-depth walkthroughs of each of these classes using example problems and data. Documented, reproducible steps are provided for using tools, and sometimes code, to do the same.

At first glance, your own business problems may seem too multidimensional to fit into one of these seemingly small and tidy boxes. For example, your problem may involve both spatial networks and flow and will certainly always involve relationships. These are not mutually exclusive aspects. When choosing an approach, try to think of what is most fundamental about the questions you are attempting to answer.

RELATIONSHIPS

One of the most valuable and fundamental uses of graphs is to express a model of the relationships that compose a defined world or system. In a way, anytime you draw diagrams on a whiteboard, you are creating a graph of sorts. Graphs enable you to explain a world in a way that can be readily absorbed. A graph presents a visual model that translates into a mental model, a way in which you can internalize an understanding of systems and factors that help inform smart business decisions.

Similar to how diagrams can be drawn informally by hand, diagrammatic graphs can be generated formally by computers. Formalisms vary by approach, but essentially, in any formal graph structure, subjects and objects are represented by nodes, and relations are expressed by links. When the goal is to understand the elements of a world and their relationships, as well as *how* they are related, graphs are an invaluable technique.

The representation of a relationship in a graph can be reduced to a line, sometimes with a particular weight to indicate strength or volume. But in reality, the underlying relationship often has more nuanced or expansive characteristics than can be shown with a simple line. If the world being displayed is reasonably small, visually expressive links, along with their nodes, can help to more fully explain the nature of relationships.

One type of relationship that is fundamental to data science in virtually any business is *correlation*. Correlations provide an indication of when and how aspects of a world are related, which can inform decisions in pursuit of business objectives. Understanding what conditions are most favorable to a particular outcome provides the basis of a strategy for action, influencing the probability of a profitable outcome by manipulating those factors that are within control. Depending on the industry, that strategy might take the form of targeted advertising, adjusting premiums based on a risk assessment, or other actions.

Figure 2-1 reveals feature relationships in a modern take on a classic data science study known as the Iris flower data set published by Sir Isaac Fisher in 1936. A technique known as a *scatterplot matrix* is used to plot 50 samples of each of three species of Iris, for each pairwise combination of four features. The features plotted in each scatterplot are found by following the row and column to the feature labels. The data here represents flower classifications and their features, but it could just as well represent customer classifications and their purchasing or risk characteristics.

IRIS FLOWER FEATURE RELATIONSHIPS

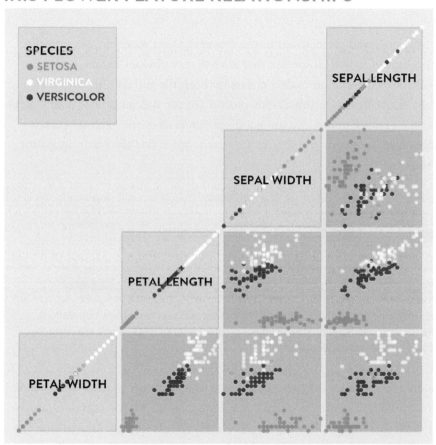

FIGURE 2-1: This modern web-based scatterplot matrix chart of the classic Iris flowers data set from Sir Isaac Fisher in 1936 shows relationships between features for three species.

All the raw data is shown here, but only two aspects of information can really be taken away from an analysis of this chart: the defining features for any species and the correlations between features, both across and within species. It appears that the species here can be identified primarily by differences in petal width and length, which seem to be strongly correlated, and there also looks to be a correlation of both sepal width and sepal length.

A correlation between petal and sepal length indicates only that both tend to grow in size together, which seems logical and not particularly interesting. If these were correlations between product purchases, however, a known affinity for one class of product would increase the likelihood of affinity for another, indicating value in marketing to those customers.

If you inspect the observed correlations in the flower data set more closely, however, you see significant disparities within species that are not very obvious in the scatterplot matrix. Figure 2-2 shows correlation matrix charts for both the full data set and all three species individually. The correlations observed across all of the species do not hold *within* all of the species. Petal length and width are good indicators of species and so are correlated at the global level. But once the species is known, one is not always an indicator of likelihood of the other.

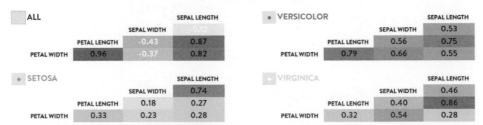

FIGURE 2-2: A series of correlation matrices constructed in a spreadsheet reveal how correlations between characteristics vary significantly within subject groups. Here, subject groups are species of Iris flowers but could also be customer profiles.

The same phenomenon occurs in business. For example, statistics may show a correlation between comic book and sports biography purchases. However, the correlation may simply be an indicator that the purchaser is a young male. If it is already known that the purchaser is a man between the age of 18 and 25, there may be no correlation whatsoever, and promoting comics alongside sports bios here would be a waste of time.

Computers are very good at modeling these kinds of relationships and computing the likelihood of other realities or behaviors given a set of known facts. Given a case of *a, b, c*, a computer can communicate the likelihood of *d, e, f.* However, without visualization of the nature of the underlying relationships and how they are interconnected, it is difficult for an analyst to gain sufficient enough understanding of the landscape to inform strategic business decisions.

Figure 2-1 and Figure 2-2 are useful charts. They share a common characteristic in that they present a collection of slices of information. However, it is impossible to take them in as a whole and come away with a big picture. An analyst would instead read the charts serially, perhaps prioritizing based on the most interesting-looking cells, and make individual observations that could be then taken away and assembled into a portrayal of the big picture in some other form. It might take the form of narrative annotation and explanation, a manually drawn diagram, or both.

On the other hand, a graph is intrinsically diagrammatic, capable of expressing the big picture without manual construction. Figure 2-3 shows one method of summarizing the same relationships between features using a graph. Features with reasonably strong correlations within any or across all of the species are linked, with dots on the links representing the scope of correlation.

IRIS FLOWER FEATURE RELATIONSHIPS

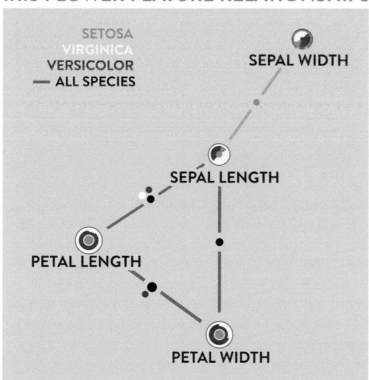

FIGURE 2-3: Graphs provide a big-picture model of how everything is related. For example, here, sepal width is linked to sepal length, and only in the case of Setosa, which are small with relatively wide sepals for their size. Petal length and width are the best indicators of species, reflected by the obvious stratification in those nodes.

Having each subject represented only once with all of its relationships, in the context of all of the other subjects and their relationships, makes it possible to see how everything is related at the big-picture level. It is also convenient for summarizing important things about each subject in the same context. Here, the distribution of values for each species is drawn in alternating homogenous and heterogeneous rings, summarizing the defining characteristics of each species. Clear radial striations in the Petal Length and Petal Width nodes indicate that they are good features for classifying flowers.

Because graphs can summarize relationships so effectively and so efficiently, they can more easily scale to allow you to show more information. For example, the number of features could easily be tripled in this case, and the big picture would still be evident (and more interesting) in Figure 2-3, easily outdistancing the effectiveness of the matrix charts for doing the same. Graphs are truly unparalleled in their capability to express interconnected relationships.

> **NOTE** Chapter 9, "Relationships," provides further examples of visualization and analysis of relationships using graphs.

HIERARCHIES

Graphs are also a great choice for gaining insights from hierarchical data. Hierarchical graphs are typically referred to as *trees*. Trees have a root parent node with links branching to a second order of nodes, which may in turn branch again, eventually reaching the leaf nodes that have no children. Each node descendant of the root has a single parent.

Trees have many business applications. Figure 2-4 reframes the Iris flower classification information as a *decision tree*. A decision tree shows sequences of decisions that lead to particular conclusions. Each node in the tree is a decision, and each link represents a path to follow based on particular criteria.

The Iris decision tree starts with the greatest distinguishing characteristic of each species, which is petal length. All 50 of the Setosa samples can be correctly identified by their characteristically short petals. If the petals are longer, petal width can be measured and an estimate made as to whether they are Virginica or Versicolor. The statistics in this case indicate how many samples will be correctly classified using this approach.

IRIS CLASSIFICATION DECISION TREE

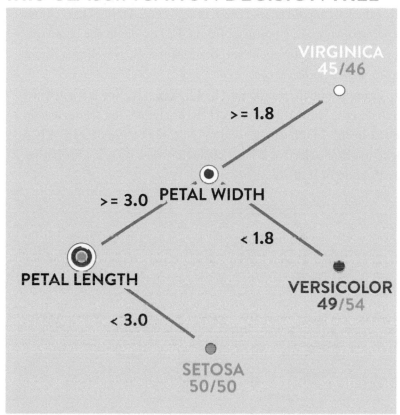

FIGURE 2-4: A decision tree articulates a series of branching paths that lead to different conclusions. Here, the flower data set shown in the previous figures is reframed to show a rudimentary process of classification based on defining features.

A decision tree can be useful as a simple rule-of-thumb approach to human decision making. It can also be a useful method of prioritizing information gathering. In the flower classification case, it is not necessary to measure anything other than petal length to make a classification decision in a third of the samples. Similar criteria priorities may exist in marketing products to individuals. For example, it may be most valuable to know gender, followed by age. You can use priorities to order fields in an online account profile, or questions in a survey, to target the most important data.

Trees are also perfect for understanding organizations. A family tree is an example of a visualization technique for an organizational hierarchy, where ancestors are placed at the root and children branch out from parent nodes. The work-life equivalent of a family tree is commonly called an *organizational chart*, or *org chart*. An org chart shows the structure of who reports to whom in a business, from CEO on down the chain of authority. Org charts provide information about corporate structure, as well as a framework for understanding corporate performance.

Figure 2-5 shows an example org chart produced by OrgVue. OrgVue is a software platform for organization design, Human Resources (HR) analytics, and strategic workforce planning. Bubble size in this graph can be used to indicate the size of staff or budget. Color can be mapped to other objective-related characteristics, such as affirmative action employment classification of staff members.

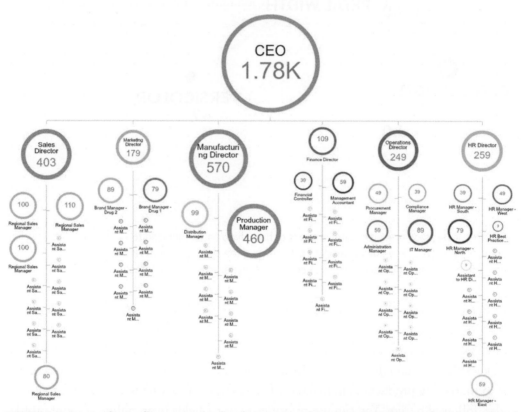

FIGURE 2-5: An org chart reflects organizational structure using a tree. Corporate performance-related characteristics such as department size and affirmative action employment classification can be mapped to size and color of each node.

An org chart provides an ideal, intuitive framework for portraying characteristics of an organization. However, when those characteristics are summative and a more precise reading of proportional contribution is desired, a *sunburst chart* may be an appropriate choice.

In Figure 2-5, the size of staff for a manager is the sum of the size of staff for each of the manager's direct reports. Each higher-level bubble represents the sum size of bubbles below. This gives an impression of department size, which is, in most cases, a sufficient level of detail. When the goal is to analyze department performance, however, more precision may be desired.

The sunburst chart in Figure 2-6 shows a similar organization with profit and loss information, as well as an additional level of detail. The tree is rooted at the center and branches out radially. Sibling nodes are represented as subdivided sectors of their parents, indicating precise proportion of the whole. In this case, nodes simply touch their parents instead of being linked with lines.

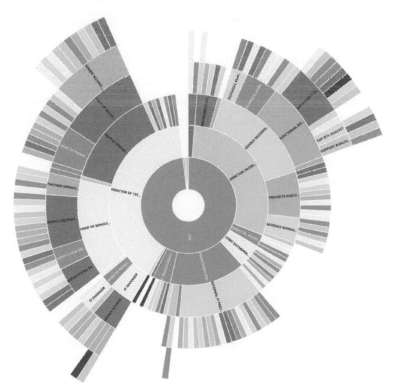

FIGURE 2-6: A sunburst chart provides an alternate representation of hierarchy appropriate for viewing organizational subdivisions by proportion of the whole. Profit and loss are shown in degrees of green and red, revealing roots of overall corporate performance.

Org charts can lend more clarity to the qualitative aspects of a tree, whereas sunburst charts tend to lend more clarity to quantitative aspects. Both are ideal choices for representing hierarchies.

NOTE Chapter 10, "Hierarchies," covers visualization and analysis of business hierarchies in depth.

COMMUNITIES

Graphs are indispensable for revealing communities, which are fundamental to understanding macro relationships and dynamics in business data. Communities in a graph visualization are similar to geospatial communities on a map in that they are qualitatively reflected by clusters of related members in close proximity, distinguishable from the field of other graph members.

Figure 2-7 shows communities of philosophers linked by influence using data extracted from Wikipedia by DBpedia. The PageRank algorithm is used to size nodes based on their degree of influence, and layouts are used to cluster nodes with common influences. Even without knowing much about philosophy, you can spot the most influential figures such as Kant, Marx, and Wolff, as well as many of the ancients like Plato and Aristotle. Communities of influence also have apparent regional tendencies, with a prevalence of German names in the mid right and British names in several clusters to the lower left.

Delving into the dynamics of influence is central to the art of persuasion in business. The popular writer Malcom Gladwell puts forth a social theory of influence in *The Tipping Point* (New York: Little, Brown, and Company, 2000), which suggests the importance of individuals he labels mavens and connectors, as well as salesmen. Graph visualization and analytics like PageRank and centrality algorithms can help reveal mavens and connectors. For example, a connector would be a hub reflected by many incoming and outgoing connections, including bridge connections to other communities. On the other hand, a maven might be more likely to show as a node with a large number of influential outgoing links.

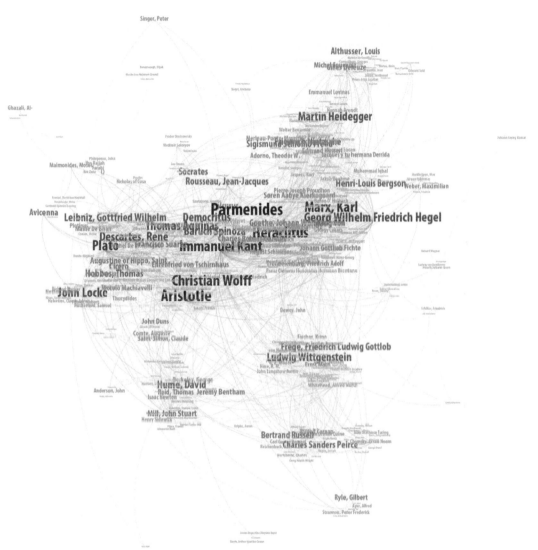

FIGURE 2-7: Visualizing a large graph reveals communities. Here, philosophers listed in DBpedia are clustered by influence. Labels characterize clusters and show key nodes.

Linking communities of buyers with products provides useful information about patterns of customer interest and purchasing. Figure 2-8 shows products that are linked to a seminal design book, marked by the large icon, through co-purchase and co-review. Where linked by review, the reviewer appears in black. Closely linked products surrounding the central product can be seen as most related, implying domain similarity, in which case the reviewers who link them and little else are more likely to be domain specialists than the effusive reviewers on the periphery. The opinions of domain specialists, most like mavens in Gladwell's social lexicon, may be particularly influential. As potential connectors, the effusive reviewers that bridge communities are also interesting because they suggest areas of cross-domain appeal.

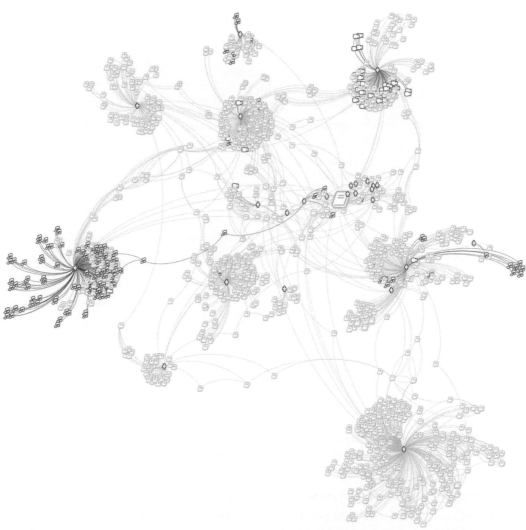

FIGURE 2-8: Graphs can be used to visualize product communities, linked here by co-purchase and co-review. Symbols reflect class of product.

For advertising purposes, however, what are more immediately relevant than hints of influence in this case are the clusters of other products that are likely to appeal to buyers of a product. Figure 2-7 uses symbols reinforced with color to reveal patterns by basic class of product. The label-based technique used in Figure 2-7 can be used instead here with product titles to provide a more nuanced (but cluttered) view of the character of products in each cluster. Chapter 14, "Big Data," provides further analysis of this data.

One of the characteristics of graph visualization of communities is that visually spatial relationships are more important than link clarity. The links produce the spatial relationship but become less important when you are reading the graph. In some cases, if the goal is simply to identify and analyze cliques, it may be clearer to remove the links.

Figure 2-9 shows computed online social communities separated into groups with links hidden. Locale is reflected by color and label, indicating composition of the group. Because the original layout is preserved, central connectors and general relationships are still apparent.

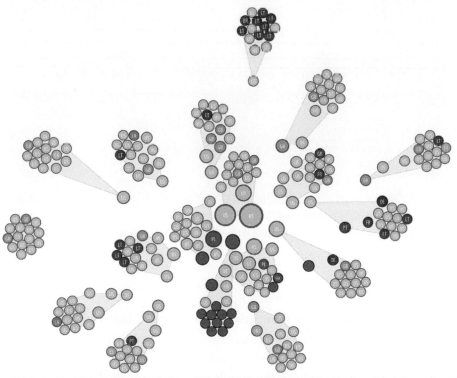

FIGURE 2-9: Hiding links can produce a clearer view if the goal is simply to identify and analyze cliques. Here, online communities are characterized by locale.

In other cases, links might represent essential information, and the lack of clarity in a community graph can be a problem. Figure 2-10 shows how communities in a highly connected graph (in this case, money flow) that would otherwise form a hairball can be aggregated and summarized visually to show interconnection. Chapter 11, "Communities," and Chapter 14 cover these examples in more detail.

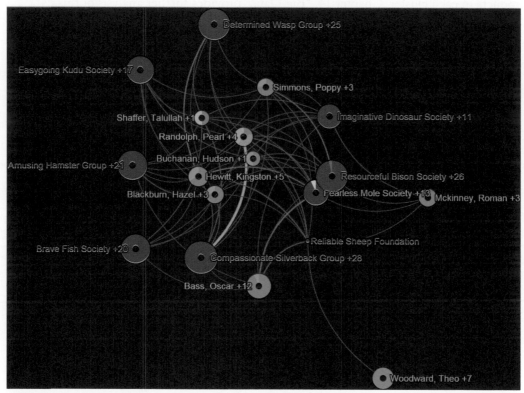

FIGURE 2-10: Communities in a highly connected "hairball" graph can instead be aggregated and summarized visually to better show community links. Here, link width and color reflect money flow.

FLOWS

The graph in Figure 2-10 shows money flow between communities but is still fundamentally structured to focus on community structure. Distance separates those communities that are least connected and brings related communities together. It is not clear which direction money flows in, and the links in the middle are still relatively dense. When the goal is to clearly understand flow, other graph techniques must be used.

The decision tree in Figure 2-4 shows a process, which is an event-oriented type of flow. One of the most important aspects of flow is that it is directional—that is, it has a source and a destination. The decision tree demonstrates one of the most fundamental principles of visualizing flow, which is that the most intuitive way to show direction is to use a consistent direction across the whole graph. The left-to-right layout of nodes in the decision tree makes it easy to see flow is left to right.

The same principle applies to graph problems that are not trees. Figure 2-11 shows a complex supply chain of materials for the textile industry. This visualization technique is known as a *Sankey diagram*. In this technique, flow always enters the same side of each node and exits on the other. Width indicates the volume of flow.

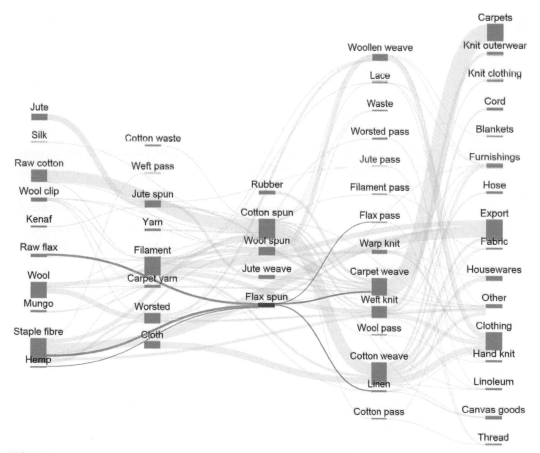

FIGURE 2-11: Sankey diagrams are an ideal graph technique for showing flow. Here, flow of materials in textile production is shown, where width indicates volume.

Sankey diagrams can also be used to show paths of customer experience. For example, Figure 2-12 shows flow through website pages. In this case, each column in the diagram represents a step in those paths, with the exception of the first, which shows something of their origin. A node may technically appear in more than one column, because web pages are organized by sequence. The red down arrows indicate the end of the road for a subset of paths.

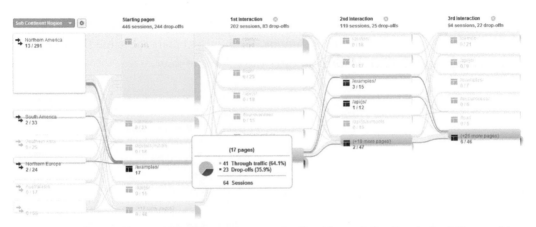

FIGURE 2-12: Flow graphs can also show customer paths through a website. Google Analytics provides this for analysts looking to boost engagement and click-through.

Flow graphs can also be combined with small multiple charts to show flow over time. Figure 2-13 is an example of how financial transaction activity between parties can be shown using Influent. Communities of similar nodes are hierarchically clustered and summarized for scalability. Figure 2-14 shows how flow of influence (in this case, steel consumption factors) can be visible even when not easily quantifiable. Correlation of time series patterns suggest complex relationships of cause and effect.

A left-to-right layout works brilliantly for indicating flow direction. However, when there is frequently an exchange of flow in both directions, you may want to use an alternative layout approach. Figure 2-15 uses a D3 *chord chart* to show reciprocal flow by modifying the width of the link on either end to reflect outgoing exports. The links in a chord chart resemble two arrows that collide in the middle and swallow one another. In this example, red links emphasize trade imbalance, and red country nodes are net exporters. Green countries are net importers.

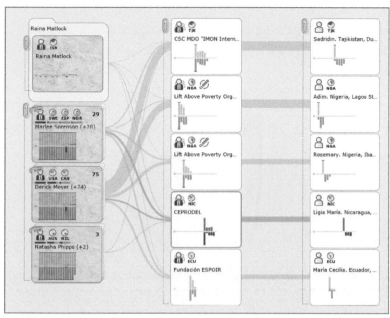

FIGURE 2-13: Flow can be combined with charts to show patterns over time, as shown here with finance.

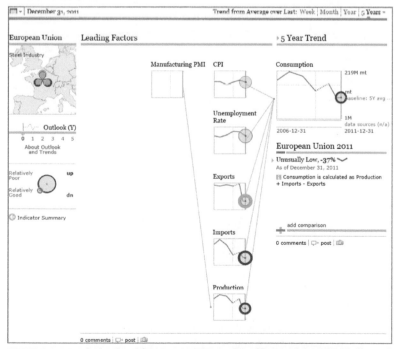

FIGURE 2-14: A behavioral factor tree shows the effects of modeled influencing factors in an outcome through correlation of pattern and inflection.

Chapter 12, "Flows," provides detailed examples of the use of graphs for flow analysis, including a case study using this data.

FIGURE 2-15: Chord diagrams show reciprocal flow between entities. Here, all reported trade of goods between countries is represented by width of link at the exporting country. Color flags trade imbalance.

Data courtesy of DESA/UNSD, United Nations Comtrade database.

SPATIAL NETWORKS

Graphs are also clearly a natural choice for showing spatial network data. In a *spatial network*, nodes already have a meaningful real-world location, which is often a communication advantage if nodes are familiar. One of the challenges, however, can be that the limited capability to move nodes can make it more difficult to make links easily readable. In Figure 2-16, a fictional subway map demonstrates how *schematic* versions of spatial network graphs can abstract angles and locations for legibility.

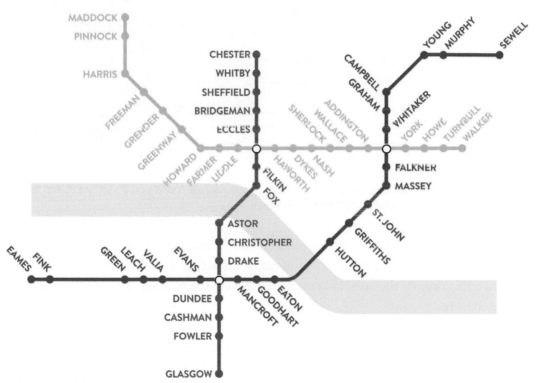

FIGURE 2-16: Schematic network diagrams abstract spatial layout to optimize legibility, as in the route map shown here.

In addition to showing how network routes and hubs are connected, graphs can also show performance characteristics of those routes and hubs. Figure 2-17 shows average winter flight delays for all airline routes flying in and out of airports across the United States. Red routes and airports indicate greater delays. The size of route and airport indicate the number of flights.

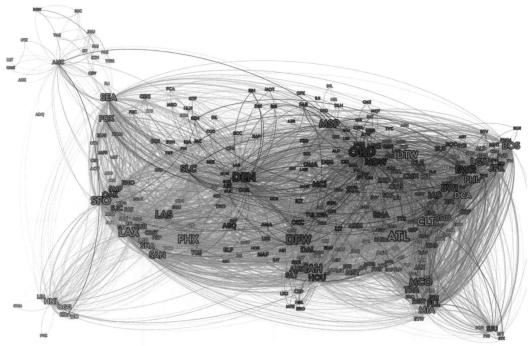

FIGURE 2-17: Average flight delays for all routes and airports across the United States are shown here in red for December 2013, revealing trends and anomalies.

The link density in Figure 2-17 is extraordinarily high, but the approach still works to reveal interesting geospatial patterns of red. It helps that airports are more likely to link to other airports that are closer by, which reduces the number of links that cross the entire country.

Although that is the case in many spatial networks, in the 1997 interstate Commodity Flow Survey data shown in Figure 2-18, every state is linked with almost every other in both directions, creating nearly 2,500 cross-country links. Furthermore, the disparity between state sizes makes it likely that flow between large states such as California and New Jersey on opposite sides of the country would obscure the view of small states in between.

A *link rose* technique was used for the graph in Figure 2-18 using Aperture JS, which summarizes outgoing flow in each direction at each node, removing links for clarity. States are colored by region to distinguish between near and far flow.

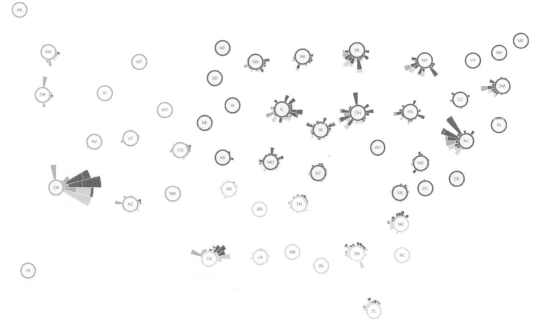

FIGURE 2-18: An Aperture JS link rose diagram summarizes flow in each direction around a node. Here, flow of commodities to other states is shown using 1997 Commodity Flow Survey data from the U.S. Department of Transportation's Bureau of Transportation Statistics.

However, when the goal is to show traffic along routes, as shown in Figure 2-17, and a large number of them exist, you can subdivide the spatial field recursively into tiles and aggregate by tile cell for better scalability. Figure 2-19 shows a tile-based visualization of shipping traffic statistics. Areas of high traffic in this graph (such as the capes of South Africa and the coast of Japan) appear in red and black. Chapter 14 provides more examples of tile-based approaches.

Graphs are an obvious fit for visualizing spatial networks. Choosing appropriate techniques depending on the objective will help to overcome challenges that spatial networks can sometimes present.

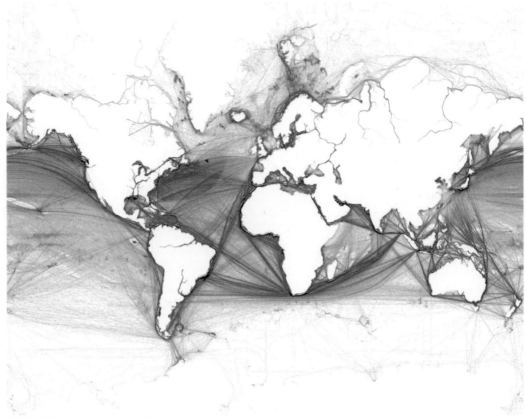

FIGURE 2-19: You can use tile-based aggregation and rendering techniques to graph a very large number of links, as in this visualization of shipping traffic over a period of a year.

NOTE Chapter 13, "Spatial Networks," provides more in-depth information on visualization and analysis of spatial networks.

SUMMARY

Graphs come in many shapes and sizes, suitable for an extremely wide variety of business problems. To choose the right approach, you must understand the relative strengths and weaknesses of each, know your data, and, most importantly, know what your objectives are. Graphs can be a solution to a problem in themselves, or they can be the organizing framework for small multiples of other types of visualization (such as line charts, bar charts, donut charts, or radial indicators, as shown in the preceding examples).

Diagrammatic relationships can be shown using expressive links and nodes, expressing a model or high-level conceptual picture of a problem. Hierarchies can be effectively visualized using trees or sunburst charts. Distant, near, nested, and overlapping communities can be revealed through clustered layouts and characterized with symbols or labels. Or, they can be grouped and summarized in more detail using computational clustering approaches.

Flows are usually best expressed as Sankey diagrams, or left-to-right trees. When flows are traded between each node, a chord diagram is an appropriate choice. In spatial networks, often a schematic approach to locating nodes and routes will help to clarify the graph. When visualizing route statistics for a large graph, a brute-force overplotting of links can still be effective in some cases, but tile-based aggregation techniques can provide greater scalability and color accuracy when expressing very dense areas of a graph.

This chapter served as an introduction of the many approaches to visualizing and analyzing graphs for business problems. The chapters in Part 2 describe the processes and tools used to do so, starting at the beginning with data, as discussed in Chapter 3.

PART 2

Process and Tools

The goal of this part of the book is to outline all the steps involved in taking raw data and transforming it into an insightful, interactive analysis of a graph data set. Various examples will be used throughout this section—such as the graph of people associated with 10,000 e-mails shown in Figure P2-1.

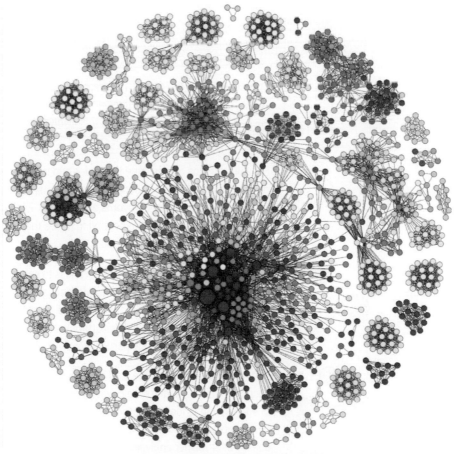

FIGURE P2-1: Graph of people connected through 10,000 e-mail messages

Whether you are exploring e-mails, tweets, market baskets, Internet networks, flight networks, or global trade flows, you usually follow a sequence of steps, as well as use various tools, to transform data into insights through analysis and visualizations.

PROCESS

Table P2-1 provides an overview of the next six chapters. Chapter 3 ("Data—Collect, Clean, and Connect"), Chapter 4 ("Stats and Layout"), Chapter 5 ("Visual Attributes"), and Chapter 6 ("Explore and Explain") walk you through the major steps, starting from data through to communicating results. Chapter 7 ("Point-and-Click Graph Tools") and Chapter 8 ("Lightweight Programming) discuss how this is accomplished using either point-and-click graph software or programming.

TABLE P2-1: Process of Visualization

STEP	EXAMPLE	DESCRIPTION
Data (Chapter 3)		Collect and clean the data. Then prepare it for use as a graph data set with explicit nodes and edges and associated attributes for each. For example, for e-mail data, this involves creating nodes and edges out of To, From, and Cc fields.
Layout (Chapter 4)		Review statistics and arrange the nodes and edges in a way that reveals insightful patterns such as components, clusters, and so on. Many different kinds of layouts are possible. For example, in an e-mail graph, this may mean identifying nodes that act as bridges between different groups of people.
Add Visual Attributes (Chapter 5)		Adjust labels, sizes, colors, and line thickness to enhance understanding. For example, with an e-mail data set, you can use additional data such as the number of messages, message size, and how recent the e-mail is to adjust visual attributes such as node size and color. This helps differentiate particular individuals of interest.
Interact, Explain, Further Analysis (Chapter 6)		Zoom, select, filter, annotate, and explain. In a social data set, zooming, filtering, and drilling down all provide ways to isolate data of interest and to identify particular individuals. You can then present or publish the results or export/integrate the results with other software for further analysis.

TOOLS

Types of tools used to create graph visualization range from point-and-click software to varying degrees of scripting and programming. Table P2-2 provides some examples.

TABLE P2-2: Tools of Visualization

TOOLSET	EXAMPLE	DESCRIPTION
Point and Click Graph Tools (Chapter 7)		You can perform graph analysis with tools such as spreadsheets and free (or at least low-cost) point-and-click graph software such as Excel, Gephi, and Cytoscape.
Programming (Chapter 8)		Some programming may be required, and some simpler lightweight programming tools are available that you can use to with graphs, including Python and JavaScript. Python is useful for data preparation. JavaScript is useful for displaying interactive graphs on web pages.

3

DATA—COLLECT, CLEAN, AND CONNECT

This chapter discusses how to get raw data that you might find in a corporate environment and turn it into data that you can use in a graph. Good insights cannot result from dirty data! Once you have an objective, you need data. Make sure the data is valid, clean, and properly organized before proceeding on to analysis and visualization. Following are the data steps that you must follow:

- **Collect**—Where is the data coming from? Graph data in corporate environments may be buried in many different data sets. This chapter discusses some of the different ways graphs may exist within common data.

- **Clean**—What is the quality of this data? Are items identified consistently? Are there many empty values? Are there duplicate entries? Are there any privacy issues? There can be many issues you must resolve while preparing data before you are able to use it with graph software.

- **Connect**—How do you turn data into graph data? You have many different ways to create graph data. Most require that you create a data set of nodes and edges, which may then be organized into one or more files. Finally, the data is ready to import into graph software.

KNOW THE OBJECTIVE

The authors once worked on a project for a senior vice president who said, "Here's some data about our staff—what can you show me?" We prepared a beautiful interactive graph visualization and he replied, "This tells me nothing I don't already know."

This precautionary story illustrates that the first step in the process of graph visualization is to understand what the objective is. If you don't have a clear objective, you cannot know which data to use, how to prepare it, and what to analyze. As you move through the analytic process, goals and objectives help guide choices in data preparation, layouts, and so on. Incremental findings along the way can be reviewed to help refine the goals.

> **TIP** Make sure you know what your goals are at the outset, and revise as needed through the process.

COLLECT: IDENTIFY DATA

Assuming there is a clear objective, the next big step—and sometimes the most difficult step—concerns data collection and data preparation. Rarely is graph-oriented data readily available and nicely formatted. One quote often repeated in network analysis is, "First you need to 'collect the dots' before you can 'connect the dots.'"

Your first challenge may be determining what data to collect. First, identify what data is available relative to your objective. Also, recall that a graph is made up of two related data sets: a set of nodes and a set of links (that is, the connections between the nodes, also called *edges*). Identify which of the data available may have information that contains links. Consider the following example.

Suppose that a senior sales rep is working with a team on a major account in a sales process that takes many months. Each team member works with different staff at the major account. The senior sales rep recognizes the importance of understanding the customer, which means understanding the various staff employed by the customer, and their relationships. Ideally, the rep wants a map of all the staff and their interpersonal relationships—that is, a graph. The rep would like to see clusters of staff, where the key communication channels are, and which staff occupies the most critical points in the network. Figure 3-1 shows an example.

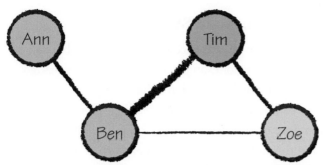

FIGURE 3-1: In this desired graph, lines indicate the relationships between individual people. The color and width of the line add extra information.

This graph data is not automatically available. Even with the best sales force automation system, there may be many elements outside of the system. There is likely a wide range of data available, including many documents (such as proposals, technical literature, pricing guides, and answers to questions), relationship databases, and many communications (such as hundreds or thousands of e-mails, phone calls, attachments, video conferences, and other interactions with the customer). None of these data sources is in a nice graph data set, but some of the communications have connections between people.

Consider e-mail data. For each e-mail, a list of people is identified in the To, From, and Cc fields that represent connections between people. For example, if someone is Cc'd in many e-mails, you might conclude that particular person is significant. From a set of e-mails, you can extract a graph. In Figure 3-1, you can see that Ann only connects with Ben on e-mails (indicated by a line between Ann and Ben). In addition to the graph of people and the connections, additional data provides additional useful insights. For example, in Figure 3-1 more e-mails exist where Ben and Tim are both included (indicated by a thicker line).

Potential Graph Data Sources

The previous scenario is an example of graph data existing buried inside transactions. Graph data can exist in many different ways in other data. Finding graph data requires that you identify within that other data both the nodes and the links between nodes. You will find that some nodes and links may already exist in other data.

Node and Link Data Sets (for Example, Flight Stats)

On rare occasions, there can be data sets that are already nicely organized with both node data and link data. One example is a flight database (for example, http://transtats.bts.gov).

Are you a frequent traveler? Ever wonder which routes have the most passengers? Or, have you found a route that has a lot of competition presumably leading to better fares? Have you ever wondered which routes have the most flight delays? There is a wealth of flight data on government websites and through the marketing departments of major airlines that can be graphed to answer these curious traveler questions.

The flight data sets at http://transtats.bts.gov consist of a primary data set containing each flight (that is, the links), and a supplementary data set containing each airport (that is, the nodes). In the primary data set, each flight can be indicated by a single record. The record indicates the city pair (that is, a link), such as ORD–LGA or LAX–ATL. Note that this particular data has directed links. ORD–LGA is a flight that starts in Chicago's O'Hare Airport and ends at LaGuardia Airport in New York City and is different from LGA–ORD, which is a flight going in the other direction. Both links are valid.

```
Flight, Origin, Destination, Distance, Duration
AA100, ORD, LGA, 836km, 1:55
DL364, LAX, ATL, 2384km, n/a
AA102, ORD, LGA, 836km, 1:55
QF32, LHR, SYD, 11711km, 22:18
...
```

> **TIP**
>
> For *directed graphs*, A-B and B-A are two different edges, and both are valid. In an *undirected graph*, A-B and B-A are the same edge, and only one pair should occur in an undirected graph.

The supplementary data set of airports lists the nodes. In this example, the individual airports (such as ORD and LAX) are the nodes:

```
Airport, Name, Latitude, Longitude, AvgFlightsPerDay
ORD, O'Hare, 41.94, -87.9, 2409
LGA, LaGuardia, 40.77, -73.87, 423
```

```
LAX, Los Angeles, 33.9, -118.40, 1218
...
```

In the case of this airline data, the graph itself is simply the nodes (airports) and links (routes between airports). Additional attributes, such as AvgFlightsPerDay, Distance, or Duration, may not be important to draw the graph but may be important in the analysis of the graph and achieving the goal. For example, finding the shortest flight in duration between London, England, and Auckland, New Zealand, would require both the graph and the duration associated with each link.

One challenge with links in general is that most graph visualization software does not handle many links between the same pair of nodes. Using the flight example, if 15 flights are listed in the flight database from ORD to LGA, some types of graph visualization software must receive summarized links (that is, a single link for ORD–LGA with an extra field indicating a count of 15 flights).

Because many airlines may serve the same route, you have multiple links per route. To consolidate multiple links into a single link, you can use a pivot table in the spreadsheet to summarize the data for each route, and then you use this pivot table as the output for the graph data, as shown in Chapter 7, and the Flight Stats spreadsheet in the Supplementary Material on this book's companion website. Or, you can consolidate multiple links programmatically, as shown in the e-mail example in Chapter 8.

Link Records (for Example, Network Logs)

Sometimes only links are identified in a data set. One example is network log files. Although log files may seem arcane, they contain a wealth of interesting information—for example, from where people are connecting into a corporate network, when and where big files are transferred out, patterns of regular activity (such as network backup), and patterns of irregular activity (such as hackers attempting to break in).

Network log files may indicate a source computer IP address and destination computer IP address in each line, identifying a link. You can extract nodes by compiling a list of all unique IP addresses in the source and destination IP addresses, as shown here:

```
Timestamp, Source, Destination, Etc
2/25/2014, 9.8.2.3, 128.2.9.87
2/25/2014, 7.6.9.5, 128.2.19.45
2/25/2014, 7.6.9.5, 128.2.9.87
...
```

For an example, see the `Network_Logs` data in the Supplementary Material on this book's companion website. This is a small sample Excel spreadsheet showing anonymous network data from an intrusion system, and it shows techniques for summarizing the link data using pivot tables. Real-world network systems can generate tremendous amounts of data that require a programmatic approach to handle the data.

Transaction Records (for Example, Purchases, E-mails)

By looking at the items that co-exist in a transaction, you can construct a graph. Nodes are the items, and links are the co-occurrence of items within any transaction. Examples of this type of graph include a wide variety of social networking (including e-mail data, as discussed earlier in this chapter), as well as multiple authors of documents such as books, news stories, or reports.

Ever wonder how websites recommend additional products you may be interested in? If you're looking at the book *Calvin and Hobbes Lazy Sunday Afternoon* (Kansas City, Mo.: Andrews-McNeel Publishing, 1989) and see four other recommended books, these additional books could be the result of a market basket analysis.

There are different ways of computing product recommendations, such as machine learning, collaborative filtering, and market basket analysis. A *market basket analysis* is a graph created by connecting all the items purchased in a single transaction (that is, all the items in that market basket are linked together).

In the case of an e-mail, a market basket is all the people involved in each e-mail. An example of e-mail data may look like this:

```
To, From, CC, Date, Size
"Joe", "Zoe",. "Tim", 12/09/2014, 156kb
"Joe", "Ben", "Ann, Tim, Zoe", 11/09/2014, 2048kb
"Joe", "Tim", "Ben, Zoe", 11/09/2014, 805kb

...
```

In this example, each row is a single e-mail, and all the people in the From, To, Cc, and Bcc fields form a set of links. Chapter 8 provides an example programming script to turn email data into a graph data set. See the Python Email data in the Supplementary Material on this book's companion website for an example of raw, anonymous e-mail data similar to what was previously transformed into node and link graph data and then visualized.

Sequence Data (for Example, Customer Paths, Patent Citations)

Sequence data is very similar to transaction data.

In a web server log, each row indicates a particular web page served to a particular user. Within each row, a client IP address and possibly a session identifier is used to indicate a particular session for a user accessing the website. By collecting all the records corresponding to a particular session, all the web pages for that session are identified, in the sequence that the user went through the website. That is, this is a set of nodes (web pages) and the associated links (sequence) that the user traveled through the site. By combining multiple paths, you might see if people take common routes through a website:

```
Time Client_Address Requested_File Status
09:55:15 12.34.56.78 GET /index.html 200
09:57:35 12.34.56.78 GET /images/logo.gif 200
09:58:22 12.34.56.78 GET /flash/splash.swf 200
09:58:35 55.44.33.22 GET /ad/advertisement.js 404
...
```

Sequences can also be found in many other kinds of data. One good example is the creation of a network of doctors based on patient visits by creating links for multiple doctors who bill for the same patient around the same time (http://bit.ly/1bgyHuk). Strong links between a pair of doctors implies a strong relationship (such as referrals). What's fascinating here is that raw transaction data of patient visits has been turned into a graph, which then reveals new, valuable information about connections between doctors.

Another example is patent citations. Each patent references prior patents. The various references can be collected to gain insights such as which patents are referenced the most.

Unstructured Data (for Example, Tweets)

Unstructured data can also be processed to extract nodes and links. A means to identify nodes and identify links is required. For example, tweets are short, 140-character messages publicly broadcast on Twitter. Tweets are a rich data source from which you can mine different kinds of nodes and links by looking for co-occurrence of hash tags (that is, user-defined topics), usernames, or stock symbols within tweets, and you can extract these to form graphs. This approach is similar to the transaction approach used with e-mail analysis described earlier. Sample raw data may look like this (for example, via tweetarchivist.com):

```
UserName, Time, Tweet
Benzinga, 01/15/2014, Is #Wendys Success at #McDonalds Expense?
$MCD $WEN http://t.co/OibzrKFiVB
SeekingAlpha, 01/15/2014, 2 Dividend Machines I Purchased Last Week
     http://t.co/hMcX5rvSxH $TGT $KO $MCD
wallstCS, 01/15/2014, RT @Jacqui_WSCS: #Starbucks Catches
     "McDonald's Syndrome" and Gets a #Stock Downgrade
     http://t.co/elwMdFbcQ4 via @wallstCS $SBUX $MCD
...
```

In this example, the co-occurrence of hash tags in the first tweet can be used to iden-tify a link (for example, #Wendys and #McDonalds). In the second tweet, co-occurrence of stock symbols for Target, Coca-Cola, and McDonald's can be used to establish links ($TGT, $KO, $MCD), and in the third tweet, a link between users can be identified (@wallstCS and @Jacqui_WSCS).

In a less-structured set of data (such as a book), nodes can be identified such as char-acters in a story. Consider *Alice's Adventures in Wonderland* (New York: HarperCollins, 1865). Characters (such as Alice, the Mad Hatter, and the Rabbit) are nodes. Links can be created such as co-occurrence of characters within a paragraph, as shown here:

```
There was nothing so VERY remarkable in that; nor did Alice think it so
VERY much out of the way to hear the Rabbit say to itself, 'Oh dear! Oh
dear! I shall be late!' (when she thought it over afterwards, it
occurred to her that she ought to have wondered at this, but at the
time it all s eemed quite natural); but when the Rabbit actually TOOK
A WATCH OUT OF ITS WAISTCOAT-POCKET, and looked at it, and then hurried
on, Alice started to her feet, for it flashed across her mind that she
had never before seen a rabbit with either a waistcoat-pocket, or
a watch to take out of it, and burning with curiosity, she ran
across the field after it, and fortunately was just in time to
see it pop down a large rabbit-hole under the hedge.
...
```

Matrix (for Example, Trade, Migration)

Sometimes a matrix of data contains the same entries in both the first column and first row.

For example, global trade flows between countries can be represented as a table of numbers (http://stats.oecd.org). Each cell represents a link, with the first column and first row indicating nodes:

```
From/To, Austria, Belgium, Denmark, ...
Austria,     n/a,  2.197b,  1.014b, ...
Belgium,  4.411b,     n/a,  3.681b, ...
Denmark,  0.753b,  1.284b,     n/a, ...
...
```

See the Trade Flow example in the Supplementary Materials on this book's companion website. In the spreadsheet, you can see a technique for transforming the matrix of links into a list of links using spreadsheet formulas.

Statistical Correlation (for Example, Stocks, News Stories)

In all the previous examples, a connection existed in the data. Graphs can also be created statistically.

For example, two stocks can be said to have a strong correlation if their prices move up and down together. This can be computed statistically as a function of the two time series of data. Raw price time series may look like this:

```
Stock, Jan-2, Jan-3, Jan-4, Jan-5,...
AAPL, 520.21, 515.98, 518.22, 514.29
GOOG, 958.37, 968.77, 978.11, 988.33
IBM, 177.34, 176.33, 175.44, 176.58
...
```

Links can be formed between every pair of time series using a correlation function (that is, stock prices that move up and down similarly are highly correlated, whereas stocks that move in opposite directions are inversely correlated), as shown here:

```
Stock1, Stock2, 1 year correlation
AAPL, GOOG, 0.94
AAPL, IBM, 0.77
GOOG, IBM, 0.66
...
```

The correlations between two time series can be computed using the correlation function `correl()` in Excel, using statistical software, or programmatically (for example, using Python). These correlation relationships can be useful. For example, an investor may like the price pattern of a particular stock (say, a tobacco stock) but would prefer to invest in an alternative stock that has a similar price pattern to the original—that is, a highly correlated stock. Real-world portfolio managers are interested in correlations— they want diversified portfolios where the stocks they own are not strongly correlated so that if the performance of one stock goes down, the other stocks do not follow.

Note that any pair of time series can be transformed into a correlation such as Google searches over time or time series of news story topics. In the Supplementary Materials on this book's companion website, see the `Stocks` example, which shows how to transform raw time series data into links based on correlations.

Two Data Types (for Example, Board Memberships)

A *bipartite graph* has two different types of nodes, with linkages between the different types. For example, a graph analysis of executives and their board memberships reveals the connections between companies via board members. The two different data types in this example are people and companies. These are the nodes. The board memberships are the links that connect a person to a company:

```
Exec, Board, Tenure
Sergey Brin, Google, 13 years
Paul Otellini, Intel, 11 years
Paul Otellini, Google, 9 years
...
```

Many Data Types (for Example, Social Links)

The idea of two data types can be extended to many different types of data. People can be connected through many kinds of commonalities—for example, LinkedIn builds connections via companies, friendships, educational institutions, group memberships, and so on. In many business cases, each type of connection may be in different databases, making the integration of this disparate data much more difficult. Be sure to keep the type of link in the data—some graph software will be able to analyze and explicitly represent these different types of links, such as Cytoscape.

Potential Hierarchy Data Sources

Hierarchies are a special type of graph. Though hierarchies may be embedded into data in a number of the techniques discussed previously, they may also be embedded in data with other techniques.

Links within a Node (for Example, Employee Data)

In one approach, a node may be described as containing a link to the next higher node in the hierarchy (that is, the "parent" for that node).

For example, a human resources database has each record indicating an employee, and the manager of each employee indicated in one of the fields. The successive chains of managers can be used to create a graph:

```
Person, Age, Income, Manager
Ann, 22, 20000, Ben
Ben, 33, 30000, Zoe
Tim, 44, 40000, Zoe
...
```

Flattened Hierarchies (for Example, Pivot Tables)

Flattened hierarchies are sometimes found in public data sets and from spreadsheets, such as exported pivot tables. In flattened hierarchies, each successive column represents the next level of the hierarchy. Each row represents a node. Links must be extracted by identifying each unique pair across successive pair of columns.

In the following example, the links are as follows:

- Technology ⇨ Software, Software ⇨ Application_Software

- Technology ⇨ Hardware, Hardware ⇨ Computer_Hardware

- Financials ⇨ Insurance and Insurance ⇨ Life_Insurance

Note that the root level is sometimes not shown as a distinct column or row, and so the node and link to the top level must be created. Following from the same example, the node would be Portfolio and the links would be Portfolio ⇨ Technology and Portfolio ⇨ Financials:

```
Sector, Industry, Sub-Industry, Company, Holdings
```

```
Technology, Software, Application Software, Adobe, 12857

Technology, Hardware, Computer Hardware, Apple, 10475

Financials, Insurance, Life Insurance, Aflac, 2934

...
```

Hierarchy Codes (for Example, Government Data)

Sometimes hierarchies are defined with alphanumeric codes. The various nodes and links can be extracted via a lookup table indicating the code.

For example, the previous data showing a financial portfolio and hierarchy can be described using standardized codes such as Global Industry Classifications (GICs), wherein the data may resemble the following:

```
Company, GICScode, Holdings

Adobe, 4510, 12857

Apple, 4520, 10475

Aflac, 4030, 2934

...
```

In this example, the numeric code can be decoded to determine the position of each item in the hierarchy. For example, in the GICs system, the first two numbers determine the sector, the next digit determines the industry, and the fourth digit determines the subindustry.

Alphanumeric hierarchies are common in some government data. For example, see the Occupations (and corresponding yEd visualization file) data set in the Supplementary Materials on this book's companion website for a hierarchical data set showing salary data by occupation in the United States.

Hierarchy as Indentations (for Example, Reports)

In some software and reports, hierarchies are made human-readable by using whitespace (for example, www.bls.gov/cpi/#data). Extracting the number of spaces in front of a label determines that node's level in the hierarchy, and the next shortest line immediately above determines the parent (that is, link) for that node:

```
CPI Expenditure Level                                          Weight

+ All items.........................................          100

+   Food and beverages...............................         14.792
```

```
+     Food........................................    13.742
+       Food at home....................................    7.816
+         Cereals and bakery products.....................    1.09
+           Cereals and cereal products...................    0.35
+             Flour and prepared flour mixes................    0.039
+             Breakfast cereal..............................    0.194
...
```

See the CPI data set in the Supplementary Materials on this book's companion website for an example.

Getting the Data

Identifying the data is only part of the problem—actually getting the data can be an interesting challenge in some corporate environments. Techniques for getting data include the following:

- **File download**—Many of the previously described data sets are available as downloadable files on the Internet from various sites. http://data.gov can be a good top-level source for U.S. data. http://stats.oecd.org or http://data .worldbank.org can be good sources for data across countries. Social network data can be accessed from a variety of sites such as http://tweetarchivist.com.

- **Report data export**—Many reporting software solutions provide a means to export data as flat files or into spreadsheets.

- **Tools**—Various software apps and plug-ins are available to make data access for a particular type of data easier. For example, NodeXL provides point-and-click access from Excel to social network data, including Twitter and Facebook. Examples of NodeXL and social data are shown in Chapters 7 ("Point-and-Click Graph Tools") and Chapter 11 ("Communities"). Google Spreadsheet provides formulas that can directly pull data from web sources such as RSS feeds and web pages.

- **Programming**—Both Internet sources and internal data sources such as databases can be accessed programmatically. (See Chapter 8, "Lightweight Programming," for more about this.)

- **Cut and paste**—When all else fails, sometimes cut and paste works. Some web-based publications use a PDF file format, and data can be cut and pasted into spreadsheets. In many software solutions, data is presented in tables where items can be selected. Try selecting data in a table-like interface and then attempt to copy it. For example, you can cut and paste e-mail data out of Outlook, as shown in Figure 3-2 and Figure 3-3. In Outlook, the e-mail list pane is a customizable table: columns such as To and Cc can be added, and columns such as Size and Date can be reformatted via right-clicks on the column headers. Then, multiple rows can be selected via Shift+click and pasted into a spreadsheet or text editor.

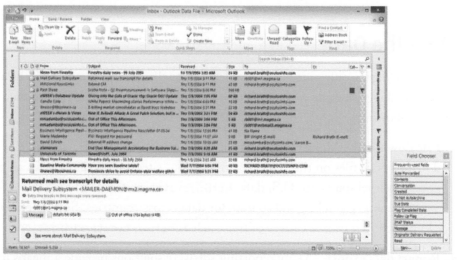

FIGURE 3-2: Often tables can be reconfigured and multiple rows selected and then copied to export the data. Here e-mail data is copied out of Outlook.

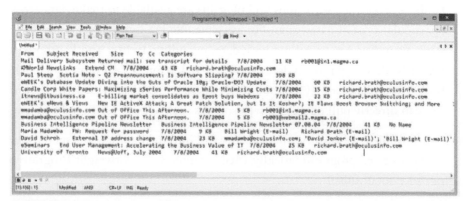

FIGURE 3-3: Then the data can be pasted into a spreadsheet or text editor, such as this freeware editor called Programmer's Notepad.

CLEAN: FIX THE DATA

Very rarely is data already in a nice format ready to use. And, too often, data is frustratingly messy. Unfortunately, most graph software is not designed to operate on messy data, and it is your task to first clean and prepare data before providing it to graph software.

Carrying on with the senior sales rep example outlined previously, let's use a data set of 10,000 e-mails as an illustration. Each person who sent, received, or was Cc'd will be a node. Links will be formed between any pair of people included in the same e-mail.

Because the actual messages are not required, only the metadata is exported: To, From, Cc, Bcc, Date, e-mail size, and so on. The exported data set ideally will look like this, with each row indicating one e-mail message between a group of people:

```
To,     From,  CC,     Date,       Size
"Ben", "Zoe", "",     12/09/2014, 156kb
"Ben", "Zoe", "Tim", 02/02/2014, 25kb
"Ben", "Tim", "Zoe", 11/18/2014, 77kb
"Ben", "Ann", "",     10/31/2014, 2048kb
...
```

Unfortunately, real data is rarely as tidy and error-free as the data shown here. A real-world e-mail data file may look more like this (with various anomalies shown underlined):

```
To,     From,        CC,          Date,       Size
"Ben", "Zoe",       "",          12/09/2014, 156kb
"Ben", "Zoe Jones", "Tim",       02/02/2014, 25kb
"Ben", "Tim",       "Tim; Zoe", 11/09/2014, 77kb
"Ben", "Ann",       76.3,        n/a,        2048kb
"Ben", "",          "",          01/01/2014, 4.2Mb
...
```

In this example of dirty data, many data-quality issues must be addressed before constructing the graph data:

- **Inconsistent node names**—Nodes are not consistently named. In this example, both "Zoe" and "Zoe Jones" refer to the same person. In real-world data, this can get quite messy. For example, in one e-mail data set you may find that "John Doe" also appeared as "john.doe@bigco.com" or "Doe, John," with or without surrounding quotes, with prefixes (for example, "SMTP: john.doe@bigco.com") and/or suffixes (for example, "John Doe (Email)"). These need to be consolidated into a single record.

- **Duplicate nodes**—Within the node data set, each node should appear only once. For example, "Zoe Jones" should occur only one time. If multiple "Zoe Jones" occur in the data and all refer to the same Zoe Jones, these should be aggregated into a single record. If two different Zoe Jones are employed, then the node should be identified with a unique identifier (for example, an e-mail address or employee number).

- **Duplicate links**—Some types of graph visualization and analysis software do not work well with many links between the same pair of nodes, and these must be consolidated. It is quite common to have many links in the data between the same pair of nodes based on additional attributes. For example, in the Flight_Stats data set provided in the Supplementary Material on this book's companion website, there may be multiple flights on a given day between a pair of cities at different times, on different airlines. If the objective is to understand the number of flights between each city pair, these must be consolidated down to a single link for that city pair. Alternatively, if the objective is to analyze each of the different carrier networks, the different links must be maintained, and the analysis tools chosen must handle multiple links between points.

- **Self-loop**—A node that has a link that connects to itself is a *self-loop*. In the third e-mail of the previous example, Tim has sent an e-mail to Ben and Zoe, but also Cc'd himself, thus creating a self-loop. Self-loops may not be relevant to the analytic objectives. Self-loops are not handled in some graph software.

- **Isolated nodes**—In the final e-mail shown previously, no From or Cc is identified. It is feasible to have nodes in data sets to which no links exist—on some occasions graph programs may have problems with unlinked nodes.

- **Links pointing to nonexistent nodes**—Although this does not occur in the previous example, in some data sets, a link may be defined between two nodes, where one of the nodes does not exist in the list of nodes. This may cause problems with some graph software.

- **Invalid data**—Unfortunately, real-world data consists of fields that may be empty, NULL, or may otherwise have invalid data. A column of numeric data may have text entries such as N/A or #ERROR. These entries should be cleaned or removed.

- **Units**—Data sets can sometimes shift units, as indicated by the final e-mail showing the size in megabytes (MB), whereas all earlier examples were in kilobytes (KB). All numeric data needs to be normalized to the same units.

There are many approaches to dealing with invalid, incomplete, and inconsistent data. A simple approach may be to remove the particular problematic record, but other approaches including inputing missing values or normalizing the data. These are beyond the scope of this book.

Depending on the data set, privacy issues may need to be addressed—for example, where people are uniquely identified by name or numbers (such as a government ID number). In an e-mail data set, the names of individuals should be replaced with numbers, letters, or generic names. Unique, generic names can be found in government registries (for example, www.ssa.gov/OACT/babynames/limits.html). Corporate policy varies at different companies, so check the appropriate guidelines. If you are uncertain, replacing personally identifying information (such as names) with other data is a good idea.

CONNECT: ORGANIZE GRAPH DATA

By definition, a *graph* is a collection of nodes and links between the nodes. Graph software almost always works with a data set of nodes and a data set of links. Even it not required, conceptually, it can be very effective to identify and organize data into a set of nodes and set of links. This will enable data exploration with a wider variety of tools if this clear separation is available.

Extending the e-mail example, the clean data may look like this:

```
To,     From,   CC,     Date,        Size
"Ben",  "Zoe",  "",     12/09/2014,  156kb
"Ben",  "Zoe",  "Tim",  02/02/2014,  25kb
"Ben",  "Tim",  "Zoe",  11/18/2014,  77kb
"Ben",  "Ann",  "",     10/31/2014,  2048kb

...
```

But, unfortunately, this data is not in a nice graph data format. The typical target format of graph data will be nicely organized into two data sets—a table of nodes and a table of links, as shown here:

```
Nodes:

"Ann"

"Ben"

"Tim"

"Zoe"


Links:

NodeA, NodeB

"Ann", "Ben"

"Ben", "Tim"

"Ben", "Zoe"

"Tim", "Zoe"
```

Furthermore, the target graph data can be much more useful if it contains additional information, such as counts, size, and recentness, which may be used later in the analysis:

```
Nodes:

Person, Number_of_Emails,  Total_kb, Most_Recent_Date

"Ann",  1,                 2048,     10/31/2014

"Ben",  4,                 7687,     12/09/2014

"Tim",  2,                 102,      11/18/2014

"Zoe",  3,                 4292,     12/09/2014


Links:

NodeA, NodeB, Number_of_Msgs

"Ann", "Ben", 1

"Ben", "Tim", 2

"Ben", "Zoe", 3

"Tim", "Zoe", 2
```

Nodes must be extracted from the To, From, and Cc fields. Similarly, links must be constructed between people within a single row—in the previous example, the first e-mail represents an e-mail from Zoe to Ben (that is, a link).

Compute the Graph

Transforming raw data into a set of nodes and a set of links typically requires some computation. You can do this via programming, or sometimes spreadsheet formulas may be sufficient (see the sample spreadsheets on the accompanying website).

Following the e-mail example, the raw data was accessed via cut and paste from Outlook to Excel. Transforming the raw e-mail data into a set of nodes and links required some programming, which will be shown in detail in Chapter 8. Essentially, for the e-mail data set, the process looked like this (for each row in the data):

1. Extract each unique node. For example, for the first e-mail, the nodes are Ben and Zoe.

2. Add these nodes to the node list and set the count (number of e-mails) to 1. If a node already exists in the node list, instead increment the count for that node by 1.

3. Each unique pair of nodes within the row is a link. In the second e-mail, the nodes are Ben, Zoe, and Tim. The unique pairs are Ben-Zoe, Ben-Tim, and Tim-Zoe. Each of these links must be added to the link list with a count of 1. If the link already exists, then instead increment the count for that node by 1.

> **NOTE**
>
> When processing links, if the links are not directed, then Tim–Zoe and Zoe–Tim represent the same link, and only one of these pairs should be in the output link list. Alternatively, if the links are directed, then Tim–Zoe represents a link from Tim to Zoe, whereas Zoe–Tim represents a different link from Zoe to Tim—and both pairs can exist in the output link list.

The results of this computation are two data sets—a set of nodes and a set of links—exactly the output desired. Although many of the examples provided in the supplementary data are small (that is, less than 10,000 nodes), you can take the same approach with much larger data sets. For data sets with millions to billions of nodes, the approach can be extended to using optimized processes, graph databases, and distributed computing.

Already, at this point, with this trivial data set, you can identify some interesting graph properties by sorting these lists. In this trivial example, the node that occurs most frequently is Ben, and the most frequent link is Ben–Zoe.

Another interesting property is the number of nodes and number of links. With four nodes and four links this is not a fully connected data set. A fully connected data set—meaning every possible link exists—would have 16 links. At four links and four nodes, it is certain that this cannot be a hierarchy either—a single hierarchy always has one less link than the number of nodes.

With the 10,000 e-mail data set, following are some of the interesting properties:

- There are 2,500 nodes. With 10,000 e-mails, this means that each e-mail is not to a different person, so some people will occur multiple times.

- There are 9,600 links, significantly less than 2,500 × 2,500 possible links (that is, a fully connected 2,500-node data set would have more than 6 million links). The ratio of the number of actual links to the maximum number of links is called *graph density*, and if the graph density is low, the graph is considered a sparse graph.

- The node with the highest count is Michael Johnson with 2,271 e-mails. Michael is the head of sales in this data set—he Cc's or is Cc'd by many people because he must coordinate between sales, marketing, technical, and executive staff.

> **NOTE**
> Graph statistics will be discussed in more detail at the beginning of Chapter 4, "Stats and Layout."

When processing the initial data, it may be useful to filter out some of the data at this early stage. For example, using an e-mail data set extracted from one person's e-mail inbox (say, Richard's e-mail) means that every single e-mail will have Richard in either the To, Cc, or Bcc fields. Later, when visualizing this data, every single link to Richard will then be drawn in addition to all the other links, thus creating a potentially cluttered view. Because it is already known that Richard is the source of the e-mail data, it may be much more effective to filter out Richard during this initial computation. In the e-mail data set, all links to Richard have been removed.

A number of scenarios exist in which it may be desirable to filter out links during the data preparation stage, such as removing some of the weaker links in massive graphs to make it faster to process the graph in later steps. For example, in the case of correlated time series for stocks, the result shown in Figure 3-4 is a fully connected graph with a link for every possible combination. Processing the data so that only the top few links for each stock are retained can result in a completely different visual layout later.

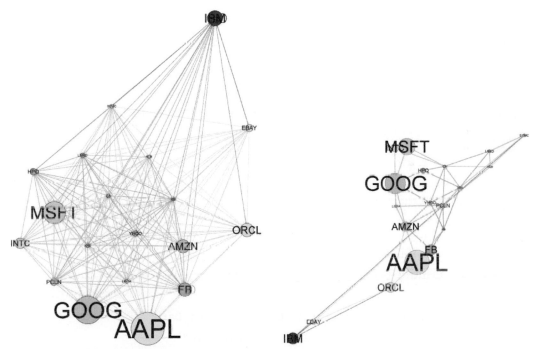

FIGURE 3-4: Same data set of stock correlations. In the left image, all links were used. In the right image, only the top three links per node were output and used.

At this point, these two data sets can be output into the appropriate file formats that can then be read by graph software. You can learn more details about the programming in Chapter 8.

Graph Data File Formats

Once data has been collected and connected, most graph analysis applications will need some way to input the graph data. Although specialized graph databases are available, in many business-analysis and smaller data-science applications, simple data files can be used to exchange graph data between graph applications.

As with many things in the fields of computer software and data, more than one file format is available for graph data. Some of the more common techniques are discussed in the following sections. A number of the supplementary examples on this book's companion website are provided in multiple formats. A few of the examples (such as Trade and CPI) include sample spreadsheets that provide examples of preparing data for different file formats on successive worksheets.

> **WARNING** Most graph software only supports a few file types, may not support all fields, and may have other issues, such as requiring specific names for some columns. Some experimentation with data preparation and data formats likely will be required.

CSV Files

A simple way to deal with graph file formats is to create two separate files—one file of nodes and one file of links—both of which are in a *Comma Separated Value (CSV)* format. These files are identified with a .csv extension. Following are a couple of examples:

```
Nodes.csv:

Person, Number_of_Emails, Total_kb, Most_Recent_Date
"Ann",  1,               2048,     "10/31/2014"
"Ben",  4,               7687,     "12/09/2014"
"Tim",  2,               102,      "11/18/2014"
"Zoe",  3,               4292,     "12/09/2014"


Links.csv:

NodeA, NodeB, Number_of_Msgs
"Ann", "Ben", 1
"Ben", "Tim", 2
"Ben", "Zoe", 3
"Tim", "Zoe", 2
```

Note the following conventions for CSV files for graph data:

- **Header row**—The top row of each file defines the name of data for each column.

- **Node column**—The first column of the node file contains the unique identifier for each node.

- **Link columns**—The first two columns of the link file contain the links. In a directed graph, the first column indicates the source nodes, and the second column indicates the destination nodes.

CSV files can be easily opened, edited, extended, and exported in many programs, including spreadsheets and text editors. CSV files can be problematic because there is no data quality enforced in their format. For example, the authors have come across CSV files with embedded tabs, extremely long fields, invalid numerical values, and so on.

GDF Files

The *GDF* file format began with a graph system called GUESS and is now commonly used with the graph software Gephi. GDF is similar to CSV files; however, both nodes and links are defined within the same file, and visual attributes such as edge widths, node sizes, colors, shapes, visibility, or even images can be defined in the file as well. The GDF file format is a good format for people who manipulate their graph data with spreadsheets. Following is an example using the simple e-mail data set:

```
EmailGraph.gdf:
nodedef> name VARCHAR, NumEmails DOUBLE, width DOUBLE, Recency VARCHAR
'Ann',1,2048,'10/31/2014'
'Ben',4,7687,'12/09/2014'
'Tim',2,102,'11/18/2014'
'Zoe',3,4292,'12/09/2014'
edgedef> NodeA VARCHAR, NodeB VARCHAR, weight DOUBLE, color VARCHAR
'Ann','Ben',1,'0,0,255'
'Ben','Tim',2,'0,255,0'
'Ben','Zoe',3,'255,0,0'
'Tim','Zoe',2,'255,0,255'
```

The file is set out with the nodes first, followed by the links. The first row of the nodes section is similar to the first row of a nodes CSV file:

- **nodedef>**—The header row starts with the keyword `nodedef>` to clearly mark out the start of the nodes section. There is no space between `nodedef` and the greater-than symbol.

- **Node column**—The first column is required to be the node column. The convention is that this column is titled `name`, and some software requires it to have this title.

- **Label column**—An optional label column is used to define the label to apply to the node. A label column is almost always very useful to have, even if it is a duplicate of the name column. It is even better to have a label that is short, for example, `'LGA'` instead of `'New York La Guardia Airport'` or `'US'` instead of `'United States'`, because long labels tend to overlap and obscure each other later in the graph visualization steps.

- **Other node columns**—Additional columns can be added, such as color, width, visibility, position, and so on. Not all graph software is going to necessarily automatically use these attributes even if they are present. Some software requires that these columns be in a specific order. For example, according to `http://gephi.org/users/supported-graph-formats/gdf-format/`, the Gephi graph visualization software documentation indicates that it supports attributes when listed as columns with the following names in the following order:

  - `name`

  - `label`

  - `visible`

  - `labelvisible`

- width

- height

- x

- y

- color

Other software (for example, GUESS) supports additional attributes such as shape and image.

- **Data types**—Each column is indicated with a title, just as with a CSV file. In addition, the final text for each column indicates the data type. This helps the graph software understand if the column should be interpreted as text or as a numeric value. This is important for defining other visual attributes, such as colors and sizes, and interactive features such as filtering. Following are some common data types:

  - VARCHAR—VARCHAR stands for VARiable CHARacter field. It defines a field as a text field. Node and link ID fields are typically VARCHAR, as are fields for labels or other text. Color could also be defined as VARCHAR, whether defined as a name (for example, 'orange') or as an RGB value (for example, '255,127,0').

  - DOUBLE—Use DOUBLE for numerical values, such as node size, edge width, population, average age, and so on.

  - BOOLEAN—Use this for an attribute such as Visible. A boolean column can only have fields set to either TRUE or FALSE.

  - INT—This is used for an integer. Typically, you use DOUBLE if you are using a number. INT is used for lookup codes such as a shape. GDF supports different node shapes (called *style*) such as circles, squares, and images where the code 1 corresponds to a square, 2 is a circle, and so on. Note that not all graph software supports the use of different shapes.

The links section is similar to the nodes section:

- **edgedef>**—The header row starts with the keyword `edgedef>` to clearly mark the start of the nodes section.

- **NodeA,** NodeB **columns**—The first two columns define the links. For directed graphs, the first column indicates the source node, and the second column indicates the destination node.

- **weight**—An optional `weight` column with numeric values defines the thickness of the links connecting nodes. This is very effective for indicating the strength of the relationship. Some caution is required when setting weights in the source data— some software will not handle negative weights; some software will truncate large numbers, and some will not. Gephi, for example, may display a massive arrow larger than the entire graph, thus obscuring everything for a large value. A safe approach is to normalize the `weight` data to the range of 1–10 or 1–50 for the first time the file is created and iteratively experiment with the visualization software.

- **Other link columns**—Additional columns can be added, such as `label` `visibility`, `color`, `directed`, and so on. The use of the `directed` column can be particularly useful if the graph has a mix of both directed and undirected links. Otherwise, if the graph has links of all one type (directed or undirected), most graph software provides a simple checkbox to declare all links as directed or undirected.

GDF files can be easily edited with a spreadsheet. To export a GDF file from a spreadsheet, save it as a CSV file, then rename the extension from .csv to .gdf.

Other Node-and-Link File Formats

Many other file formats exist. You may want to use a more structured file format, such as GML or GraphML. These formats potentially offer more features, but there is the complementary challenge in that these features may not be used by the target graph software.

One approach might be to transform data into these other formats by using graph analysis software (for example, Gephi) that can load and export a wide variety of different graph file formats. Another approach might be to use some lightweight programming, discussed further in Chapter 8, to transform and output your desired data into the target format.

Graph Modeling Language (*GML*) is a fairly straightforward format, very similar to GDF—that is, a single file of nodes and links. It does offer more flexibility (for example, defining edges that are non-straight lines as a list of points). Unfortunately, GML does not identify data type. A basic GML file may look like this:

```
EmailGraph.gml:

graph [
    directed 0
    node [ id 1 label "Ann" numEmail 1 totalKb 2048 ]
    node [ id 2 label "Ben" numEmail 4 totalKb 7687 ]
    node [ id 3 label "Tim" numEmail 2 totalKb 102 ]
    node [ id 4 label "Zoe" numEmail 3 totalKb 4292 ]
    edge [ source 1 target 2 numMsg 1 ]
    edge [ source 2 target 3 numMsg 2 ]
    edge [ source 2 target 4 numMsg 3 ]
    edge [ source 3 target 4 numMsg 2 ]
]
```

> **NOTE** Details on GML file format are available at `http://www.fim.uni-passau.de/fileadmin/files/lehrstuhl/brandenburg/projekte/gml/gml-technical-report.pdf`.

GraphML is a Graph XML file format. It is more verbose than GML or other graph data file types because GraphML uses XML standards for encoding data. GraphML is used as the file format for the graph visualization software yEd. Note that yEd includes a lot of detail in its GraphML file, and other graph software that can read GraphML files may ignore, skip over, or generate warnings for these additional attributes. GraphML provides useful features such as data type identifiers, as is shown in the top section of the following sample file:

```xml
<?xml version="1.0" encoding="UTF-8"?>
<graphml xmlns="http://graphml.graphdrawing.org/xmlns">
  <key id="NodeLabel" attr.name="Label" attr.type="string" for="node" />
  <key id="NumMail" attr.name="NumMail" attr.type="double" for="node" />
  <key id="TotalKb" attr.name="TotalKb" attr.type="double" for="node" />
  <key id="NumMsg" attr.name="NumMsg" attr.type="double" for="edge" />
  <graph edgedefault="undirected">
    <node id="Ann">
      <data key="NodeLabel">Ann</data>
      <data key="NumEmail">1</data>
      <data key="TotalKb">2048</data>
    </node>
    <node id="Ben">
      <data key="NodeLabel">Ben</data>
      <data key="NumEmail">4</data>
      <data key="TotalKb">7687</data>
    </node>
    ... more nodes ...
    <edge source="Ann" target="Ben">
      <data key="NumMsg">1</data>
    </edge>
    ... more edges ...
  </graph>
</graphml>
```

> **NOTE** GraphML is well documented at http://graphml.graphdrawing.org/primer/graphml-primer.html.

JavaScript Object Notation (JSON) is a different open standard alternative to XML that works well with JavaScript and web-based interactive visualizations. d3.js is a popular visualization library that does use some graphs, and, as shown in the following example, a graph can be represented in JSON:

```
{
  "nodes":[
    { "name":"Ann","numEmail":1,"totalKb":2048 },
    { "name":"Ben","numEmail":4,"totalKb":7687 },
    [ "name":"Tim","numEmail":2,"totalKb":102 },
    { "name":"Zoe","numEmail":3,"totalKb":4292 }
  ],
  "links":[
    { "source":0,"target":1,"value":1 },
    { "source":1,"target":2,"value":2 },
    { "source":1,"target":3,"value":3 },
    { "source":2,"target":3,"value":2 ]
  ]
}
```

Essentially, this is a list of nodes, denoted as "nodes":[] and a list of links, shown as "link":[]. Each individual node object is shown in braces ({}) as a set of attribute:values. Note in this example that the links do not reference nodes by name. Instead, links reference the nodes by the index number of the node in its list, with the first item having an index of zero. For example, the link { "source":1,"target":3,"value":3 } is a link from source node index 1 (Ben) to target node index 3 (Zoe). All of the data is wrapped in a single set of braces to indicate the overall graph object.

Some tools will output JSON, but the format can vary. Gephi can load data and save data in a variety of formats, including export JSON via a Gephi plug-in. Its JSON format follows a similar pattern with some minor variances—for example, Gephi uses the term "edges," whereas d3.js uses the term "links." For the same data set shown previously, Gephi will output JSON like this:

```
{
  "edges":[
    {"source":"Ben","target":"Tim","id":"1422",
        "attributes":{"Weight":"2.0"},"color":"
        rgb(153,153,153)", size":2.0},
```

```
        {"source":"Ann","target":"Ben","id":"1421",
            "attributes":{"Weight":"1.0"},"color":"rgb(153,153,153)",
            "size":1.0},
        {"source":"Ben","target":"Zoe","id":"1423",
            "attributes":{"Weight":"3.0"},"color":"rgb(153,153,153)",
            "size":3.0},
        {"source":"Tim","target":"Zoe","id":"1424",
            "attributes":{"Weight":"2.0"},"color":"rgb(153,153,153)",
            "size":2.0}
    ],
    "nodes":[
      {"label":"Tim","x":3.358,"y":0.669,"id":"Tim",
          "attributes":{"numemails":"2.0"},"color":"rgb(153,153,153)",
          "size":4.0},
      {"label":"Ben","x":0.759,"y":0.063,"id":"Ben",
          "attributes":{"numemails":"4.0"},"color":"rgb(153,153,153)",
          "size":100.0},
      {"label":"Ann","x":-3.696,"y":0.833,"id":"Ann",
          "attributes":{"numemails":"1.0"},"color":"rgb(153,153,153)",
          "size":28.6},
      {"label":"Zoe","x":-0.422,"y":-1.566,"id":"Zoe",
          "attributes":{"numemails":"3.0"},"color":"rgb(153,153,153)",
          "size":57.0}
    ]
  }
```

Other Data Formats

In some cases, the target software may use data in a format that is not a list of nodes and a list of links.

Matrix layouts are used by some software where all the possible links are expected. For example, the d3.js chord diagram example uses a two-dimensional (2D) matrix of data to define the links.

PUTTING IT ALL TOGETHER

The essential first steps in graph analysis and visualization are to acquire the right data and to answer the objective. To recap, following are the key steps to getting data:

- **Objective**—Prior to collecting data, ensure that the objective is known. This will help establish what data needs to be collected and how it can be prepared. For example, the question of whether to maintain multiple links between nodes or aggregate them into a single link must be understood in the context of the overall project goals.

- **Collect**—Graph data can exist in data in many different ways. It may be necessary to collect data from multiple sources and/or evaluate the data to determine if there is a way that links could be resident in the data and potentially extracted (for example, by spreadsheets or programmatically).

- **Clean**—Unfortunately, real-world data may often have quality issues, and for graphs, you have additional concerns to address. Some graph software cannot handle self-loops, duplicate links, missing nodes, or Null values.

- **Connect**—Data must be transformed into a format that graph software can use—typically a list of nodes and links. Once prepared, the data must be output, and you have various file format alternatives. CSV, GDF, GML, and JSON can all be straightforward to use when preparing spreadsheets or via programming.

SUMMARY

In any kind of data analysis or data visualization, data is required. It is quite feasible for a project to fail with inadequate data and poor preparation. Therefore, take care to identify the right data and prepare it appropriately.

With a well-defined objective and the right data, you can proceed to the next step—graph analysis and visual layout, as described in Chapter 4. Finally, you can start to look at some the statistics and the organization of the graph visually.

4

STATS AND LAYOUT

Once graph data is prepared, it can be analyzed and visualized. The next goal is to get a high-level understanding of the graph:

- Is it all connected together or in many separate parts?

- Is it a hierarchy?

- Is it sparse, or is it densely connected?

- Are there obvious clusters?

These are the questions that this chapter addresses.

Statistics can provide a wealth of information, and some high-level statistics will answer questions about size, density, and number of separate graphs.

Layouts are an important visual technique to get a sense of the graph structure. Different layouts will reveal different aspects of the graph, enabling different types of analyses and supporting different types of stories.

A wide variety of node-and-link layouts can provide different ways of revealing the connections, groupings, and sequences in graphs. Other types of graph layouts focus on other properties of a graph, revealing flows, hierarchies, or multiple attributes.

BASIC GRAPH STATISTICS

You can compute a wide variety of graph statistics. Which graph statistics are relevant depends, in part, on your objective. Some of the simpler graph statistics are outlined here, such as density, degree, and centrality.

Size (Number of Nodes and Number of Edges)

As described in Chapter 3, "Data—Collect, Clean, and Connect," you can collect various simple graph statistics (such as graph size statistics—that is, number of nodes and number of edges) during the data preparation. Graph size statistics are used to establish how to best proceed further. Consider the following:

- Graphs with hundreds to hundreds of thousands of edges can be processed on a local computer, whereas graphs with millions to billions of edges require a multi-computer graph analysis approach.

- Graphs with thousands of edges can be directly visualized, whereas larger graphs require a strategy or interface for selecting and filtering down to smaller, more manageable subsets of the graph.

Size statistics also provide a quick validation that the graph data imported correctly into the target analysis and visualization software. Does the software show the same number of nodes and edges as noted when the data was prepared?

Density

Graph density is the ratio of actual edges to the maximum possible edges. A fully connected graph (that is, a *dense graph*) will have every node connected to every other node—for n nodes, the maximal graph will approach n^2 edges for a directed graph (or $\frac{1}{2}\,n^2$ nodes for an undirected graph). Density is a good summary statistic. A large dense graph can take a long time to process. Visualizing dense graphs can result in cluttered graphs with too many lines to visually decipher.

Keep the following in mind:

- **Dense graphs**—You can use, filter, extract, and visualize dense graphs in many ways. A *market basket analysis* (which is a graph of all products purchased together) is a dense graph, because almost every product combination is purchased given enough transactions. Depending on the objective, a dense graph may be

  - Reduced to just the top edges, for example, by filtering out edges below a set threshold or by retaining only the top *n* edges for each node.

  - Visualized using techniques that can work well on fully connected graphs (such as a chord diagram or matrix), or visualized using a node-and-link technique, with edges removed via edge filtering.

- **Sparse graphs**—By contrast, a sparse graph has a low number of edges compared to the maximum number of edges. Graphs that have the number of edges on the order of one, two, or three times the number of nodes are often good for visualizing, and many different layout techniques will work well.

- **Hierarchy** A density less than one hints that the graph could be a hierarchy and/or has multiple components. A *hierarchy* (or *tree*) is a sparse graph with a density where the number of edges is one less than the number of nodes for a single tree. If you have multiple separate trees, the difference between the nodes and edges indicates the number of trees.

Number of Components

A *component* is a completely disconnected subgraph from the rest of the graph. The number of components is the number of these distinct disconnected subgraphs. You can measure each component for size by counting the number of nodes and edges within that component. A single node with no connections is an *isolated node*.

When visualizing a graph with multiple components, use a layout that clearly separates the different components. Edges that crisscross make it more difficult to visually distinguish the different components, as shown in Figure 4-1.

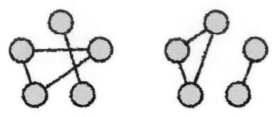

FIGURE 4-1: Different components are easier to identify if they do not overlap in the graph layout.

Degree and Paths

The famous graph game "Six Degrees of Kevin Bacon" is incorrectly named! For those unfamiliar with the game, a randomly named movie actor is linked to Kevin Bacon through other actors, where each pair of actors must have co-starred in a movie together. The challenge is to connect the random actor to Kevin Bacon in as few edges as possible (for example, "How many steps does it take to connect Arnold Schwarzenegger with Kevin Bacon?") This game is so popular that a number of websites exist to find the shortest path between an actor and Kevin Bacon (for example, http://oracleofbacon.org). The answer to previous question, by the way, is only two steps to connect Schwarzenegger and Bacon (for example through Tom Arnold or John Cleese).

Path

A *path* is a sequence of edges that connect a pair of vertices. The *distance* between any two nodes can be thought of as the shortest path between a pair of nodes in the graph and is measured as the number of edges used to create this route.

Average path length is a property of the entire graph that indicates the average number of edges across all the shortest paths for every possible pair of nodes in a network. Intuitively speaking, it measures how many edges must be travelled across to get from one place in the network to another.

The *diameter* of a graph is simply the largest of all the shortest paths between each pair of nodes in the graph. Graph diameter can be an interesting measure to get a sense of how spread out or how compact the graph is. Different layouts can emphasize (for example, force-directed) or hide (for example, chord) the sense of diameter. A layout that emphasizes diameter will emphasize the outermost leaves, as well as make the center more visually apparent. Figure 4-2 shows an example.

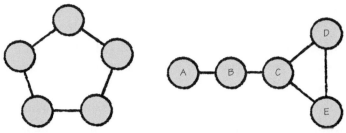

FIGURE 4-2: The two graphs shown here each have five nodes and five edges. The left graph has a diameter of 2. The graph on the right has a diameter of 3 (for example, from A to D).

In business applications, paths are interesting when there is a sequence being analyzed, such as paths through a website, or a *customer journey* to purchase a new vehicle. The goal of the analysis may be to minimize the number of steps in the path, reduce the number of abandoned shopping carts, or make each step in the journey a positive experience.

Referring back to the Kevin Bacon game, the target of the game is to find the shortest path (in less than six steps) to Kevin Bacon. The game could be more accurately renamed to "Shortest Path to Kevin Bacon." The reference to six degrees is a reference to earlier social network theory that everyone in the world is only six steps away from any other person in the world. When talking about graphs, the term *distance* is used to measure lengths of paths whereas the term *degree* (discussed next) is a property of a node.

Degree

Node degree is the number of edges connecting to a given node. A node with degree zero is a node with no edges—it is an isolated node. A node with degree one has only a single edge and is often called a *leaf node*.

When considering the entire graph, the *average degree* is simply an average of the degree of all nodes. When the average degree is higher, each node has high connectivity, the graph is densely connected with a large number of edges, and dense graphs tend to become more difficult to lay out nicely (for example, there will often be many more crossing lines).

The *maximum degree* can be particularly interesting. For example, in a social network, the node with the maximum degree is the one with the most connected nodes. The assumption in "Six Degrees of Kevin Bacon" is that Kevin Bacon is a highly connected person—that is, that he has a very high degree, making it easy to connect to him.

High-degree people in social networks can be critical in the success of spreading a message or spreading a virus. Consider Gaëtan Dugas, an early HIV case in the 1980s. Gaëtan is node "0" in the graph shown in Figure 4-3. Through the analysis of relationships across various states (shown as two letters), cases were sequenced (shown as numbers) and connected back to Gaëtan. He became known as "patient zero" because he was the earliest known patient in this study.

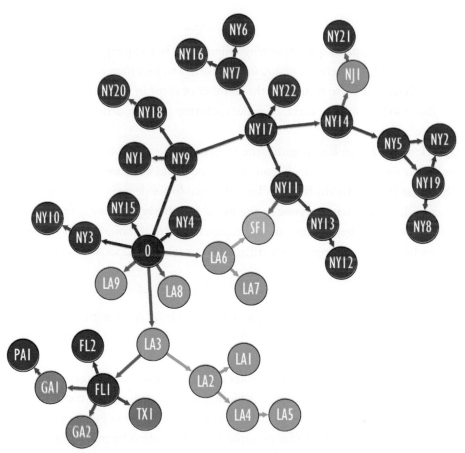

FIGURE 4-3: This graph is from an early study of HIV where patient 0 is the first HIV case and also the highest degree, making him suspect as an early source.

Original source: American Journal of Medicine, *March 1984*

(redrawn based on http://en.wikipedia.org/wiki/File:AIDS_index_case_graph.svg*)*

NOTE

This graph was re-created in Gephi. For a more detailed graph and more information on Gaëtan, see http://en.wikipedia.org/wiki/Ga%C3%ABtan_Dugas.

Centrality

Centrality is an attempt to identify the nodes at the center of the graph. You can measure centrality in many different ways:

- *Degree centrality* is the simplest. This is simply the node with the highest degree (that is, the highest number of connections). In a social network, this is the very well-connected person, and the importance of this person is that he or she will likely know what's going on around him or her because he or she is so well-connected.

- *Betweenness centrality* measures the number of times that a particular node is a member of the shortest path between two other nodes.

- *Closeness centrality* measures the average distance to all other nodes from each node. In a social network, this could be a VIP for which all communications pass through a few intermediaries (for example, an assistant or a spouse), but acts as a bridge between different clusters.

- *Katz centrality* sums all of the weighted distances to all other nodes from a given node. The further away a node is from the measured node, the lower the weight and the lower the contribution to centrality.

- *Eigenvector* centrality is similar to Katz centrality, but it is a recursive approach where a node is more likely to be central if its neighbors are central.

- *PageRank* centrality is famous as the method used by Google to rank pages. Similar to Katz and eigenvector, it additionally weights nodes by other factors, such as the degree of the node.

So, is Kevin Bacon at the center of all actors? Perhaps Bacon has starred in a large number of epic movies with casts of thousands and, therefore, has the highest degree resulting in degree centrality. Or, perhaps Bacon has been in only a few movies but is connected with some extremely well-connected actors for betweenness centrality. The answer also depends on the data. With each new movie, every actor's centrality score can shift.

These subtle differences can be important when discussing relative importance of different nodes in a network, as shown in the diagrammatic social network in Figure 4-4.

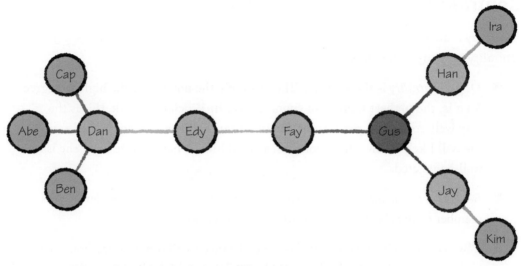

FIGURE 4-4: This small social network shows different key central people.

- Dan has the highest degree centrality (that is, has the most connections). Dan is important because he has the most immediate friends.

- Gus has the highest betweenness centrality, meaning Gus most frequently occurs on the shortest path. If a message needs to travel between any two people, Gus is mostly likely to be on the path.

- Fay has the best closeness—that is, the shortest average distance to all other nodes. Starting a message at Fay gets the message to everyone else in the fewest number of steps. Note that even though Fay (and Edy) each have only two edges, they occupy the critical bridge between the left and right sides of the graph.

Viral Marketing Example

A small real-world example can illustrate many of these statistical concepts and exhibit many similar properties to the schematic diagram shown in Figure 4-4. If you happily forward e-mails, you may be generating data that marketers can analyze. The image in Figure 4-5 is the result of a viral e-mail campaign for a single e-mail starting at John (blue node) and then forwarded successively through a number of people.

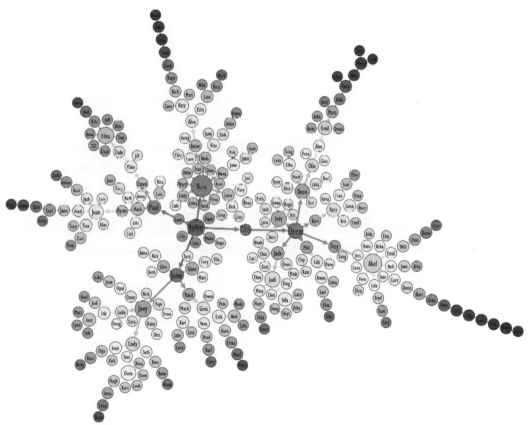

FIGURE 4-5: This network shows the spread of a viral e-mail starting with John. Statistics help identify some of the key nodes.

- *High degree* people are shown by node size. Vern and Abel distribute e-mails widely.

- *Betweenness centrality* is represented by text size. John and Drew have the highest betweenness centrality—and each is at the center of respective halves of the network.

- *Closeness centrality* is represented by color. The central horizontal spine—John, Tiny, and Drew—are the deepest blue.

- *Furthest away* is Yuko (purple, far right) as measured by closeness centrality. Betweenness and degree do not differentiate between leaf nodes, but closeness does.

- Note that Tiny has only two connections but is in a critical position joining the two halves of the network.

This example shows some of different, critical roles that various nodes have in this social network and how some of those roles can be revealed through both statistics such as centrality and the visual representation. The statistics also hint at some of the potential characteristics of these people. For example, although people such as Tiny or Trey may have very low degree (that is, very few edges), the edges that they do have are highly influential. Expressed differently, access to Tiny and Trey may be limited, but if they can be accessed, they can open up new large clusters.

> **NOTE** This data set is available in the supplementary materials under `ViralMarketing`. Note that the data has been cleansed, and names are not actual names.

LAYOUTS

Many different kinds of layouts can reveal different structures in the graph.

Node-and-Link Layouts

One common method for drawing graphs is to draw nodes as markers, and edges as lines connecting them (also referred to as *links*). Table 4-1 provides more detail.

TABLE 4-1: Node-and-Link Layouts

TYPE	EXAMPLE	DESCRIPTION
Force-Directed		These layouts mimic physical forces, with forces pushing nodes apart, and links pulling connected nodes together.
Node-Only		These layouts are used in conjunction with force-directed layouts, particularly with large graphs.
Time-Oriented		These layouts are used where time is an element of the graph. A time-based ordering facilitates seeing the sequence.
Top-Down		These layouts are a traditional organizational layout of a hierarchy—top-down or left-right.
Radial		Sometimes a circular layout for graphs and hierarchies are effective.

Other Layouts

You can use a variety of other graph layouts and techniques for analyzing graphs visually. Some of these are shown in Table 4-2.

TABLE 4-2: Other Layouts

TYPE	EXAMPLE	DESCRIPTION
Maps		When geographic coordinates are available, you can organize the nodes based on location, and add a map.
Chord Diagram		This is a circular layout that can be useful for showing directional flows.
Adjacency Matrix		Links are represented within a matrix.
Treemap		This is an area-based representation of a hierarchy.
Hierarchical Pie		This is a circular area-based representation of a hierarchy with explicit levels.
Parallel Coordinates		This is usually not used for graph analysis but can be used for interacting with some types of graphs, such as bipartite graphs (for example, network security).

The choice of layout is important. Perception of the graph can be highly influenced by different layouts. Figure 4-6 shows a tiny graph with four nodes and six edges represented in four different ways. In the left diagram, all the nodes are evenly spread out around the perimeter, but two links are crossed. The second diagram has no crossed links, but the node in the center of the triangle perceptually is different than the ones around the edges, leading to a potentially erroneous conclusion that the center node has higher centrality than the others. The third diagram has all the nodes in a line, but two are centered and two are at the ends. The final diagram shows a completely different representation using filled areas to represent nodes and a shared boundary between areas to represent an edge.

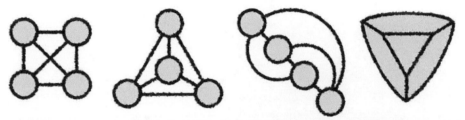

FIGURE 4 6: This shows the same graph drawn four different ways. All nodes have the same number of connections but appear differently relative to their neighbors in the right three graphs.

Force-Directed Layout

A highly popular technique used to lay out graphs is a *force-directed layout*. The approach is appealing because it seems intuitive, can work on most any type of graph, and can work for large-sized graphs. The approach essentially pulls together nodes that are connected and may push apart nodes that are not connected.

This is sometimes called a "spring" layout. In other words, links are considered as springs, and the springs will stretch and compress if needed but have a set size when they are at rest. Typically, all the nodes and springs start in a random layout, and the springs are recomputed iteratively until the forces cancel each other out.

Force-directed layouts are popular because of the intuitive outcome—nodes that are far away from each other are likely many steps away from each other, and nodes that are physically close to each other are likely only a step or two away from each other. Figure 4-7 shows an example of a force-directed layout applied to a channel-flipping data set. This is data from a television viewer, with each node representing a different television channel and a link indicating a click changing from one channel to the other.

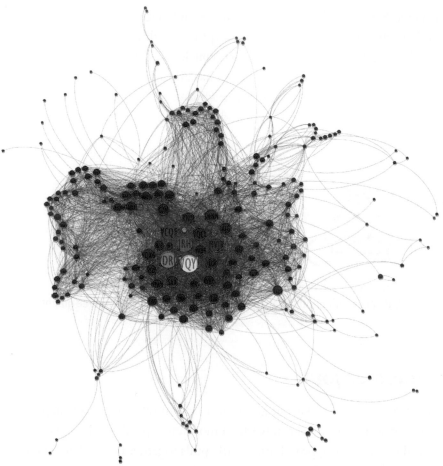

FIGURE 4-7: Nodes are television channels, and links are clicks from a remote control showing a person flipping from one channel to another.

At first glance, this may appear chaotic with thousands of purple links. Visually, this can be read as follows:

- In the center are approximately two dozen nodes dominated by a half dozen yellow and orange large nodes. With so many links around them, they are in a sea of purple links. These are the most-watched television channels, such as VQRI and VDRU, which are major national broadcast networks (station identifiers have been replaced with these generic names). Also, because they are very close to each other, the person is most frequently clicking from one of these channels in the center to another adjacent channel.

- Immediately above and to the left of the largest nodes is a cluster of medium-sized purple nodes (for example, GAN, GANPE, GANZE, and so on). This is a collection of specialty cable channels that have a high degree of connection between them, forming a distinct cluster.

- Tiny nodes near the perimeter of the image surrounded by a lot of white are stations with low viewership. They tend to have very few, very long lines connecting them back to the rest of data—meaning that these are channels that are not clicked through from very many other channels.

- Long tendrils of channels radiate out from the center. These tendrils represent channels that are most commonly clicked through in a sequence, and the start of the clicking sequence is more likely to start at the end of the tendril closer to the center. The many purple links to and from various nodes indicate many paths to and from these channels. These tendrils tend to be channel packages (for example, a set of basketball channels or a set of baseball channels).

To get a nice force-directed layout requires using one or more force-directed layout algorithms. Some graph packages provide a number of different algorithms with many settings. Some use the names of researchers; some use generic names.

Some common layout algorithms may include the following:

- **Fruchterman Reingold**—The *Fruchterman Reingold layout* algorithm can be a good place to start. It lays out the graph in a fairly compact circle, and separate components stay within this circle, as opposed to flying away as found in some other layout algorithms. The downside to Fruchterman Reingold is that all nodes tend to be the same distance apart, and separate components may not be readily apparent. Fruchterman Reingold is highly dependent on the layout before it is run, so a better result may occur after first running one of the other layouts.

- **Force Atlas**—The *Force Atlas layouts* can produce good layouts pulling strongly connected nodes together and weakly connected nodes apart. Force Atlas may require more iterative experimentation with parameters. If available, try Force Atlas 2, and try adjusting parameters such as "Prevent Overlap," "LogMode," and "Scaling." Scaling adjusts the ratio of the attraction force along the links and the repulsion between nodes. Force Atlas can work well for dense graphs and fully connected graphs where the edges have weights associated with them. Force Atlas sometimes is less effective when the graph is very sparse, or the graph has many components.

■ **Yifan Hu**—*Yifan Hu* is somewhat similar to Force Atlas. It can be fast on large data sets. Whereas Force Atlas tends to get different results tweaking various parameters, Yifan Hu tends to come up with a similar layout. Yifan Hu does not take into account node sizes, edge weights, and so on, in the software package Gephi.

To get a sense of how these different algorithms compare, Table 4-3 shows the results of these algorithms on a few different data sets (all done using Gephi).

TABLE 4-3: Samples of Different Layout Algorithm Results with Different Types of Graphs

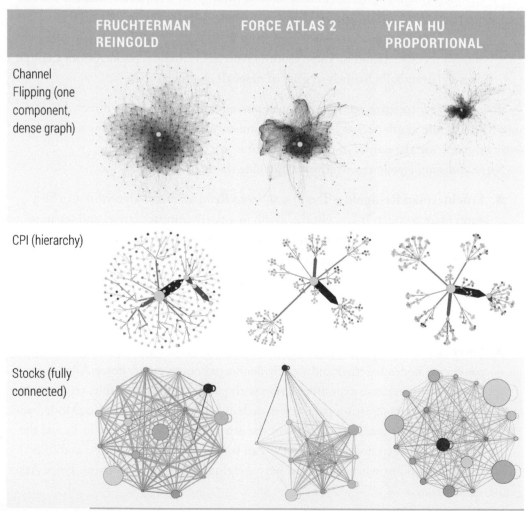

	FRUCHTERMAN REINGOLD	FORCE ATLAS 2	YIFAN HU PROPORTIONAL
Channel Flipping (one component, dense graph)			
CPI (hierarchy)			
Stocks (fully connected)			

More: Organic, Prefuse, Force, Spring, and SOM

In different graph packages, there will be completely different layout algorithms. For example, Cytoscape has force-directed layouts such as Organic, Prefuse, Force, Spring, and Inverted Self Organizing Map (SOM). Where do you start? Sometimes you should try them all! Figure 4-8 shows the different results on the channel-flip data.

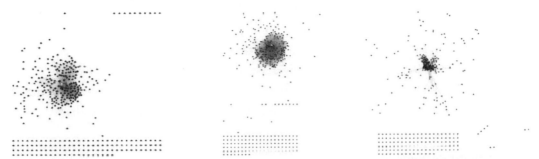

FIGURE 4-8: This shows Cytoscape's layout of the television channel browsing data using Organic, Prefuse, and Spring layouts

In all these layouts, it is apparent that there is one large densely connected cluster, with a number of more weakly connected channels around the center. The big difference between the defaults in these algorithms seems to be the density of the center of the clusters and how far spread out some of the outliers are. At the heart of all force-directed algorithms are the forces. In most cases, you have control over these settings.

> **NOTE** Getting a nice force-directed layout almost always requires some experimentation with different algorithms and different settings.

Force Settings and Other Settings

Force-directed layouts are, by definition, controlled by their forces. Getting a good layout often involves going beyond the defaults and adjusting some of the force attributes, such as attraction, repulsion, and gravity.

- **Attraction/repulsion**—Adjusting the ratio between attraction/repulsion is one important consideration. This may be set as a single parameter (for example,

Relative Strength in Yifan Hu, Scaling in Force Atlas, or both in Gephi) or as multiple parameters (for example, Attraction and Repulsion in Force-Directed layout in Cytoscape). If all the nodes are in a blob, increasing repulsion can help push the nodes apart.

- **Gravity**—Gravity is similar to attraction, but it applies to all nodes, even when not connected. Turning up gravity can bring very distant nodes back toward the center, but turning up gravity too high will create a packed circle.

- **Edge weight**—The strength of the attraction can be the same for all nodes, or it can be based on weight of the edges. Strong weights will pull nodes closer together. Edge weight is an attribute provided with the data. This is perhaps the most important additional attribute to include when you prepare your data.

Other Layout Settings

Beyond basic control over forces, each layout algorithm will have a bewildering set of additional settings. Some are self-explanatory (such as no-overlap, which is a useful setting to turn on). Others may be vague. Experimentation with these settings is required.

Many other possible settings are available, including linear versus logarithmic, temperature, and so on. For example, in the previous comparisons, note that the CPI Force Atlas 2 example has edge weight influence 0.2 and scaling 50, whereas the Stocks Force Atlas 2 example is LinLog with gravity 8.

> **TIP**
>
> Getting the wrong balance between attraction and repulsion can cause most of the nodes to collapse into a big blob or fly out toward infinity. Simply adjust the forces and try again.

Force-directed layouts can be finicky. When using default Force Atlas 2 settings for the Stocks graph included in the supplemental material, it completely disappears off the screen (that is, expands so quickly as if to disappear). If your graph expands too much, try increasing the attraction/gravity and/or switching to a logarithmic mode. If it all the nodes are in a tight blob, try increasing the repulsion, reducing gravity, or, if available, forcing no-overlap.

Speed, Iteration, and Approximation Settings

Some settings are related to the speed and quality of the layout. Force-directed algorithms step through each node, incrementally adjusting the position of each one to resolve the forces. They repeat these steps hundreds or thousands of times—this is the number of *iterations*. Reducing the number of iterations increases the speed but reduces the quality. Similarly, settings that increase speed, or increase approximations, will reduce quality.

Interacting with Force-Directed Layouts

You can interact with force-directed layouts in different ways, including the following:

- **Interactive layout**—The iterative nature of force-directed layouts can be a benefit. You can make adjustments while it is running or at stops between iterations. You can adjust attraction and repulsion settings and see the impact while you watch. You can watch a cluster of intertwined nodes appear to be stuck together, and you can help disentangle these nodes interactively by dragging a few nodes out—way out—and the other nodes will follow.

  In some software, you must wait for the iterations to finish before you can click and drag nodes. In this case, you can still adjust the nodes and then run the algorithm again (but make sure that the algorithm does not reset all the positions each time you run it in the settings).

- **Label Adjust and other tweaking layouts**—There may also be some additional layouts that are intended to be run after a force-directed layout. The Label Adjust layout minimally pushes nodes around to minimize the overlap of labels. Similarly, the Noverlap layout pushes nodes around to minimize overlapping nodes.

- **Mix-and-match layouts**—Because the layouts are iterative, you can also start with one layout and a little bit of another layout. In this mode of experimenting with different layouts, it can be useful to slow down the layout algorithms—each one has a speed setting (or a *step size*) that can be reduced. The e-mail graph shown in the introduction to Part 2 (Figure P2-1) started with a Force Atlas 2 layout and then has some Fruchterman Reingold added.

Node-Only Layout

Sometimes you have so many links that it's not worth showing all of them. Using a force-directed layout implies that the distance between adjacent nodes indicates the strength of the connection between those nodes. For large graphs, thousands or millions of links clutter the view, making it impossible to see patterns. Instead, the links can be removed from the display and the clusters and adjacencies are still visible.

For example, the http://internet-map.net by Ruslan Enikeev shown in Figure 4-9 includes 350,000 websites with many millions of links. By showing only the nodes, the viewer can see relative clustering and implied relationships.

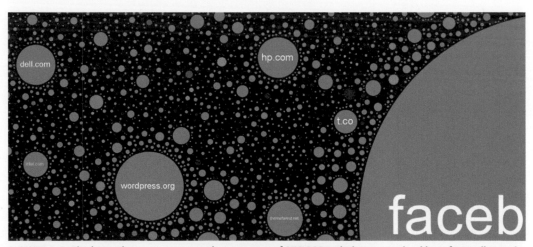

FIGURE 4-9: The http://internet-map.net shows a map of 350,000 websites, organized by a force-directed layout.

Copyright 2014 by Ruslan Enikeev (used with permission)

Some care should be taken with this approach. It is feasible for nodes that are not actually close to each other to be close in a force-directed graph, particularly with sparse graphs and only gravity pushing nodes apart. In fact, a graph with no links, but some gravity to pull nodes together and some repulsion to keep some spacing between nodes, can create a nice-looking, but meaningless, layout.

Time Oriented

Some kinds of graphs have nodes organized by time. Patents have references to earlier examples—each reference is a directed edge. Tracking down successive references generates a directed graph. Consider an example.

A client involved in a patent investigation was excited at the prospect of visualizing the relationship between patents. A typical force-directed layout results in a visualization that clearly shows clustering such as Figure 4-10, which was created with Cytoscape using the Prefuse layout. However, there is no sense of time—two nodes beside each other may have occurred at completely different times.

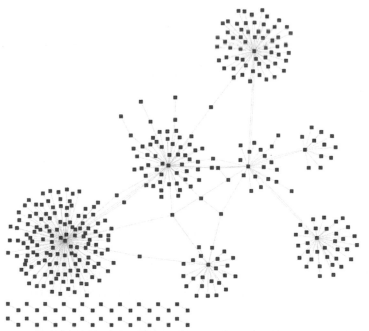

FIGURE 4-10: In this force-directed layout of patent citations, any indication of which nodes came earlier and which nodes came later is not visible.

This is a perfect example of where a force-directed layout is ineffective. The time element is an essential feature in understanding this data. To better understand which items came first and which items came later, a layout is needed where the sequence is preserved. A hierarchical layout, or a *directed acyclic graph (DAG)* layout, will preserve order so that the direction is always pointing down (or right).

The layout in Figure 4-11 is the same patent data (using the hierarchical layout from Cytoscape) with the earliest patents at the top and later patents toward the bottom. Although the layout isn't as compact as the previous force-directed layout, it provides a clear indication of precedence—the earlier patents are always above later patents. For any particular patent of interest, links going up are prior patents cited by this particular patent, and links going down are later patents that have cited this particular patent. This visual relationship of before and after is the basic approach used in the interactive exploration of massive time-based networks.

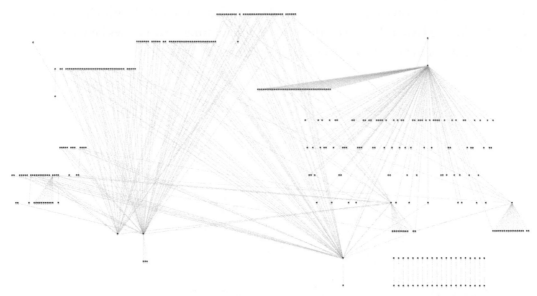

FIGURE 4-11: In this hierarchical layout of patent citations, earlier patents are above later patents.

Note that time is not explicitly depicted. You cannot look at a particular patent and make a determination about what time that patent occurred. Near the bottom-right corner of the image are a dozen components of two nodes each. The layout only indicates which came first and which came second. If one pair occurred in the 1930s and another pair came in the 1970s, this can only be determined by interacting with the nodes of interest.

Top-Down and Other Orthogonal Hierarchies

Hierarchical data may be displayed in a "traditional" top-down hierarchy. This is similar to the previous time-oriented approach, except that the data is strictly a hierarchy of data.

One interesting consideration is whether to set out the hierarchy as top-down or, alternatively, left-right or bottom-up. Another consideration regards labels. If the hierarchy is wide, it will be difficult to fit labels on it. On the other hand, if the hierarchy is turned sideways, there will be much more space horizontally to fit in the labels. Figure 4-12 and Figure 4-13 show the same hierarchy previously shown in Figure 4-5 with a force-directed layout, only this time with a hierarchical layout created in yEd.

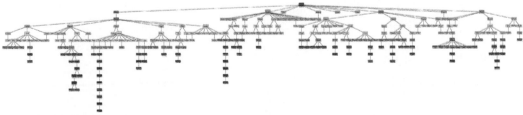

FIGURE 4-12: This hierarchical layout of the viral marketing example uses the same data as shown in Figure 4-5. The top-down layout results in a wide graph, making it difficult to label nodes.

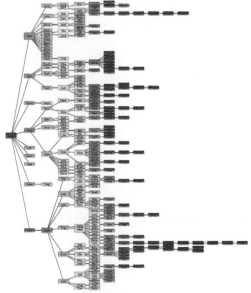

FIGURE 4-13: In this hierarchical layout of the viral marketing example shown in Figure 4-5, a left-to-right orientation allows more space for node labels.

With larger hierarchies, a strictly top-down or left-right approach is often unusable because the graph becomes too long and narrow. Alternatives to purely top-down or left-right are other orthogonal layouts that alternate between top-down/left-right, or otherwise organize nodes into a hierarchy of blocks. Figure 4-14 shows an organizational chart for more than 4,000 managers within 6 levels from the CEO, in this case generated with the yEd compact tree layout. The CEO is the tiny yellow dot in the top-left corner.

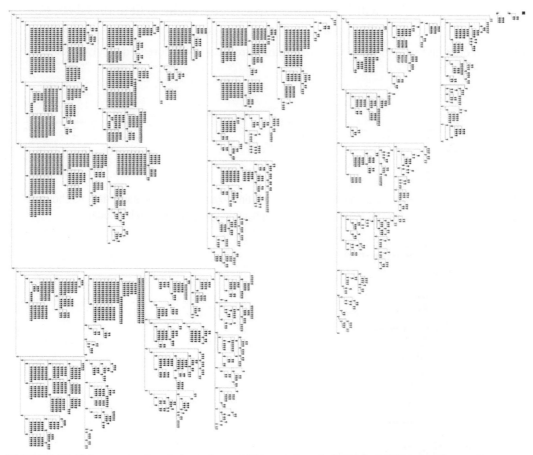

FIGURE 4-14: This organizational chart shows 4,000 managers in 6 levels at a large-scale company.

Radial Hierarchy

A radial hierarchy can be preferable to a top-down or left-right hierarchy, particularly when hierarchies are very wide. As always, a number of variations exist. In yEd, the radial hierarchy generates a nice hierarchy with successive circular shells, as shown in the left of Figure 4-15. The radial hierarchy may work well with hundreds of nodes but can be problematic with larger hierarchies.

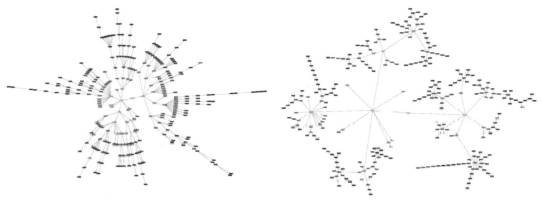

FIGURE 4-15: Radial hierarchy and circular hierarchy of viral e-mails.

An alternative circular layout will set out each successive level as another set of circles around each successive node—as shown on the right side of Figure 4-15. It may not be particularly appealing on this hierarchy with a few hundred nodes but can work well with even larger hierarchies. It tends to look good on hierarchies where intermediate nodes in the tree tend to have degrees higher than 3 or 4 so that the circular shape is more visibly apparent.

Figure 4-16 shows a hierarchy of more than 4,000 managers in a Fortune 500 company. The president is the person shown near the bottom left of the image as a light yellow dot. People with more direct reports are clearly more visible surrounded by larger circles of nodes. And you can get a sense of circles made up of smaller circles. The upper-left quadrant of the image shows in the center a direct report of the CEO, surrounded by many smaller bubbles showing successive levels of managers and sub-managers. Comparing these various levels of bubbles provides a much stronger sense of who is responsible for different areas of the company, compared to the traditional organizational chart showing only one or two levels seen back in Figure 4-14.

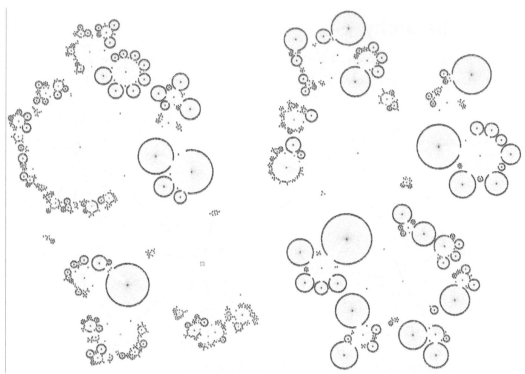

FIGURE 4-16: This is a circular layout of 4,000 managers.

Geographic Layout and Maps

Sometimes, nodes correspond to cities or countries, and you may want to lay out the visualization geographically. Physical networks, such as air traffic, rail traffic, electrical grids, pipelines, and many supply-chain networks are the kinds of data that have geographical coordinates associated with them. Once longitude and latitude coordinates are available for each node, the x and y values for each node can simply be set to these coordinates and then displayed in any graph software that supports setting x and y coordinates based on user-provided data. Figure 4-17 shows domestic passenger air traffic across the continental United States set out geographically.

Sometimes graphs on maps end up with too many nodes overlapping each other, typically in densely populated areas, such as the East Coast of the United States The incredible density of airports in Figure 4-17 obscures many of the airports. Instead of achieving exact geographical layout, a better approach might be to start with a geographical layout and then shift the nodes automatically to reduce overlap. The result will be easier to view with less overlap, and the relative location of nodes to each other will be similar. Compare Figure 4-17 and Figure 4-18 to see the difference.

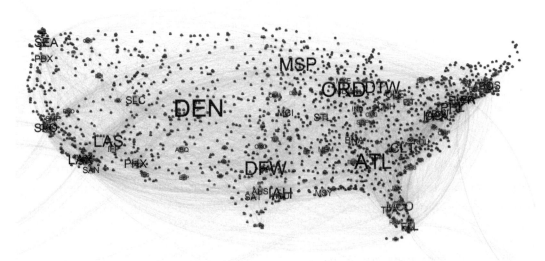

FIGURE 4-17: This shows air traffic in the continental United States. Airport size indicates the number of cities served by that airport (that is, node degree). Edge color indicates the number of passengers (dark for few, bright green for many).

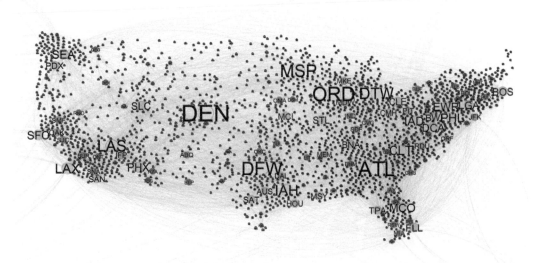

FIGURE 4-18: This geographical layout shows airports shifted to reduce overlap.

Chord Diagrams

When viewing flows that go in each direction between a pair of nodes, the challenge can be representing the magnitude of the flows in each direction, as shown in Figure 4-19.

FIGURE 4-19: This shows bidirectional flows with overlapping links, curved links, and a chord link.

A *chord diagram* represents flow in each direction by joining the nodes on opposite sides with a single chord, where the thickness of the chord indicates the magnitude of the outbound flow from that node. By visually comparing the sizes at either end of the chord, the viewer has a sense of the total flow in each direction. Visually comparing both ends indicates the difference between the two. Figure 4-20 indicates trade flow between major countries depicted as a chord diagram. Chord diagrams will be discussed more in Chapter 12, "Flows."

Global Trade Flow, 2010 ($USD)

FIGURE 4-20: This shows trade flows between countries.

Adjacency Matrix

The connections between nodes can be shown in a matrix. The row header and column header indicate the nodes, and a filled square in the matrix indicates an adjacency (that is, a link) between two items, based on which row and which column it is associated with.

In the example shown in Figure 4-21, the colored matrix indicates all the edges between every pair of stocks. The diagonal is white—these are self-loops and not relevant in this analysis. The number in the cell is the correlation, which ranges from negative one to positive one, and can be considered an edge weight.

For a directed graph, the rows represent source nodes and the columns represent target nodes. The colors of the cells on either side of the diagonal will be different. For an undirected graph, the colors are symmetric across the diagonal, and the lower diagonal does not need to be drawn.

	XRX	PCLN	YHOO	CA	PBI	LINTA	GOOG	AMZN	LNKD	MSFT	FB	HPQ	NCR	INTC	AAPL	SYMC	ORCL	EBAY	IBM
XRX		0.96	0.95	0.95	0.92	0.89	0.88	0.86	0.85	0.83	0.81	0.80	0.75	0.73	0.62	0.45	0.09	-0.29	-0.67
PCLN	0.96		0.96	0.96	0.94	0.94	0.91	0.93	0.81	0.85	0.87	0.73	0.77	0.73	0.73	0.29	0.14	-0.33	-0.79
YHOO	0.95	0.96		0.92	0.94	0.93	0.92	0.92	0.77	0.87	0.84	0.74	0.68	0.79	0.70	0.28	0.18	-0.28	-0.70
CA	0.95	0.96	0.92		0.89	0.91	0.91	0.86	0.83	0.89	0.77	0.82	0.79	0.80	0.62	0.37	0.06	-0.36	-0.71
PBI	0.92	0.94	0.94	0.89		0.91	0.90	0.91	0.76	0.80	0.86	0.69	0.62	0.69	0.74	0.31	0.24	-0.34	-0.69
LINTA	0.89	0.94	0.93	0.91	0.91		0.95	0.95	0.65	0.84	0.80	0.74	0.63	0.77	0.72	0.13	0.26	-0.29	-0.69
GOOG	0.88	0.91	0.92	0.91	0.90	0.95		0.91	0.67	0.89	0.71	0.81	0.57	0.83	0.63	0.17	0.22	-0.33	-0.62
AMZN	0.86	0.93	0.92	0.86	0.91	0.95	0.91		0.61	0.76	0.84	0.66	0.53	0.66	0.79	0.05	0.34	-0.29	-0.74
LNKD	0.85	0.81	0.77	0.83	0.76	0.65	0.67	0.61		0.66	0.73	0.65	0.83	0.55	0.42	0.71	-0.19	-0.28	-0.61
MSFT	0.83	0.85	0.87	0.89	0.80	0.84	0.89	0.76	0.66		0.57	0.80	0.66	0.92	0.48	0.18	0.01	-0.33	-0.58
FB	0.81	0.87	0.84	0.77	0.86	0.80	0.71	0.84	0.73	0.57		0.41	0.68	0.48	0.83	0.27	0.27	-0.21	-0.81
HPQ	0.80	0.73	0.74	0.82	0.69	0.74	0.81	0.66	0.65	0.80	0.41		0.55	0.74	0.32	0.37	-0.11	-0.40	-0.38
NCR	0.75	0.77	0.68	0.79	0.62	0.63	0.57	0.53	0.83	0.66	0.68	0.55		0.58	0.40	0.50	-0.20	-0.21	-0.64
INTC	0.73	0.73	0.79	0.80	0.69	0.77	0.83	0.66	0.55	0.92	0.48	0.74	0.58		0.39	0.11	0.05	-0.29	-0.46
AAPL	0.62	0.73	0.70	0.62	0.74	0.72	0.63	0.79	0.42	0.48	0.83	0.32	0.40	0.39		-0.06	0.45	-0.29	-0.74
SYMC	0.45	0.29	0.28	0.37	0.31	0.13	0.17	0.05	0.71	0.18	0.27	0.37	0.50	0.11	-0.06		-0.31	-0.04	-0.09
ORCL	0.09	0.14	0.18	0.06	0.24	0.26	0.22	0.34	-0.19	0.01	0.27	-0.11	-0.20	0.05	0.45	-0.31		0.15	0.02
EBAY	-0.29	-0.33	-0.28	-0.36	-0.34	-0.29	-0.33	-0.29	-0.28	-0.33	-0.21	-0.40	-0.21	-0.29	-0.29	-0.04	0.15		0.40
IBM	-0.67	-0.79	-0.70	-0.71	-0.69	-0.69	-0.62	-0.74	-0.61	-0.58	-0.81	-0.38	-0.64	-0.46	-0.74	-0.09	0.02	0.40	

FIGURE 4-21: This adjacency matrix shows stock correlations. All edges are equally visible.

Matrix diagrams can be effective when the graph is fairly dense and where the goal is to analyze links. For an analyst trying to understand which stocks are strongly correlated and which are not (see the Stock example data set), the task is focused on all the edges. The matrix diagram in Figure 4-22 shows all the correlations—that is, all the edges—as a colored matrix with the detailed data values and all edges are equally visible.

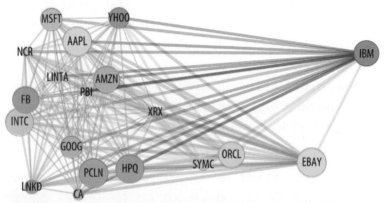

FIGURE 4-22: Using this force-directed graph of stock correlations, the assigned task requires analyzing links, but some links are difficult to see.

However, while showing the overall clustering pattern, the force-directed diagram (Figure 4-22) makes it more difficult to see all the links. Some links are very long, and others are not visible at all. Furthermore, the intuitive understanding of distance between nodes is useful for understanding the overall graph but is not effective for comparing individual links.

Look closely at the relationship between Symantec (SYMC) and Oracle (ORCL) versus eBay (EBAY) and IBM. In the matrix, eBay-IBM is stronger (0.4, light orange) than Symantec-Oracle (-0.3, reddish). But in the force-directed diagram, Symantec-Oracle is much closer together than eBay-IBM, and the link between Symantec-Oracle is difficult to perceive.

Sorting of matrix diagrams helps reveal some of the higher-level patterns. You can do simple sorting using a tool such as Excel and more advanced sorting with some light programming. By convention, the same sorting is always applied to both the rows and columns. Using Excel and sorted adjacency matrices are discussed in more detail in Chapter 7, "Point-and-Click Graph Tools."

Treemap

A *treemap* is a representation of a hierarchy as a series of nested rectangles completely filling the plot. The size of each rectangle is based on a quantity. You can visibly see the proportion of each item relative to its peers in the group.

Figure 4-23 (created with MicroStrategy Analytics Desktop) shows a treemap of U.S. inflation data as indicated by the various components that make up Consumer Price Index (CPI). The size of each box indicates the portion of the component within the CPI, and the color indicates the percent change over the first decade of the 2000s. Large items contribute significant weight to the CPI—the cost of housing is the single largest expense. Bright green items have increased the most—gasoline costs went up significantly in the 2000s. Bright red items have gone down the most—television prices have dropped significantly (for example, a 55-inch television would have been very expensive in 2000 and much more affordable in 2010).

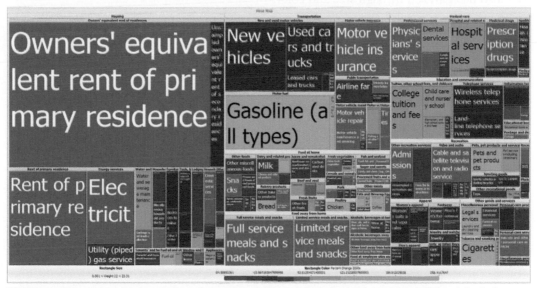

FIGURE 4-23: In this treemap of the U.S. Consumer Price Index, size indicates the weight of the index, and color indicates the change from 2000 to 2010.

Hierarchical Pie Chart

The authors were once working on a project for a Fortune 500 financial firm. The top executive for capital markets said to us, "I want a treemap so I can see what our whole portfolio looks like. But it can't be a treemap—50 percent of the people have no idea what it is, and the other 50 percent love them. I need something that is intuitive for everyone." The authors created a visualization based on a hierarchical pie chart that was successfully deployed to all the users.

Also known as a *sunburst chart*, the *hierarchical pie chart* is a close cousin of the treemap. A treemap focuses on the leaves of the tree (the boxes), and the intermediate levels of the tree are compressed into thin strips. As shown in Figure 4-24, in the hierarchical pie, the intermediate levels are on successive rings, and each of these intermediate levels can also be analyzed through size and color.

Parallel Coordinates

Often, in the analysis of graphs, the topology of the graph is not the objective, even though you may be analyzing graph data.

The *parallel coordinates* technique is *not* a graph layout. But it is extremely useful for the analysis of data with many attributes. Network log data contains graph information—source computers and target computers—as well as a wide variety of other fields (such as timestamp, ports, country, and so on).

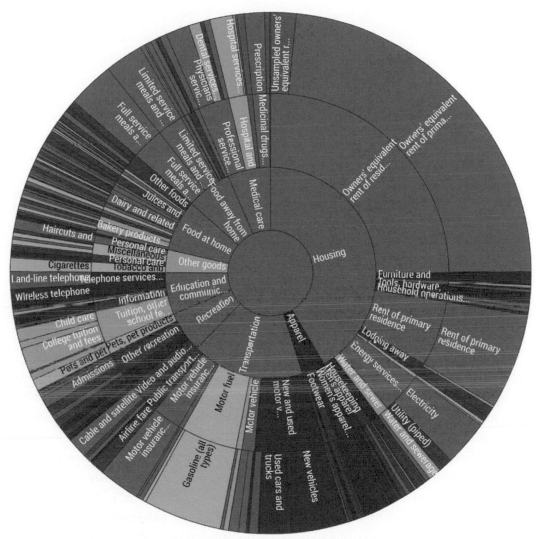

FIGURE 4-24: This hierarchical pie chart of the U.S. Consumer Price Index uses same data as Figure 4-23.

As shown in Figure 4-25, the parallel coordinates representation shows each field as a vertical line ranging from the minimum value to the maximum value. Each row of data becomes one zigzag line crossing over each field at the location corresponding to the data value.

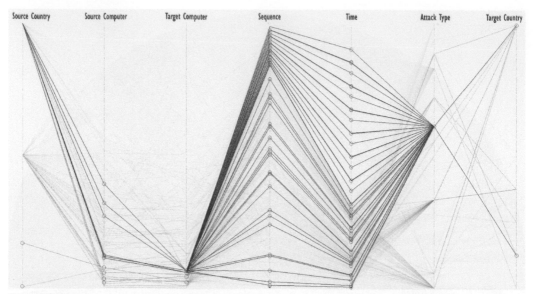

| Source Country | Source Computer | Target Computer | Sequence | Time | Attack Type | Target Country |

FIGURE 4-25: With this parallel coordinates visualization, you can view network security log file data with one attack type highlighted.

In Figure 4-25, anonymous network security data is plotted with the vertical axes representing source country, source computer, target computer, sequence, time (in seconds), attack type, and target country. The thin colored lines zigzagging across represent individual rows from the log file, with color indicating the attack type. In the snapshot, one attack type (registry reads) has been highlighted as bright red lines. The red lines emanate from one source country in the upper left and proceed through a few source computers (where the red lines cross the second axis "source") and primarily attach only a few target computers (where the red lines cross the third axis "target"). These attacks have occurred throughout the overall sequence and timeframe (where the red lines cross the fourth axis and fifth axis). The sixth axis is the attack type, and all of these lines are of the same attack type, and, therefore, all meet at one point.

In practice, parallel coordinate plots are used interactively to isolate data of interest, either by direct interaction with the plot—such as the click on the particular attack type as discussed previously—or via clicks on adjacent charts. Successive clicks can then be used to further isolate the data of interest.

Following with the previous example, it seems that a few computers are particularly targeted. These can be further isolated. In Figure 4-26, only one of the targeted computers of the registry reads attacks has been highlighted in bright red, as can be seen in the third column of the parallel coordinate plot, as well as the ninth item in the far-right bar chart. Visual inspection shows that this particular target computer is attacked from two different source computers (second column) and that these events occur at regular intervals over time (fifth column and also the timeline chart below). With this extra insight, combining link analysis with other variables, the security specialist may be able to reach a conclusion—for example, this is an expected regular event, and this is not an attack.

Parallel coordinate plot and linked-chart multi-variate analysis isn't the target of this book. However, it is a highly recommended data exploration and analysis technique that can be effective for analyzing some types of graphs.

NOTE   The graph in Figure 4-26 was created with Mondrian (http://www.rosuda.org/Mondrian).

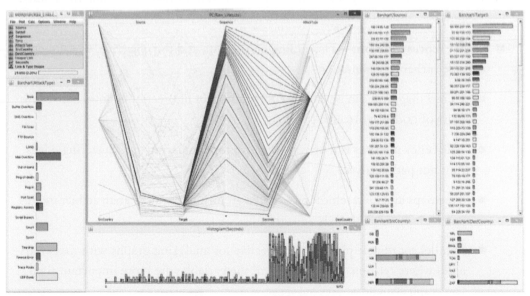

FIGURE 4-26: This isolates an attack type on only one target computer, with additional charts providing context.

PUTTING IT ALL TOGETHER

Statistics and layout are the starting points for analyzing and understanding graphs. To recap, following are key elements to keep in mind:

- **Statistics**—A profile of the entire network (such as size, density, number of components, average degree, and diameter) helps you to understand the nature of the graph, and assists you when it comes to visualizing the graph. Statistics such as degree and centrality help identify particular nodes of interest.

- **Node-and-link layout**—The node and link layout is a very common way to represent a graph and can be laid out with many different techniques.

  - Force-directed layouts are very popular, particularly with larger and denser graphs.

  - Time-ordered graphs can work well with directed graphs.

  - Circular and orthogonal layouts can work well for hierarchies and directional flows.

- **Other representations**—Depending on the data and the objective, you should consider other representations.

  - Chord diagrams can be effective for analysis of bidirectional flows between pairs of nodes in directed graphs.

  - Adjacency matrices can be very effective for comparing and clustering edges (but not path analysis).

  - Treemaps and hierarchical pies can be an intuitive way to analyze hierarchies, particularly when there is a magnitude.

  - Parallel coordinate plots can be effective for analyzing graphs with many variables where relationships between all the variables are more important than the graph structure.

SUMMARY

The first level of analyzing a graph is to get a high-level understanding of the graph. Creating some overall statistics and generating a graph layout can provide a good understanding of the types of relationships in the graph.

You should consider different kinds of layouts, depending on the objective and the nature of the graph, ranging from a variety of node-and-link layouts to other types of layouts such as adjacency matrixes, chord diagrams, treemaps, and, in some cases, parallel coordinates.

Once you have a layout, you must consider what data you want to reveal about the nodes and edges, and how to reveal it. Chapter 5 provides a discussion on the use of size, color, labels, line styles, and so on, to show this information in the graph.

5

VISUAL ATTRIBUTES

Once you have a basic graph with a reasonable layout, applying visual attributes is the next step. In a business environment, there is often much more data about nodes and edges, such as age, income, gender, frequency of purchases, type of relationship, strength of relationship, and so on. These can be perceived by using visual attributes such as colors, line widths, sizes, labels, and so on. Choosing the right visual attribute takes advantage of our human perception. For example, a bright red item pops out from gray ones, or larger items are more visually dominant than small items.

Following are some important attributes examined in this chapter:

- **Node attributes**—Not all nodes are the same. Which has the most connections? Which is the oldest? Which has the biggest change? Use visual attributes such as color and size to reveal node data.

- **Link attributes**—Which links have the strongest connections? What are the different types of links? In what direction do the links point? Visual attributes such as color, line width, and arrows show link data.

- **Labels**—Who is that? What is that node? Perhaps one of the most important elements (particularly in smaller graphs), labels should not be an afterthought, but carefully planned so that they are clear, legible, and informative.

Consider a portion of the e-mail visualization discussed in the previous chapters. Figure 5-1 shows a subset that represents people in the family of one of the authors e-mailing each other. Nodes represent people, and the links represent e-mail transfers between the users.

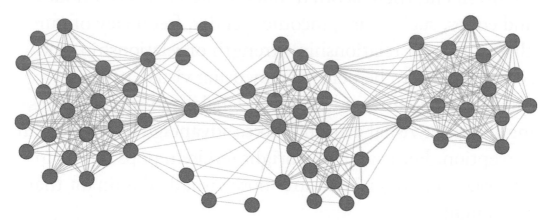

FIGURE 5-1: In this graph of e-mails among family, the graph shows three clusters but doesn't reveal additional details such as the number of e-mails, the size of e-mails, and who the people are.

The graph without any sizes, colors, or labels only reveals three clusters in the family and hints that a few people act as bridges between these clusters. But who are these people? Who sends the most e-mails? Who connects the different groups? What's different between these clusters? These are the sorts of questions best answered by adding visual attributes to the graph.

ESSENTIAL VISUAL ATTRIBUTES

Table 5-1 shows a few basic visual attributes that are effective in almost every graph for showing additional data attributes or graph statistics.

TABLE 5-1: Basic Visual Attributes

ATTRIBUTE	EXAMPLE	DESCRIPTION
Node size		Shows magnitudes or quantities such as counts or sums
Node color		Shows different categories, or shows positive/negative numeric values
Label		Shows individual identity of a node or link
Edge weight		Shows the strength of a connection between nodes
Edge color		Shows categories (such as the type of connection) or numeric values (such as how recent the connection is)
Edge type		Shows direction via arrows, or shows other attributes via line styles

As shown in Table 5-2, beyond the essentials, many additional attributes are useful for showing data or for increasing the visual clarity of graph.

TABLE 5-2: Additional Visual Attributes

ATTRIBUTE	EXAMPLE	DESCRIPTION
Bundled edges		Use these for aesthetics or to reveal relationships about connections.
Shapes		Use unique shapes to show a few different categories (for example, male/female, up/down, and so on).
Images		Use an image for a node (for example, a photo, a flag, an icon, a pie chart, bar chart, or sparkline).
Transparency, border color, arrow shape, font family, label offset, shadows, gradients, and more		There are other visual attributes that are less commonly used, sometimes because they are not available in a particular program, because they may be more obscure, or because they do not visually pop out as much as attributes such as size or color.

The availability of these visual attributes varies widely by software package. Depending on which software you are using, it can be challenging to find where to adjust the visual properties. In most cases, there will be one place in the software to adjust the visual attribute globally across the entire visualization (for example, set all colors to blue, set all lines to a particular thickness, set all shapes to circles), and this setting is usually easier to find. There will then be another place in the user interface to connect a visual attribute to a data value. This is referred to as a *style mapping* (in Cytoscape), *properties mapper* (in yEd), or *partition and ranking* (in Gephi).

Connecting data to visual attributes is different in each graph software package. In some packages, the options may be fairly limited, whereas other packages are highly flexible. For example, Cytoscape provides more visual attributes and more precise settings than some other graph software but may be more difficult to use.

KEY NODE ATTRIBUTES

Nodes often represent nouns. Some of the nodes in the examples so far in this book have been people, stocks, television channels, categories of purchases, websites, web pages, computers, and countries. Nouns often have additional attributes such as size, age, income, gender, viewers, profit, errors, or populations. Even if other data attributes are not available, you can use graph statistics such as degree and centrality. All of these additional data attributes are not visible in the layout of the graph, but you can show them by using a variety of visual attributes. In particular, the visual attributes of size, color, and label are very strong visual cues that can effectively indicate information and are configurable in most graph software packages.

Node Size

Size is a useful visual attribute for data that represents a *magnitude*. Data such as counts and sums in graph statistics (such as degree, that is, a count of the number of connections) are good candidates to represent with size. Data that is not negative or zero works well. Fields such as number of followers, total sales, page count, market capitalization, total bytes, weight, number of likes, number of passengers, total trade, and proportion of a whole can all work well. These are all non-negative data examples.

If the data has zero values, consider having a minimum size instead of zero, which is an invisible node. If the data has both positive values and negative values (for example, profit or loss), consider setting size to the absolute values and color to the sign (for example, positive to cyan and negative to red).

In most software, you will have some indication of the original range of your data values. In the e-mail data for Figure 5-1, the number of e-mails among family members ranges from 1 to 36, and the total size of e-mails for each family member ranges from 9KB (for example, short messages) to 1,300KB (for example, messages with image attachments). Note that the range is fairly small for the number of e-mails (the largest number of e-mails is 36 times the smallest), whereas it is larger for total size (the largest e-mail is 140 times larger than the smallest). This range may impact how you configure size.

Accurate Size

You may want people to be able to look at the graph and visually estimate relative sizes. In this case, you want a node that is visually twice as big to represent data that is twice as large. Note that *node size* is an *area*. This means that a node that is twice as big in area is, in fact, only 1.4 times as wide and high as the smaller node. Figure 5-2 shows accurately sized nodes based on the number of e-mails sent.

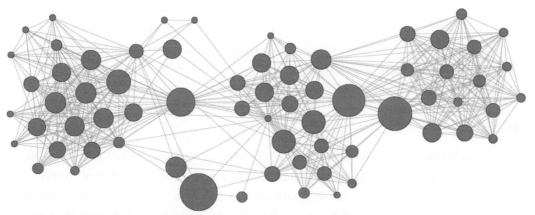

FIGURE 5-2: E-mails between family members are shown here with nodes accurately sized based on number of e-mails from 1 to 36. There are a few people who send a large number of e-mails, and the left cluster clearly has larger nodes (more e-mails) than the right cluster.

> **WARNING**
> If you want size to accurately represent data, inspect the resulting visualization to validate the sizes by comparing different nodes. Some software scales sizes linearly to the data (incorrect for accuracy), and some software scales sizes to the square root of the data (correct for accuracy).

You may want to add a column to the node data that is a square root of the intended size data, in case your software doesn't automatically use the square root of the size. If you intend to have accurate sizes, it can be useful to have a legend or otherwise indicate the sizes of some of the different nodes, including the largest and smallest nodes.

Relative Size

Relative sizes can be useful, too, particularly where the dynamic range is more than a couple orders of magnitude. The problem with extremely large ranges and accurate sizes is that some nodes are teeny dots (for example, a single pixel), and other nodes are so large that they completely overwhelm (or obscure) other nodes, as shown in Figure 5-3. In this case, relative size can be effective. With relative sizes, nodes that represent larger data are visually bigger, and nodes that represent smaller data are visually smaller.

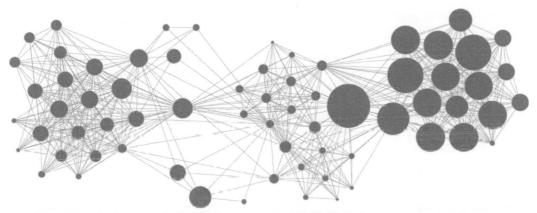

FIGURE 5-3: E-mails between family members are shown here with nodes accurately sized based on e-mail size. The smallest nodes are a few kilobytes, and the largest are megabytes. The huge range makes teeny nodes almost disappear and large nodes overwhelm.

If no scale or legend is visible, it is better to assume that sizes are relative until you have a way to verify them.

Minimum Size, Overlap, and Other Options

Very small nodes may be difficult to see or even accidentally ignored. If your data has some very small values, an alternative approach to relative size is to set a *minimum size*.

When using a wide variety of node sizes, you can end up with items overlapping or obscuring other nodes. As described in Chapter 4, "Stats and Layout," some layouts enable you to adjust node locations by node size (for example, a no-overlap setting). Alternatively, you should ensure that small nodes draw on top of large nodes or have large nodes be more transparent than small nodes.

Another approach for nodes with a very large range of values is to use color instead of size. Note that people are able to discriminate a wider range of sizes than they are able to discriminate color, so typically it will be better to use size.

Node Color

Color is a powerful visual indicator of data. Color has different attributes such as *hue* (for example, red, yellow, orange, green), which is different than *brightness* (for example, ranging from dark green to light green), both of which are different from *saturation* (for example, ranging from vivid red to muted red to gray with a bit of red). Hue also has perceptual connotations. For example, use red for hot, warning, or loss; blue for cold or night; green for profit; and so on. Using color semantics can help the viewer more quickly understand the representation. It is important to understand a little about color because you can use color in three main ways to add information to nodes or edges:

- Magnitude
- Positive and negative values
- Categories

Magnitude

Similar to node size, you can use color to show magnitudes (such as counts or size) by using a *quantitative color scale* (also called a *sequential color scale*). In this use of color, typically you define the color for the lowest value and the highest value. The chosen color scale should vary from a dark color to a light color over the range of values. People perceive brightness of the color and will see patterns based on brightness. Therefore, you should use a set of colors that vary in brightness in proportion to the numeric values they represent. For this reason, you should not use a "rainbow color scale," because the brightness varies inconsistently, as shown in Figure 5-4. If you take away the hue (such as with a low-contrast projector or a black-and-white hard copy), the variation in brightness across the colors is very apparent.

FIGURE 5-4: The rainbow color scale (left) does not consistently increase in brightness, as shown in the grayscale image of the same rainbow color scale (right). *Do not* use a rainbow color scale for magnitude.

Examples of good choices include simply varying from a dark hue to a bright version of that same hue. Or, pick a dark color (such as blue) and a related bright color (such as cyan). Figure 5-5 shows an example.

FIGURE 5-5: The upper row contains color scales that vary only in brightness. The second row has color scales that vary in both brightness and a bit of hue. Both are effective, but the lower color scale is more interesting and can be more effective.

Extending the e-mail example introduced at the beginning of this chapter, Figure 5-6 shows node size indicating number of messages, and node color indicating total e-mail size from yellow indicating small e-mail size to red indicating large e-mail size.

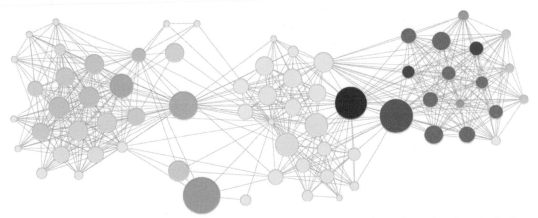

FIGURE 5-6: In this graph of family e-mails, nodes are sized by number of e-mails, and node color indicates the total size of e-mails ranging from tiny e-mails in yellow to large e-mails in red.

Combining multiple visual attributes to show different data attributes can yield some interesting insights that are otherwise hidden in the data. Figure 5-6 is the first example in this chapter where two visual attributes are used to show two different data attributes. On the left, nodes are yellow (small e-mails) and have a slightly larger node size (more e-mails), whereas on the right side nodes are orange (large e-mails) and have a smaller node size (fewer e-mails). The interpretation is that the right side represents family members who like to send fewer, bigger messages (for example, photos), whereas the left side represents family members who send more textual messages back and forth.

Positive and Negative Values

For numerical values that diverge from a baseline (such as positive and negative numbers), a diverging color scale draws attention to the opposite ends of the scale. As shown in Figure 5-7, the center color is typically close to the brightness of the background color (for example, yellow or beige for a white background), and the ends are typically vivid colors (such as red and greenish-blue, or orange and blue).

FIGURE 5-7: Diverging color scales are effective for data where you want to focus on the values at either extreme, such as the extreme positive and negative values.

Any applications tracking changes in prices and values (such as investments, CPI, migration, or net trade flows) may use a diverging color scale to differentiate between positive and negative directions, as well as draw attention to the magnitude at the extremes.

Figure 5-8 shows diverging color scales for income data by various occupations (available from www.census.gov or www.bls.gov). The diverging color indicates percent change in income over the ten-year period from 2001 to 2010, with a diverging color scale set at 25 percent (the rate of inflation over the same period). The darker the color is, the greater the divergence. Oranges to reds indicate real wages that have decreased over the period, and greens indicate real wages that have increased. Gray is used to indicate no data.

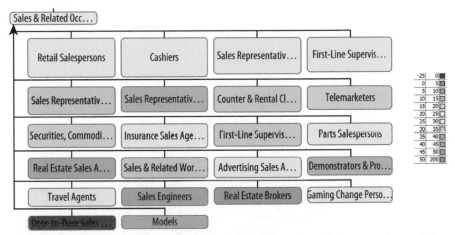

FIGURE 5-8: Sales occupations in the United States are colored by percent change in income from 2001 to 2010, using a diverging color scale centered at 25 percent—the inflation over the same period. Gray indicates no data.

In this example, it is easy to see that door-to-door sales' incomes have decreased the most, while models' incomes have significantly increased. Most sales occupations are light orange, indicating a modest increase in wages, but a bit less than the level of inflation over the same period. A larger version with all the occupations is available in the Supplementary Materials on this book's companion website.

Categories

Many different kinds of categories exist: professions, gender, religion, tags, and so on. Any quantity can be turned into a category, too—for example, age can be turned into a few age groups. Using color to show categories is effective for up to ten or so categories— because each color needs to be clearly distinguishable from other colors. Recall that people perceive brightness as a strong cue, so color choices for categories should leverage the natural brightness associated with different hues, as shown in Figure 5-9.

FIGURE 5-9: Uniquely distinguishable colors are useful for differentiating categories.

Figure 5-10 shows the top 4 levels of a Fortune 500 company's organizational chart with 12 different job categories color-coded. Executives are in yellow in the hub of each cluster. Engineers are in cyan, predominantly in the upper-left cluster, and the blues are administrative roles (including finance, tax, real estate, facilities, construction, and so on). The administrative roles tend to have a few people in almost every cluster.

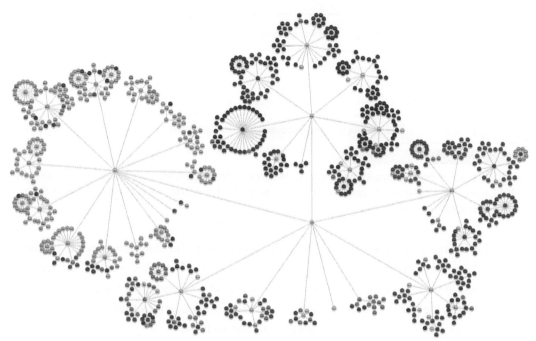

FIGURE 5-10: This hierarchy of a Fortune 500 company is color-coded by job category (for example, engineers in cyan and administration in blue).

Color Blindness

One extra challenge with color is creating palettes that are effective for color-blind people. About 1.3 percent of the population has a form of red-green color blindness. Vischeck.com provides a quick means to transform a color image into what it looks like for someone with different forms of color blindness. Using Vischeck for red-green color blindness with the previously shown diverging color scales results in what is shown Figure 5-11.

Using pure red and pure green for diverging color is usually considered ineffective for the color blind—the red-green diverging colors in the figure have blue mixed with the green to create some difference. Note how the blue-orange palette appears to have more differentiation.

FIGURE 5-11: Two color scales. The upper image shows the original color scale, and the lower image shows the color scale after simulating red-green color blindness (using `vischeck.com`).

NOTE

Numerous websites exist that can generate good colors. ColorBrewer (`colorbrewer.org`) is a well-known resource for creating effective color palettes of all three examples. You can also use a color recommender (`http://aperturejs.com/colorrecommender/index.html`) to generate palettes.

Labels

Labels can be one of the most important enhancements to a graph. Labels unambiguously identify specific nodes (or links). The topology may reveal that there is a critical node connecting two clusters, and the color may indicate importance, but a label is required to reveal the specific identity of the node. Interactions such as tooltips or selection (discussed in Chapter 6, "Explore and Explain") can reveal node identity, but it is important to remember that those interactions are lost once the graph is shown as an image in a PowerPoint presentation, a printout, or a PDF file.

Labels can be tricky to use. Some earlier examples in this book show nice short names such as Chad or Zoe, whereas real-world names are much longer. Even the generic names applied to the e-mail data result in rather long labels, as shown in Figure 5-12. Label legibility is an immediate problem—some labels are difficult to read because of overlap, and some are difficult to read against dark node colors.

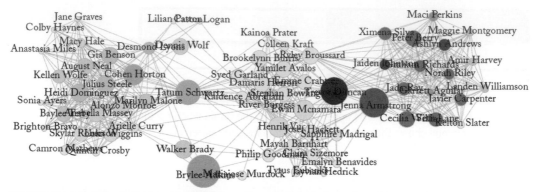

FIGURE 5-12: Labels applied to the family e-mail example include such problems as labels overlapping and labels that are difficult to read against dark colors.

Reducing Label Width

In node and link diagrams, nodes tend to be fairly "squarish" in proportion (such as circles, stars, and so on). Layouts tend to position the nodes based on distance without any special regard to horizontal versus vertical distance. Labels, however, tend to be wide, resulting in problems with long labels reaching across multiple nodes and interfering with other labels. A few remedies exist for managing label width:

- **Condensed fonts/narrow fonts**—A wide variety of specially designed narrow fonts are available, and this is the perfect time to use them because they are 25 percent to 50 percent narrower than standard fonts. Though most Windows users will be familiar with Arial Narrow, other choices may already be available on your system (as shown in Figure 5-13), including fonts such as Myriad Pro Condensed, Gill Sans Condensed, or even Gill Sans Extra Condensed (which is an extremely narrow font).

  If you have limited choices for narrow fonts, a few nice open source condensed fonts are available (in other words, no fee for commercial use) such as Open Sans Condensed and Miso (available, for example, from `http://fontsquirrel.com`). Gill Sans Extra Condensed is used in Figure 5-14. Be careful, though—the narrower the font, the larger the font size required to maintain readability.

Leonardo da Vinci	Standard Helvetica
Leonardo da Vinci	Helvetica Condensed
Leonardo da Vinci	Arial Narrow
Leonardo da Vinci	Franklin Gothic Medium Condensed
Leonardo da Vinci	Rockwell Condensed
Leonardo da Vinci	Myriad Pro Condensed
Leonardo da Vinci	Gloucester Extra Condensed
Leonardo da Vinci	Gill Sans Condensed
Leonardo da Vinci	Gill Sans Extra Condensed Bold

FIGURE 5-13: Condensed fonts are 25 percent to 50 percent narrower than standard fonts—useful for labeling graphs.

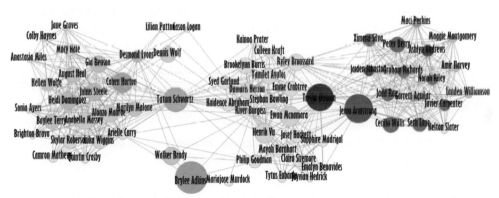

FIGURE 5-14: This is the same family graph using Gill Sans Extra Condensed. You can reduce the amount of overlap by using narrow fonts.

- **Short labels**—Long labels can often be shortened, although shorter labels may not automatically exist in the source data. In the e-mail example, names can be shortened to first initial plus surname, as shown in Figure 5-15.

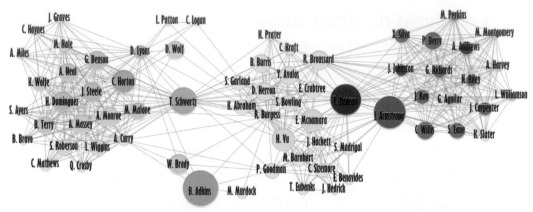

FIGURE 5-15: Shortening labels reduces overlap and makes the scene much less cluttered.

Improving Label Legibility

Even with short labels and narrow fonts, some text will still be difficult to read over lines and nodes. The readability of text depends on the amount of contrast against the background. As shown in Figure 5-16, an orange label on a purple background of the same brightness will be difficult to read—contrast is required.

Michael Faraday   **James Maxwell**

FIGURE 5-16: Labels that have the same brightness (or darkness) as their background are more difficult to read.

Therefore, if black labels are on top of dark nodes and lines, they will be difficult to read. You can improve legibility in many ways:

- **Change colors of nodes and/or links**—Adjust the range of colors of the underlying node to increase contrast. Following from the previous example, brightening all of the node colors results in labels that are easier to read.

- **Tweak node positions**—Depending on the software used, you may find tools to automatically adjust node positions for improved label visibility, or the capability to simply move and drag an offending node or two. Figure 5-17 shows an example.

- **Adjust label position**—Placing a label above or below a node may be more effective than placing the label over the node. Not all graph software provides this option.

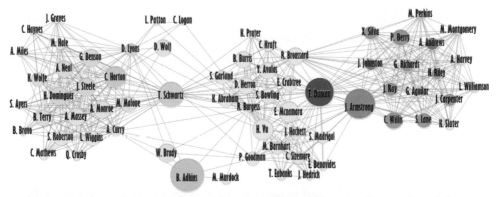

FIGURE 5-17: This graph of family e-mails has node color brightened and a couple node locations slightly shifted to improve label visibility.

- **Change label colors**—In some cases, the label color can be switched depending on the color of what is behind it, such as pie hierarchy in Chapter 4 (Figures 4-23 and 4-24).

- **Labels only**   Remove the nodes completely and use only the label as the node. As shown in Figure 5-18, labels can also vary in size, color, and other attributes based on data, so this is feasible, although the range of colors and sizes must be tweaked.

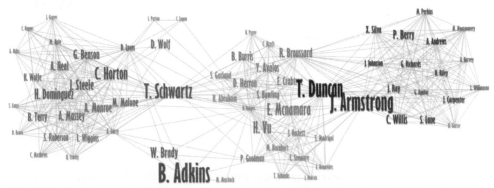

FIGURE 5-18: This graph of family e-mails uses labels to indicate three data attributes. Label size indicates number of e-mails, label color indicates total size of e-mails (from small in amber to large in dark red and purple), and the label text indicates the specific sender.

- **Smaller labels**—Although smaller fonts reduce overlap to improve legibility, they are more difficult to read. Depending on the device (for example, a laptop), 8 to 10 points could be considered a minimum size. Ultra-high-quality printers available at high-end print shops can produce readable fonts down to 4 points, although 4 points may be too small for some people to read, so 5 or 6 points may be a better minimum size, even with access to these high-quality printers.

Reinforcing Labels

Label size and color can be used to reinforce node size and color. In Figure 5-19, the underlying nodes vary in size and color. The labels on top also vary in size and color using the same attributes as the nodes (although the label colors are much darker versions of the node colors). This approach can reinforce the other visual attributes, look more visually appealing, and improve readability (somewhat) if labels partially overlap.

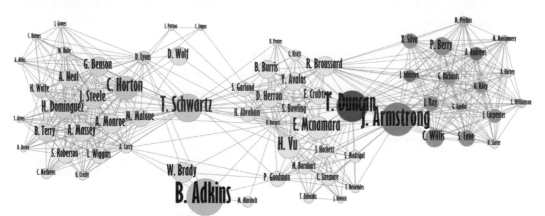

FIGURE 5-19: Colors and size of labels reinforce the color and size of the underlying nodes.

In general, the approach of using one data attribute to set two or more visual attributes is called *redundant encoding*. Some redundant encoding can be considered to be good because, as viewers learn the visualization, they see these different cues representing the same thing, and it helps them understand it. In Figure 5-19, it seems logical to have smaller labels on smaller items and larger labels on larger items—the redundant encoding here acts as an aid to the viewers.

KEY EDGE ATTRIBUTES

Edges, like nodes, may have many attributes associated with them. Edges represent relationships. There can be different types of relationships, including directions, quantities, measurements, and statistics. Weight, color, and line style are key visual attributes for revealing additional data about edges.

Edge Weight

Edge weight is common in many data sets and is important for many layout algorithms. Visually, edge weight is simply the thickness of the edge between two nodes. In the e-mail data set, edge weight has already been included in all the previous examples because the particular force-directed layout used edge weight as part of its calculations. However, the edges were all drawn fairly thin to de-emphasize edge weight. As shown in Figure 5-20, edge weight can be increased, revealing connections where there have been many e-mails.

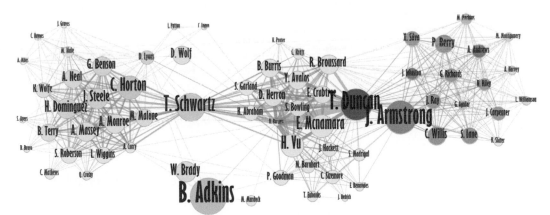

FIGURE 5-20: Edge weight shows number of e-mails between people. Trevor Duncan (red node) is involved in many e-mails with many other people.

As edge weight becomes thicker, transparency of the edges can help; otherwise, all the edges can become a big blob.

Edge Color

Edge color can show data attributes in a very similar way to node color. All the guidelines discussed previously regarding color and the different types of color scales (sequence, diverging, categoric) apply to edge color as well. Again using the e-mail example, in Figure 5-21, edge color is added to indicate the recency of the e-mails between each pair of people, ranging from red (recent) to blue (old).

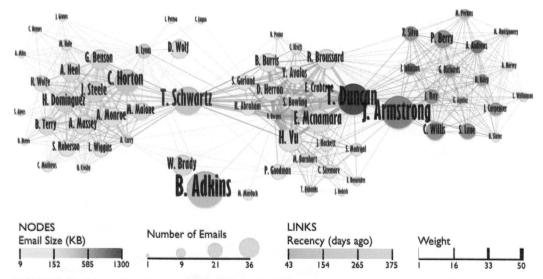

FIGURE 5-21: Edge color shows recency of e-mails, with newest e-mails in red and oldest e-mails in grayish-blue. The cluster on the right has been more active recently than the cluster on the left.

> **TIP**
> If you have many overlapping edges, having different edge colors as well as a bit of transparency will help viewers distinguish between them.

Edge Type

Edge type is a broad category covering many different line styles associated with edges, including arrows, dashes, and curves.

Arrows are critically important for indicating flow in directed graphs when edges are lines. (Note that, instead of arrows, the chord diagram uses width at the start and the end to indicate flow.)

Curved edges are often used in conjunction with arrows so that arrows in both directions between a pair of nodes do not overlap and can be clearly distinguished. This curvature does not need to be very large—a small curvature means the flows in either direction can be easily compared. Figure 5-22 shows trade flows as edges with arrows and a very slight line curvature so that the flows do not overlap and so that the opposite flow is almost immediately adjacent. For example, the flow from China to the United States (bright pink) is much larger than the flow from the United States to China (purple), whereas the flow to/from Canada and the United States is almost equal.

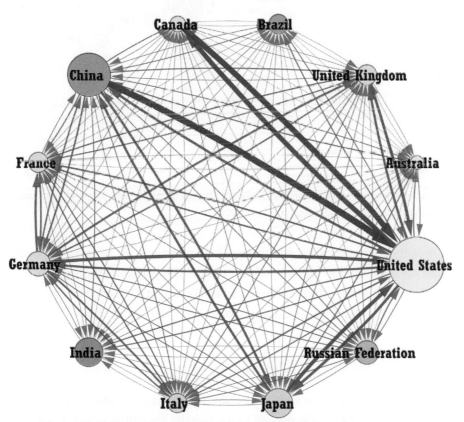

FIGURE 5-22: In this graph of trade flows of the top 12 countries (by 2012 GDP), curved arrows indicate direction of flow, and edge color and width indicate value of trade flow. Subtle curvature keeps the opposite flow close for comparison.

Curved edges are sometimes used in undirected graphs—they can be used to reduce apparent connections between a series of nodes all in a row; and sometimes curved edges are used because they are aesthetically pleasing. Figure 5-23 shows curved edges on the e-mail data set.

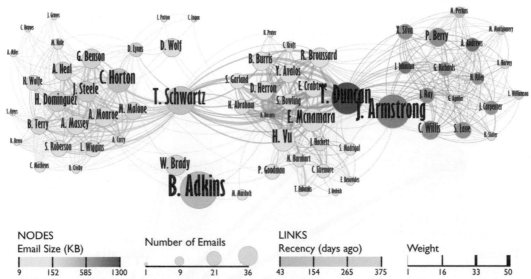

FIGURE 5-23: This shows edge curvature, color, and thickness, as well as labels with size and color, and nodes with size and color. A legend is provided for reference.

Dashes can be useful for indicating different types of connections. In an organizational chart, dashed lines are often used to indicate indirect relationships. Different categories of connections may also exist in other data. For example, in the airline data set, dashes could be used to differentiate routes with only freight service or non-regularly scheduled service.

COMBINING BASIC ATTRIBUTES

Combining multiple attributes such as node size, color, labels, edge weight, edge color, and curvature can transform dense information into a visually appealing graph image. It is important to provide all the detailed information about the visual attributes in a legend, or at least a caption with the graph, so that the viewers can decode the image. Also, although you can encode many attributes using all these attributes, you must be careful not to make the image so complex that the viewer struggles to decode what it means. Given all the combinations, a legend is a very useful aid.

Consider Figure 5-23, the graph of family e-mails. Some people may consider it too complicated because it now encodes five different data attributes across seven different visual attributes!

So, how do you interpret the graph in Figure 5-23? To recap, the set of nodes represents the (anonymous) family and friends of the author, not including the author. The visual attributes are configured as shown in the legend and described as follows:

- **Node size**—This represents the number of e-mails the person was included in (also node label size).

- **Node color**—This represents the overall number of bytes sent, ranging from a few (yellow) to a large number (red). This is also shown in a very dark version of the same color for the node label.

- **Label**—This indicates the name of the person (generically anonymous).

- **Edge weight**—This represents the total kilobytes sent between a pair of people.

- **Edge color**—This represents the most recent e-mail between a pair of people, ranging from red (very recent) to blue (a year ago).

The topology and the thick edges (many e-mails) show the importance of T. Schwartz in connecting the left cluster to the center cluster. Schwartz sends many e-mails, but big e-mails. Schwartz is the primary connector between the center cluster (direct family) and the left cluster (a set of in-laws and cousins).

Note that B. Adkins (shown large at the bottom) is also in a similar bridging position to Schwartz, but B. Adkins' role is different. Adkins is large because Adkins sends a lot of e-mails to the author (who is not otherwise shown in this graph). However, Adkins rarely copies other people (all the lines are thin and the color is close to yellow). Adkins is simply communicating a lot of short e-mails directly with the author—that is, Adkins is a *point-to-point communicator*, not a *broadcast communicator*.

J. Armstrong and T. Duncan (and, to a lesser extent, R. Broussard) connect the central cluster to the right cluster (another set of in-laws). This is the side of the family that likes to send bigger e-mails, as shown by the orange node color indicating larger e-mails than the yellow e-mails. (Armstrong and Duncan often send photos of family gatherings.) The Duncan/Armstrong side has also been active more recently, with edge colors closer to red. Unlike Schwartz and Adkins, the Duncan/Armstrong pair both communicate fairly heavily.

So what does all this mean? If you need to get a message out with the widest reach, you should contact Schwartz and one of Duncan/Armstrong pair. And, if you have a secret, it is likely safe to share it with Adkins.

BUNDLES, SHAPES, IMAGES, AND MORE

You can manipulate many more visual attributes to enhance visual aesthetics and/or add additional data. Each software package should (hopefully) offer all the basic attributes previously discussed, but additional attributes available can vary widely. The earlier e-mail examples in the chapter were created with Gephi, but the following examples have been created with other software.

Bundled Edges

An exciting attribute to emerge in recent years is *bundled edges*. These are not quite the same as curved edges. The idea is to simplify the visual depiction of the graph (particularly when it has many edges) by grouping edges together (particularly when the edges are close to each other). This could be considered perhaps an aesthetic attribute or a type of layout attribute.

Figure 5-24 shows bundled edges for the e-mail example (created with Cytoscape using the Bundle Edges feature). Note how the relationships indicated by Broussard, Duncan, and Armstrong differ from Figure 5-23. Previously, Duncan seemed to be the key link bridging between the middle cluster to the right cluster. But with edge bundling, alternative paths between middle and right clusters through Armstrong and Broussard are now more visually apparent.

Shape

You can use shape to represent a few categories of data. Typically, you will have a few shapes to pick from, such as a circle, square, or triangle (for example, in Cytoscape). Figure 5-25 shows the same Fortune 500 organizational chart as seen in Figure 5-8 colored by job category, but now with shape applied to indicate region (for example, squares indicate people located in the European Union, and diamonds indicate people in North America).

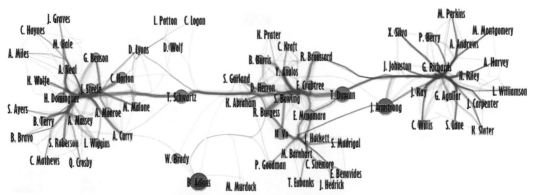

FIGURE 5-24: Bundled edges simplify the image by clustering edges traveling similar paths.

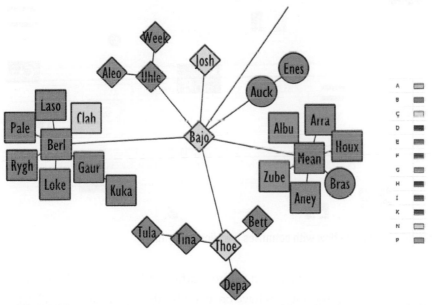

FIGURE 5-25: In this portion of a Fortune 500 company hierarchy, shapes vary to indicate region. (The full version is provided in the Supplementary Materials on this book's companion website.)

Node Image

Instead of shapes or colors, you can use images for nodes. The simplest case can be literal images of items, such as flags for countries in a view of trade flow, portraits for people in a social network, or photos of products. Figure 5-26 shows a simple example of trade flow data using images of flags for each node (created with NodeXL).

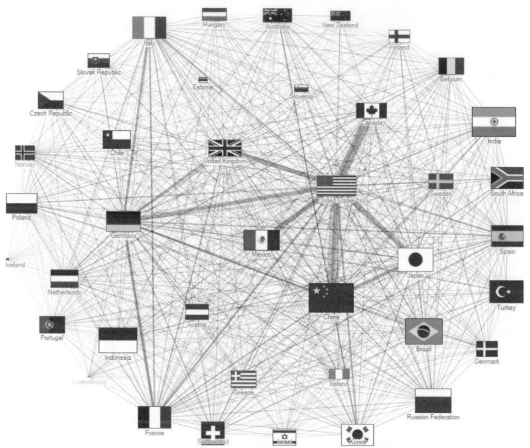

FIGURE 5-26: The international trade flow with countries is indicated by flags.

The approach using images can be extended to show different kinds of attributes as an adjunct to other node attributes. The authors have created visuals such as mini pie charts or mini-line charts used in graphs on some particular occasions. This requires extra effort to generate all the images and then to configure the graph software to use the images. But you can use this approach to reveal information that would otherwise be difficult to show (such as trends).

Node Border

You have already explored edge type. Similarly, the *node border* has attributes such as line weight, line style, and line color that you can use to indicate additional data. Extending the occupation example, you can set node size to the number of people in a particular occupation. You can set node color to a diverging color scale indicating change in wages over the ten-year period from 2001 to 2010. Additional data includes the median income—how much money did the typical person in this occupation earn? Although you could potentially use font size or font color, there could be challenges with layout or legibility of the font over the colored background.

In Figure 5-27 (created with yEd), the outline color has been set to the income level, with dark purple indicating low income (below $20,000—for example, cashiers) ranging to a bright cyan indicating a high median above $140,000 (none in this image are in the highest income category). Note, per the example shown in Figure 5-8, models are the darkest green, indicating a large increase in income (up over 50 percent), but the overall median income is low ($30,000 to –$40,000—presumably the median model is not a supermodel). The sales engineers have also increased in bright green (up 45 percent to 50 percent), and their income is fairly high, too ($80,000 to $100,000).

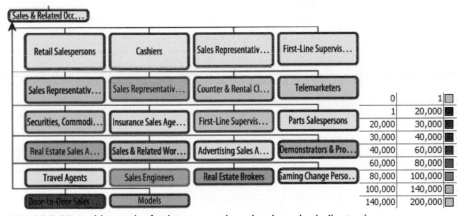

FIGURE 5-27: In this graph of sales occupations, border color indicates income.

More Attributes

Many more attributes are available than have been addressed here. The authors have added visual attributes to graphs such as glows, drop shadows, multi-line text labels, multiple font styles, three-dimensional (3D) nodes, gradient edges, pie chart and doughnut chart nodes, dozens of shape types, and more. Although all these advanced attributes are feasible, they each have different caveats and may not be easily accessible in many graph visualization packages. Feel free to experiment with some of the advanced features, but beware that the results may not be as effective as intended, and keep in mind how the use of these features relates back to the overall objective.

Interference and Separation

Combining many visual attributes results in interference and/or legibility issues. Some attributes still visually pop out (such as size), but other attributes such as colors or font styles may be more difficult to distinguish—particularly if the same visual attribute is being used multiple times (for example, color for both node fill and node outline).

Figure 5-28 shows the sales occupation data with color being used to indicate both change in income (node fill color) and total income (node outline color). Note that the bright red fills may be easily perceived, but the bright cyan outlines require effort to visually scan across all the boxes to see them.

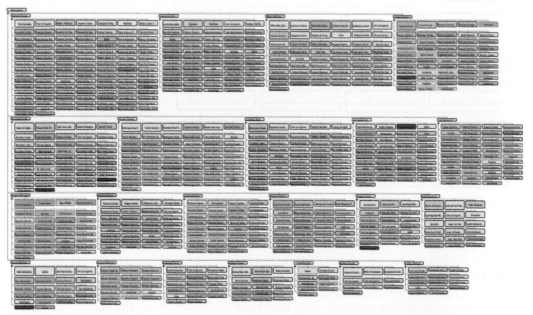

FIGURE 5-28: In this representation of occupation data, node fill color indicates income change, and node outline color indicates overall income. Note that the outline colors do not visually pop out.

In general, care is required when adding many extra data attributes. Ensure that the most important data for the objective incorporates the visual attributes that visually pop out (such as size and node fill color). Don't add extra data that isn't relevant to the analysis. In the occupation income example, if change in income was not important to the objective, you can use node fill color instead for the important attribute.

When you have many equally important data attributes and you use them as support for successive points in an analysis, you might consider using two images or three images. In each case, use a consistent layout, but then, in successive versions, vary the attribute of interest. For example, Figure 5-29 shows the occupation data first colored by change in income and then colored by median income.

PUTTING IT ALL TOGETHER

Node, edge, and label attributes can increase the information delivered by a graph, as well as increase its clarity and appeal. Basic attributes such as size, color, and labels can be used effectively to add data in any graph. Keep in mind the following:

- Node size is an effective attribute for conveying non-negative quantities.

- Node color is effective and visually appealing for conveying information such as categories, quantities, or diverging values.

- Labels are extremely useful for identifying nodes, as well as potentially showing information via label color and size. Good labels require effort and should not be an afterthought.

- Edge weight (that is, line thickness) is very effective for indicating the strength of the relationship.

- Like node color, edge color can be visually effective for differentiating among edges (for example, categories), as well as quantities or diverging values.

- Edge type (such as arrows and curvature) is useful for directed edges.

- Bundles, shapes, images, borders, and other advanced attributes can enhance the visualization, but beware of cluttering the visualization or making it confusing.

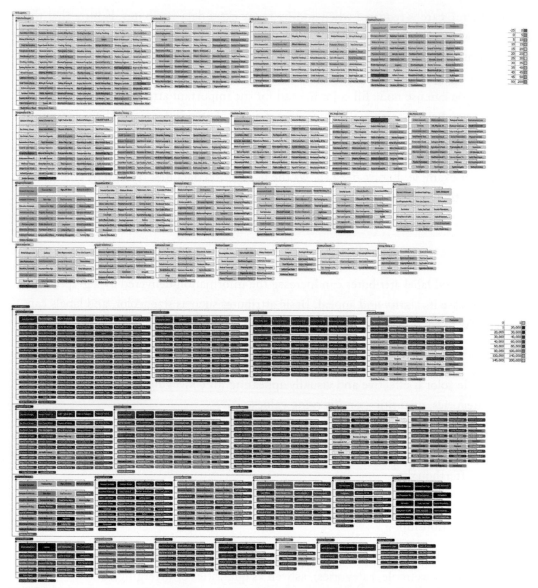

FIGURE 5-29: Here, occupation data is represented first by percent change in income (red-green) and second by income bracket (purple-cyan). In both examples, the extreme values can be easily perceived.

SUMMARY

Applying visual attributes can be one of the most exciting steps in creating a graph—the story of the data starts to be revealed as visual attributes add information on top of the topology. Starting with the basics of size, color, and labels can be an effective way to add information and to increase visual clarity in a graph. Many more attributes are available but should be approached with some caution because a graph can be made more complicated and more difficult to understand if too many different or advanced attributes are combined at once.

A legend is extremely useful to include as well. Once two or three different visual attributes are used, it is important to be able to quickly and easily recall the configuration.

Just as the visual attributes help reveal the graph's story, interaction becomes the next step in understanding the graph. As you'll see in Chapter 6, interactions enable you to explore the graph in more detail, zooming in, filtering out weak edges or small nodes, probing for data details, isolating subsets, and so on, which can help the viewer gain additional insights.

6

EXPLORE AND EXPLAIN

After getting data, visually laying out the graph, and attaching data to visual attributes, you may want to explore the network in more detail to gain some insights. The interesting patterns described in the various examples in the previous chapters may not be so obvious in your graph. In many cases, some amount of interactive analysis is required before patterns emerge. Often, initial graphs look like "a hairball" or "a plate of spaghetti." Do not despair. Most graph software packages contain interactive features to explore the graph in more detail, which are the topics of this chapter. For example, zoom and identification interactions let you explore graph details. Filters and selection help you focus on items of interest and hide less relevant items.

Assuming that you do gain some insights, in most situations you will want to share those findings with other people. Whether those findings appear in a PowerPoint presentation, whitepaper, or poster, you will want to help the viewer see those patterns, too. The second portion of this chapter covers enhancements such as annotations, labels, legends, and explanations to help you convey your findings.

EXPLORE, EXPLAIN, AND EXPORT

Upon first viewing a graph, the viewer (whether the graph author or the presentation audience) may have some basic questions:

- What am I looking at?

- Are there some landmarks?

- What is this node (or link)?

- What is it connected to?

Basic interactions are used in conjunction with graph layout and the configuration of visual attributes to do a first-level assessment and understanding of the graph. Then, interactions such as filtering and isolation provide a powerful means for exploring the graph, in addition to topological analysis (such as exploring neighbors, exploring paths, and modifying the graph).

For presentation, more context is required for the audience. It may be helpful to add a legend, add annotations, and sequence a story to help the viewer understand the graph. Additionally, you may provide an export of data so that the viewer can do further analysis.

Table 6-1 shows the various interactions involved with this process.

TABLE 6-1: Interactions

TYPE	EXAMPLE	DESCRIPTION
Zoom and pan		Go from an overview with all of the context down to a local neighborhood by zooming and panning. Capabilities to rotate, scale, and translate offer similar effects for different purposes.
Identify		Hover and/or click to identify the specific node, confirm the visual attributes, or inspect the detailed data.
Filter		Set criteria to remove items that do not match, and focus only on the items that do match. Explore the graph based on statistical graph properties or other data properties.

TYPE	EXAMPLE	DESCRIPTION
Isolate		Select a subgraph, move it to its own workspace to lay it out again, focus on specific properties, and so on.
Neighbors		Assess the immediate neighbors, or reach out two or three steps away to see what a particular node can reach.
Paths		Explore the routes from one node to another. How many hops are needed?
Drag, move, modify, delete, group, and so on		Adjust the scope of the network. Isolate subgraphs, move nodes, modify properties, delete irrelevant nodes, and group related nodes.
Explanation Sequence		Explanation requires a logical sequence to tell a story about data. For example, you may start from an overview and step toward a specific observation.
Annotate		Mark particular nodes, edges, or parts of the graph that are relative to the story.
Legend		Add a legend to aid the viewers in understanding what they are looking at, as well as explain all the visual attributes.
Export		Generate images and data sets for further presentation and/or analysis.

ESSENTIAL EXPLORATORY INTERACTIONS

In this section, an example consisting of a market basket analysis steps through the various interactions using a real-world data set of purchases. As a quick recap, a *market basket analysis* is a graph where nodes are products purchased, and edges occur when two products are purchased together.

The apocryphal "beer and diapers" data mining story is an example of a market basket analysis. The story claims that a convenience store retailer noticed a large number of purchases included both beer and diapers and then adjusted the store layout by placing diapers near the beer to increase beer sales. Although this particular story may never have actually happened, this type of correlation between goods purchased together is fundamental to market basket analysis. You see this every day when using website interfaces such as Amazon (people who purchased X also purchased Y) and Netflix (people who viewed A also viewed B) or when observing marketers who look at potential impulse purchases (for example, items bought with a wide variety of other items). This type of analysis can be computed in different ways; graph analysis is only one approach.

> **NOTE** For a detailed account of the beer and diapers story, see: `www.dssresources` `.com/newsletters/66.php`.

Market basket graphs tend to be very dense. When aggregating data across thousands of baskets, it is not uncommon for two unrelated items to get purchased together a few times. Because market basket graphs are dense, interaction is required to explore the graph and gain insight.

The example of a market basket analysis in this chapter uses anonymous data from a hardware store to view more than 300,000 items purchased in more than 10,000 basket purchases. The graph has approximately 8,000 products and 180,000 links. The first half of this chapter shows the various types of interactions used to do an exploratory analysis. Gephi is used for the screen shots, but Cytoscape or other graph software could have been used. You can see the same graph in more detail using the `MarketBasket` examples in the Supplementary Materials available on this book's companion website.

The initial view of the data in Gephi may look like a square with random node layouts, as shown in Figure 6-1. The nodes have been sized and colored by the total revenue for that item (pink is low revenue, and deep purple is high revenue). The edges have been colored by the frequency at which each pair of products has been purchased.

FIGURE 6-1: This initial market basket graph looks like a square with random node layouts.

On such a large graph, layout takes time. In Figure 6-2, the layout has been done using a Yifan Hu multi-level layout in Gephi and required approximately 5 minutes to compute. The visual results indicate a disconnected graph with one very big component, a few very small components, and a number of isolated dots. The isolated dots are simply individual products that were purchased with no other products. Examples of some of these individual product purchases include specialized tools or parts.

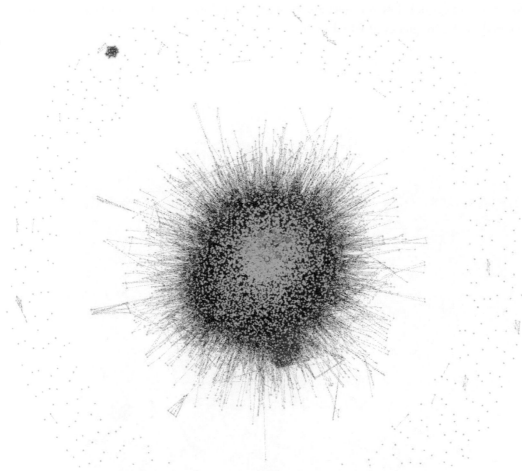

FIGURE 6-2: This market basket graph has a force-directed layout applied, indicating one large component, a few small components, and many isolated dots.

Zoom and Pan (and Scale and Rotate...)

Navigating around a graph is a fundamental requirement, and because no standard exists, each software package implements zoom and pan differently. You might try the following:

- **Zoom via mouse wheel (or drag vertically along the center of the mouse on Mac)**—Generally, a mouse wheel is supported for zooming, and the cursor is the center point for the zoom. Gephi, yEd, and NodeXL support a mouse wheel, but Cytoscape does not.

- **Pan by pressing the right mouse button and dragging**—In many graphical applications, if you press the right mouse button and then click and drag, you can easily pan around the scene. This works in Gephi and yEd. In Cytoscape, the right-click-and-drag action is linked to zoom.

- **Pan by pressing center mouse button, clicking, and clicking and dragging**—In Cytoscape and NodeXL, you can press the center mouse button, click, and then click and drag to pan.

- **Pan using the scrollbars**—If available, you can use scrollbars to pan.

Scaling, translating, and rotating are used to alter node positions. Scaling can be used to space the nodes closer together or further apart without changing the line widths, font sizes, node sizes, and so on. This can be effective if you want to make the graph a bit more dense without having to increase the size of all the elements separately.

> **TIP** Zoom and pan are not the same as scale and translate. Zoom and pan change your viewpoint, while scale and translate change the positions of nodes.

Scaling, translating, and rotating can be very effective when you are working with parts of a graph. For some of the examples in this book, the automatic layouts left huge gaps between different parts of the graph. You can select a portion of the graph and drag it closer (that is, translate it), and possibly add a bit of rotation and scale, to help make the graph more dense while still preserving the overall layout. Scale, translate, and rotate functionality can vary widely between software. Chapter 7, "Point-and-Click Graph Tools," provides further information on these.

In the market basket analysis, it may be interesting to zoom in on some of the small components. Using zoom and pan, you can quickly focus on the little component in the upper-right corner of the graph in Figure 6-2, as shown zoomed in Figure 6-3.

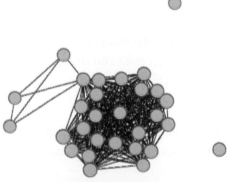

FIGURE 6-3: These small components in a market basket graph are related spare parts that were purchased together.

This particular component is a collection of nodes that represent obscure replacement parts that, on occasion, may be purchased together.

Identify

In the 1990s, the authors were building a visualization of a banking network. At one point, the CEO heard about the project and decided to see it firsthand. Because he was a very action-oriented CEO, he immediately took control of the mouse. Although the authors had identified some very interesting red nodes in this network, the CEO first went to the big nodes—the well-known familiar nodes—to identify them. This helped him confirm his intuitive understanding of what he was seeing. By recognizing and validating these known points first, he could gain confidence before proceeding to explore the anomalies. It also helped to establish some landmarks in the visual scene—he could refer to the known large nodes and the relationship of other nodes to the known nodes.

You can identify data points in multiple ways. Labels, if already added, are excellent but can show only a small amount of data. Tooltips, if available in the graphing software, can be effective because they are immediately adjacent to whatever you are pointing at. Most software packages have an information panel beside the graph somewhere.

For example, you could use the yEd Properties View panel (discussed in more detail in Chapter 7), which is typically in the lower-right corner. Cytoscape typically displays a panel at the bottom. Note that, in some software, you must go into a particular mode to access the details for a node. For example, in Gephi, you must click the following icon for the Edit Selector, which, in turn, opens a detail panel in the upper-left corner: 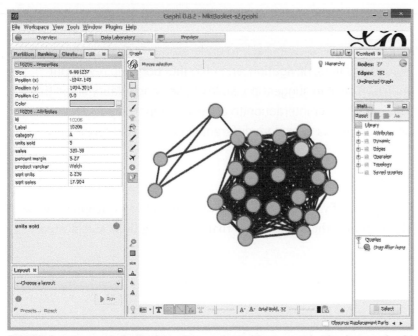.

Picking any item and inspecting the details panel helps you validate what you're seeing. In many software packages, the detail panel is also an editor where you can edit the data and possibly other graphical attributes.

> **TIP** You can identify a few nodes at random to spot-check the validity of the data and confirm the visual mapping.

Getting back to the market basket analysis, any node can be selected and inspected, as shown in Figure 6-4, which shows a snapshot of Gephi with the detail panel in the upper-left corner. Here you can see that the item is product number 10206, that 5 units were sold for a total of $320.58 in revenue, and the product name is Welch (which is not the real product name because the real data is confidential). Note that all the attributes are editable, including color, which has been changed here to yellow to make the selected node stand out in the screen snapshot.

FIGURE 6-4: One node (yellow) has been selected from a market basket graph with the details shown in the upper-left panel in Gephi.

Filter

If you look back at Figure 6-2, you notice that there is still the challenge of the giant component with too many edges to be clearly distinguishable. *Filtering* is a fundamental operation in all data visualization—a way to easily remove some of the data that is currently not of interest so that you can focus on what remains. Filtering doesn't actually delete the data. It just visibly hides the data, and usually you can make all the data visible again by simply adjusting the filter values, turning off the filters, or deleting the filters.

Filters are particularly important for exploratory analysis. By adjusting filter settings, you can quickly isolate and segment the graph by various data attributes and statistical properties. Sometimes these adjustments are goal-oriented to a particular line in an inquiry (for example, what's connected to this specific node), or sometimes it may be more about formulating various hypotheses (for example, are products from the lighting and the flooring departments connected, and, if not, what else is connected to lighting). By adjusting filters and settings (plus zoom and identify), you can start to explore different parts of the graph, and gain some understanding about what's happening in different areas.

> **NOTE**
>
> *Exploratory data analysis* is an approach to understanding data visually. Interactions such as filters, navigation, and identification help reveal patterns and outliers. This can suggest possible causes and relationships that can be the basis for further interaction to uncover supporting evidence. You can use multiple iterations to explore different scenarios and reveal new insights.

In the market basket graph, if you use Gephi, you can see that you can apply a wide variety of filters. In this example, the hypothesis is that interesting links and clusters exist in the giant component, but with many irrelevant connections—because eventually someone will purchase any two products together in a basket. Therefore, the following filters are applied to explore this further:

- **Giant component**—This is a topology filter that removes all the small components and isolated nodes. This reduces the data set from 8,000 nodes down to 7,400 nodes, with no significant change on the edges (still approximately 180,000 edges).

- **Edge weight**—Many items are bought together with very low frequency almost at random. These low-frequency purchase pairs are noise-obscuring more interesting patterns. So, a filter on edge weight set to a threshold of 4 immediately removes any edges that occurred three or fewer times. Note that, in Gephi, when the two filters are combined, all nodes that are now isolated or part of smaller components are also removed. This reduces the graph incredibly quickly down to 1,600 nodes and 6,300 edges, as shown in the left image in Figure 6-5.

The same idea of filtering may be achieved in different ways in different software. For example, in Cytoscape, filtering is achieved by using selection tools available via the Select menu and filter tools in the Select panel. Using the same market basket data in Cytoscape, first a filter is created in the Select panel based on column data of edge weight. The filter is set to select edges of weight above 3 and then applied (with the Apply button). This selects the target edges of weight 3 or higher.

Note, however, that the nodes they are connected to are not selected. The Selection menu is then used to Select ⇨ Nodes ⇨ "Nodes connected by selected edges." This results in a similar subset to the approach used in Gephi.

All the other nodes and edges are still cluttering the view. In Cytoscape, you can hide selections. In this case, you can invert the selected nodes and selected edges, and then you can hide the selection—all via options under the Select menu.

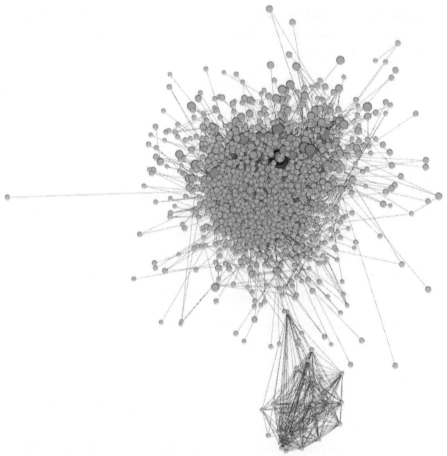

FIGURE 6-5: By filtering the market basket down to edges for only three or more purchases together, you can reduce 180,000 edges down to 6,300 edges.

Isolate and Redo Layout

In Figure 6-5, note that the center of the cluster is still too dense to see any edges. So, you can redo the layout in conjunction with filtering.

But, you may also like the original layout, have become familiar with it, and may want to return to it. Because force-directed layouts can achieve a different layout every time, you must save this layout. In some graph packages, you may want to save different versions of the file each with different filters and layouts so that you can easily return to them.

Graph software may offer ways to manage multiple subsets of a graph, each with a different set of nodes, edges, and layout. For example, Cytoscape allows a selected portion of a graph to be copied and managed as a separate network (File ⇨ New to create new graph instances, and the Network tab to manage different networks). Gephi offers multiple *workspaces*. In this market basket analysis using Gephi, you can select all the points (using the rectangle selection). Then, you right-click to pop up a context menu. Choose "Copy to… New Workspace" to access workspaces via a menu in the bottom-right corner.

Now, you can apply a new layout to this filtered subset of nodes. For example, using Force Atlas 2 layout with Prevent Overlap turned on, Scaling set to 0.6 (so the layout does not spread out too far), and LinLog Mode turned on (to enhance separation of clusters), you can produce a layout with more visually distinct clusters as shown in Figure 6-6.

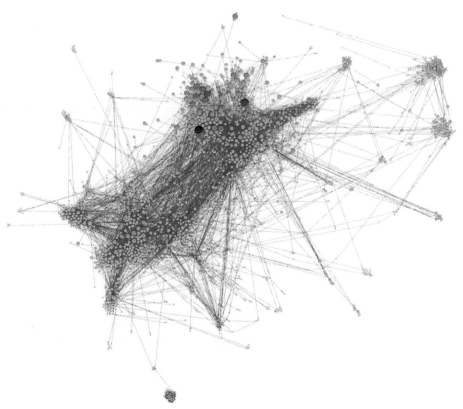

FIGURE 6-6: This market basket with clusters is more apparent after a new layout.

Gephi incrementally refreshes the screen while calculating the new layout, which is generally useful for exploratory analysis:

- You can see nodes moving and keep track of them as the layout shifts to a new position. You don't have to re-learn the layout after the layout finishes calculating.

- You can interact while the layout is still adjusting positions. You can pick nodes and even drag them while the layout is continuing to adjust. This can help disentangle some parts of the graph faster than waiting for the layout to disentangle it.

By creating a new layout on this isolated subset of the graph you see clusters that are much more distinct. For example, there is a cluster at the bottom as shown in Figure 6-7, which is connected by a single thin edge that may seem worthy of investigation.

FIGURE 6-7: A cluster of do-it-yourself books appears at the bottom of the market basket analysis.

Using identification interactions, individual items can be investigated. In this cluster are do-it-yourself books, indicating people are likely to purchase multiple books. As shown in Figure 6-8, the books connect back to the central cluster through a small cluster of clearance books and then to the large cluster via two high-degree nodes—one of which is an extension cord, and the other of which is a tape measure. These are both common items that might be needed at the start of a project.

FIGURE 6-8: Discount books (pink—near bottom) are connected to the larger clusters via two nodes—extension cords and tape measures (highlighted).

MORE INTERACTIVE EXPLORATION

You can also use a wide variety of other analytical interactions, depending on the software package you are using. Some of these interactions might be available as separately downloadable add-ins. Some more common types of analysis are identifying neighbors, finding paths, deleting/modifying data, grouping, and so on.

Identifying Neighbors

Neighbors are the nodes directly connected by a single edge to a specific node. Because this is often of interest in graph analysis, Gephi automatically highlights the immediate neighbors of any node that the mouse is on top of. In Cytoscape, you can use buttons on the main toolbar to highlight the neighbors of a selected node.

In Gephi, this technique of highlighting the immediate neighbors applies to any selection. Using Gephi for the market basket analysis, you can select all the nodes in the top-right cluster, which highlights all the neighbors to all the selected nodes, as shown in Figure 6-9.

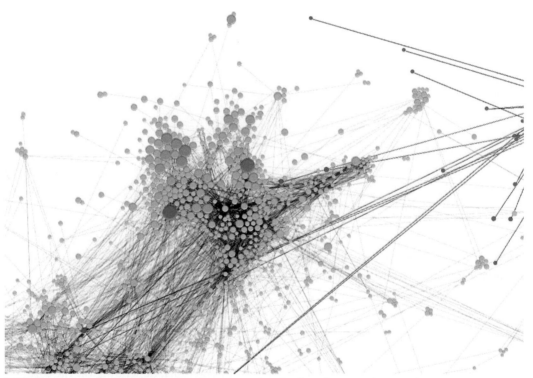

FIGURE 6-9: Light fixtures have only a few connections back to the central mass of products including smoke detectors and extended warranties.

Without interaction, it is easy to see that the cluster is distinct with only a few edges going back to the center. Now, with the neighbors highlighted, you can identify the individual nodes that connect this cluster to the center. This cluster happens to be light fixtures, and the connected products in the center are items such as smoke detectors and extended warranties. You can also see a number of products in the cluster immediately below that are joined. These are products associated with household painting. This implies a reasonable degree of connection between lighting products and painting products.

Paths

In Chapter 4, "Stats and Layout," you learned about paths in the context of a viral marketing example (see Figure 4-5). In that discussion, you read about a marketer who was very interested in understanding the paths to get information to flow between people, particularly if the marketer does not have a direct connection with their target audience.

A *path analysis* can also be useful in a market basket analysis to see how close, or how far apart, some different products may be. For example, when you look at the graph in Figure 6-6, you can see three distinct clusters near the top-right corner. Whereas the first two clusters appear to be interconnected, the third cluster seems to be somewhat independent. You can select individual products from the upper cluster and the lower cluster, and find paths such as this, rather than the tenuous path shown in Figure 6-10. Trying a few different combinations can yield some shorter examples than what is shown in Figure 6-10, but the general conclusion is that the paths between them are fairly indirect.

FIGURE 6-10: The connection from a product in the top-right cluster to a product in the middle-right cluster is highly indirect.

Sometimes it can be tricky to track a particular node in a dense graph. You can modify the label, for example, with a *; change the node shape (for example, to a star); or change the node color (for example, to bright yellow). Alternately, put a sticky note on the computer screen with an arrow to temporarily mark the specific node of interest.

Deleting

Sometimes you have situations in which you want to remove one node. An *ego-network* is a graph of all the neighbors of one node and all their connections. Applying an ego-network analysis to the extension cord from the market basket analysis reveals a network shown in Figure 6-11.

FIGURE 6-11: This shows all the products purchased with the extension cord (in green).

However, because it is already known that all items are connected to the extension cord, it is no longer necessary to display the extension cord node and its associated edges—all those edges are obscuring further analysis. Selecting the extension cord node and deleting it makes the rest of the graph somewhat easier to decipher, as shown in Figure 6-12. In this particular graph, another product also seems to act as a bridge between the left and right clusters—it is a power strip.

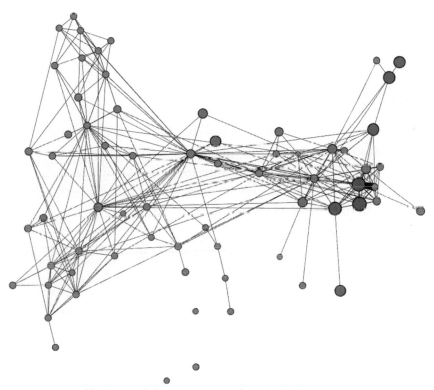

FIGURE 6-12: This shows all the products purchased with the extension cord, with the extension cord removed. A second product, near the center, is also highly connected to both the left and right sides.

Grouping

Grouping is useful when you've identified that certain nodes are associated because they are similar (for example, extension cord and power strip) or because they have been strongly clustered together (for example, books). In this case, some graph software will allow items to be grouped together. Ideally, a node that represents a group of items should be visually distinct from other nodes such as different shapes.

Depending on the software, sometimes nodes can be grouped together, moved, and then ungrouped/expanded as a way to move around sets of nodes.

Iterative Analysis

Exploratory analysis is iterative—you visually inspect, form a hypothesis, narrow down via filtering or selection, identify, and repeat. Within this process, changing the layout, visual attributes, and sometimes fixing bad data are also part of the iterative process. Through the process of analysis and iteration, you can become more familiar with the graph and the data, which, in turn, spurs additional questions and can yield successive insights.

In the market basket analysis, various insights can result from the analysis. For example, you could use the two clusters near the top-right corner in Figure 6-6 to justify a standalone store—these products do not have a strong reliance on other product categories. Or, you could see that books connect back to some more general products—the books stand relatively alone, but if they were located more closely to the general products, perhaps they would sell more. Or, you might see that general hardware products could be sold with the do-it-yourself books in bookstores. With successive iterations, insights can be improved or new insights can result.

For many of these interactions (particularly when exploring connections, paths, and neighbors), more pixels can help make the details visible. For example, one of the authors' workstations provides double the resolution of current HD displays, and another workstation has five times the resolution of HD, as shown Figure 6-13. Thus, the different workstations can aid in different interactions.

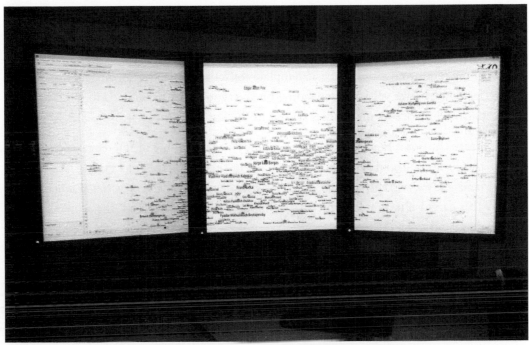

FIGURE 6-13: More pixels are useful when interactively exploring larger graphs.

EXPLAIN

After you have completed all the work of collecting data, laying out graphs, connecting visual attributes, and finding insights, it is likely that you will want to share those insights with other people.

In general, telling a story with a graph must be done carefully, or the impact can simply be one of confusion. Early in his career, one of this book's authors received one type of this reaction from his boss who said, "There's too much here. What am I supposed to look at? Where am I supposed to look? How am I supposed to know, or is the goal to overwhelm?"

Sequence of a Data Story

You can tell a story in many ways. After years of trial and error, one of this book's authors now tends to use a fairly basic template for telling data stories, although there can certainly be better versions, depending on the type of story you need to tell. The approach roughly follows the process set out in the last few chapters:

1. **State the goal.** Starting with the goal provides the frame of reference as to why the audience should even be thinking about this problem. For example, *"Identify strategies for microstores: an analysis of complementary product categories to standalone."* This can also indicate the metrics of importance, the data used, the scope of the data, and the analysis.

2. **Provide an overview.** The overall visual representation of a graph may be unfamiliar and confusing to some viewers, with colored dots and lines everywhere. A high-level indication should focus on the following:

   2a. What are the nodes? An example might be, *"Nodes are products we sell."*

   2b. What are the edges? An example might be, *"Links indicate when two products have sold together."*

   2c. What do the size and color indicate? An example might be, *"Nodes are sized and colored by revenue. The link width indicates the number of times two products were purchased together."*

   2d. Identify a few familiar recognizable data points. This moves the story from the general concept into specific familiar information that is relevant. An example might be, *"So, for example, this big purple node represents light bulbs, our top-selling item. Or, this wide line represents the connection between screwdrivers and screws."*

3. **Provide a specific analysis.** Once the audience is familiar with the objective, the structure, and a few data points, individual patterns can be identified and explained. An example might be, *"These two clusters to the upper-right corner represent lighting products and paint products. Note that they are not strongly connected to our other products—meaning that we could consider a microstore based purely on this product segment."*

4. **Explain the anomalies.** The audience may be interested in what is highly visible, such as outliers and anomalies (for example, the discrete little cluster in Figure 6-3). These should not be ignored but explained as part of the process to help familiarize the viewer with what may be important or unimportant. If these anomalies are unimportant, it might be useful to completely remove them if the presentation is brief or include them and explain them away immediately after step 2d. An example might be, "*These little clusters off to the side are obscure products purchased together—but they are not purchased together with our core products.*"

5. **Filter and drill down.** When you use a subset of data or you use a new layout, there is a change of context. This context shift must be conveyed clearly, or the viewer can be confused. Sometimes a sequence of images may aid the explanation. An example might be, "*From this larger graph, we can extract only the products that sell with an extension cord, shown here as a green dot, and then we can remove the extension cord to more clearly see that there are two different clusters of products that sell with extension cords.*"

How the explanation is to be conveyed depends on how the story is told:

- A *presentation* such as a PowerPoint benefits from a verbal story, during which the presenter controls the discussion and flow, but the viewers do not have the capability to inspect the data, zoom in, nor control how long to linger on an image.

- A *distribution* such as a PDF file can allow the viewers to review the data, visualizations, and analysis at their own pace, and potentially zoom in to inspect details and read small labels.

- An *interactive analysis* such as an interactive version on a web page (or a saved file, graph software, and accompanying directions) allows the viewers to do some explorations on their own. In this scenario, the end viewer has more control (or even full control) over the analysis.

In the case of a presentation, some of the story elements can be verbal but should be backed up with a corresponding visual element such that the viewers can still decode what they are seeing should they arrive late or otherwise miss a point being made. In the case of a PDF or other distributed document, these story elements must be made an explicit visual element.

Legends

In most cases, some form of legend should be added. Ideally, you should include a nice legend, similar to a map legend, which visually indicates the range of data that is desirable. Some graph software (such as Cytoscape) provides a legend that you can export. Some graph software (such as yEd or Gephi) provides some visual indicators when configuring the visual attribute, which can potentially be captured with a screen capture. Unfortunately, these techniques result in graphical legends that are not necessarily self-explanatory to the casual viewer, so you may want to create one, such as the one in Figure 6-14, using drawing tools (for example, PowerPoint or Illustrator).

Product Sales

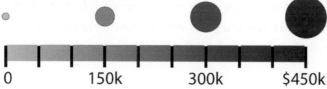

0   150k   300k $450k

Number of pairs purchased

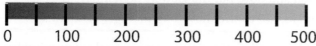

0   100   200   300   400   500

FIGURE 6-14: This is a legend for the market basket visualization.

Another alternative is to put a brief text legend below or beside the graph, such as one including the following:

- *Nodes* indicate products.

- *Node size* indicates product revenue from $0 to $450K.

- *Node color* similarly indicates revenue from $0 (pink) to $450K (deep purple).

- *Links* indicate pairs of products purchased together.

- *Link width and color* indicate frequency of pairs purchased from 1 (narrow, dark blue) to 500 times (wider and green).

Annotations

In the process of telling a data story, you may refer to specific items such as "the large purple node" or "the node at the bottom of the screen." This can be somewhat ambiguous because there may be multiple nodes close to the stated criteria.

You can clearly identify nodes or edges of interest by changing the color or adding a label. You can add labels selectively to only a few items by adding an extra column of data to the nodes data and then entering notes on only the items that you want to be labeled, as shown in Figure 6-15.

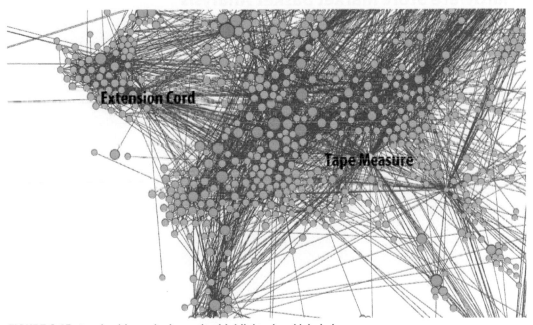

FIGURE 6-15: Graph with particular nodes highlighted and labeled.

In some software, other enhancements include shifting the label (so as not to obscure the node), changing the shape, changing/adding other visual attributes, or adding direct annotations.

Often, you may want to add other annotations (such as arrows, circles around particular items, or outlines around a particular cluster). Because most graph software doesn't provide general drawing tools, you must add these types of annotations in other software, such as Adobe Acrobat, Adobe Illustrator, or Microsoft PowerPoint. Cytoscape does have some text and drawing annotation tools available via the right-click context menu.

Figure 6-16 shows a complete explanation of the hardware store market basket analysis graph created with Gephi and with titles, explanations, a legend, and annotations added via Adobe Illustrator. Note that some minor enhancements were done to the graph prior. For example, node spacing was increased by using the Noverlap Gephi plug-in, and graph preview options (such as a slight transparency) were tweaked to node edges to improve the legibility of the output graph prior to output as SVG. The SVG was directly imported to Adobe Illustrator, enhancements were added, and then it was output as a PDF file (or other high quality format, such as EPS).

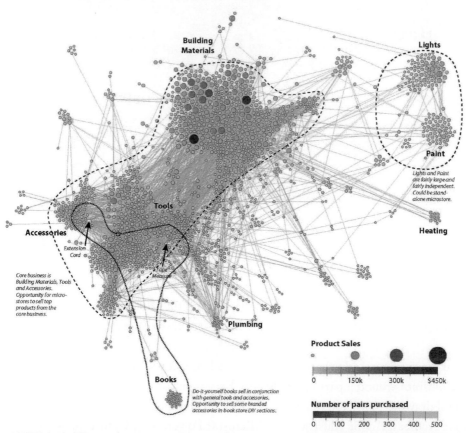

Hardware Store Market Basket Analysis
to evaluate product subsets for new microstores

This graph indicates all products which were purchased together at least three times.
Links between products indicate which pairs were purchased together.

FIGURE 6-16: This market basket analysis includes an explanation, legend, and annotations. The graph was created in Gephi and exported as SVG, and then additional information was added in Adobe Illustrator.

Figure 6-17 shows a similar analysis with explanation for the same hardware store market-based analysis, created using Cytoscape instead of Gephi. In this example, a Cytoscape graph was exported to a .png image. The image was inserted into PowerPoint with various text and outlines added. Since Cytoscape can generate and export a legend, a portion of the Cytoscape legend has been added to the PowerPoint file.

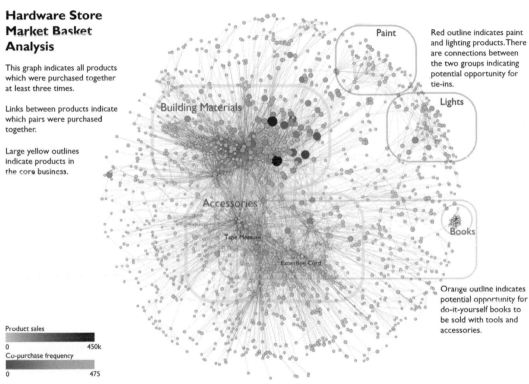

Hardware Store Market Basket Analysis

This graph indicates all products which were purchased together at least three times.

Links between products indicate which pairs were purchased together.

Large yellow outlines indicate products in the core business.

Paint

Red outline indicates paint and lighting products. There are connections between the two groups indicating potential opportunity for tie-ins.

Lights

Building Materials

Accessories

Tape Measure

Extension Cord

Books

Orange outline indicates potential opportunity for do-it-yourself books to be sold with tools and accessories.

Product sales
0   450k
Co-purchase frequency
0   475

FIGURE 6-17: This is the same market basket data with similar analysis and story. This version was created in Cytoscape and exported as .png, and then additional information was added in Microsoft PowerPoint.

Export Data Subsets, Graphs, and Images

Finally, you may need to provide data subsets, images, or graph files of the results as part of the explanation. Most graph software provides the capability to export all of these.

Data Files

You learned about various graph file formats in Chapter 3, "Data—Collect, Clean, and Connect." There can be many reasons to export graph data, including the following:

- **Subgraph**—One benefit of graph export is that a small, isolated subgraph can be exported, resulting in a smaller file size and less exposure to possibly confidential data.

- **Enhanced graph data**—Other graph statistics (such as degree or centrality measures) can be exported with the graph data and then used by other software.

Image Files

Images are often a desired output. Following are a few important points about exporting images:

- **Bitmap images**—Bitmap images (such as .png, .jpg, or .jpeg files) may look nice but will be simply the pixels that you see on the screen. Zooming in on a bitmap image will show a grainy image with no additional useful information. Bitmap images produced at typical screen resolutions are okay for PowerPoint presentations and hard copy. Higher resolutions are required if the target output is larger (such as a poster). In this chapter, most of the images are bitmap screen shots from the actual interactive session.

- **Vector images**—Vector images (such as PDF or SVG files) represent the image as geometry (lines, circles, text, and so on). These can be scaled up and zoomed in, and small fonts can become readable when zoomed in. However, in vector formats, fonts may change to a different style if a font is not available on the viewer's computer. The location of labels may not be exactly as located in the original software. Sometimes the document may be clipped with part of the graph missing. For the latter problem, the SVG export tends to have fewer cropping problems. Although SVG can be viewed directly in a recent web browser, PDF is a more common, more familiar format, and there is an additional step to convert SVG into a PDF file (for example, via Adobe Illustrator). In most of the other chapters of this book, high-quality vector-based images are used.

Interactive Web Applications

As graph visualization software packages add more features, direct export of the graph into an interactive web application will become available. This feature is expected soon in Cytoscape.

PUTTING IT ALL TOGETHER

Exploration, explanation, and export are various interactions with a graph that help achieve insight, share insights, and use those insights.

Many of these interactions are used together to enable exploratory analysis of a large graph by providing an easy means to aid the formulation of a hypothesis, test assumptions, explore relationships, and sift through the graph. You can repeat this process iteratively to test a wide variety of ideas to gain a wide variety of insights:

- **Navigate**—Zoom and pan are essential to move between an overall context and a view of local detail.

- **Identify**—Accessing all the data associated with a node via mouse-over or mouse-click establishes which nodes are which, helps establish landmarks within the scene, and allows for inspection of detail data.

- **Filter**—Interactive filtering enables exploratory analysis of a large graph and provides a quick means to isolate subsets of the graph based on any data attributes.

- **Isolate**—You can isolate and then analyze graph subsets separately, including re-layout, changing attributes, and any other exploratory interactions.

- **Neighbors**—Adjacencies indicate the direct relationships to a particular node.

- **Paths**—You can use paths to identify a route though a large graph to understand how to connect from one point to another.

- **Delete/move/modify**—You can delete individual nodes (for example, to see what connections remain with a target node removed), move them to make patterns more clear, or modify them to stand out (for example, by changing shape).

- **Group**—You can combine multiple nodes.

After gaining a number of insights, you should consider the following when communicating these findings to other people:

- **Sequence**—Use a story to explain the objective, what the configuration is, and what patterns can be seen.

- **Legend**—Add legends so the viewer knows what the visual attributes are.

- **Annotate**—Add annotations to call out specific nodes.

- **Export**—Export data or images for reports and presentations.

SUMMARY

Interactive exploration is often the stage where insights are found in a graph. Gain proficiency with the interactive tools in your graph software to sift through subsets of data, understand neighbors and paths, and isolate parts of the graph.

To share insights, assemble an annotated story that explains the findings step-by-step and provides images and/or exports of graph data. The full sequence provides the recipient with the objective, the data used in its representation, and the visual findings in a concise explanation that can be delivered to all stakeholders.

In this chapter, the interactions discussed are implemented in different ways in different point-and-click graph software. Chapter 7 discusses some of the graph software packages available, some of their unique strengths, and how some of the essential interactions work.

7

POINT-AND-CLICK GRAPH TOOLS

As you've read through the previous chapters, you have learned about the process for graph analysis and visualization. It's now time to consider the tools that you can use to analyze and visualize graphs.

A number of good point-and-click graph analysis and visualization tools are available to explore modestly sized graphs. These tools can provide quick insights without requiring any programming. Note that point-and-click tools are not necessarily as quick and easy to use as you might expect, so allow time to learn the software and its idiosyncrasies.

In the writing of this book, the following point-and-click tools have been used. No single point-and-click tool is best; each tool has specific strengths.

- **Excel**—This is effective for data cleansing, data preparation, and the visualization of small-scale matrices. Free alternatives (such as Google Spreadsheet) can be used for some of these tasks. (See http://products.office.com/en-us/excel or http://docs.google.com.)

- **NodeXL**—This is a free plug-in for Excel that provides direct graph import from social networks and e-mail, as well as some visualization capabilities. (See http://nodexl.codeplex.com/.)

- **Gephi**—This is a free, popular graph analysis and visualization software package with extensive data import/export capabilities, rich layout capabilities, and additional third-party plug-ins. (See `https://gephi.github.io/`.)

- **Cytoscape**—This is a free, powerful graph analysis and visualization software package with some capabilities beyond Gephi, including multiple links between the same pair of nodes, and a very wide variety of visual attributes. (See `http://www.cytoscape.org/`.)

- **yEd**—This is a free graph layout and analysis package with a wide variety of edge layouts and labeling options. (See `www.yworks.com/en/products/yfiles/yed/`.)

This chapter takes a closer look at each of these tools.

EXCEL

The spreadsheet has evolved beyond a simple data calculation tool into a sophisticated and flexible repository for collecting, analyzing, and summarizing data from multiple sources.

For preparation of graph data, Excel can be an effective tool in helping you summarize links, extract nodes, or enhance the data with additional attributes. For example, Excel is utilized to enhance data in the "Community Topic Analysis," in Chapter 11, "Communities." Because the need to summarize links and/or create nodes can be a common task with most graph data sets, let's take a look at a quick illustration.

Summarizing Links

As discussed in Chapter 3, "Data—Collect, Clean, and Connect," network logs and air traffic data may have many links between a pair of nodes, but some graph analysis will permit only one link between a pair of nodes (or two directed links). You can use Excel's PivotTable functionality to summarize all the data corresponding to a source and destination node, thus consolidating multiple links into a single link.

As a simple example, raw link data from air traffic data may appear as shown in Figure 7-1. Note that an additional column has been added (E) to concatenate the origin and destination into a single cell, which will be used to create the summaries in the next step into directed links.

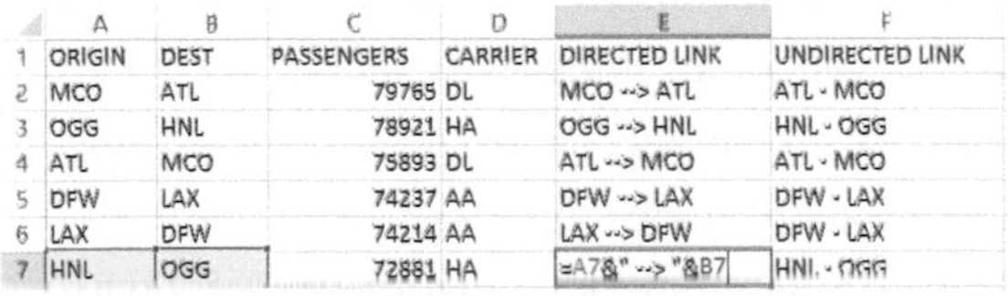

	A	B	C	D	E	F
1	ORIGIN	DEST	PASSENGERS	CARRIER	DIRECTED LINK	UNDIRECTED LINK
2	MCO	ATL	79765	DL	MCO --> ATL	ATL - MCO
3	OGG	HNL	78921	HA	OGG --> HNL	HNL - OGG
4	ATL	MCO	75893	DL	ATL --> MCO	ATL - MCO
5	DFW	LAX	74237	AA	DFW --> LAX	DFW - LAX
6	LAX	DFW	74214	AA	LAX --> DFW	DFW - LAX
7	HNL	OGG	72881	HA	=A7&" --> "&B7	HNL - OGG

FIGURE 7-1: This sample raw flight data in Excel has a `DIRECTED LINK` column and `UNDIRECTED LINK` column added.

For undirected links, column F instead places the origin-to-destination order of the nodes into a consistent node1-node2 pair in alphabetic order using the formula `=IF(A7<B7,A7&" - "&B7,B7&" - "&A7)`. In cells E5 and E6, note how `DFW-->LAX` is different from `LAX-->DFW`, whereas in cells F5 and F6 they are the same.

In the next step, as shown in Figure 7-2, the links are aggregated into a single link per origin-destination using a PivotTable in the spreadsheet, with the rows set to the `DIRECTED LINK` column created previously, and summaries based on counts and sums.

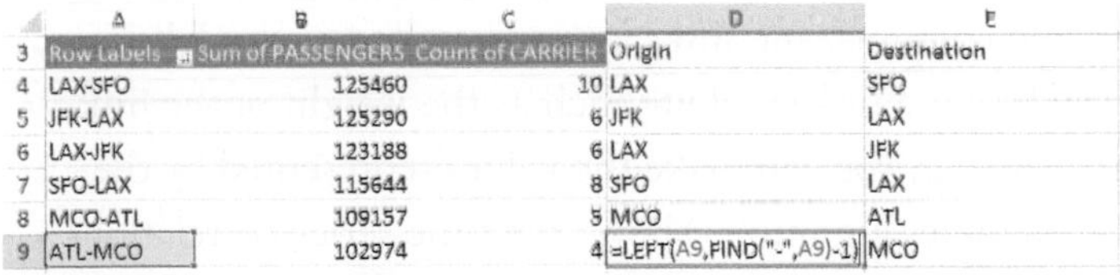

	A	B	C	D	E
3	Row Labels	Sum of PASSENGERS	Count of CARRIER	Origin	Destination
4	LAX-SFO	125460	10	LAX	SFO
5	JFK-LAX	125290	6	JFK	LAX
6	LAX-JFK	123188	6	LAX	JFK
7	SFO-LAX	115644	8	SFO	LAX
8	MCO-ATL	109157	5	MCO	ATL
9	ATL-MCO	102974	4	=LEFT(A9,FIND("-",A9)-1)	MCO

FIGURE 7-2: These links have been aggregated with a PivotTable. The last two columns are added to separate the origin and destination.

The first three columns are the PivotTable. The final two columns have been added to split the route back into corresponding references to the origin and destination nodes. As a result, each row represents a single consolidated link ready to use in the graph software. Figure 7-2 shows summarized directed links—note how rows 5 and 6 are the links JKF-to-LAX and LAX-to-JFK. If the data were summed based on undirected links, there would be only a single entry for JFK-LAX.

See the `AirTrafficData-Jan2013.xlsx` Excel spreadsheet in the `FlightStats` folder of the Supplementary Materials on this book's companion website for an example.

Extracting Nodes

The previous example had both a data set of nodes and a data set of links where the links were summarized. But in some data sets no separate list of nodes is available, such as network logs. In network log data, each record lists a connection (that is, a link). These links may need to be summarized. In addition, a set of nodes must also be extracted.

Extracting nodes can be done by utilizing a similar approach with PivotTables with summaries based on nodes. Because you have two columns of nodes (for example, source and target), you must create two PivotTables, one for each column. You can then concatenate these to create the node list, and if duplicate nodes exist, you can remove them.

See the NetworkLogs Excel spreadsheet in the supplemental materials for an example.

Adjacency Matrix Visualization in Excel

Most people wouldn't think of Excel as a graph visualization environment. However, Excel can be handy for visualizing adjacency matrices (which were first discussed in Chapter 4, "Stats and Layout"). An *adjacency matrix* is simply a grid where nodes are represented as the titles to rows and columns, and links are represented as the cells in a matrix. The number in the cell indicates a link attribute such as the weight of the link.

Using Excel's conditional formatting, you can make the values represented by the links more visually explicit. For example, Figure 7-3 shows the time series correlations between 20 topics. *Time series correlations* indicate how two different items move together over time. In this example, topics are based on a list of popular on-line topics from a list published by *Time* magazine a few years ago. When two topics are popular at the same time, they are highly correlated (green). Two topics that are popular at opposite times are inversely correlated (red), and topics with no correlation are yellow.

Simply viewing all the connections as a color-coded matrix is not sufficient to see clusters or patterns. The only visible pattern is the green diagonal line through the center, which simply indicates that any topic is perfectly correlated with itself, and this is not an interesting insight.

Rearranging the data in Excel can improve your capability to see clusters. A simple approach may be simply to sort by a particular column (and also do the sort in the corresponding row to preserve the same order in both rows and columns). This is a good start and shows how all the other items are correlated to one specific topic.

FIGURE 7-3: This adjacency matrix in Excel shows trend correlations between topics. Clusters are not visible.

Topics	Colson Whitehead	Jennifer Weiner	Maureen Johnson	R.L. Stine	William Gibson	Amazon MP3	Comcast	H&R Block	Harvard Business Review	JetBlue Airways	Netflix	Richard Florida	Southwest Airlines	Starbucks	Threadless	Whole Foods Market	Zappos	Alyssa Milano	Ashton Kutcher
Colson Whitehead	1.00	0.11	0.08	0.01	-0.08	0.06	-0.01	-0.06	-0.08	0.05	0.07	-0.06	-0.06	0.11	0.03	-0.04	0.08	-0.10	0.04
Jennifer Weiner	0.11	1.00	0.32	-0.31	-0.35	0.40	0.11	-0.17	-0.38	0.30	0.43	-0.40	-0.34	0.28	0.29	-0.24	0.38	-0.44	0.22
Maureen Johnson	0.08	0.32	1.00	-0.21	-0.42	0.60	-0.18	0.10	-0.41	0.22	0.67	-0.53	-0.48	0.40	0.25	-0.49	0.50	-0.50	0.44
R.L. Stine	0.01	-0.31	-0.21	1.00	0.23	-0.18	-0.24	0.15	0.29	-0.25	-0.26	0.27	0.07	-0.18	-0.26	0.10	-0.24	0.27	-0.17
William Gibson	-0.08	-0.35	-0.42	0.23	1.00	-0.64	-0.27	0.06	0.87	-0.70	-0.44	0.78	0.43	-0.58	-0.76	0.21	-0.75	0.86	0.09
Amazon MP3	0.06	0.40	0.60	-0.18	-0.64	1.00	0.12	-0.04	-0.64	0.36	0.68	-0.68	-0.47	0.58	0.50	-0.50	0.76	-0.71	0.26
Comcast	-0.01	0.11	0.18	0.24	0.27	0.12	1.00	-0.12	-0.31	0.36	-0.01	-0.18	0.17	0.44	0.43	0.20	0.33	-0.24	-0.21
H&R Block	-0.06	-0.17	0.10	0.15	0.06	-0.04	-0.12	1.00	0.16	0.09	0.04	0.15	0.20	-0.02	-0.18	-0.05	-0.04	0.06	0.06
Harvard Business Review	-0.08	-0.38	-0.41	0.29	0.87	-0.64	-0.31	0.16	1.00	-0.74	-0.46	0.82	0.44	-0.56	-0.81	0.17	-0.79	0.88	0.10
JetBlue Airways	0.05	0.30	0.22	-0.25	-0.70	0.36	0.36	0.09	-0.74	1.00	0.33	-0.63	-0.19	0.55	0.68	-0.01	0.68	-0.72	-0.13
Netflix	0.07	0.43	0.67	-0.26	-0.44	0.68	-0.01	0.04	-0.46	0.33	1.00	-0.61	-0.52	0.65	0.30	-0.56	0.73	-0.55	0.55
Richard Florida	-0.06	-0.40	0.53	0.27	0.78	-0.68	-0.18	0.15	0.82	-0.63	-0.61	1.00	0.54	-0.57	-0.67	0.36	-0.80	0.83	-0.12
Southwest Airlines	-0.06	-0.34	-0.48	0.07	0.43	-0.47	0.17	0.20	0.44	-0.19	-0.52	0.54	1.00	-0.36	-0.36	0.27	-0.48	0.50	-0.25
Starbucks	0.11	0.28	0.40	-0.18	-0.58	0.58	0.44	-0.02	-0.56	0.55	0.65	-0.57	-0.36	1.00	0.57	-0.18	0.81	-0.61	0.21
Threadless	0.03	0.29	0.25	-0.26	-0.76	0.50	0.43	-0.18	-0.81	0.68	0.30	-0.67	-0.36	0.57	1.00	-0.03	0.73	-0.77	-0.15
Whole Foods Market	-0.04	-0.24	-0.49	0.10	0.21	-0.50	0.20	-0.05	0.17	-0.01	-0.56	0.36	0.27	-0.18	-0.03	1.00	-0.37	0.35	-0.40
Zappos	0.08	0.38	0.50	-0.24	-0.75	0.76	0.33	-0.04	-0.79	0.68	0.73	-0.80	-0.48	0.81	0.73	-0.37	1.00	-0.83	0.20
Alyssa Milano	-0.10	-0.44	-0.50	0.27	0.86	-0.71	-0.24	0.06	0.88	-0.72	-0.55	0.83	0.50	-0.61	-0.77	0.35	-0.83	1.00	-0.04
Ashton Kutcher	0.04	0.22	0.44	-0.17	0.09	0.26	-0.21	0.06	0.10	-0.13	0.55	-0.12	-0.25	0.21	-0.15	-0.40	0.20	-0.04	1.00

For example, in this data set, you can sort both vertically and horizontally by *Harvard Business Review* (an influential business publication), as shown in Figure 7-4. Although this shows items that correlate with *Harvard Business Review* (as shown in Figure 7-5), only one other cluster is readily apparent when zoomed out across the large data set of 80 topics.

Topics	Harvard Business Review	National Science Foundation	Alyssa Milano	William Gibson	The Lancet	Richard Florida	Homer Simpson	The Onion	Southwest Airlines	Reuters	Brian Wilson	R.L. Stine	Ana Marie Cox	Whole Foods Market	H&R Block	Ashton Kutcher	John Hodgman	Claire McCaskill	Michael Ian Black
Harvard Business Review	1.00	0.95	0.88	0.87	0.87	0.82	0.74	0.51	0.44	0.38	0.33	0.29	0.20	0.17	0.16	0.10	0.01	0.01	0.00
National Science Foundation	0.95	1.00	0.92	0.89	0.89	0.86	0.71	0.50	0.50	0.42	0.30	0.28	0.21	0.25	0.13	0.01	0.00	0.02	0.00
Alyssa Milano	0.88	0.92	1.00	0.86	0.85	0.83	0.68	0.42	0.50	0.43	0.26	0.27	0.21	0.35	0.06	-0.04	-0.01	0.00	-0.02
William Gibson	0.87	0.89	0.86	1.00	0.80	0.78	0.74	0.45	0.43	0.38	0.33	0.23	0.16	0.21	0.06	0.09	-0.01	0.00	-0.01
The Lancet	0.87	0.89	0.85	0.80	1.00	0.80	0.68	0.44	0.40	0.39	0.31	0.38	0.25	0.28	0.09	-0.06	0.03	0.06	0.01
Richard Florida	0.82	0.86	0.83	0.78	0.80	1.00	0.62	0.46	0.54	0.43	0.22	0.27	0.13	0.36	0.15	-0.12	0.04	0.03	-0.03
Homer Simpson	0.74	0.71	0.68	0.74	0.68	0.62	1.00	0.42	0.28	0.28	0.32	0.23	0.19	0.05	0.07	0.17	0.00	-0.02	-0.03
The Onion	0.51	0.50	0.42	0.45	0.44	0.46	0.42	1.00	0.31	0.26	0.10	0.16	0.19	-0.02	0.08	0.01	0.03	0.00	0.05
Southwest Airlines	0.44	0.50	0.50	0.43	0.40	0.54	0.28	0.31	1.00	0.31	-0.01	0.07	0.07	0.27	0.20	-0.25	-0.01	-0.01	0.08
Reuters	0.38	0.42	0.43	0.38	0.39	0.43	0.28	0.26	0.31	1.00	0.12	0.09	0.13	0.17	0.01	-0.09	0.02	0.01	0.06
Brian Wilson	0.33	0.30	0.26	0.33	0.31	0.22	0.32	0.10	-0.01	0.12	1.00	0.03	0.16	-0.13	-0.07	0.21	-0.02	-0.02	0.06
R.L. Stine	0.29	0.28	0.27	0.23	0.38	0.27	0.23	0.16	0.07	0.09	0.03	1.00	0.22	0.10	0.15	-0.17	0.05	0.01	-0.10
Ana Marie Cox	0.20	0.21	0.21	0.16	0.25	0.13	0.19	0.19	0.07	0.13	0.26	0.22	1.00	-0.07	-0.07	-0.06	0.02	-0.02	0.13
Whole Foods Market	0.17	0.25	0.35	0.21	0.28	0.36	0.05	-0.02	0.27	0.17	-0.13	0.10	-0.07	1.00	-0.05	-0.40	0.04	0.06	-0.13
H&R Block	0.16	0.13	0.06	0.06	0.09	0.15	0.07	0.08	0.20	0.01	-0.07	0.15	-0.07	-0.05	1.00	0.06	-0.05	-0.03	-0.12
Ashton Kutcher	0.10	0.01	-0.04	0.09	-0.06	-0.12	0.17	0.01	-0.25	-0.09	0.21	-0.17	-0.06	-0.40	0.06	1.00	-0.05	-0.04	0.06
John Hodgman	0.01	0.00	-0.01	-0.01	0.03	0.04	0.00	0.03	-0.01	0.02	-0.02	0.05	0.02	0.04	-0.05	-0.05	1.00	0.00	-0.01
Claire McCaskill	0.01	0.02	0.00	0.00	0.06	0.03	-0.02	0.00	-0.01	0.01	-0.02	0.01	-0.02	0.06	-0.03	-0.04	0.00	1.00	-0.03
Michael Ian Black	0.00	0.00	-0.02	-0.01	0.01	-0.03	-0.03	0.05	0.08	0.06	0.06	-0.10	0.13	-0.13	-0.12	0.06	-0.01	-0.03	1.00

FIGURE 7-4: This adjacency matrix is sorted based on correlations to *Harvard Business Review*

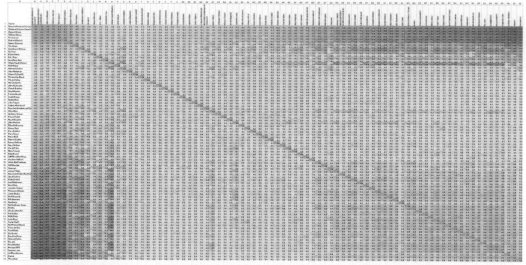

FIGURE 7-5: This zoomed-out adjacency matrix shows all 7,000 links sorted by *Harvard Business Review*.

Using Excel Visual Basic for Applications (VBA), you can program more advanced clustering. For example, you could use a naive cluster sort in which each successive row and column is sorted so that the next item is the closest to the previous item, which results in an adjacency matrix, as shown in Figure 7-6. This reveals a number of smaller, highly correlated clusters all along the diagonal, and some strong inverse correlation clusters as well.

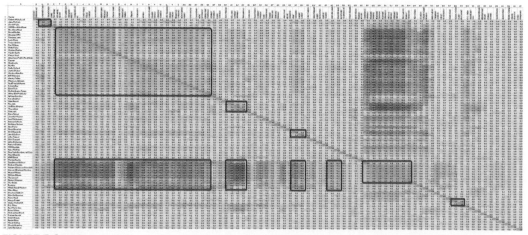

FIGURE 7-6: This zoomed-out adjacency matrix shows successive sorting via a macro. More distinct clusters are visible.

As shown in rows 3 and 4 in Figure 7-7, zooming in shows a little cluster with John McCain and Sarah Palin. You can find more advanced (and more efficient) VBA clustering algorithms online.

Topics	Colson Whitehead	John McCain	Sarah Palin	CNN Breaking News	Breaking News	RetailMeNot	Amazon MP3	Coupons.com	Lady Gaga	Tracy Jordan	Fred Wilson	Nikki Finke	Michael Pollan	Taylor Swift	Kanye West	American Public Health	Zappos	Starbucks	Netflix
Colson Whitehead	1.0	0.2	0.1	0.1	0.1	0.1	0.1	0.1	0.0	0.1	0.1	0.1	0.1	0.1	0.0	0.1	0.1	0.1	0.1
John McCain	0.2	1.0	0.8	0.3	0.0	0.0	0.0	0.1	-0.2	-0.1	0.1	0.1	0.1	0.0	0.0	0.2	0.1	0.1	-0.2
Sarah Palin	0.1	0.8	1.0	0.3	0.2	0.2	0.1	0.2	0.0	0.1	0.2	0.1	0.1	0.1	0.1	0.2	0.2	0.1	0.0
CNN Breaking News	0.1	0.3	0.3	1.0	0.5	0.2	0.2	0.2	0.1	0.2	0.2	0.2	0.2	0.1	0.0	0.2	0.2	0.1	0.2
Breaking News	0.1	0.0	0.2	0.5	1.0	0.8	0.7	0.7	0.6	0.7	0.6	0.5	0.5	0.6	0.2	0.4	0.7	0.6	0.8
RetailMeNot	0.1	0.0	0.2	0.2	0.8	1.0	0.9	0.8	0.8	0.8	0.7	0.6	0.7	0.8	0.2	0.5	0.8	0.7	0.8
Amazon MP3	0.1	0.0	0.1	0.2	0.7	0.9	1.0	0.8	0.7	0.8	0.7	0.6	0.7	0.7	0.2	0.4	0.8	0.6	0.7
Coupons.com	0.1	0.1	0.2	0.2	0.7	0.8	0.8	1.0	0.8	0.8	0.7	0.7	0.8	0.7	0.2	0.5	0.7	0.5	0.6
Lady Gaga	0.0	-0.2	0.0	0.1	0.6	0.8	0.7	0.8	1.0	0.8	0.5	0.7	0.7	0.7	0.2	0.4	0.6	0.3	0.7
Tracy Jordan	0.1	-0.1	0.1	0.2	0.7	0.8	0.8	0.8	0.8	1.0	0.7	0.7	0.7	0.7	0.2	0.5	0.7	0.5	0.6
Fred Wilson	0.1	0.1	0.2	0.2	0.6	0.7	0.7	0.7	0.6	0.7	1.0	0.8	0.7	0.6	0.3	0.6	0.6	0.6	0.5
Nikki Finke	0.1	0.1	0.1	0.2	0.5	0.6	0.6	0.7	0.5	0.7	0.8	1.0	0.7	0.6	0.2	0.4	0.5	0.5	0.3
Michael Pollan	0.1	0.1	0.1	0.2	0.5	0.7	0.7	0.8	0.7	0.7	0.7	0.7	1.0	0.6	0.2	0.5	0.5	0.4	0.4
Taylor Swift	0.1	0.0	0.1	0.1	0.6	0.8	0.7	0.7	0.7	0.7	0.6	0.6	0.6	1.0	0.6	0.5	0.6	0.4	0.6
Kanye West	0.0	0.0	0.1	0.0	0.2	0.2	0.2	0.2	0.2	0.2	0.3	0.2	0.2	0.6	1.0	0.3	0.2	0.2	0.2
American Public Health Asso	0.1	0.2	0.2	0.2	0.4	0.5	0.4	0.5	0.4	0.5	0.6	0.4	0.5	0.5	0.3	1.0	0.4	0.4	0.3
Zappos	0.1	0.1	0.2	0.2	0.7	0.8	0.8	0.7	0.6	0.7	0.6	0.5	0.5	0.6	0.2	0.4	1.0	0.8	0.7
Starbucks	0.1	0.1	0.1	0.1	0.6	0.7	0.6	0.5	0.3	0.5	0.6	0.5	0.4	0.4	0.2	0.4	0.8	1.0	0.6
Netflix	0.1	0.2	0.0	0.2	0.8	0.8	0.7	0.6	0.7	0.6	0.5	0.3	0.4	0.6	0.2	0.3	0.7	0.6	1.0

FIGURE 7-7: This is a close-up of a successively sorted spreadsheet showing the tiny cluster of McCain and Palin near the top left.

NODEXL

Excel is a popular program partially because the graph data is visible and editable directly in Excel, making it easy to adapt, extend, add to, and modify the data using spreadsheet formulas. NodeXL is a free Excel plug-in specifically designed for automating the collection of social network data, organizing the data for graphs, and visualizing graphs. NodeXL makes it particularly easy to import data from a variety of social networks and applications, including Twitter, Flickr, Facebook, YouTube, Outlook, Exchange Server, and more.

NodeXL Basics

NodeXL provides a *template spreadsheet* that you can use to organize a graph and configure its visual attributes. As shown in Figure 7-8, a *ribbon toolbar* across the top of Excel aids with data acquisition, analysis, filters, export, help, and so on. A *visualization window* assists with interactive exploration of the graph.

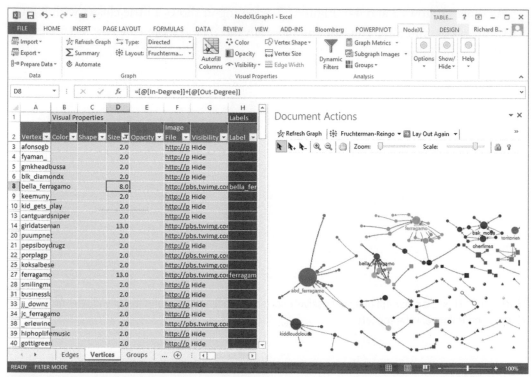

FIGURE 7-8: NodeXL is an Excel plug-in with templates you can use to easily configure the graph. Mouse over any cell for configuration hints.

NodelXL Worksheet

NodeXL provides all the features and flexibility of Excel, such as familiar toolbars, formulas, and filters. The worksheet templates make it easy to configure and manipulate the graph. Each column heading includes a brief comment that indicates how to use the cells in that column. (Point at the little red comment triangle to see the comment.)

The following are some useful Excel worksheet functionality:

- **Formulas**—You can set visual attributes using Excel's formulas. You can use standard Excel formulas such as setting cell F3 to be = R3 + 2. Since the NodeXL template sets up the graph data in Excel tables, you can also use Excel column references, which work similar to named ranges in Excel. For example, if one column is named MyData, then a formula in another column can be set to reference the initial column by name—for example, =sum([MyData]). To reference the data in the column corresponding to the same row as the formula, the column reference is prefixed with a @—for example, =[@MyData]. For example, in the graph in Figure 7-8, note the following:

- Node size is set to the sum of In-Degree and Out-Degree, as shown here:

  `=[@In-Degree]+[@Out-Degree]`

- Node label is set to the Twitter name if the node size is large, as shown here:

  `=IF([@Size]>8,[@Vertex],"")`

- **Column Filters**—Every data attribute can be used as a filter using Excel's column filter drop-down menus. For example, social network data may result in many small nodes or nodes without any edges. Use the drop-downs to remove all the nodes without edges, as shown in Figure 7-9.

FIGURE 7-9: You can use Excel's filters to remove items from the visualization.

NodeXL Menu and Ribbon Toolbar

Clicking the NodeXL menu provides a ribbon toolbar to access many NodeXL features, such as the following:

- **Import**—This button provides a drop-down, many with wizards to assist in acquiring data from many different data sources (including data that may be in other Excel spreadsheets).

- **Prepare Data**—This button provides functionality to automatically summarize edges (that is, remove duplicate edges) and create nodes from edges. This can be easier than creating PivotTables, as discussed earlier in this chapter.

- **Autofill Columns**—Visual attributes can be configured via this pop-up window, as a faster and easier alternative to using Excel formulas.

- **Filters**—This provides a pop-up window to dynamically filter numeric values via interactive slider bars.

- **Graph Metrics**—Statistics such as degree, centrality, and pagerank can be calculated using this pop-up window, as well as text associated with social network data. The statistics will be added as additional columns and additional worksheets.

Social Network Features

One of the differentiators for NodeXL from other point-and-click graph software is its specific functionality for the analysis of social networks. It provides tools that make it easy to acquire social network data, load it into Excel, extract social network–specific data such as top hashtags, and follow links back to web sources.

Social Network Data Acquisition

Compared to manually collecting data and creating a graph as described in Chapter 3, NodeXL makes social data acquisition much easier (although it may not collect a large amount of historical data). To facilitate data acquisition from a social network, NodeXL provides wizards to walk you through the process. Figure 7-10 shows the Twitter Search import wizard you can use to search for all tweets containing the word "fendi" (a luxury fashion brand). Note that you must authorize NodeXL to access your Twitter account (the wizard provides steps to complete this).

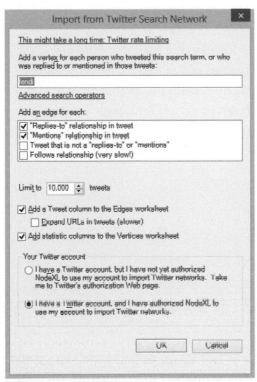

FIGURE 7-10: This shows Twitter search data acquisition in NodeXL.

Social Network Analytics

NodeXL's graph analytics provide some unique functions for analysis of the text often associated with social network data, such as words, top items, top hashtags, top domains, and top mentions (Figure 7-11). You can then display this extracted information in labels or tooltips.

14	Top Domains in Tweet in Entire Graph	Entire Graph Count
15	bit.ly	68
16	elle.com	18
17	instagram.com	6
18	thepetitionsite.com	6
19	twitpic.com	6

FIGURE 7-11: NodeXL provides functionality to extract top domains, words, hashtags, and URLs in tweet data.

Big Tooltips

Clicking a node in NodeXL automatically scrolls Excel to the corresponding row in the spreadsheet. But even faster, NodeXL provides tooltips as you move across any node so you don't have to scroll around in the spreadsheet. By default, the tooltips include useful information beyond the label. For example, as shown in Figure 7-12, with Twitter data, the tooltip includes the most recent tweet. Because the data that appears in the tooltips is simply a column, different data can be shown in the tooltip via formulas.

FIGURE 7-12: You can access the text data associated with a node easily via tooltips.

Images

NodeXL also provides the capability to specify a unique image *per each node*. With social data, this means that user images can be added. These images can be automatically added when importing social data such as Twitter searches. The image URL is placed in the Image File column on the Vertices worksheet. Note that you must set the node shape to Image in order for the image to appear. Using labels and images in a brand network provides a view of the brand ecosystem—that is, co-mentioned brands. Figure 7-13 shows other Twitter users with many followers co-mentioned with "fendi" (on a Sunday in May 2014).

Workflow

If you right-click nodes, you see a large context menu. When using Twitter data, selecting the final item on the menu opens a web browser on that user's Twitter stream. NodeXL enables you to add custom menu items by simply defining the actions in two columns so that various actions can be available by clicking a node.

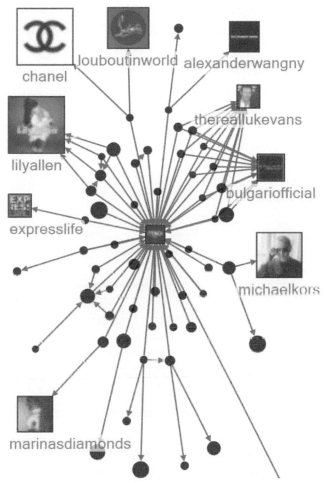

FIGURE 7-13: This shows brands co-mentioned with "fendi," sized by the number of followers for each brand.

Layout

NodeXL provides some basic layouts and a few force-directed layouts (such as Fruchterman-Reingold and Harel-Koren). One nice feature in NodeXL layouts is the capability to put each component in a separate box, accessed via NodeXL Toolbar ⇨

Layout ⇨ Layout Options. In contrast, without this feature, different components may remain tangled together (as may happen with the Fruchterman-Reingold layout) or float far away in some other layouts.

By placing each component in separate boxes, the visible separation is clear. For example, in Figure 7-14, a collection of tweets referencing the term "fendi" can be clearly separated into components connected to the official brand versus other components that may reference "fendi."

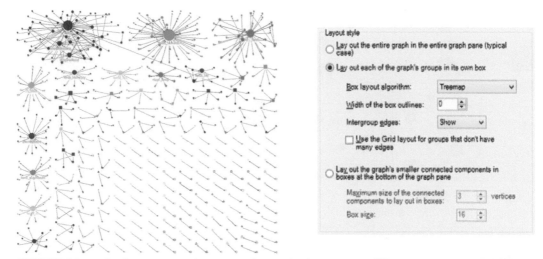

FIGURE 7-14: Putting layout groups in separate boxes clearly separates different components in NodeXL.

As you will see shortly, Gephi provides more flexibility with layouts by offering more graph layout algorithms, more parameters, and direct interaction with layouts. One approach is to create and organize the basic attributes in NodeXL and then export/import the data into Gephi or other software to utilize more features beyond those offered by NodeXL. This approach is used in Chapter 11, which analyzes social network communities starting with NodeXL and then moving to Gephi.

GEPHI

Gephi is a highly popular, free, open source program with strengths in providing a wide variety of graph import/export formats, statistics, many interactive layout algorithms, flexible filtering, high-quality output, and various plug-ins for data import/export, analysis, and layout. Gephi is available in a number of languages, including English, Spanish, Russian, Chinese, and Japanese.

Gephi Basics

As shown in Figure 7-15, the main window in Gephi is surrounded by panels for configuring the visualization. Immediately after loading data, you can use the layout and visualization panels to the left to configure a visualization. Panels to the right provide stats, filters to sift out data, and summaries. Immediately surrounding the visualization window are numerous buttons for directly interacting with the graph itself.

NOTE

A number of online tutorials are available for getting started with the basics of Gephi.

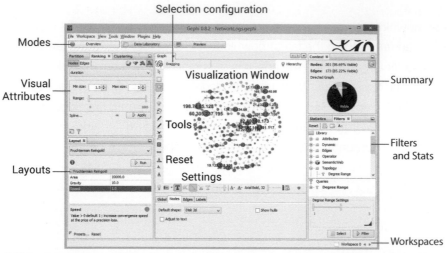

FIGURE 7-15: In the main Gephi window, the visualization is surrounded by a wide variety of interactive tools.

Interactive Layout

At the core of graph visualization, graph layout is often a challenging problem. Gephi provides force-directed layout algorithms (such as Force Atlas and Fruchterman-Reingold), with which you can interact while they are running. Furthermore, you can apply different layouts, with each starting where the previous left off. Adjusting layouts while the layout algorithm is still running can be extremely useful in many situations, including the following:

- **Tweaking parameters**—Are nodes spreading out too much? Increase the gravity and see the nodes start drifting closer together. Did you increase gravity too much? Tweak it again.

- **Moving a node**—Is there a node tangled in with some others? Drag it off to the side. Repeat as necessary to untangle portions of the graph.

- **Moving many nodes**—By default, dragging affects the node immediately under the tip of the cursor. Adjust *selection size*, which enables you to select and move a region of nodes easily. First, to drag, select the hand icon in the selection tools. To adjust the size of the dragging, click the word "Dragging" immediately above in the selection configuration region (see Figure 7-16), and then adjust the drag diameter.

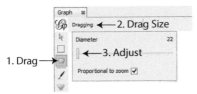

FIGURE 7-16: To adjust node positions, click on the drag icon (1). To adjust the size of drag region, click the dragging micro-menu (2) and adjust the slider bar (3).

Applying layouts in succession can be effective for clarifying and improving readability. Consider the following:

- **Force-directed adjustment**—You can use the Force Atlas layout to tweak another layout—for example, to pull it closer together. You can apply Fruchterman-Reingold to pull apart the densely packed areas of the graph, while at the same time pulling in far-flung nodes.

- **Small shifts**—Layouts such as Noverlap (that is, no overlap) and Label Adjust help shift node positions slightly to improve the visual clarity of cluttered areas or increase spacing to improve readability.

> **TIP**
>
> Gephi makes it easy to mix and match different layouts, but be sure you save layouts that you like. It may be impossible to re-create a force-directed layout.

In conjunction with layout, basic navigation is simple. You can use a mouse wheel to zoom, and you can drag with the right mouse button to pan. If you happen to navigate to an empty screen, you can use the Reset Zoom button.

Graph Statistics and Visual Attributes

Graph statistics can be computed using the Statistics panel. Tooltips provide hints regarding each metric. Computing a metric will generate a report showing the distribution of the metric.

Visual attributes are set under the Partition, Ranking, and Clustering panel. Gephi allows a few visual attributes to be connected to data attributes, such as node size, node color, label size, and label color. The term "partition" corresponds to discrete category data, such as "male" and "female" categories in gender data. The term "ranking" corresponds to a quantity, such as the numeric values provided with income data.

Filtering

Gephi's Filter panel provides a set of folders organizing different types of filters and operations, such as filters on ranges of numeric values, text searches, network topology, and so on. Filters are configured by dragging and dropping filters from the library into the Query section in the lower part of the panel, and they are turned on using the Filter button.

Multiple queries can be configured by dragging multiple filters into the Query panel. If you click between different queries, you toggle between different filter states. Complex queries comprised of multiple filters are created by adding another filter to an existing query.

The filtered results of a particular query can be added back to the data or copied or moved to a new workspace.

Overview vs. Preview Modes

Unlike any other graph software, Gephi has the following two visual modes, which can be a bit confusing, particularly when a feature is available in one mode but not the other:

- **Overview**—The overview mode is the main mode for exploring graphs. It provides a rich interactive analytic environment for adjusting layouts, configuring visual attributes, adjusting filters, and otherwise exploring the graph.

- **Preview**—The preview mode is a prepublication environment for tweaking visual attributes in advance of generating high-quality visual output. Preview mode is usually used after most of the analysis has been done in overview mode. Unlike the highly interactive overview mode, any change made in preview mode requires you to explicitly click the Refresh button to redraw the graph.

TIP   If you plan to explore a graph only interactively, you don't need preview mode.

Note that each mode provides inconsistent features and different defaults (at least, as of this writing), particularly with respect to visual attributes such as the following:

- **Sizes**—The size of edge width, node labels, and nodes may be different than the preview and may need to be scaled.

- **Colors**—Color may appear slightly different in overview mode versus preview mode. For example, edge colors appear darker in overview than preview. Nodes in overview are outlined in a dark version of the node color, but this not available in the preview mode.

- **Curved links**—These are available only in preview mode.

- **Labels**—In overview mode, only labels above a particular size will appear, whereas in preview mode all labels are shown.

> **TIP**
>
> If you want high-quality output of the scene, use the preview mode and export as PDF or SVG files. Toggle back and forth between overview and preview modes to check what it looks like, rather than trying to get it perfect in overview mode first.

Caveats

Gephi is powerful but quirky. Although it can generate great-looking graphs and provide a good experience while you are interacting with the layout, it can be frustrating during other tasks.

Data

Gephi offers a fairly wide variety of data import and export formats. You can use it to convert graph data from one file format to another. However, it does not support every feature in every file format. For data import, it also offers useful feedback on issues found during data import, which can be very helpful in preparing data.

Gephi works fairly well with GDF files, and GDF files can be easy to generate using tools such as Excel. However, you *must* follow Gephi's assumed column naming conventions.

Similarly, with comma-separated value (CSV) files, you *must* name the columns in order for Gephi to utilize the data. The nodes file requires a column named `ID` and should have a column named `Label`. The links file requires a `Source` column and `Target` column, with optional `Label` and `Weight`. Although you can reconfigure labels later in Gephi, the authors haven't found anywhere to reset weight, so it looks like you must set it up during the data load.

Interface

You must search through the interface to find various features, sometimes buried under tiny arrows or drop-down menus or associated with a non-obvious icon (move the mouse over the icon for a tooltip) or combination of icons (for example, for the Edit panel to see a node's contents, ensure that both the arrow and arrow with a question mark are selected). Following are some particularly tricky points:

- **Node size**—When setting a data value to node size, by default, Gephi will apply the size based on width, not area. Thus, a node that represents a number twice as large as another number will have four times the area. As shown in Figure 7-17, Gephi provides a *spline interpolation function* that can be useful for addressing this size issue.

  Interpolators are also useful for color. For example, if the source data is skewed with many low values and one high value, the resulting color variation may be difficult to discern. You can use an interpolator to spread out the small values over a larger range and compress the high values.

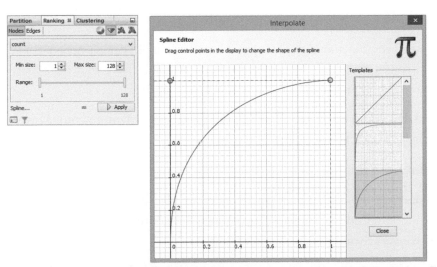

FIGURE 7-17: In Gephi, when you are configuring a data value to a visual attribute, you can configure the default linear interpolation with the spline interpolator such as this curve, which is similar to a square-root interpolation.

- **Identification**—Identifying nodes is a common task. In Gephi, you can do this with either labels or the Edit panel. Given Gephi's quirky interface, a few steps are required:

1. Turn labels on (using the first T button in the lower toolbar).

2. Scale the labels to a reasonable size (the second slider bar in lower toolbar, as shown here).

3. Set the label size to a data value. The benefit here is that the smallest labels can be made to disappear, thus reducing clutter and improving readability. You set this via a drop-down menu in the Ranking tab, with the Nodes sub-tab and the A-with-diamond icon, as shown in Figure 7-18.

FIGURE 7-18: You can set text size to data.

Plug-ins

Plug-ins extend the functionality of Gephi. However, plug-ins aren't necessarily robust or stable. Anyone can author a plug-in and make it available. Save your work first, before using a plug-in. Following are a few commonly used plug-ins:

- **Noverlap**—Use this to adjust positions of nodes slightly so that none overlap. This one is very useful.

- **OpenOrd**—This is a fast force-directed layout algorithm.

- **GeoLayout**—This is a layout where nodes are placed geographically using latitude/longitude coordinates. If your data has addresses or ZIP codes, you must first convert them into latitude/longitude.

- **MapOfCountries**—This draws a map behind the geolayout. Note that sometimes issues arise with alignment, column names, drawing in preview mode with curved edges, and there is no apparent way to remove the map once it has been added.

- **Force Atlas 3D**—This is a three-dimensional (3D) layout you can use when Gephi is in 3D mode. However, in most cases, 3D is not going to be effective because it will result in more nodes being obscured by other nodes.

> **NOTE**
>
> Gephi is available at `https://gephi.org/`. Links to a quick-start guide and tutorial as well as plug-ins, and so on, are available from the main page.

CYTOSCAPE

Cytoscape is another powerful freeware graph analysis and visualization software package. It was originally developed for analysis of biological data, but it works for any kind of graph data. Some of the terminology is a bit different than with other packages. For example, Cytoscape uses *network* to refer to a *graph* and sometimes uses *interaction* to refer to an *edge*. It has a number of features beyond other packages, such as the capability to handle multiple links between a pair of nodes, a much wider range of visual attributes that can be connected to data more flexibly than with other software, and a variety of plug-ins from the Cytoscape App Store.

Cytoscape Basics

As shown in Figure 7-19, Cytoscape presents a straightforward interface you can use for creating and interacting with the visualization. Toward the bottom of the screen, a data table, by default, always updates to show the details for whichever nodes and links are currently selected. In the visualization window, nodes and links can be selected using the conventions found in many software packages — that is, click to select, click and drag to select a block of items, Shift+click to add additional items to the selection, and Ctrl+click to remove an item from the selection.

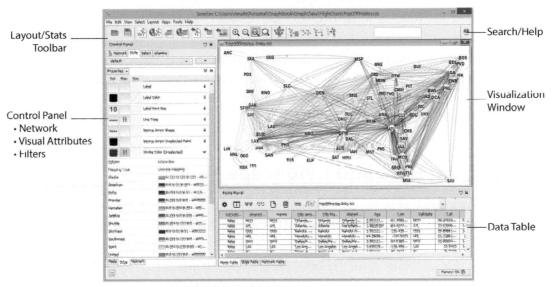

FIGURE 7-19: This is the main window of Cytoscape.

You can find graph statistics under the Tools menu and apply them to any selected subset of the graph.

Layouts in Cytoscape are not as interactive as in Gephi. You pick a layout from the Layout menu, and the new graph layout appears. Adjusting a layout requires trial and error. Select Layout ⇨ Settings, adjust a property, select Layout again, and repeat until you are satisfied with the results. One alternative is that you can generate the layout in another program (for example, Gephi or yEd), export it as GraphML, and then import it into Cytoscape.

If you already have x and y positions for nodes (for example, latitude and longitude, or positions generated in other software), you won't find a layout for these. Instead, Cytoscape provides visual attributes for node x and node y positions.

Although Cytoscape does not have layouts that tweak node positions in the current version, it does make it easy to click and drag to move nodes or groups of nodes or apply layouts to a selected subset of the graph.

Selection and filtering work together. You can select parts of the graph via click, click-and-drag, the Selection menu, or filters. You can then act upon this subset—for example, you can group it together (via right-click), collapse it into a single node (via right-click, and thereafter collapse and expand via double-click), place it into new network workspaces (created via File ⇨ New, and accessed under the Network tab in the Control Panel), and so on.

Importing Data into Cytoscape

Getting data into Cytoscape can be the first challenge. If you have difficulties importing data, Cytoscape works well with GraphML files, and GraphML files can be generated with most other software. Note that Cytoscape does not support data of type float in a GraphML file, and Gephi, for example, exports some items as type float. You can use a text editor to simply replace any references to float with double.

To import flat files of links and nodes (such as CSV or text files), the data import into Cytoscape is very flexible, which means that it has many settings. You can import these flat files by following a specific sequence:

1. First, load the links data via the Import Network from the following File button (or File ⇨ Import ⇨ Network ⇨ File menu):

As shown in Figure 7-20, a detailed dialog box appears, where you must identify the following:

- Source node (called *Source Interaction*)

- Target node (called *Target Interaction*)

- Type of link (called *Interaction Type*), which you can leave empty if there is only one type of link between nodes

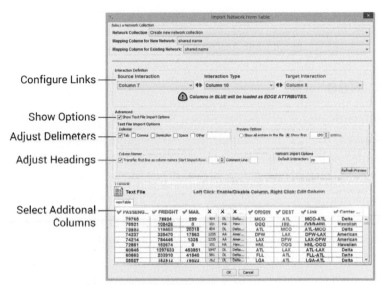

FIGURE 7-20: With Cytoscape text file import, you can configure many items to get the data to import correctly.

2. This dialog box has many settings: so click Advanced ⇨ Show Text File Import Options, which enables you to configure the following:

- **Field separators**—Adjust the delimiters as needed (for example, turn off spaces so that names do not get split into separate columns). Note that separators inside quotation marks are still treated as separators, so "New York, NY" will, unfortunately, be split into two columns if commas are set as separators. Tab-delimited text files (.txt) are a safer choice than comma-delimited files (.csv).

- **Header row**—Make certain that the header row is not treated as data, but instead treated as column names.

- **Check desired data columns**—Data columns are *not* automatically imported. You must click the X and change it into a check mark to select the column for import.

3. A graph is displayed after the links are loaded, but you must still load all the node properties. Click the Import Table from the following File button (or File ⇨ Import ⇨ Table ⇨ File), which enables you to import the node file. Similar to the link file, you need to set the options, delimiters, headings, and so on.

4. Note that Cytoscape does not like items that are empty or null. You are better off putting in a zero or space for an otherwise empty item.

Visual Attributes

Cytoscape is powerful with regard to visual attributes. Just about any visual attribute can be connected (*mapped*) to data. For example, beyond size and color, Cytoscape offers node border color, node border width, node transparency, label font, edge line type, edge transparency, edge visibility, and so on.

You can access the visual attributes under the Style tab. The panel shows a list of visual attributes organized by tabs at the bottom to switch between node attributes and edge attributes. Note that additional visual attributes may be available under the Properties drop-down. Each visual attribute has three settings:

- **Default**—This button sets the default value for the attribute (for example, set the edge color to black).

- **Map**—This button defines the mapping to translate data values into visual attributes (for example, set the edge color based on passenger volume data).

- **Bypass**—This button allows an override value for the attribute for the currently selected subset of the graph. For example, all the links associated with one node could be set to bright red. This is useful to draw attention to part of the graph or otherwise mark specific nodes and edges of interest.

While referring to Figure 7-21, follow these steps to configure a visual attribute:

1. First, in the Control Panel, under the Styles tab, find the attribute of interest (for example, Edge Stroke Color) and expand it. This will show additional rows to set the column to connect the attribute to and the type of mapping to apply.

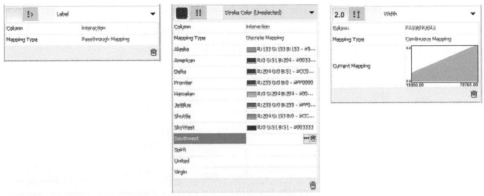

FIGURE 7-21: You can configure visual attributes in Cytoscape.

2. Then, you must connect it to a column of data. The row labeled "Column" will initially say "-- select value --". Click the text "-- select value --" and a drop down-menu will appear listing the data columns. Pick one.

3. Finally, you must set a Mapping Type, also initially set to "-- select value --". You can choose from three types of mapping:

   - *Passthrough* literally passes the value right through to the attribute. This is appropriate for labels.

   - *Discrete* enables each unique data value to be independently connected to a unique variation of the visual attribute (for example, unique shapes or unique colors). Use this for category data, particularly when you have fewer than ten or so categories. Click into the attribute field to set the attribute for that category. Any item left blank gets the default property, set previously in the Defaults section.

   - *Continuous* transforms numeric data into a range of visual attributes. Click the graphic to open the editor. You can create multiple levels and set values at each level.

As an example of discrete mapping, Figure 7-22 shows airline passenger traffic data for the top 500 routes between U.S. cities, and Figure 7-23 shows the settings from the Visual Mapping Browser. The multiple links between nodes are immediately apparent. For example, four different connections between Honolulu and Los Angeles (HNL-to-LAX) are shown in the lower left of Figure 7-22. Using Edge Stroke Color, a unique color has been set per airline. The major hubs per airline are visible where an airport with high degree has many lines of the same color—for example Delta in Atlanta (ATL) and Minneapolis (MSP), American in Dallas (DFW), and so on.

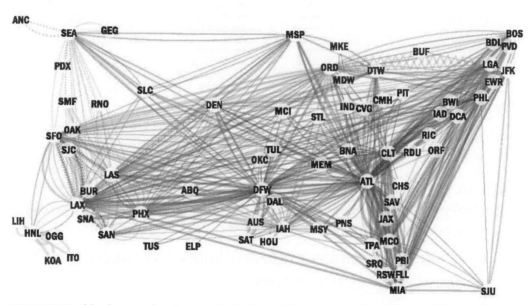

FIGURE 7-22: This shows major air routes in the United States, colored by airline. See Figure 7-23 for the visual mapping in Cytoscape.

However, some of those links can be difficult to see, because some airlines may only have a few flights in the top 500, and it can be difficult to create a color palette with more than a half dozen or so distinct colors (whereas here there are a dozen airlines). Therefore, Edge Line Type is used to further differentiate the edges for those airlines that fly only a few routes, making them much more readily visible. For example, Alaska Airlines appears as dotted lines in the top left; Virgin Airlines appears as a fishbone pattern between San Francisco (SFO), Los Angeles (LAX), and Las Vegas (LAS); and

Shuttle appears as the zigzag edge between Chicago O'Hare (ORD) and New York LaGuardia (LGA).

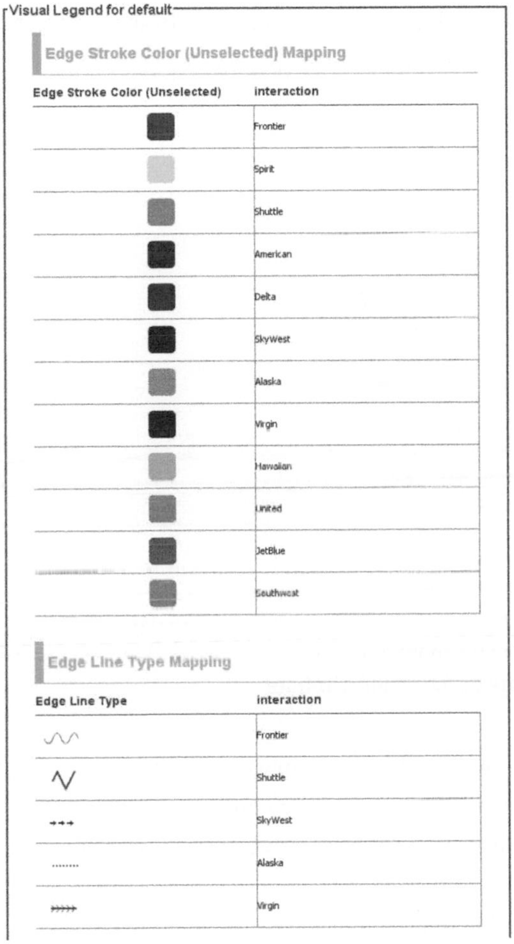

FIGURE 7-23: This discrete visual mapping in Cytoscape uses edge color and edge line type to indicate airlines.

Finally, Cytoscape also provides the capability to export a legend for the visual mappings, under an unlabeled button near the top-right corner of the Style panel. This will create a nicer legend than a screen shot, as shown in Figure 7-23.

For continuous mapping, Cytoscape offers more control over the connection of the data to visual attributes than most other packages. For example, topic correlation (discussed earlier in this chapter) ranges from 1 (strongly correlated) to –1 (inversely correlated), with 0 indicating no correlation. To show these edges, you could show 1 and –1 as thick, but 0 as thin. Cytoscape can do this as shown in Figure 7-24.

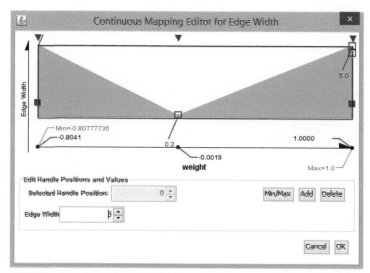

FIGURE 7-24: The Continuous Mapping Editor in Cytoscape enables you to change how the range of the data is applied to the range of the visual attribute.

Similarly, you can adjust edge transparency or any other continuous attribute at various levels. Figure 7-25 shows the topic correlation graph with the continuous mappings for edge color, edge transparency, and edge width set, as shown in Figure 7-26. Note how some highly correlated topics may not be close together but are still highly visible because the thick green connection remains visible over the other thinner, more transparent connections (such as John McCain and Sarah Palin or Nancy Pelosi and Claire McCaskill).

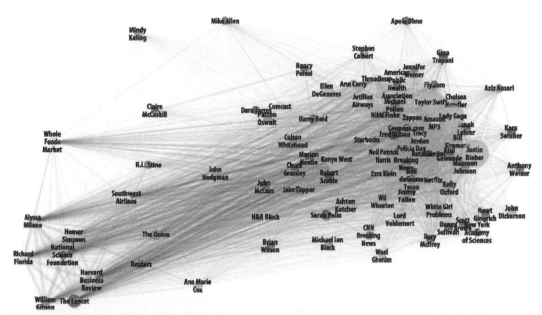

FIGURE 7-25: Topics that trend similarly are joined by thick green lines. Topics that are inversely correlated have thick red lines between them. Topics with no correlation have transparent thin brown lines.

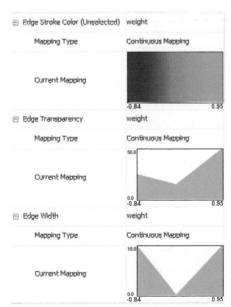

FIGURE 7-26: This shows visual mapping for the topic correlation graph in Figure 7-25.

Apps Menu

Like Gephi, Cytoscape provides a variety of plug-ins via the Apps menu. Though many are specific to biological research, Cytoscape provides general-purpose plug-ins as well, including the following:

- **Venn and Euler**—This displays a graph as an approximate Venn diagram (discussed in Chapter 11).

- **Clustering**—A variety of clustering apps are available, such as ClusterViz, which provides multiple clustering algorithms and diagrams of each cluster.

- **Path analysis**—You can use PathExplorer to find the shortest path between a pair of nodes.

> **NOTE**
>
> You can download Cytoscape from www.cytoscape.org/. Note that multiple versions of Cytoscape are available. Download the latest version. Links to documentation are also available.

YED

Unlike some of the open source graph tools outlined here, yEd is produced by the commercial software company yWorks, which has a long history of producing software for drawing and laying out graphs. yEd is a free version of its software.

yEd has strong capabilities for creating and editing graphs via point-and-click. Coming from a commercial background, the software is robust (that is, it doesn't crash), and it supports undo/redo.

> **WARNING**
>
> In some graph software, clicking on the background deselects items. But in yEd, gratuitous clicks in the main window creates new nodes!

yEd can produce specialized types of graphs such as flowcharts, class diagrams, and process management diagrams with the expected styles associated with the special graph types. yEd provides a number of robust layouts, good label handling, and, particularly unique to yEd, the capability to route links with multiple bends according to layout rules.

yEd Basics

Figure 7-27 shows the basic layout of the screen when you are working with yED.

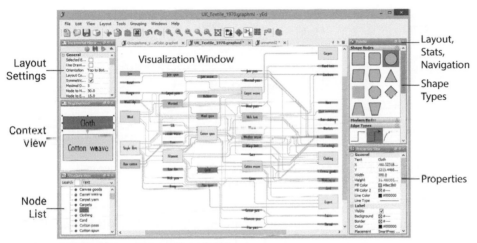

FIGURE 7-27: This shows an overview of yEd.

GraphML is the native file format for yEd. You can export GraphML formats from other graph software and import them into yEd. yEd also has direct Excel import functionality, including the capability to directly import an adjacency matrix or node/edge lists.

You can compute a few graph statistics from the Tools menu and directly apply them to node attributes such as color.

yEd has some effective and popular layout algorithms. Some of yWorks' graph layouts are embedded in Cytoscape. One part of yWorks' business is selling the graph layout algorithms for embedding into other software. The Organic Layout is a force-directed layout. Other layouts (such as Hierarchy, Circular, and Radial) can be effective with some graphs.

One of yEd's powerful features is layouts for edges. After the nodes have been positioned, try some of the edge layouts. For example, Organic can subtly bend lines to avoid overlapping lines with nodes that they do not connect with, as shown in Figure 7-28. Note how the link from Drew to Trey bends around the other nodes.

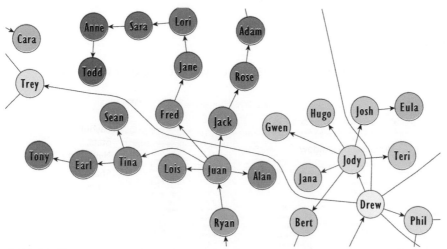

FIGURE 7-28: yEd's edge routing layouts can, for example, bend edges to neatly weave in between nodes, rather than overlapping and causing potential misinterpretation.

yEd is packed with functionality, and some items may be a bit difficult to find. Scale, Rotate, Mirror, and so on, are under the Tools ⇨ Geometric Transformation menu. Visual attribute configuration in yEd is hidden under the Edit ⇨ Properties Mapper menu. yEd provides a broad range of visual attributes that can be connected to data, such as border color, tooltips, gradient fills, line type, and arrow style.

As shown in Figure 7-29, the Properties Mapper dialog box offers the following:

■ The Configurations list shows all the previous configurations that have been made and named. You can copy a previous configuration if it has desirable settings.

■ The Mappings list (center) shows all the visual attributes for the current configuration. Each item (Data Source, Map To, and Conversion) has a drop-down menu. You can define the mapping once all three have been set.

■ Selected Mapping (bottom) indicates the data values and the corresponding visual attribute setting.

The visual attribute mappings are applied in the order listed. You can use the same visual attribute multiple times, and only the last mapping will be effective. You can return to previous mappings by changing the order.

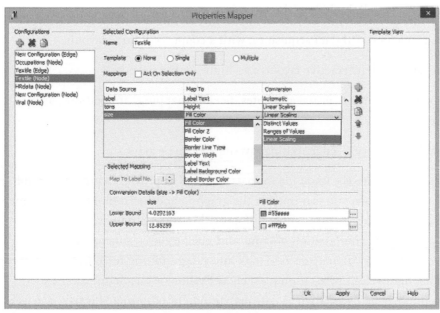

FIGURE 7-29: This shows the yEd Properties Mapper.

It is easy to override visual attributes. For example, you can select any combination of nodes and edit their properties in the property view. In addition, a wide variety of shapes and various icons are available (such as people, computers, flowchart symbols, and so on).

You can download yEd from www.yworks.com/en/products_yed_about.html. Detailed help documents and tutorials are also available.

SUMMARY

Different point-and-click tools are available for working with graphs, from acquiring and processing data, computing graph statistics, visualizing graphs via various layouts and attributes, and providing interactions to explore and filter the graph. Although each tool offers a breadth of features across statistics, visualization, and interaction, each offers some unique features as well, including the following:

- NodeXL provides social data acquisition with a couple of unique layouts.

- Gephi provides rich interactive layouts and high-quality outputs.

- Cytoscape provides many visual attributes, flexible mapping, annotations, and interactive output.

- yEd provides a variety of edge routing layouts and shape types.

Furthermore, you can use common file formats such as GraphML to process a graph partially in one tool, and then you can transfer the graph to another tool. However, some care is required because some features are not supported in some products.

Sometimes, though, no combination of point-and-click tools is sufficient for the task. Under these circumstances, you may need to look into programming to achieve your objectives. Simple, lightweight programming such as Python or JavaScript can be used to accomplish some specific tasks (such as data preparation or customized interactive web visualizations). Lightweight programming is the subject of Chapter 8.

8

LIGHTWEIGHT PROGRAMMING

Sometimes you need to go beyond what has been prepackaged even in the most flexible point-and-click software. In graph analysis, programming typically becomes useful in a few areas. This chapter provides some code examples for both Python and JavaScript. Each section starts with a simple introductory example and then builds progressively to more detailed examples.

Often data isn't quite right and must be cleaned or transformed into a graph. Python is an excellent programming tool for programming novices (and even experts) to quickly create some code to manipulate graph data. Examples in the first part of the chapter include cleaning data—extracting nodes from a data set with only links, and extracting both nodes and links from a data set not organized as a graph (for example, e-mail).

Although Gephi and Cytoscape may seem powerful, sometimes you may want to use other types of visualizations, or perhaps you want to put an interactive graph on a web page. JavaScript is one way to build out lightweight visualizations. The second part of the chapter focuses on JavaScript, the drawing format Scalable Vector Graphics (SVG), and the visualization library D3. The discussion builds incrementally from simple geometry, through simple graphs with rectangular and circular layouts, to interactive force-directed graphs.

PYTHON

If you've ever done any programming, Python is quick to learn, has a straightforward syntax, and is fairly forgiving. Python provides object-oriented programming concepts, but if you want, you can do everything procedurally. If you are comfortable using Excel, Python is not a big jump.

> **NOTE** Note that Python had some changes between version 2 and version 3. All the examples shown here utilize Python version 3 or later.

Getting Started

To use Python, you must first download a recent version from `Python.org`. It's also handy to have a nice text editor that provides syntax highlighting. One of this book's authors uses Programmer's Notepad (`www.pnotepad.org/`), whereas the other uses Sublime Text (`www.sublimetext.com`).

The emphasis in this book is not on the basics of programming Python. If you are already familiar with programming, you may find all you need is a Python 3 cheat sheet (such as `www.cogsci.rpi.edu/~destem/gamedev/python.pdf` or `www.ar-python.com/wp-content/uploads/mementopython3-english.pdf`). Be aware that the biggest quirk in Python is that indentation matters in loops and `if` statements. Many other useful books, websites, and programming resources are available for Python, including the following:

- `Python.org` online documentation (`https://docs.python.org/3/`)

- *Beginning Programming with Python for Dummies* (Indianapolis: Wiley, 2014)

If you get stuck at some point, likely your question has already been answered on a programming Q&A website such as `http://stackoverflow.com/questions/tagged/python`.

Cleaning Data

Many data sources can be messy. Python is a good tool for data cleansing and preparation. Perhaps long labels must be shortened, or accents must be removed because your graph software cannot handle them. Consider the following example of data that must be cleaned:

```
From, To, CC, Date, Size
"Joé", "Zoë", "Timothy", 12/09/2014, 156kb
"Joé", "Ben", "SMTP:Ann@mail.co; Timothy; Zoë", 11/09/2014, 2048kb
"Joé", "Timothy", "Ben; Zoë", 11/09/2014, 805kb
"Joé", , "Ben", 11/01/2014, 22kb
```

The following Python script reads each line, replaces Timothy with Tim, removes a leading STMP:, removes the domain name from the e-mail address, and strips out Unicode characters:

```python
import re
import unicodedata

filein = open("origData.csv","r")
fileout = open("cleanData.csv","w")

for line in filein:
    line = line.replace("Timothy","Tim").replace("SMTP:","")
    line = re.sub("@[a-zA-Z0-9_.-]*","",line)
    line= "".join(x for x in unicodedata.normalize("NFKD",line)
             if unicodedata.category(x)!="Mn" )
    fileout.write(line)

filein.close()
fileout.close()
```

The first two lines of this script import Python libraries that add functionality to Python. The first one is for handling regular expressions (re), which is a way to do search and replace on string patterns. The second provides Unicode data functionality (that is, handling strings with complex characters from a wide variety of languages).

The next two lines open the original data file and the output data file. Then, the main loop reads each line from the input file and processes it:

- `line.replace("oldstring","newstring")` is a simple find and replace. `replace()` can be chained in a sequence for multiple substitutions.

- `re.sub()` is used to perform *regular expression* substitution. To remove the domain name from an e-mail, the expression `@[a-zA-A0-9_.-]*` matches an initial `@` symbol followed by a character that is any of the following for any length after the `@` symbol: lowercase (a-z), uppercase (A-Z), numeric (0-9), underscore, period, or dash. Whatever is matched is replaced with nothing (`""`).

- `"".join(x …)` starts with an empty string and then successively adds a new character `x`, going through each character in the `line` and normalizing the character from Unicode to ASCII when the character is not of type `Mn` (non-spacing mark). This line is an example of finding a good solution on stackoverflow.com. It is much nicer solution to substitute characters with a close ASCII character, rather than just dropping out accented characters using a regular expression. Simply searching in a web browser for programming questions (such as "python remove accents from string") will often return useful code snippets showing how other programmers have solved similar issues. In this example, the web search returned `http://stackoverflow.com/questions/517923/what-is-the-best-way-to-remove-accents-in-a-python-unicode-string`.

Running this script across the sample e-mail data shown previously results in the following output:

```
From, To, CC, Date, Size
"Joe", "Zoe", "Tim", 12/09/2014, 156kb
"Joe", "Ben", "Ann; Tim; Zoe", 11/09/2014, 2048kb
"Joe", "Tim", "Ben; Zoe", 11/09/2014, 805kb
"Joe", , "Ben", 11/01/2014, 22kb
```

Extracting a Set of Nodes from a Link Data Set

Sometimes a data set may consist of only a set of links. Network logs are one example discussed earlier in Chapter 3, "Data—Collect, Clean, and Connect." Another example is the following data set of writers and their influences was extracted from dbpedia.org:

```
subject          influence
Frank Herbert    Edgar Rice Burroughs
Frank Herbert    H. G. Wells
Frank Herbert    Jules Verne
J. G. Ballard    William S. Burroughs
J. G. Ballard    Alfred Jarry

  ...
```

dbpedia.org is an online resource of structured data from Wikipedia. DBpedia can be queried to extract data, including graph data sets. You can find an overview of DBpedia's data sets at http://wiki.dbpedia.org/Datasets. You can enter a simple query at http://dbpedia.org/snorql/.

As an example, if you want to focus on science fiction writers and their influences, you can see the data collected for a sample writer such as Stephen King (http://dbpedia .org/page/Stephen_King). One of the fields is influencedby, which is a list of other science fiction writers that Stephen King was influenced by. (This means that data for a social network of writers is in DBpedia.) To extract data from DBpedia, you use the query language SPARQL. (SPARQL and related graph database technology is discussed more in Chapter 14, "Big Data.") For example, you can enter the following SPARQL query on http://dbpedia.org/snorql (note that data and fields on DBpedia can change—scripts may not necessarily work as is):

```
SELECT * WHERE {
?subject dbpedia2:genre :Science_fiction.
?subject rdf:type foaf:Person.
?subject <http://dbpedia.org/ontology/influencedBy> ?influence.
}
```

> **TIP** You can use SPARQL queries directly in Gephi with the Semantic Web Import plug-in.

The resulting data is a set of links with the author being the source node, and the corresponding influence being the target node. While this query generates a fairly simple data set, the query can be enhanced to add a variety of additional data attributes. For example, data available may include birthdate, nationality, description, nicely formatted label, list of works, and so on.

Given the file of links, the programming task is to extract a set of nodes. The approach used here is as follows:

1. Open the link file.

2. For each line in the link file, take the source node and the target node and add them to a list of nodes, checking to make sure that nodes are not duplicated.

3. Write out the node file.

CSV File and Lists

Python has a comma-separated value (CSV) reader library with functionality to make it easy to parse .csv and tab-delimited (.txt) files. The following code opens the .csv file and calls a function to add two nodes per each row:

```
import csv
# open the link file
with open ("SciFiWriters.txt", "r") as inputfile:
    datareader = csv.reader(inputfile, delimiter="\t")
    # skip the header row
    next(datareader, None)
    # process each row: add source node and target node
    for row in datareader:
        addNode(row[0])
        addNode(row[1])
```

The first line imports the Python csv library. The next two lines open the text file SciFiWriters.txt as read-only ("r") and set the delimiter to tab ("\t") as opposed to the default, which is a comma. The file has a header row (subject influence), which is skipped over using next(datareader, None).

The csv library turns each row of input into a list data structure. You can access each field in the list using an *index* (referred to in Python as a *slice*). The index is an integer, starting at zero for the first item. For example, consider a data row in the data file:

```
Stephen King      Edgar Allan Poe
```

The first item is accessed using row[0], which returns Stephen King, while row[1] returns Edgar Allan Poe, and so on. You can reference the entire row simply using row.

Each row is processed with a for loop. For each row, the function addNode is called. The function addNode takes one argument: the node ID (that is, the person's name). addNode is called twice, first for the source node (the first two items in the row), followed by the target node (the next item in the row of data).

Collecting Nodes in a Hashmap

At the beginning of the Python script, the addNode() function is defined (def), which adds and updates nodes in a global *hashmap* declared in nodemap={}. A hashmap is a type of data structure that allows for efficient access of items using a *unique key*. Conveniently, nodes in graphs must have a unique ID, so this ID can be used as the key for a hashmap. In addition to the key, hashmaps can store additional values, lists, or objects. Here the hashmap is used to store node objects:

```
nodemap = {}

# define function to find or add a node; and adjust its count
def addNode(name):
    if name in nodemap:
        node = nodemap[name]
        node["count"] += 1
    else:
        node = {"nodeid": name, "count": 1}
        nodemap[name] = node
    return
```

An empty hashmap is initially defined (nodemap = {}). The addNode function is defined with one arguments passe in: name, which is the unique node ID (that is, the author's name, or the name of the influencer).

The first line inside the function (if name in nodemap:) checks to see whether the key name has already been used in the hashmap. If false (such as the first time calling addNode), the else section is called. In the else section, a new node is defined using name:value pairs (node = {"nodeid": name, "count": 1), and then the node is added to the nodemap using the key (nodemap[name] = node).

On successive calls to the function addNode, in some cases the node already exists, and name in nodemap will be true. In this case, the variable node will be assigned to the already existing node object retrieved using the key node = nodemap[name]. With the retrieved node, any value stored with this node can be adjusted using the appropriate name to access it. For example, incrementing the count for the number of times this name has occurred is done with node["count"] += 1.

Writing Out the Node Hashmap

The final step is to write out the file, which steps through all the nodes in nodemap and writes out a node on each successive row in the file.

```
#write out nodes
with open("nodes.txt", "w", newline="") as nodefile:
    formatter = csv.writer(nodefile, delimiter="\t")
    formatter.writerow(["Id","Count"])
    for name in nodemap:
        node = nodemap[name]
        formatter.writerow([node["nodeid"],node["count"],
            ])
```

Opening the file is similar to reading, except it's set for writing ("w"). A header row is written first, and then a loop iterates through each key (that is, name) in the hashmap (for name in nodemap:).

The key is used to retrieve the node with node = nodemap[name]. Writing each row requires passing a single object to the formatter. Because the data must be in a specific order to match the column headers, each data item is placed in order (for example, node["nodeid"], node["count"], and so on), and the overall set is placed into a list (denoted with square brackets, []) and passed to the formatter.

The Python script and the sample data set are available in the Supplemental Materials on this book's companion website. The overall Python script looks like this:

```python
import csv


nodemap = {}


# define function to find or add a node; and adjust its count
def addNode(name):
    if name in nodemap:
        node = nodemap[name]
        node["count"] += 1
    else:
        node = {"nodeid": name, "count": 1}
        nodemap[name] = node
    return


with open ("SciFiWriters.txt", "r") as inputfile:
    datareader = csv.reader(inputfile, delimiter="\t")
    # skip the header row
    next(datareader, None)
    # process each row: add source node and target node
    for row in datareader:
        addNode(row[0])
        addNode(row[1])
```

```
#write out nodes
with open("nodes.txt", "w", newline="") as nodefile:
    formatter = csv.writer(nodefile, delimiter="\t")
    formatter.writerow(["Id","Count"])
    for name in nodemap:
        node = nodemap[name]
        formatter.writerow([node["nodeid"],node["count"],
            ])
```

The resulting link and node files can then be imported into graph software. For example, Figure 8-1 shows this data set plotted in Gephi.

FIGURE 8-1: This is a graph of science fiction writers and their influences extracted from Wikipedia data.

Transforming E-mail Data into a Graph

E-mail data is an example of a data set that requires more effort to transform into a graph. It may be possible to find point-and-click software that automatically imports e-mail data (for example, NodeXL), but there may be other requirements (such as data cleansing or anonymization), or different metrics requiring you to create a simple program to process the data. The core task is to transform data that originally may look like this sample e-mail CSV file into a set of nodes and links:

```
From, To, CC, Date, Size
"Joe", "Zoe", "Tim", 12/09/2014, 156kb
"Joe", "Ben", "Ann; Tim; Zoe", 11/09/2014, 2048kb
"Joe", "Tim", "Ben; Zoe", 11/09/2014, 805kb
"Joe", , "Ben", 11/01/2014, 22kb
```

The node data is a list of all the unique e-mail participants, and the link data is a list of all the occurrences of e-mails between two participants, aggregated into a single link with an associated weight representing the number of communications between the two participants. The approach to process e-mail data programmatically into a graph is similar to the previous example, with a bit more effort to prepare the data, and an extra step to generate links:

1. Open the data file.

2. For each line in the data file,

    a. Create a distribution list of all the people involved in the e-mail.

    b. Add each person to a list of nodes, checking to make sure that nodes are not duplicated.

    c. For each pair of people, define a uniquely named link (that is, source-target), and add that to a list of links, making sure that links are not duplicated.

3. Write out the node file and link file.

Opening the file and starting the loop to process each row is similar to the previous example, except the default comma delimiter is used.

```
with open ("emailSample.txt") as datafile:
    datareader = csv.reader(datafile)
    # skip the header row
    next(datareader, None)
    # process each row: add source node and target node
    for row in datareader:
```

Processing each row has a few more steps than before. Some data preparation is done first. For example, the e-mail size, stored in row[4], is in a string such as 25kb, so the kb is removed, and the remaining string is converted into an integer.

```
kb = int(row[4].replace("kb",""))
```

Creating a Distribution List

The list of people in the e-mail distribution is spread out across three columns (from, to, cc), and each of these can contain zero, one, or many people. To make this easier to work with, you create a distribution list, as shown here:

```
distlist = [];
for i in range(0,3):
    names = row[i].replace('"','').split(';')
    for name in names:
        name = name.strip()
        if (name!=""):
            distlist.append(name)
```

First, you create an empty list to assemble all the names.

```
distlist = [];
```

Then you create a loop to go through the first three items in the row, (that is, the from, to, and cc fields).

```
for i in range(0,3):
    names = row[i].replace('"','').split(';')
```

For each field, there may be multiple people, which are separated with semicolons, whitespace, and quotation marks. You create a list of names by first removing the outer quotation marks and splitting the field based on the semicolons.

This list of names is then iterated through. Any extraneous spaces are removed via strip(). Because a field can be empty (for example, no one was CC'd), there is also a check for an empty name. If the name is not empty, it is appended to the distribution list.

```
for name in names:
    name = name.strip()
    if (name!=""):
        distlist.append(name)
```

The overall data preparation to create the distribution list for this one e-mail looks like this:

```
for i in range(0,3):
    names = row[i].replace('"','').split(';')
    for name in names:
        name = name.strip()
        if (name!=""):
            distlist.append(name)
```

Creating Nodes

Now you can create the nodes, one for each person in the distribution list for this e-mail, along with additional information such as the size of this e-mail, using the addNode function as shown here:

```
# create the nodes
for name in distlist:
    addNode(name,kb)
```

At this point, let's review the addNode function at the beginning of the script file. It is similar to the previous science fiction example, but with a slight modification. This time, addNode has two parameters passed to it—the node name and the size of the e-mail. In addition to name and count, the node data will also track the total e-mail size.

```
def addNode(key, kbytes):
    if key in nodemap:
```

```
        node = nodemap[key]
        node["count"] += 1
        node["size"] += kbytes
    else:
        node = {"id": key, "count": 1, "size": kbytes}
        nodemap[key] = node
    return
```

Creating Directed Links

Creating links is similar to creating nodes. A source node and target node are required. Given that the order of the original data was from, to, cc, the first name on the distribution list is the source, and all subsequent names are targets. For example, for a distribution list with four items (Joe, Tim, Ben, Zoe), you create three links (Joe-Tim, Joe-Ben, and Joe-Zoe).

```
# create directed links:
for i in range(1,len(distlist)):
    addLink(distlist[0],distlist[i],kb)
```

The addLink function is similar to the addNode function. For a link, the key can be the unique link that is the combination of the source and target nodes.

```
def addLink(src, tgt, kbytes):
    key = src + "..." + tgt
    if key in linkmap:
        link = linkmap[key]
        link["count"] += 1
        link["size"] += kbytes
    else:
        link = {"src": src, "tgt": tgt, "count": 1, "size": kbytes}
        linkmap[key] = link
    return
```

Creating Undirected Links

Depending on the objective, you may want to identify connections between all people on a distribution list based on the assumption that all people who are copied on a message are linked together. In this case, you want to use undirected links instead of directed links between all people in the distribution list. You can use the same addLink function to create each link, but you have more links to create. Each person in the distribution list is part of the same e-mail, and you create a link between each unique pair of people. For example, for a distribution list with four items (Joe, Tim, Ben, Zoe), you create *six* links (Joe-Tim, Joe-Ben, Joe-Zoe, Tim-Ben, Tim-Zoe, and Ben-Zoe).

Another requirement is that you should create only a single link between a pair of people. For example, Ben-Zoe is the same link as Zoe-Ben. To avoid duplication of links, always define the links in alphabetical order.

To generate all the unique person-pairs, you use two loops to walk through all the combinations of people.

```
# create undirected links:
for i in range(0,len(distlist)):
    for j in range (i+1,len(distlist)):
        if distlist[i] < distlist[j]:
            source = distlist[i]
            target = distlist[j]
        else:
            source = distlist[j]
            target = distlist[i]
        addLink(source,target,kb)
```

Writing out the Node and Link Files

The final step is to write out the resulting files. This is similar to the file written in the previous example. The entire script for creating the e-mail graph is as follows (using undirected links), with the file write at the end:

```
import csv


nodemap = {}
linkmap = {}
```

```
# define function to find or add node; and add to its count and size
def addNode(key, kbytes):
    if key in nodemap:
        node = nodemap[key]
        node["count"] += 1
        node["size"] += kbytes
    else:
        node = {"id": key, "count": 1, "size": kbytes}
        nodemap[key] = node
    return


# similar function to add/update links
def addLink(src, tgt, kbytes):
    key = src + "..." + tgt
    if key in linkmap:
        link = linkmap[key]
        link["count"] += 1
        link["size"] += kbytes
    else:
        link = {"src": src, "tgt": tgt, "count": 1, "size": kbytes}
        linkmap[key] = link
    return


# open the file and skip the header row
with open ("emailSample.txt") as datafile:
    datareader = csv.reader(datafile)
    next(datareader, None)

    # process each email
    for row in datareader:
        # size of this email
        kb = int(row[4].replace("kb",""))
```

```
        # create a distribution list of all the people in this email
        distlist = [];
        #loop through distribution fields: from, to and cc:
        for i in range(0,3):
            # split apart when the field has multiple names
            names = row[i].replace('"','').split(';')
            for name in names:
                name = name.strip()
                # add the name to the distribution list
                if (name!=""):
                    distlist.append(name)
        # create the nodes
        for i in range(0,len(distlist)):
            addNode(distlist[i],kb)


        # undirected graph:
        # create links between each pair in thedistlist
        for i in range(0,len(distlist)):
            for j in range (i+1,len(distlist)):
                if distlist[i] < distlist[j]:
                    source = distlist[i]
                    target = distlist[j]
                else:
                    source = distlist[j]
                    target = distlist[i]
                addLink(source,target,kb)


#write out nodes
with open("nodes.csv", "w", newline="") as csvfile:
    formatter = csv.writer(csvfile)
    formatter.writerow(["Node","NumEmail","SumSize"])
    for key in nodemap:
        node = nodemap[key]
```

```
        formatter.writerow([node["id"],node["count"],node["size"]])

    #write out the links
    with open("links.csv", "w", newline="") as csvfile:
        formatter = csv.writer(csvfile)
        formatter.writerow(["Source","Target","NumEmail","SumSize"])
        for key in linkmap:
            lk = linkmap[key]
            formatter.writerow([lk["src"],lk["tgt"],lk["count"],
                lk["size"]])
```

For the trivial e-mail data set using Joe, the resulting node and link files can be read into graph software. On the left of Figure 8-2 are Gephi visualizations showing directed links, and undirected links are shown on the right.

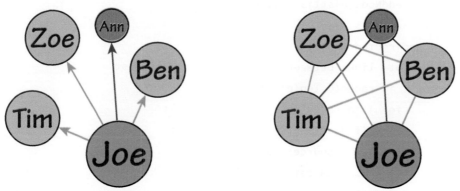

FIGURE 8-2: This is the result of the simple e-mail data processing, imported into Gephi and visualized, with directed links on the left and undirected links on the right.

This same script can be used on a much larger list of e-mails. Figure 8-3 shows the visualized result of the same script (with undirected links) used on a data set of 10,000 e-mails.

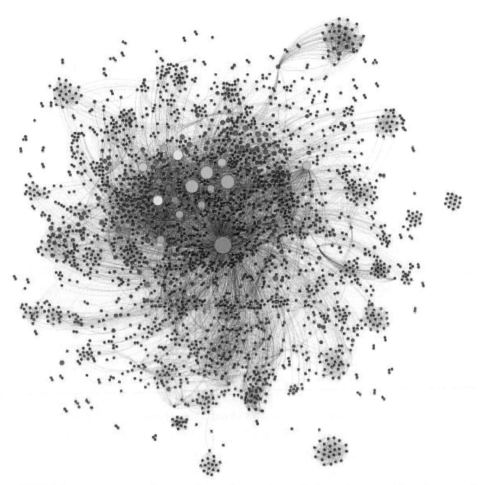

FIGURE 8-3: The same e-mail processing script can be applied to a data set with 10,000 e-mails.

Graph Databases

Python is a handy scripting language for processing small graphs. For huge graphs, a graph database is likely required. Chapter 14 discusses graph databases in more detail.

JAVASCRIPT AND GRAPH VISUALIZATION

JavaScript is the programming language of the web browser—the ubiquitous interface to almost everything. You can use JavaScript to view graph data interactively in the browser, which is particularly useful if you want someone else to see and interact with your graph.

Many different libraries and technologies are available for drawing things in the browser using JavaScript, including SVG, Canvas, ProtoVis, Raphael, D3, and P5, to name a few. SVG and Canvas are more popular with novices interested in low-level drawing. D3 and P5 are popular libraries for making interactive graphics in a browser, but D3 specifically has a data visualization focus.

If you are new to web-based development, the following examples are in HTML. They can be saved as .html files and opened directly in a web browser. Modern web browsers also provide built-in developer tools to inspect the web page in the browser. For example, in the web browser Chrome, the developer tools are accessed under the customization menu More Tools… ⇨ Developer Tools. This opens a panel with many tabs, allowing for various diagnostics on the current web page.

D3 Basics

Before getting started, first you may want to download D3.js (typically just referred to as D3) from d3js.org. If you will be working with D3 and always have an Internet connection, this step isn't needed. You may also want to view the many examples and documentation available at the same website.

Because D3 is a comprehensive library that allows for a wide range of data visualizations, this part of the discussion provides only a simple introduction to D3 and an example using graph functionality in D3. For more general review of D3, many books and online tutorials are available, including the following:

- Scott Murray's book, *Interactive Data Visualization for the Web* (Sebastopol, CA: O'Reilly Media, 2013), with a number of nice online tutorials at http://alignedleft.com/tutorials/d3/

- Mike Dewar's book, *Getting Started with D3* (Sebastopol, CA: O'Reilly Media, 2012)

- Dashing D3.js tutorial at https://www.dashingd3js.com/table-of-contents

Don't expect to see the same speed or the capability to handle as many nodes compared to desktop software. D3 is based on the underlying technology SVG, which is not fast, but the graphics have a wide variety of visual attributes. When you create a visualization in D3, the D3 code is creating and modifying SVG in the browser dynamically. To use D3, you don't need to know all the details of SVG. However, when debugging D3 using the browser's developer tools, you will see SVG code, so it is useful to look at some simple SVG first before getting into D3.

SVG

You can draw graphics on an HTML page using SVG. The following is a simple HTML page that draws a couple of circles in SVG:

```
<!DOCTYPE html>
<meta charset="utf-8">
<body>

<svg width="500" height="500">
  <circle cx="100" cy="100" r="75" fill="orange"/>
  <circle cx="300" cy="150" r="50" fill="yellow" stroke="blue" />
</svg>

</body>
```

The initial section simply identifies that this is an HTML page (first two lines) and starts off the body of the HTML document (third line). The SVG object defines an area of 500 by 500 pixels on the page in which to place SVG graphical objects. The origin is in the top-left corner, with the positive x-axis going to the right, and positive y-axis going down.

The next two lines define SVG circle objects, the first being a circle with center (cx and cy) at (100,100), a radius (r) of 75 pixels, and filled with orange. The second circle is farther to the right (cx is 300), farther down (cy is 150), smaller (r is 50), and filled in yellow with a blue outline. In the Chrome browser, it looks like Figure 8-4.

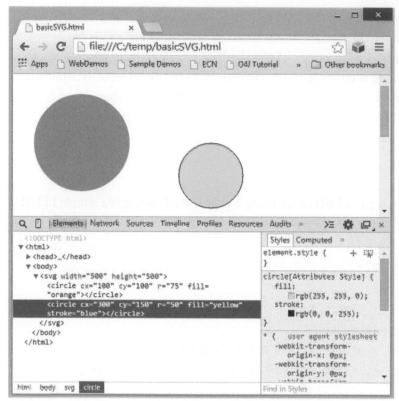

FIGURE 8-4: You can use SVG to draw two simple circles on a web page.

The bottom half of the browser has the developer tools opened, accessed from the top-right menu (or using Ctrl+Shift+I in Chrome). Using the Inspector window, you can see the exact HTML that is being drawn and point at any item on the page (for example, a circle) to highlight the corresponding HTML below.

D3 and SVG

D3's approach is to use JavaScript to generate the SVG dynamically when the JavaScript is executed. You can script the same scene previously shown in Figure 8-4 in D3 as follows:

```
<!DOCTYPE html>
<meta charset="utf-8">
<body>
```

```
<script src="http://d3js.org/d3.v3.min.js"></script>
<script>
var svg = d3.select("body").append("svg")
    .attr("width", 500)
    .attr("height", 500);
svg.append("circle")
    .attr("cx", 100)
    .attr("cy", 100)
    .attr("r", 75)
    .attr("fill", "orange");
svg.append("circle")
    .attr("cx", 300)
    .attr("cy", 150)
    .attr("r", 50)
    .attr("fill", "yellow")
    .attr("stroke", "blue");
</script>
```

```
</body>
```

After the initial HTML definition, the first script object loads the D3 JavaScript visualization library directly from the D3 website so that the rest of the scripts on this page can use D3. The rest of the page is JavaScript that creates the SVG dynamically when the code is executed.

The next three lines use JavaScript *method chaining* to create the SVG region.

```
var svg = d3.select("body").append("svg")
    .attr("width", 500)
    .attr("height", 500);
```

Each successive step of the chain performs one action and returns an object for the next method. To understand what is happening, read these three lines from left to right:

- `var svg =`—Define the variable svg.

- `d3`—Call the d3 library.

- `.select("body")`—From the d3 library, use the `select` method to pick and return the object "body" on the web page.

- `.append("svg")`—Add a new object, after all the other objects contained in body of type svg. This returns the svg object, on which you can now set attributes.

- `.attr("width",500)`, `.attr("height",500)`—Set some attributes associated with the svg object. In this case, svg has attributes of width and height that are being set to the variables width and height. Each time `.attr` is used, the same object is returned, thereby allowing more attributes to be set in successively chained methods. Note that the final item on a method chain has a semicolon to indicate the end of the chain.

At the end of this sequence, the SVG drawing area is set up but is otherwise empty with no content. The next five lines of D3 code create the first circle:

```
svg.append("circle")
     .attr("cx", 100)
     .attr("cy", 100)
     .attr("r", 75)
     .attr("fill", "orange");
```

This example simply takes the svg variable previously defined, pointing to the new svg object, and appends to it a new circle SVG object. This object has various circle attributes defined. Similar code is used to make the second circle.

Running this in a browser with the Inspector window open shows the HTML, script, and all the SVG code that was created by the script, as shown in Figure 8-5.

D3, Data, and SVG

Creating individual objects is cumbersome, particularly when you are trying to create a lot of objects, with each one connected to data. D3 provides methods that make it easy to create a set of graphical objects, each one connected to a successive data item from a list of data.

The JavaScript code that you create in D3 will need data in order to draw a graph. To accomplish this, you can do one of the following:

- Embed the data directly in the JavaScript code.

- Fetch the data from a web service.

- Load the data from a local data file such as a .csv file.

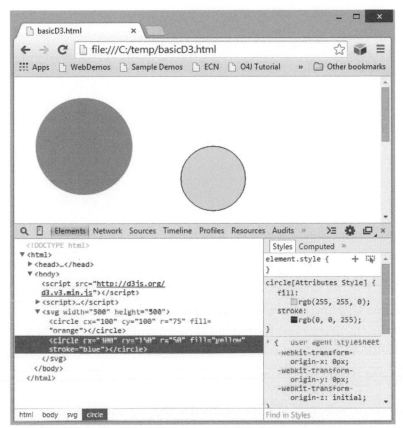

FIGURE 8-5: These are the same circles as before, but this time the script creates the SVG portion on-the-fly when the script executes.

Accessing data from local files is blocked by many web browsers for security reasons, so for the purposes of the examples presented here, let's use data directly in the code or simply extract it into a separate JavaScript file.

This next example has a list of data, [20,50, 75, 40]. Four circles are created based on this data.

```
<!DOCTYPE html>
<meta charset="utf-8">
<body>

<script src="http://d3js.org/d3.v3.min.js"></script>
<script>
var myData = [20,50,75,40];
```

```
var svg = d3.select("body").append("svg")
    .attr("width", 500)
    .attr("height", 500);
svg.selectAll("circle")
    .data(myData)
  .enter().append("circle")
    .attr("cx", function(d,i) { return (i*100+100); })
    .attr("cy", 100)
    .attr("r", function(d) { return d; })
    .attr("fill", "orange")
    .attr("stroke", "blue");
</script>


</body>
```

In this example, the data is defined near the top as a JavaScript list (var myData = [20,50,75,40];), and then each circle can be created in D3 based on the data. There is a bit more to the method chain to set up the geometry based on data:

- svg—Start with the svg object.

- .selectAll("circle")—Select all objects contained in the svg object of type circle. No circle objects have been created yet, so this is just a placeholder for objects that are about to be created.

- .data(myData)—This identifies which data will be connected to the graphical objects (that is, the list of four values).

- .enter().append("circle")—The enter portion now sets up the selection specifically for those objects that do not yet exist (that is, the new objects that are *entering* the scene). For each of those items, a graphical circle object is appended.

- .attr("cx", function(d,i)—Instead of a single value, a function is used. The function has two parameters available for working with data. d references the data for this specific node, so, for example, d for the first item is 20. i is an iterator, which starts at 0 and increases by 1 for each successive data item.

- `return (i*100+100);`—The function returns a value based on the iterator `i`, which is multiplied by 100 (so the circles are spaced out by 100 pixels each) and 100 is added as a padding so that the first circle isn't cut off.

- `.attr("cy", 100)`—This simply sets the y value to a constant of `100`.

- `.attr("r", function(d) { return d; })`—The radius is based on a `function` of the data value (that is, the data from the array is directly mapped to the size of the circle).

- `.attr("fill", "orange"), .attr("stroke", "blue");`—Set the fill and outline color of the circles.

Figure 8-6 shows the result of this code.

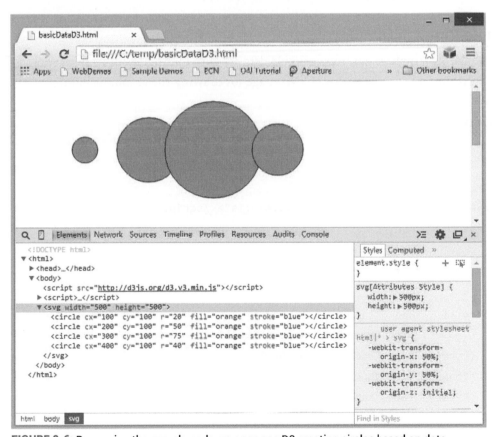

FIGURE 8-6: By running the sample code, you can see D3 creating circles based on data.

Where the circles partially overlap, you can see how each successive circle is drawn on top of the previous circle. All the SVG is drawn in the sequence listed. You should be aware of this sequence so later on when you draw a graph, links are not drawn over the top of the nodes or labels drawn last.

D3 and Graphs

D3 is all about data visualization, and not simply graph visualization. Examples provided with the library include non-graph visualizations such as bar charts, scatterplots, and box plots, as well as general graph visualizations such as node-link graphs, chord diagrams, and Sankey diagrams. Other examples include hierarchy-specific visualizations such as dendograms, collapsible trees, treemaps, and sunbursts.

A Simple Graph in D3

Let's start with a simple graph from a simple data set with four nodes and four edges. Following is the code for the entire HTML page for drawing the graph, including the data:

```
<!DOCTYPE html>
<meta charset="utf-8">

<body>
<script src="http://d3js.org/d3.v3.min.js"></script>
<script>

// this is the graph data
graph = {
 "nodes":[
     {"name":"Ann","NumEmail":1,"SumSize":100},
     {"name":"Ben","NumEmail":4,"SumSize":500},
     {"name":"Tim","NumEmail":2,"SumSize":200},
     {"name":"Zoe","NumEmail":3,"SumSize":400}
   ],
  "links":[
```

```
        {"source":0,"target":1,"NumEmail":1,"SumSize":100},
        {"source":1,"target":2,"NumEmail":1,"SumSize":100},
        {"source":2,"target":3,"NumEmail":1,"SumSize":100},
        {"source":1,"target":3,"NumEmail":2,"SumSize":300}
    ]
}


// set up the drawing area
var width = 500,
    height = 500;
var svg = d3.select("body").append("svg")
    .attr("width", width)
    .attr("height", height);


// some variables for layout assistance
var pad = 50;
var num = Math.sqrt(graph.nodes.length);
var scale = (width - pad * 2) / (num+1);


// draw the nodes
var node = svg.selectAll(".node")
    .data(graph.nodes)
  .enter().append("circle")
    .attr("r", 15)
      .attr("cx", function(d,i) { return scale * (i / num) + pad; })
      .attr("cy", function(d,i) { return scale * (i % num) + pad; });


// draw the links
var link = svg.selectAll(".link")
    .data(graph.links)
  .enter().append("line")
    .style("stroke","blue")
      .attr("x1", function(d,i) { return scale * (d.source / num)
```

```
        + pad;})
    .attr("y1", function(d,i) { return scale * (d.source % num)
        + pad; })
    .attr("x2", function(d,i) { return scale * (d.target / num)
         + pad;})
    .attr("y2", function(d,i) { return scale * (d.target % num)
         + pad; });
```

```
</script>
</body>
```

The first four lines set up the web page and load the D3 library. This is followed by the beginning of the script, where the first portion includes the graph data. The graph data is defined in JavaScript as follows:

- A list of nodes is contained in square brackets ([]).

- Each node is an object contained in curly braces ({}).

- Each attribute is identified by its name and value pair ("itemtype": "value").

Note that the links refer to the nodes based on the node order. For example, the first link has a source node 0 (Ann) and a target node 1 (Ben). In JavaScript, complex data objects such as this graph can be accessed by *dot notation*. For example, graph.nodes is a reference to the list of nodes, and graph.nodes[0].name would have the value Ann.

```
<script>
```

```
// this is the graph data
graph = {
  "nodes":[
      {"name":"Ann","NumEmail":1,"SumSize":100},
      {"name":"Ben","NumEmail":4,"SumSize":500},
      {"name":"Tim","NumEmail":2,"SumSize":200},
      {"name":"Zoe","NumEmail":3,"SumSize":400}
   ],
  "links":[
      {"source":0,"target":1,"NumEmail":1,"SumSize":100},
```

```
    {"source":1,"target":2,"NumEmail":1,"SumSize":100},
    {"source":2,"target":3,"NumEmail":1,"SumSize":100},
    {"source":1,"target":3,"NumEmail":2,"SumSize":300}
  ]
}
```

The SVG drawing area of the web page is created next. In this example, the width and height have been set up as separate variables so that they can be referenced later when calculating layouts.

```
// set up the drawing area
var width = 500,
    height = 500;
var svg = d3.select("body").append("svg")
    .attr("width", width)
    .attr("height", height);
```

In drawing the graph, you can place nodes anywhere in this 500-pixel-by-500-pixel area. So, you first set up some variables to assist in a layout.

```
// some variables for layout assistance
var pad = 50;
var num = Math.sqrt(graph.nodes.length);
var scale = (width - pad * 2) / (num);
```

With this code, you do the following:

- You don't want nodes right on the edge of the drawing area and partially chopped off, so you allow for some padding around the edges (pad=50).

- A simple layout algorithm is a grid-like layout incrementing the position of each successive node and wrapping it after reaching the end of line. Because the code should be generic to handle different graphs, the number of items per line should depend on the total number of items. Here, num is set to the square root of the total number of nodes (graph.nodes.length). For example, for 4 nodes, the number of nodes per row will be 2; for 100 items, the number of nodes per row will be 10.

- The spacing between the items is handled by a scale factor, based on the number of items to fit in a given width (less the padding on both sides).

Now, you can create each node in D3 based on the graph.node data.

```
// draw the nodes
var node = svg.selectAll(".node")
    .data(graph.nodes)
  .enter().append("circle")
    .attr("r", 10)
    .attr("cx", function(d,i) { return scale * (i / num) + pad; })
    .attr("cy", function(d,i) { return scale * (i % num) + pad; });
```

In this case, there is a bit more to the method chain to set up the nodes:

■ svg—Start with the svg object.

■ .selectAll(".node")—Select all objects contained in the svg object of class node, which are about to be created.

■ .data(graph.nodes)—Identify the data (that is, the list of nodes in the graph object) to connect to the graphical objects.

■ .enter().append("circle")—Create a graphical circle per each node in the list.

■ .attr("r",15)—Set attribute r (that is, the radius) to 15 pixels.

■ .attr("cx", function(d,i) {return scale * (i / num) + pad; })—Set circle x position to a function. The function returns a value based on the iterator i divided by number of items per line (num), scaled by the scale factor, and moved over by pad to adjust for padding.

■ .attr("cy", function(d,i) {return scale * (i % num) + pad; })—The function for the y position is similar, using a modulus (%) operator to wrap the y value after each column is completed.

Similar to the previous example, at this point, a set of circles has been created. The next portion generates all the lines corresponding to links. This code is very similar to the circle code, except that SVG line objects have different attributes—x1 and y1 refer to the starting x and y coordinates of the line, and x2 and y2 refer to the ending x and y coordinates of the line.

```
// draw the links
var link = svg.selectAll(".link")
    .data(graph.links)
```

```
.enter().append("line")
  .attr("stroke","blue")
  .attr("x1", function(d,i) { return scale * (d.source / num)
      + pad;})
  .attr("y1", function(d,i) { return scale * (d.source % num)
      + pad; })
  .attr("x2", function(d,i) { return scale * (d.target / num)
      + pad;})
  .attr("y2", function(d,i) { return scale * (d.target % num)
      + pad; });
```

The function for x1,y1, and so on, is a bit different for the lines, too. For the nodes, the iterator is used so that node 0 is placed based on a function of the iterator. For the links, the graph.links.source attribute provides a numerical index to the corresponding source node. In the .data step of this chain, the links are connected to the list of links (that is, graph.links). Then, when each line is created for a link, the function provides the parameters d and i, where d is a reference to that link's data, so d.source indicates the index to the source node, and d.target indicates the index to the target node.

Figure 8-7 shows the result of this example code.

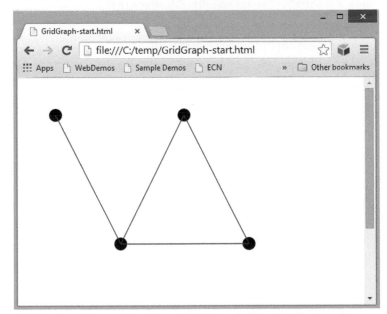

FIGURE 8-7: This very simple graph is drawn in D3 using the sample code provided.

If you look closely, you will see that the blue lines are on top of the nodes. You can fix this easily by putting the links section of the code before the nodes section of the code. This means that the nodes will draw on top of the links.

Using Different Data

Because the example code was written to be fairly flexible, you should be able to change the data set and otherwise use the same code. Now, let's substitute the data to use the same data set as presented in Chapter 5, "Visual Attributes" (that is, a data set with approximately 70 people sending e-mails to each other), in JavaScript format. The data is available in JavaScript form in the Supplemental Materials on this book's companion website.

> **NOTE** If you need to change from CSV format to JavaScript data format, you can either write a Python script, or use an online CSV-to-JavaScript Object Notation (JSON) converter (for example, search for CSV2JSON in Google).

This e-mail data has a few more attributes. For example, for nodes, it has attributes such as shortname and recency, as shown here:

```
{ "id": 0, "name": "Maci Perkins", "shortname": "M. Perkins",
    "numEmail": 3, "sumSize": 448102, "recency": 200},
{ "id": 1, "name": "Garrett Aguilar", "shortname": "G. Aguilar",
    "numEmail": 2, "sumSize": 433735, "recency": 200},
{ "id": 2, "name": "Jada Ray", "shortname": "J. Ray",
    "numEmail": 6, "sumSize": 701842, "recency": 145},
```

Figure 8-8 shows the results of using this data. The layout algorithm automatically adjusts to fit all the data, because the scale factor and number of items per row are based on the size of the data.

Changing the Layout

Some other types of layouts are fairly straightforward to calculate. The grid layout shown in Figure 8-8 isn't perfectly a grid and could be improved by rounding numbers rather than just using floating-point numbers.

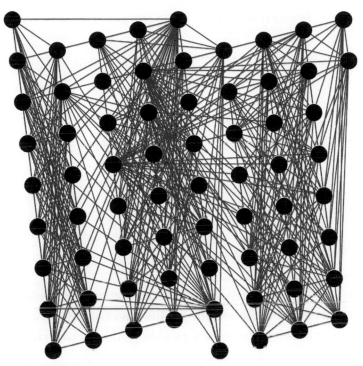

FIGURE 8-8: You can use the same e-mail data set as presented in
Chapter 5 to draw this graph in D3.

A circular layout requires only high-school trigonometry to calculate, as shown here:

```
// angle and radius for layout assistance
var ang = 2 * Math.PI / graph.nodes.length;
var rad = width / 2.5 ;

// create the links
var link = svg.selectAll("line").data(graph.links).enter()
    .append("line")
  .style("stroke", "blue")
  .attr("x1", function(d) { return(rad * Math.còs(d.source*ang)
      +.5*width); })
  .attr("y1", function(d) { return(rad * Math.sin(d.source*ang)
      +.5*width); })
```

```
    .attr("x2", function(d) { return(rad * Math.cos(d.target*ang)
        +.5*width); })
    .attr("y2", function(d) { return(rad * Math.sin(d.target*ang)
        +.5*width); });


// create the nodes and set out in a circular layout
var node = svg.selectAll("circle").data(graph.nodes).enter()
    .append("circle")
    .attr("r", 6)
    .attr("cx", function(d,i) { return(rad * Math.cos(i*ang)
        + .5*width); })
    .attr("cy", function(d,i) { return(rad * Math.sin(i*ang)
        + .5*width); });
```

In this example, ang sets out the angle to increment each node based on the number of items (measured in radians). rad sets the radius slightly smaller than two times the width of the SVG area so that there is a bit of space left for padding. This is essentially a scaling factor.

The x,y location of the nodes and link end points is then a function, where x is a cosine of an angle (index times the angle increment), scaled by the radius (r), and offset by half the SVG area. (Otherwise, it would be centered around the top corner, not in the center of the screen.)

Figure 8-9 shows the results of using the circular layout.

Adding Visual Attributes and D3 Scales

Each SVG object supports a variety of visual attributes, outlined in detail in the SVG specification (www.w3.org/TR/SVG11/Overview.html). Following are a few quick improvements:

■ Outlines around nodes

```
attr("stroke", "white")
```

■ Line transparency

```
.attr("stroke-opacity", 0.25)
```

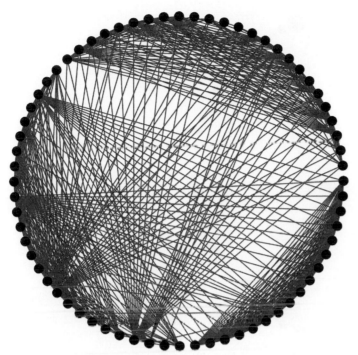

FIGURE 8-9: Using the same data, you can create a circular layout.

Just like x and y values, visual attributes can also be set to data attributes.

- Node radius set to number of e-mails per node

```
.attr("r", function(d) {return Math.sqrt(d.numEmail)*2; })
```

- Line width set to link weight

```
.attr("stroke-width", function(d) {return d.weight *0.2; })
```

Now the visualization looks like Figure 8-10.

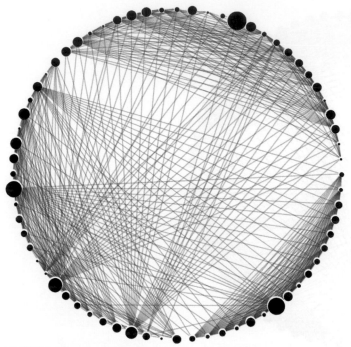

FIGURE 8-10: Using visual attributes, you can show e-mail data with nodes sized based on data.

Setting sizes based on data directly isn't a good idea. To get the line weight right, the data was multiplied by 0.2, which probably will not be the right value for a different data set. D3 provides built-in *scales* to transform data attributes (based on whatever the domain of the raw data is in) into the numerical values relevant to the range appropriate to the visualization (such as sizes or even colors). You do this in three steps:

1. Determine the range.

2. Define a scale.

3. Use the scale when creating the visual attribute.

For example, for the nodes, you can use a JavaScript loop to calculate the minimum and maximum values of the data to establish the range of the raw data first, as shown here:

```
// calculate min/max values
var minEmail = 0, maxEmail = 0,
    minRecent = 0, maxRecent = 0;
for (var i = 0; i < graph.nodes.length; i++) {
    var minEmail = Math.min(minEmail, graph.nodes[i].numEmail);
    var maxEmail = Math.max(maxEmail, graph.nodes[i].numEmail);
    var minRecent = Math.min(minRecent, graph.nodes[i].recency);
    var maxRecent = Math.max(maxRecent, graph.nodes[i].recency);
}
```

You then set up a size scale and color scale, as shown here:

```
// set up a size scale and a color scale
var nodesize = d3.scale.sqrt()
    .domain([minEmail,maxEmail])
    .range([2,15]);
var nodecolor = d3.scale.linear()
    .domain([minRecent,maxRecent])
    .range(["yellow","red"]);
```

Here, D3 scales are defined using d3.scale, followed by the mapping function. D3 provides some built-in mappings, such as square root (useful for mapping data to sizes of things) and linear (useful for most other cases). Then, you specify the domain and range, each as a list of values. Because you have the min and max values, you use these in the list to identify the domain. Then, in the range, you provide the values for the min and the max in the visualization. D3 will interpolate between the values provided. For example, for node size, D3 will interpolate between a minimum size of 2 and a maximum of 15. D3 scales will also interpolate colors. In this example, a color scale is created where D3 will interpolate between the colors listed, yellow to red.

Finally, you use the scale functions when the data is assigned to the visual attribute, as shown here:

```
.attr("r", function(d) { return nodesize(d.numEmail); })
.attr("fill", function(d) { return nodecolor(d.recency); })
```

Figure 8-11 shows how the visualization now appears.

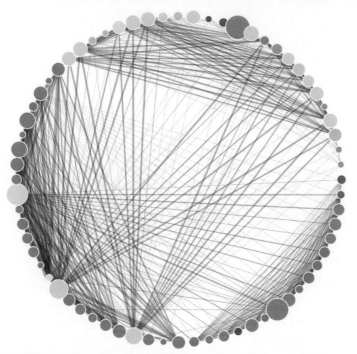

FIGURE 8-11: By using visual attributes, you can show e-mail data with color coding.

Adding Interaction

Although the visualization steps just discussed perhaps create a result that is visually appealing, it doesn't reveal the details of any of the items. A tooltip would be a simple and highly useful interaction to add. SVG conveniently provides a `title` object that contains text. You can add the `title` object to any SVG object, and most browsers will show the `title` as a tooltip. Adding the following code creates a `title` for the circles:

```
node.append("title")
   .text(function(d) { return d.name + "\n # email: " + d.numEmail; });
```

The text in the `title` object is set to a function that returns a string containing the node name and also the number of e-mails. The \n is a newline character that puts the number of e-mails on a second line in the tooltip.

Adding Explanations

Adding explanations to D3 visualizations is easy. The entire capabilities of HTML are available. You can add an HTML heading and paragraph to explain what the viewer is seeing (for example, colors and sizes) and perhaps an interesting observation or two. Following is an example of how to do this:

```
<body>
<h1> A graph of emails </h1>
<p> Nodes show idividual people sending emails. Size is proportional to
the number of emails sent, color is related to recency (most recent
senders are yellow, older are red). Note how the lower right is  a
group of senders that are fairly thin links and fairly old. Point
at any node for details.</p>
```

Figure 8-12 shows the page with the explanations.

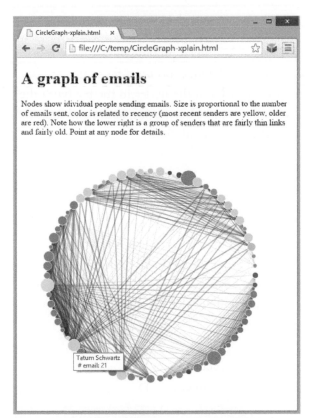

FIGURE 8-12: Using HTML, you can add a tooltip and explanations to a circular graph.

D3 Springy Graph

Instead of programming layouts manually, D3 provides some automated layouts, including a *force-directed layout* specifically designed for graphs. Force-directed layouts are sometimes called *spring layouts* because the links act like springs pulling nodes together. Chapter 4, "Stats and Layout," discusses force-directed layouts in more detail. Spring layouts are a bit more complex than the layouts previously discussed. Spring layouts *iterate* over and over, changing the layout each time to resolve the forces between all the nodes. You have a number of items to set up in order to use the springy layout.

First, set up the force-directed graph layout system prior to creating the SVG scene. In the following code, `charge` sets repulsion between nodes to minimize node overlap, `linkDistance` sets desired link length, and `size` sets the overall area available:

```
var force = d3.layout.force()
    .charge(-250)
    .linkDistance(100)
    .size([width, height]);
```

Next, the force system is connected to the data. You must provide the force system with the list of nodes and the list of links. Note that the links do *not* refer to the nodes by name, but rather by the number implied by the order of the nodes in the file (with the first node starting at 0). This is consistent with how you've been using nodes and links up to this point. The final method (`start`) starts the force calculations:

```
force
    .nodes(graph.nodes)
    .links(graph.links)
    .start();
```

This final piece of the code defines functions that update attributes on the nodes and links each time the force calculations update. Note that these functions reference the data attributes x and y (for example, d.source.x, d.target.y, d.x). When the data is connected to the force system, D3 adds an x and y attribute to the source, target, and node to keep track of the positions.

```
force.on("tick", function() {
    link.attr("x1", function(d) { return d.source.x; })
        .attr("y1", function(d) { return d.source.y; })
```

```
        .attr("x2", function(d) { return d.target.x; })
        .attr("y2", function(d) { return d.target.y; });


    node.attr("cx", function(d) { return d.x; })
        .attr("cy", function(d) { return d.y; });
    });
]);


</script>
```

At this point, the springy graph is ready to run.

Click-and-Drag Nodes

D3's springy layout also provides a nice interaction: the capability to drag nodes while the layout is updating. When the nodes are created, a `call` method is added that refers to the `force.drag` function. This built-in function automatically responds to `drag` events on the target object, changing the object's x and y position to the new mouse position.

```
        .call(force.drag);
```

When dragging any node, all the other nodes update as well, with the entire graph appearing to be bouncy, hence the reference to a springy graph. The resulting graph shown in Figure 8-13 now has clusters much more obvious than in the circular layout or the grid layout.

Labels

It is nice to add labels to a graph. You can use the SVG `text` element to add labels. The `text` element has many attributes, including font family, alignment, `font-size`, x, y, and also a `dx`, `dy` for nudging text. (In the following example, the label is nudged down a half a character.) Because `text` labels must be on top of the nodes and lines, `text` is the last visual object added to the scene.

```
    var label = svg.selectAll("label").data(graph.nodes).enter().append
        ("text")
    .attr("text-anchor", "middle")
    .attr("font-family", "Arial")
    .attr("dy", "0.5em")
```

```
.attr("font-size", function(d) {return nodesize(d.numEmail); })
.text(function(d) { return d.shortname; })
.call(force.drag);
```

Note that `call(force.drag)` has been moved to the text, because the text is on top of the circle, and, therefore, a mouse click will hit the text, not the circle. Similarly, the tooltip will not appear when the mouse is over the label, so you need to add the `title` to the label as well.

```
label.append("title")
.text(function(d) { return d.name + "\n # email: " + d.numEmail; });
```

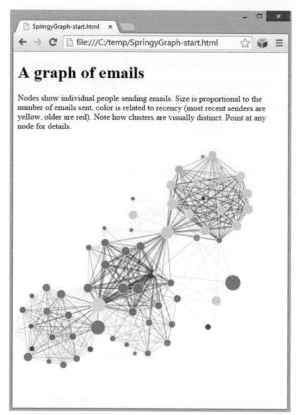

FIGURE 8-13: In the springy graph of e-mails in D3, clusters are much more obvious.

Also note that the text x and y position is not set in the label creation. These positions must update as the forces are updated. The x,y positions must be set in the springy layout update function, just like the nodes.

```
label.attr("x", function(d) { return d.x; })
       .attr("y", function(d) { return d.y; });
```

Figure 8-14 shows the labeled graph.

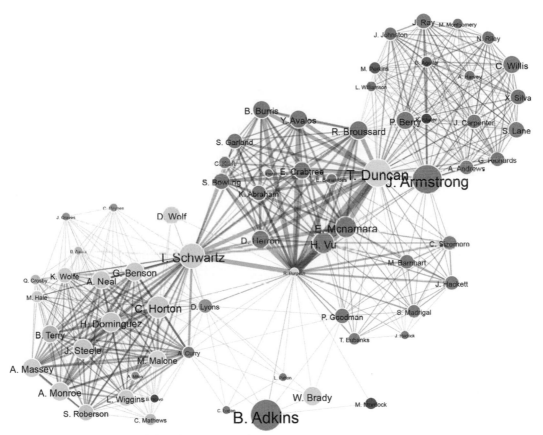

FIGURE 8-14: This shows a labeled springy graph.

Full Springy Graph Code

You have inserted and modified a lot of code since the start of this section on D3. The following code represents the visualization in Figure 8-13 (also available in the

Supplementary Materials on this book's companion website). Note that the data is now in a separate file, simply referenced in its own script object.

```
<!DOCTYPE html>

<meta charset="utf-8">


<body>
<h1> A graph of emails </h1>
<p> Nodes show individual people sending emails. Size is proportional
to the number of emails sent, color is related to recency (most recent
senders are yellow, older are red). Note how clusters are visually
distinct. Point at any node for details.</p>


<script src="http://d3js.org/d3.v3.min.js"></script>
<script src="familyEmail.js"></script>
<script>


// calculate min/max values
var minEmail = 0, maxEmail = 0,
    minRecent = 0, maxRecent = 0;
for (var i = 0; i < graph.nodes.length; i++) {
    var minEmail = Math.min(minEmail, graph.nodes[i].numEmail);
    var maxEmail = Math.max(maxEmail, graph.nodes[i].numEmail);
    var minRecent = Math.min(minRecent, graph.nodes[i].recency);
    var maxRecent = Math.max(maxRecent, graph.nodes[i].recency);
}


// set up a size scale and a color scale
var nodesize = d3.scale.sqrt()
    .domain([minEmail,maxEmail])
    .range([2,15]);
var nodecolor = d3.scale.linear()
    .domain([minRecent,maxRecent])
    .range(["yellow","red"]);
```

```
// set up the graph drawing area
var width = 500;
var height = 500;
var svg = d3.select("body").append("svg")
    .attr("width", width)
    .attr("height", height);

// set up the force system
var force = d3.layout.force()
    .charge(-250)
    .linkDistance(100)
    .size([width, height]);
force.nodes(graph.nodes)
    .links(graph.links)
    .start();

// create the links
var link = svg.selectAll("line").data(graph.links).enter().append
    ("line")
  .style("stroke", "blue")
  .style("stroke-opacity", 0.25)
  .style("stroke-width", function(d) { return d.weight *0.2; });

// create the nodes as circles
var node = svg.selectAll("circle").data(graph.nodes).enter().append
    ("circle")
  .attr("r", function(d) { return nodesize(d.numEmail); })
  .attr("fill", function(d) { return nodecolor(d.recency); })
  .attr("stroke", "white");

// add labels to the nodes
var label = svg.selectAll("label").data(graph.nodes).enter().append
```

```
      ("text")
   .attr("text-anchor", "middle")
   .attr("font-family", "Arial")
   .attr("dy", "0.5em")
   .attr("font-size", function(d) {return nodesize(d.numEmail); })
   .text(function(d) { return d.shortname; })
   .call(force.drag);

// "titles" are text strings that appear as tooltips
label.append("title")
   .text(function(d) { return d.name + "\n # email: " + d.numEmail; });

node.append("title")
   .text(function(d) { return d.name + "\n # email: " + d.numEmail; });

// force.on tick updates the location of the graphics each calc cycle
force.on("tick", function() {
    link.attr("x1", function(d) { return d.source.x; })
        .attr("y1", function(d) { return d.source.y; })
        .attr("x2", function(d) { return d.target.x; })
        .attr("y2", function(d) { return d.target.y; });

    node.attr("cx", function(d) { return d.x; })
        .attr("cy", function(d) { return d.y; });

    label.attr("x", function(d) { return d.x; })
        .attr("y", function(d) { return d.y; });
  });

</script>
</body>
```

This example merely scratches of surface of what is possible for visualizing graphs using JavaScript. This is just an introduction to D3 and much more could still be added. For example, refinements could include the following:

- Show only big labels.

- Highlight a selection and its immediate neighbors.

- Better handle label overlap.

More JavaScript graph examples appear in the following chapters:

- Chapter 12, "Flows," includes examples of a circular chord diagram of trade flow using D3.

- Chapter 12 includes examples of a Sankey flow diagram using Aperture JS.

- Chapter 13, "Spatial Networks," includes examples of a link rose diagram using Aperture JS.

Beyond these, you can find numerous examples at d3js.org. Other libraries (such as Aperture JS) and various books, websites, and online forums provide more information.

SUMMARY

Python and JavaScript are free, well-documented languages with extensive references online and in books.

Python is a fairly easy-to-use scripting language for manipulating graph data for tasks such as data cleansing, as well as extracting nodes and/or links from graph data.

JavaScript is useful for creating browser-based interactive visualizations of graph data. The underlying SVG library provides browser-based support for drawing graphics, and higher-level libraries such as D3 provide capabilities for connecting these graphics to data, as well as specific functionality for graphs (such as force-directed layouts).

Until now, the focus of the book has been on the basics of using graphs—the process and the tools. The next part of this book shifts to various types of analyses for which graphs are useful, starting with relationships in the Chapter 9. Links describe relationships between things and can be used to find interesting connections between things (such as fraud).

PART 3

Visual Analysis of Graphs

This part of the book considers some of different types of graphs and example of associated analyses over the next five chapters. Table P3-1 provides a broad overview of these chapters.

TABLE P3-1: Overview

TOPIC	DESCRIPTION
Relationships (Chapter 9)	Graphs may have any number of links between a pair of nodes. For some types of applications (such as fraud analysis), it is important to keep all links between these nodes and have techniques to analyze the many different connections.
Hierarchies (Chapter 10)	Beyond organizational charts, hierarchies are used in many applications to organize data. Hierarchies are a unique type of graph. They can have unique representations (such as treemaps) or be used in combination with other types of graphs (such as visitor path analysis).
Communities (Chapter 11)	The clustering of nodes in graphs reveals communities. Enhancing node and link data, filtering, grouping, and additional analytic techniques can help refine the qualities to define these communities and make them visually apparent (such as in social network data).
Flows (Chapter 12)	Graphs are often used to indicate flows between nodes, whether communications, money global trade, or web traffic. Flow visualization has unique representations and associated analyses such as Sankey diagrams and chord diagrams.
Spatial Networks (Chapter 13)	For graphs based on spatial data (such as airline traffic, electrical grids, or brain topography), the data can be plotted directly based on the spatial coordinates associated with the nodes and links. Because the relative position of nodes is predetermined, there can be challenges and specific approaches for working with this data.

9

RELATIONSHIPS

Connections are what define a graph. Without links, nodes are just a table of data. While most of this book has discussed links as only one or two links between nodes, oftentimes there are multiple links. For many objectives, these multiple links may be aggregated into a singular link. However, for some types of analyses and applications, you want to keep those many links and then have approaches to view, filter, and separate different subsets of the graph based on these links. Applications where it is important to find and identify a few anomalies in the data (such as fraud detection or cybersecurity) are examples where it is important to retain the individual links.

LINKS AND RELATIONSHIPS

At very simple level, you have undirected links. You can perform a lot of graph analysis at this level, and most of the examples in the book up to this point utilize undirected links. You have also seen a few examples with directed links.

But in the real world, relationships can be much more complex than simple directed and undirected links. For example, let's say that you are a user of LinkedIn. You can query a particular person, and if you are directly connected, the relationship is immediately shown. LinkedIn will also show all the types of connections between you and the other person (for example, field of study, skills and expertise, location, school, group, and so on). Figure 9-1 shows the many links between the two authors of this book.

In Common with David

FIGURE 9-1: Many types of links connect the two authors on LinkedIn's social network.

Most of the time, using LinkedIn, you will see only single links between people, such as the direct connection between the authors. However, being able to see the multiple links provides additional insights not available with summary links. In this particular LinkedIn example, the links indicate common connections based on work, school, skills, and groups, which could be used as a basis for starting a discussion or searching for commonality with other parties.

Note that some graph software (such as Gephi) handles only one link between a pair of nodes (or two directed links). Other graph software (such as Cytoscape) may handle many links between pairs of nodes. The next few examples use Cytoscape. You must ensure that all the links are visibly displayed. Cytoscape, for example, contains a "level of detail" feature that turns off the display of fine details such as labels and multiple links when you are zoomed out and then turns them on when you zoom in. You can validate that all the links are visible by zooming in and out, or you can make all links and labels visible by using the View ⇨ Show Graphic Details menu.

Similarities in Fraud Claims

Insurance fraud is a significant problem. Although it might be perceived as a victimless crime, insurance fraud can affect innocent people directly through injury or damage and also increases insurance premiums for everyone using insurance.

One way to explore potential fraudulent claims is to analyze similarities between insurance claims. One person may have multiple valid claims after a series of accidents or after a series of thefts. But a fraudster may attempt to obfuscate multiple claims by slightly altering personal information (for example, filing one claim under the name Jeff Benson and another under the name Geoff Bensen) or using slightly different address (for example, 34 Main Street versus 34a Maine Street).

Figure 9-2 shows an export of some data from a fraud analysis system and that has been loaded into Cytoscape. Each node represents an insurance claim, and each edge represents one type of similarity between two claims. The visual attributes of the edges have been set so that similarities are color-coded (for example, purple for similar phone numbers, green for similarly named involved parties, and red for similar vehicle identification numbers, or VINs). A similarity is represented as dashed for a weak connection, with a solid line for an exact match.

Notice the multiple different fraudulent components (that is, separate clusters). At the top left is a component with connections between various claims that all have similar phone numbers (purple connection). In reality, this may not be a fraudulent cluster (the phone numbers could be different extensions from one place of business).

The lower-left component has similar phone numbers but also has quite a few claims with similar VINs (red links). This may be a set of claims with people all using the corporate phone number, and vehicles may have similar VINs because they may be part of a company's fleet of vehicles and purchased in a single large transaction.

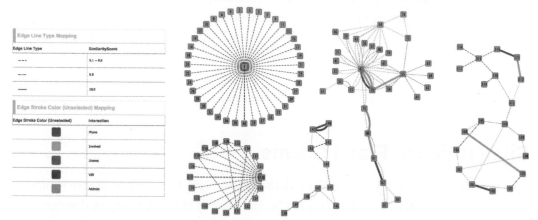

FIGURE 9-2: Different clusters of suspect insurance claims are linked by similarities.

In the middle of Figure 9-2, stretching from top to bottom is an interesting component showing many similarity types and multiple connections between a pair of claims, including similar people names (green), similar phone numbers (purple), and similar addresses (brown). A number of nodes have many connections, and these highly connected nodes are each somewhat unique. Notice that claim 44 (near the top) is mostly connected by similarly named people, whereas 55 (right) is mostly connected by similar phone numbers.

Claim 42 shares three solid connections (two people and one vehicle) with claim 70, which is likely the same vehicle and occupants (for example, a spouse), but claim 42 is also suspiciously linked to other claims in a wide variety of similarities. Claim 42 is a claim worth exploring further.

The first step is to investigate the immediate details available in the graph. The data was exported from the fraud system, including the item labels of the similarity match. By selecting the edges around node 42, you can see the details for each link in the Table panel, as shown in Figure 9-3. You will notice similar names (note that the real data has been modified here to reflect fictional names). Based on this set of matching names (as well as phone numbers and addresses), a fraud investigator may be inclined to go back to the various connected claims and open an investigation.

shared name	Δ Item1 Attribute	Item2 Attribute	SimilarityScore
43 (Involved) 42	Suzie Mayer	Susan Mayer	9.7
72 (Involved) 42	Susanna Mayer	Susan Mayer	9.2
71 (Involved) 42	Susan Meier	Susan Mayer	9.1
70 (Involved) 42	Susan Mayer	Susan Mayer	10.0
73 (Involved) 42	Susan B. Mayer	Susan Mayer	9.5
45 (Involved) 42	Sue Mayer	Susan Mayer	9.6
46 (Involved) 42	Sue Ellen Mayer	Susan Mayer	9.1
57 (Involved) 42	Brie Van de Kamp	Bree Van de Kamp	9.7
58 (Involved) 42	Bree vanden Kamp	Bree Van de Kamp	9.2
59 (Involved) 42	Bree Van Kamp	Bree Van de Kamp	9.2
70 (Involved) 42	Bree Van de Kamp	Bree Van de Kamp	10.0
74 (Involved) 42	Bree de Camp	Bree Van de Kamp	9.2

FIGURE 9-3: Some of the connection attributes indicate similar names.

Cybersecurity

Internet security is an incredibly important topic. Massive data breaches, compromised credit cards, and insecure accounts grab news headlines every few months. Hackers use many different techniques to probe for weaknesses, exploit vulnerabilities, and launch attacks. Security personnel have a variety of tools to detect anomalies on their networks, which may reveal weaknesses or indicate potential attacks. These tools generate data, such as log files, where each line in the log file indicates the IP address of source and target computers (that is, links), as well as different attack types (that is, types of links). You can analyze this information and plot it with graph software.

Network logs can be enormous, so prior to visualizing, it may be effective to narrow down the scope of data, such as a particular time range, a subset of computers, attack types, or other attribute filters. Figure 9-4 shows 1,000 links from an intrusion-detection system, with the IP addresses and specific attack types anonymized. This has been visualized using Cytoscape.

> **TIP** Cytoscape may show only some links and labels by default. To turn on *all* links and labels, choose View ⇨ Show Graphic Details.

Source computers (that is, potential attackers) are represented as triangles, and target computers are represented as circles. Each link indicates a single row from the log file created by the intrusion software—that is, an anomalous network event that could be related to an attack. There are 19 different types of links as indicated in the legend associated with Figure 9-4. About eight to ten unique colors can be reasonably distinguished when used as thin lines, so line type (for example, solid, dashed, wavy, zigzag, arrowed, and so on) is combined with color to create uniquely identifiable lines. Even though there are three variations of purple lines, each one has a unique line type, for example, dashed purple for Spoof, solid purple for Teardrop, and an arrow line for Timeout Error.

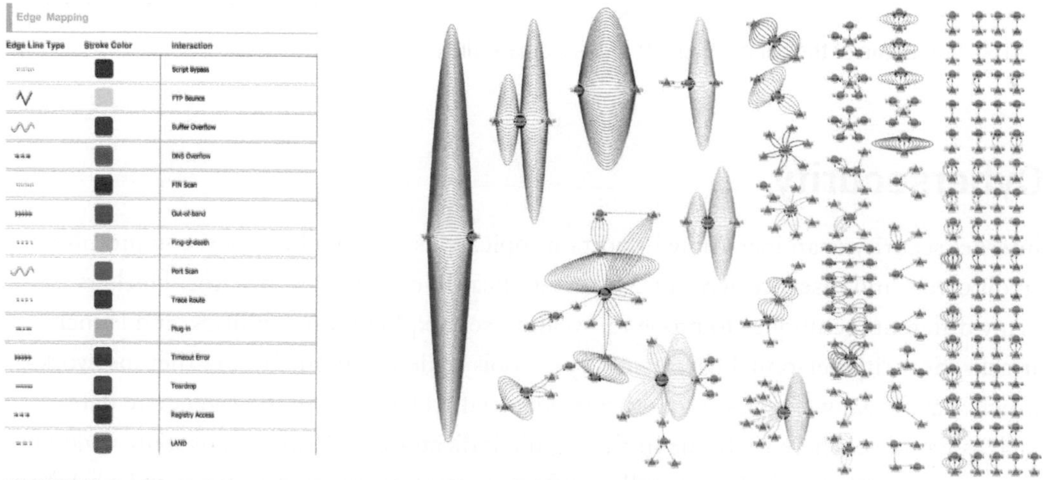

FIGURE 9-4: This graph of anomalous events on a computer network shows nodes representing computers, and a wide variety of events indicated by link color and line type.

You can see many different components in the resulting visualization. In most components, all the links in that component are the same color. The giant purple component is comprised of only two nodes and about 100 links, all of the same type. This may indicate some behavior that is anomalous to the intrusion system but possibly benign or expected by the network administrators (perhaps some form of data update or a configured download script).

On the other hand, some components have multiple types of links. The large component near the bottom left is shown larger in Figure 9-5. The triangle near the center (128.70.100.158) is a potential attacker using multiple attack types against different target computers (circles), along with potential collaborators (other triangles). This could be indicative of suspect behavior.

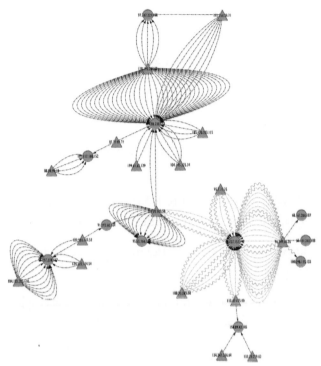

FIGURE 9-5: In this visualization of a suspect component, note that the computer near the center generates multiple different kinds of attacks against multiple targets.

Note that other small components could represent bigger threats. Some attack types may be frequent but relatively harmless, whereas other attack types may be rare but highly dangerous and indicative of an expert attacker. Let's assume that DNS and FTP attacks are important to identify. Only four DNS Overflow attacks between a single source and target are hidden in the field of two-node components on the left side of Figure 9-4, and enlarged in Figure 9-6. Similarly, only two FTP attacks (shown as a yellow zigzag link) exist in this data, hidden in two different small components.

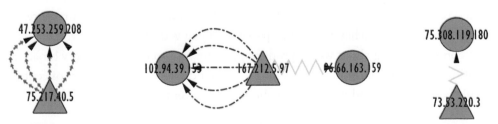

FIGURE 9-6: Some specific specialized attacks may be easy to miss in the larger graph shown in Figure 9-4.

E-MAIL RELATIONSHIPS

Social networks are full of fuzzy relationships. You can extract and transform this data into multiple different link types to explore and better understand the relationships. Following are some of the many different sources of social data that may contain multiple types of relationships:

- An address book or directory may provide metadata such as department, tenure, and responsibilities of a person.

- A sales system or customer relationship management (CRM) system may contain metadata such as job title, management level, responsibilities, and so on.

- Content analysis (for example, keywords in an e-mail title) may indicate useful information, such as products or opportunities.

- E-mail addresses can be used to differentiate between types of e-mails (for example, bob@us.ibm.com is likely a different kind of relationship than bob789@gmail.com).

- From, To, CC, and BCC can be used to identify how close the relationship is. A From-To relationship indicates a direct communication between two people. A From-CC relationship indicates a potentially weaker relationship, where a person may simply be informed of status.

Using one of the author's e-mails as an example, links have been created that identify different products and strategic relationships in e-mails between a pair of people. Coloring link types by these relationships can then reveal who is involved in which types of discussions, as shown by the color legend associated with this graph in Figure 9-7.

A subset of this graph was discussed in Chapter 5, "Visual Attributes." Figure 9-7 shows a much larger graph (2,000 nodes and 10,000 edges) than the previous examples. Here, the patterns are difficult to discern at a high level. You can see many components and various colors in the largest component (top right), but many overlapping links are obscuring each other, even when using transparency. If you want to focus on which people are communicating about which products, you are able to make only very broad generalizations about this large cluster, such as that it tends to be more blue left of center, more purple below center, and more reddish-brown above center.

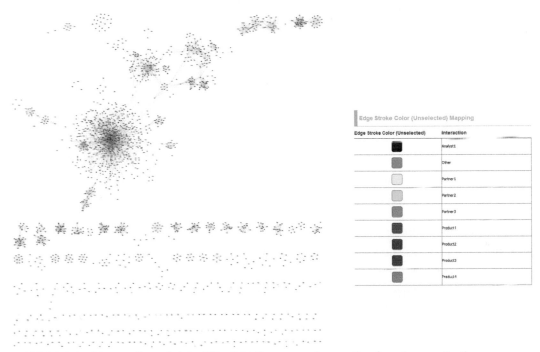

Edge Stroke Color (Unselected)	Interaction
	Analyst1
	Other
	Partner1
	Partner2
	Partner3
	Product1
	Product2
	Product3
	Product4

Edge Stroke Color (Unselected) Mapping

FIGURE 9-7: In this e-mail graph, it is difficult to discern much more than broad generalizations.

Spatial Separation

One effective way of comparing portions of graphs is to use *spatial separation*. You can separate each subgraph of interest into its own window. Because the layout has not changed, you can make visual comparisons across the separate windows using the same *landmarks* in each graph to aid in orientation. Landmarks such as the Eiffel Tower in Paris help visitors orient themselves in a city. Landmarks in a graph are particular nodes or portions of a graph that are visually distinct, such as a large node or a cluster of a few nodes that form a unique pattern.

To create this spatial separation, you use filtering and isolation. You place each successive filtered graph into a new network based on the selection.

In Cytoscape, the workflow to filter and isolate is as follows:

1. Create a new filter using the Filter tab in the Control Panel under the Select tab.

2. Define the filter (for example, on link type and choose the types).

3. Add additional filters, if needed (for example, add another link type).

4. Select Apply Filter to select only those links.

5. Expand the selection to include adjacent nodes (Select ⇨ Nodes ⇨ Nodes connected by selected edges).

6. Expand the selection to include other immediate neighbors, if needed (Select ⇨ Nodes ⇨ First Neighbors of Selected Nodes).

7. Make the selection a new graph in a new visualization window (File ⇨ New ⇨ Network ⇨ From selected nodes, selected edges).

In the e-mail graph introduced earlier, most of the product discussions occur in the largest component (as shown in the top right of Figure 9-7). As shown in Figure 9-8, using Cytoscape, you can isolate this component and separate each product subgraph. Figure 9-9 shows a larger, clearer version of the three product graphs, with the three largest nodes highlighted as landmarks in each graph to facilitate comparisons.

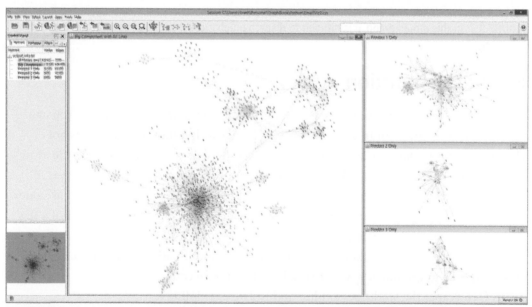

FIGURE 9-8: The large graph (center) has too many overlapping links to distinguish different groups. Each type of link is isolated and separated out in the three graphs at right.

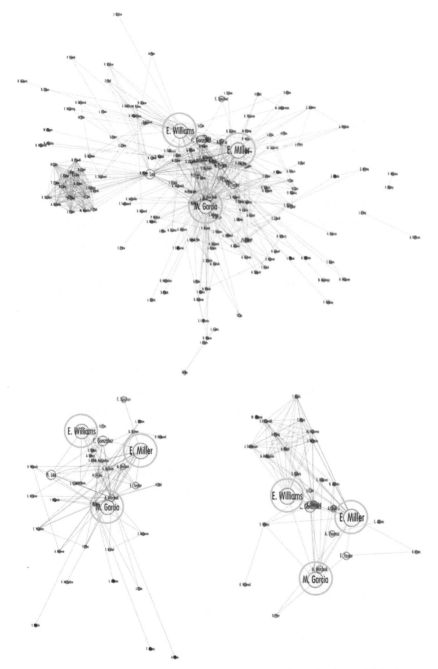

FIGURE 9-9: This shows the three different product subgraphs from within the same e-mail graph. The three largest nodes (upper management) are highlighted in each graph to facilitate visual comparison between graphs.

When you visually inspect these three subgraphs, you see that the three largest nodes are involved in all products—Miller, Williams, and Garcia are upper management. The blue product is the largest subgraph, which indicates that conversations tend to be broader, bringing in more people (that is, more connections) into conversations. For example, a large cluster on the left side represents a technology customer for that product, as well as technology-oriented discussions. The purple product contains a number of thin lines moving out. The furthest nodes out are customers, and conversations are very focused on only a person or two. The brownish-red product is quite small in terms of people and contains an interesting cluster above the management, which does not appear in the other two products. These nodes represent a distributor who is largely responsible for selling this product.

All the approaches discussed so far require using graph software that can handle many links between nodes. The rest of this chapter shows how multiple links between nodes can be handled by software that is limited to only one undirected link or a pair of directed links between nodes. This will be accomplished by transforming links into nodes.

ACTORS AND MOVIES

Another means you can use to analyze larger, complex, multilink graphs is to transform links into nodes. In this example, consider the Kevin Bacon game (described in Chapter 4, "Stats and Layout"), where actors are connected to other actors by movies in which they have both been co-stars.

Wikipedia contains data on films including stars in each film. Wikipedia's metadata is organized and accessible via `http://dbpedia.org`, where queries can be made interactively using SPARQL, a query language for databases in the Resource Description Format (RDF). A sample DBpedia query is shown in Chapter 8, "Lightweight Programming" and discussed in more detail in Chapter 14, "Big Data." This example is based on a DBpedia query that extracted a dataset of 20,000 movies and 21,000 actors on Wikipedia. The raw data is a list of links, movies, and actors, as shown here:

```
101 Dalmations        Glenn Close
101 Dalmations        Jeff Daniels
102 Dalmations        Glenn Close
02 Dalmations         Gérard Depardieu
```

A snapshot of the data is provided in the Supplemental Materials on this book's companion website.

You can then process the result of the query (for example, using Python, as described in Chapter 8, "Lightweight Programming") into a set of nodes and set of links ready to visualize. You have a couple of options with regard to how this data can be represented as a graph.

Following the general approach of this chapter, one way to see how actors are linked together is to have actors as nodes and movies as the links that join actors together. As shown in Figure 9-10, visualizing in this way directly results in a massive graph that can take a long time to lay out and does not reveal many insights.

FIGURE 9-10: This graph of actors connected by movies does not provide many insights.

Almost all of the graph is tied up in one giant component (top) with too many connections to reveal any patterns. Other teeny clusters indicate films with connections between the co-stars but otherwise not connected to any other film. For example, the large yellow dot near the bottom center represents Adolf Hitler, which is connected to other Nazi generals via links that represent the movie *Triumph of the Will*. These actors did not appear in any other films, which is why there are no connections to other movies.

Another large yellow dot is labeled "Napoleon," which seems surprising because Napoleon died before the era of moving pictures. In this case, "Napoleon" refers to an Indian actor named Kumaresan Duraisamy, whose stage name is Napoleon. This little example hints at some of the challenges when using open source Big Data. Though it is promising, you are prone to experiencing a wide variety of errors, omissions, and anomalies when using open source data such as Wikipedia, as opposed to a better curated data set.

Extracting a smaller network for a specific analysis may be closer to a specific objective, such as an analysis of the co-stars of Leonardo DiCaprio. Figure 9-11 shows the ego network corresponding to Leonardo DiCaprio. You can extract an ego network in Cytoscape by following these steps:

1. Select the ego node by entering the node name in the search box.

2. Expand the selection using Select First Neighbors of Selected Node, available as a button on the toolbar or under the Select ⇨ Nodes menu.

3. Put the selection set into a new graph window using New Network from Selection, available as a button on the toolbar or under the File ⇨ New ⇨ Network menu.

4. Apply a layout algorithm to this subgraph from the Layout menu.

Each node represents an actor. Each link represents a movie in which two actors starred. Straight links indicate a single movie. Curved links indicate a second or third movie in which both actors co-starred. (You can mouse over any link to see the name of the movie.) The nodes are sized by the number of links the actor's Wikipedia page has, and color is based on the number of times the actor appears in the overall data set. Thick lines indicate movies that have more links in Wikipedia (for example, *The Aviator* or *Inception*), as opposed to movies that have few links (for example, *Don's Plum*).

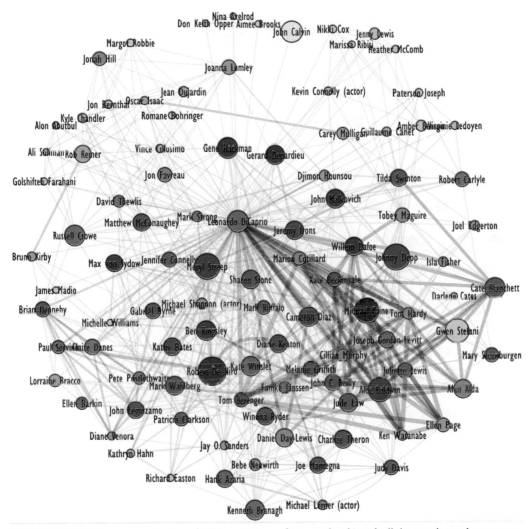

FIGURE 9-11: In this representation of all the co-stars of Leonardo DiCaprio, links are drawn between a pair of actors that acted on the same film together.

The result is a data set that shows who DiCaprio has acted with, but it doesn't show which movies connect people together, leaving some vital information accessible only via tooltips. Although it is possible to turn on the movie names, too many exist, and they obfuscate the display. Furthermore, overall, the scene seems cluttered with all the links between all the actors. However, if you remove all the links that do not directly connect to DiCaprio, you get an underwhelming visualization, as shown in Figure 9-12.

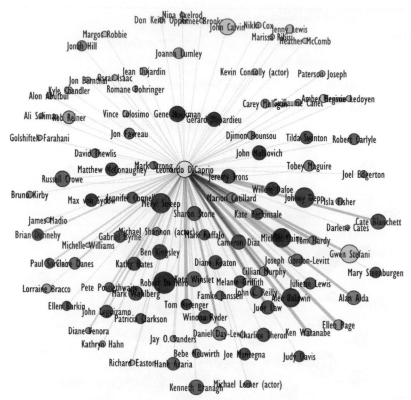

FIGURE 9-12: All the costars of Leonardo DiCaprio showing only the links to DiCaprio is an underwhelming visualization.

LINKS TURNED INTO NODES

Now, consider the simple LinkedIn graph discussed at the beginning of this chapter. In that example, the links between David and Richard are shown also explicitly as nodes.

An alternative graph representation for the DiCaprio example is to transform the graph (using programming, such as Python) so that both actors and movies are nodes and links are used to indicate an actor starring in a movie. If you extract the ego network for Leonardo DiCaprio from this data set, with the first level including movies and the second level including co-stars, you get a graph as shown in Figure 9-13.

This is called a *bipartite graph*, or *bigraph*. It is called bipartite because it's made up of two kinds of nodes that are never directly connected. In this case, you have actors connected to movies, and movies connected to actors. You must go through one to get to the other.

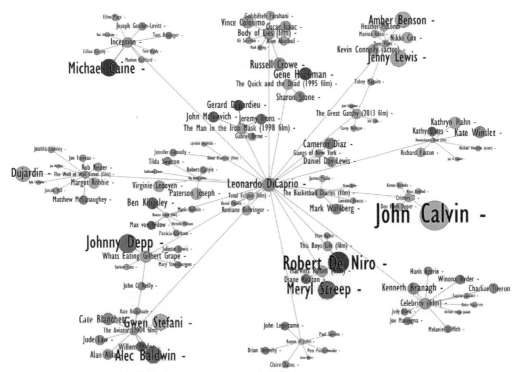

FIGURE 9-13: This version of the graph shows all of DiCaprio's movies and co-stars.

This movie and actor data appears much cleaner and more informative when presented as a bigraph, as opposed to the two graphs shown in Figure 9-11 and Figure 9-12. The two connections of John C. Reilly to DiCaprio are clearly visible (via *What's Eating Gilbert Grape* and *The Aviator*). What's missing are all the connections between actors through non-DiCaprio movies. Also, the movies that actors share in common are explicitly represented as unique nodes, and the common connection is now visually explicit.

Note the example shown in Figure 9-13 was created using Gephi. You can extract an ego network in Gephi by following these steps:

1. Use the Ego Network Filter, available in the Filter panel under the Topology folder.

2. Set the filter to the node ID of interest (for example, Leonardo DiCaprio) and Depth to the distance of interest (for this example, Depth was set to 2).

3. Click the Filter button to apply the filter.

4. Right-click one of the nodes and select Copy to...New Workspace.

SUMMARY

You can use many types of connections to join networks together. Representing these many connections can be a challenge, and the solution depends on the objective of the analysis.

You may have scenarios in which you must see those many links between nodes, particularly in applications such as fraud or network analysis, where the objective is to sift through and identify anomalies or identify specific linkages. Working with different link types can also reveal different subgroups within the graph. (This theme is addressed in more detail in Chapter 11, "Communities.")

Furthermore, links can be transformed and represented as nodes in a bipartite graph, which offers added flexibility, and can reveal different visual patterns when combined with filtering.

Many scenarios exist where the many links between nodes can be simplified into a single link and analyzed, as discussed in many of the other chapters throughout this book.

As the actor and movie graph was successively filtered and simplified, simple graphs similar to hierarchies started to emerge. Chapter 10 discusses hierarchies.

10

HIERARCHIES

The word "hierarchy" means a group of individuals or things arranged in a specific order. It is often associated with a social order found in every office (as might be expressed on an organizational chart) or other organizations such as schools, associations, and so on.

More generally, hierarchies are a special type of graph. Hierarchies have no cycles (that is, no loops) and can be depicted in unique ways such as treemaps and pie hierarchies. Hierarchies can be effective for unique types of analysis such as decision trees. Also, hierarchies can be extracted from more complex graphs and used as a way to organize and analyze the graph.

ORGANIZATIONAL CHARTS

Organizational charts have existed for more than a century. With the beginnings of large companies after the Industrial Revolution, organizational charts were recommended by early managers not necessarily as a tool for analysis but as a tool for command and control. In *Graphic Methods for Presenting Facts* (New York: Engineering Magazine Company, 1914), Willard Cope Briton wrote, "If such a chart is made, there will be fewer cases of conflict or of short-circuiting of orders." Figure 10-1 shows an example of an early organizational chart.

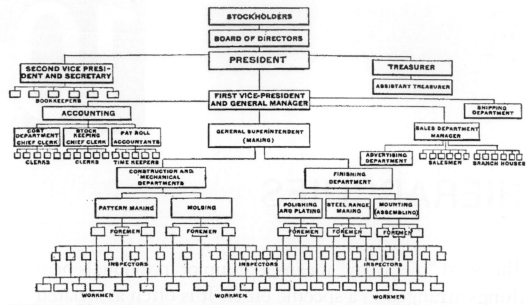

FIGURE 10-1: This organizational chart is for a stove manufacturing company from the 1910s. Image courtesy Prelinger Library (www.prelingerlibrary.org).

Source: Graphic Methods for Presenting Facts (New York: Engineering Magazine Company, 1914),
Willard Brinton Cope.

Organizational charts evolved from earlier genealogy charts. Some early genealogy charts were beautifully illustrated and conveyed a wealth of information beyond lineage. For example, Figure 10-2 shows the genealogy of French royalty in the fourteenth century as published in an 1820s publication (courtesy of www.davidrumsey.com). For this chart, the following conventions were used:

- Nodes indicate people, with black circles for men, diamonds for women, and crowns for rulers.

- Italics indicate spouses.

- Icons indicate date of death.

- Diamond-shaped line styles indicate illegitimate offspring.

- Small caps indicate rulers, and all-caps denote distinct branches.

- Wider portions of the tree have unique background shading.

The image conveys a lot of information in a dense layout that is highly readable and easy to understand.

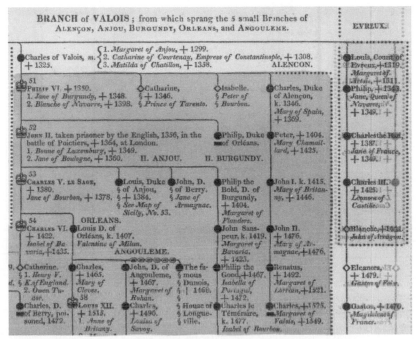

FIGURE 10-2: This chart shows the genealogy of French royalty conveying a lot of detailed information via font styles, icons, and line styles.

Source: A Complete Genealogical, Historical, Chronological, And Geographical Atlas *(Philadelphia: M. Carey and Son, 1820) by M. Carey and M. Lavoisne. Image courtesy of* www.davidrumsey.com.

NOTE

You can view this map online by visiting www.davidrumsey.com/luna/servlet/view/search?q=image_no=%221642040%22.

Like the genealogy chart, organizational charts can similarly layer in additional information using visual variables such as node shape, node size, line width, and so on. Figure 10-3 shows a chart from the 1910s Pujo Committee Report.

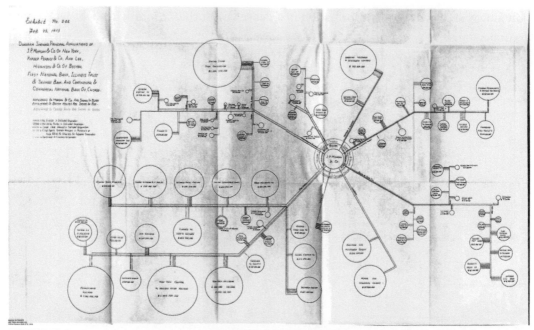

FIGURE 10-3: This chart shows J.P. Morgan's social network from 1913. A tree depicts J.P. Morgan's and other banking company affiliations across American industry, with line styles indicating different kinds of affiliations, and bubble size indicating market value.

Source: Arsene P. Pujo, Chairman of the U.S. House of Representatives Banking and Currency Committee, "Money Trust Investigation: Investigation of Financial and Monetary Conditions in the United States Under House Resolutions Nos. 429 and 504: 1912-1913."

> **NOTE**
>
> You can view this report online by visiting publicintelligence.net/pujo-committee-money-trust-wall-street-banking-cartel-investigation-1912-1913.

This chart depicts a hierarchy starting with J.P. Morgan (at the center of the chart), through other big financial institutions to major American companies with the connection lines indicating different types of relationships such as large stock holdings, directors, or trustees. The outcome of the committee investigation was a report concluding that significant resources and capital were controlled by 341 directors held across 112 corporations by members of a small group of financial institutions, with J.P. Morgan figuring in prominently. These findings led to new extensions to antitrust laws.

These organizational and genealogical charts depict hierarchies that are a special kind of graph that can be useful when analyzing and depicting graphs.

TREES AND GRAPHS

In graph terminology, a hierarchy can be called a *tree*. In a tree, no paths are cycles (circular paths), and there exists only one path between any two nodes. The number of links in an *undirected tree* is always equal to the number of nodes less one. Beyond the idea of a social hierarchy, many different data sets are trees or, more importantly, can be analyzed as trees.

The trees shown in Figure 10-2 and Figure 10-3 are extracted from larger graphs. For example, the genealogy chart (Figure 10-2) has references to other family trees as royalty married across families from different countries. Or, in the case of the Pujo Committee Report (Figure 10-3), directors of large companies may have had connections across companies without being connected to J.P. Morgan.

Any graph can be turned into a tree to answer simple questions about the graph. A *spanning tree* is a graph where some of the edges have been discarded so that no cycles remain—leaving a tree. Figure 10-4 shows a graph and a corresponding spanning tree. Note that many different spanning trees can be created from the same graph, so the edges that are kept should correspond to the objective.

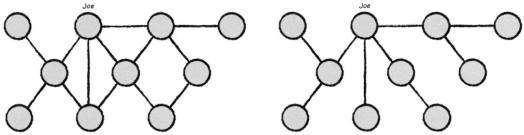

FIGURE 10-4: On the left, you see a graph, and on the right, a spanning tree of the same graph. In this spanning tree, only the links that connect a node back to Joe on the shortest path remain.

Consider the graph shown earlier in this book in Figure 9-10, which showed movie actors connected to each other via movies in which they had acted. The graph in Figure 9-10 had a single giant component with approximately 20,000 actors. The task was an analysis of a specific actor, Leonardo DiCaprio, and his connections. This resulted in a smaller, but still highly connected, graph.

Instead, you could create a tree representing all the connections to DiCaprio. The first level of connection to him is his co-stars (or, in tree terminology, the *children* of DiCaprio). The next level shows people who have co-starred in movies with these people not including DiCaprio or his co-stars, and so on. Note that if a different star was of interest (say, Christopher Walken), the tree should be extracted again because the process described earlier creates the optimal tree (that is, shortest paths) for the root actor.

> **TIP** Highly connected networks can be locally analyzed to a specific node by extracting a tree.

Ideally, using a tool, you should be able to automatically extract the tree from the graph. However, for this example, a spanning tree filter was not found in the popular graph visualization toolkits, so a Python script was created instead.

The script essentially starts with a single node of interest (for example, Leonardo DiCaprio) and then walks through the entire list of links. If the link contains Leonardo DiCaprio, then that node is added to the list of links in the tree. If the link is a duplicate (that is, it includes DiCaprio and the list already contains the same co-star, from a second movie), that link is thrown away. At the end of the first pass, what remains is a tree containing all the first-level links to Leonardo DiCaprio and a slightly shorter list of links. This process is then repeated, using the first-level tree as the set of nodes of interest. The process repeats for as many levels as desired.

This results in the graph shown in Figure 10-5. At only two levels of connection, Leonardo DiCaprio is connected to more than 3,300 actors from the original 20,000 actor data set.

Popularity (as measured by the frequency of nodes occurring from the original Wikipedia data extract) is used to size nodes. Larger nodes tend to occur for actors who have appeared in many films documented in the Wikipedia data set (such as Michael Caine, Christopher Lee, Robert De Niro, Prakash Raj, and Amitabh Bachchan). Connections can be visibly traced to DiCaprio (highlighted in green). So, for example, Donald Sutherland (near the bottom) can be connected to DiCaprio via Robert De Niro. Amitabh Bachchan and Christopher Lee (also near the bottom) are both two steps away from DiCaprio and can be connected via Ben Kingsley.

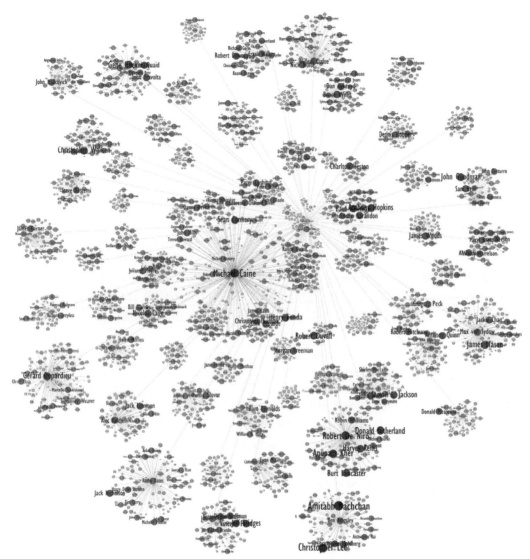

FIGURE 10-5: You can see actors connected to Leonardo DiCaprio within two steps.

The actor network is a type of graph known as a *small world network,* which means that there are many connections in the graph, and within a few steps, many of the other nodes can be reached. Using the Python script to extract the tree, you can find that the connections to Leonardo DiCaprio expand rapidly as follows:

■ The first level results in 102 direct connections to DiCaprio.

- The second level (shown in Figure 10-5) connects DiCaprio to 3,393 actors, either directly connected or only one step away.

TIP

Six Degrees: The Science of a Connected Age (New York: W.W. Norton & Company, 2003), a book by Duncan Watt, uses academic research on graphs (such as small world networks) and presents them along with real-world examples in an easily readable format for a general audience.

- The third level expands to 13,310 actors—already encompassing more than 60 percent of the actors in this component.

So, while a tree-based approach can help filter out the complexity of the graph to answer some questions local to a node, in this type of small world network, even a tree will rapidly expand and can become difficult to draw. Interestingly, there are many more possible ways to draw a hierarchy than simply using a node-link representation.

DRAWING A HIERARCHY

You can draw hierarchies in many different ways and use them to reveal different patterns. One very common business use of hierarchies is aggregations of constituent components—for example, sales of various products by category, cost of all the constituent elements that make up a product, indexes composed of stocks by sector, contributions to profitability by business unit, or organization of a workforce.

Instead of using a node-and-link representation, a *treemap* or a hierarchical pie chart can be used to represent a hierarchy. A node-and-link representation has a lot of space between nodes, whereas the treemap and pie hierarchy fill the space. In the case of the treemap, rectangles indicate quantities, and thick boundaries differentiate between levels in the hierarchy. For the pie hierarchy, wedge sizes indicate quantities, and successive subdivisions from the center out indicate levels of hierarchy.

Figure 10-6 shows the same hierarchy drawn three times depicting a grouping of the United States in 1800 with objects sized based on the population of each state.

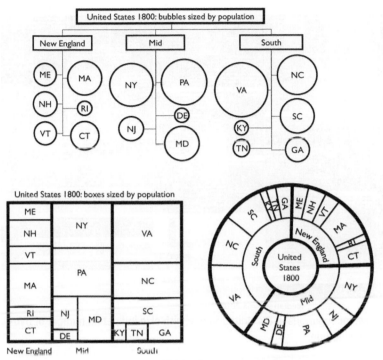

FIGURE 10-6: The same hierarchy of U.S. states from 1800 is shown as a node-and-link hierarchy (top), treemap (left), and hierarchical pie chart (right).

Figure 10-7 shows a treemap of data from occupations in the United States based on data from the U.S. Bureau of Labor Statistics as of 2010 (www.bls.gov/oes/). Each rectangle is sized by the number of people with that occupation and colored by the median income ranging from dark blue (earning $20,000 or less per year) to light green (earning more than $125,000 or more per year).

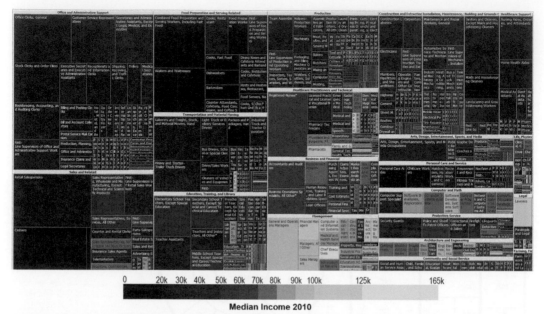

FIGURE 10-7: This treemap shows occupations in the United States with size indicating number of people employed, and color indicating income.

The treemap makes it very apparent which occupations have the most people (for example, retail salespersons, near the lower left) and regions of high income (for example, management, a set of rectangles near the middle bottom, mostly green). Food preparation (a group of rectangles near the top left) is almost uniformly colored by low wages—despite the glamour associated with food preparation on U.S. reality television shows.

> **TIP** Color encoding where the brightness consistently increases while the hue slightly varies can provide more distinctly perceivable levels than just varying brightness. This also orders the patterns perceptually so that brighter colors always represent a higher numeric value than a darker color.

A treemap can be very effective for displaying two variables by size and color. However, some deficiencies may make it difficult to answer some types of questions. For example, although each square is apparent, the median for a group is not discernible. Sales (lower left) exhibits quite a bit of variability, including some higher-income orange and even a bit of green, whereas Construction (upper middle) tends to be largely purple. The question of which group has the higher median income cannot be answered by this treemap.

Instead, a hierarchical pie chart (sometimes referred to as a *sunburst* chart) can be effective for showing intermediate aggregations. Figure 10-8 shows the same occupation income data set with the same color scheme. The outer perimeter shows the individual occupations (the *leaf nodes*), and successive levels toward the center indicate successive summaries.

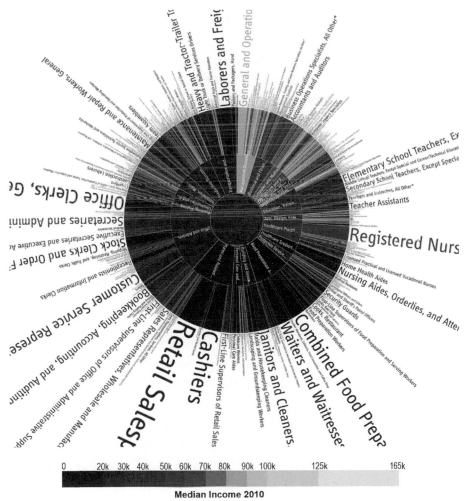

FIGURE 10-8: This hierarchical pie chart shows occupations sized by number employed and colored using median income.

For example, near the 7 o'clock orientation, you can see some labels at the perimeter with occupations such as First-Line Supervisors of Retail Sales, Cashiers, Retail Sales Sales Representatives, and so on. Moving closer toward the center, you see a wedge labeled "Sales and Related," which corresponds to the aggregation of all the outer wedges connected to it.

Looking at the chart, you can answer the previous question regarding median income of Sales versus Construction. Near the bottom (at the 7 o'clock orientation), Sales is blue, while Construction on the left (at the 10 o'clock orientation) is purple, meaning that Construction has the higher median income.

Note that the individual occupations are now slivers around the perimeter and vary in size indicating the number of people employed in an occupation. Some slivers are thin and difficult to discern. Interactive versions of hierarchical pies allow the user to drill down and drill up by clicking wedges (to drill down) or the center (to drill up). This enables the user to explore large hierarchies.

NOTE To see an example of this, visit www.jasondavies.com/coffee-wheel/.

Both treemaps and hierarchical pie charts are effective at showing two data attributes via size and color. A *node-and-link graph* can display the tree data and potentially use more visual attributes to convey additional information. Figure 10-9 shows the use of the same data as a graph. Cytoscape provides a wide variety of visual attributes that can be used to encode data, and here the node outline has been made wider and colored to indicate change in income.

In the node-and-link graph view, the intermediate nodes are prominent, just as they were in the hierarchical pie chart. The additional outline color indicates the change in median income over the 10-year period from 2000 to 2010, a period when many jobs were moved offshore.

Outline color is dark gray between 0 percent and 30 percent change in income. Because the threshold over the 10-year period was 30 percent, 30 percent is set as the Consumer Price Index (CPI), a widely used measure of inflation. Effectively, a change in income under 30 percent does not keep up with inflation.

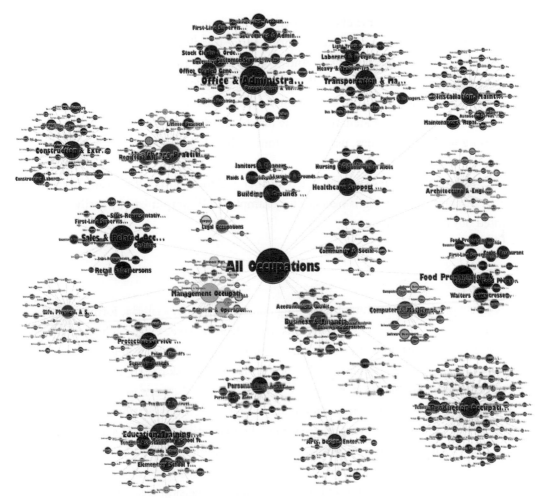

FIGURE 10-9: This shows occupations in a node-and-link graph, sized by number employed, and colored by median income. Also, an outline color per node indicates change in income between 2000 and 2010.

An actual decline in income is shown in bright red and can be seen scattered across a few occupations in different sectors such as Coaches, Chiropractors, Locomotive Firers, Forest Fire Inspectors, and Door-to-door Salespersons. On the other hand, bright green outlines indicate median income growth above the rate of inflation, and these can be seen clustered in a few major occupational areas (such as Management, Business & Finance, Life Sciences, and Architecture & Engineering).

Note that the color scheme chosen for the nodes ranges from a very dark blue to a very light green—creating a conundrum for labeling. Reading text depends on the contrast between the text and the background. One solution is to adjust the range of colors for the nodes so as not to be so dark. But this is not feasible here because the colors should be the same across all three different visualizations in order to be comparable. Instead, a white outline is added around the text to clearly separate it from dark nodes. When using text with outlines, use a heavy font such as bold or black; otherwise, thin font details can disappear.

Note that the leaf nodes are now much smaller and more difficult to read. If detail is required, interactive zooming is needed (for example, PDF output can be easily zoomed) or printed out to poster size.

DECISION TREES

Decision trees predict an outcome by dividing data by successive criteria, forming a hierarchy. The game "Twenty Questions" works like a decision tree. With each successive question, the player attempts to eliminate a significant portion of possible answers. Each decision point is a branch in the tree. The best strategy is to ask questions that quickly narrow down the possible answers.

The approach is often used in database marketing, where data attributes such as age, income, gender, and employment are used to make marketing decisions such as which credit card offer to mail out to a prospective customer. Perhaps you've been on a phone call with a cable service provider to address some concern and been offered an Internet upgrade, followed by an offer for additional channels. A decision tree has been created and is being used to prompt the call center operator to make successive offers. If done well, the caller is receiving offers that are meaningful and relevant.

Decision trees can be created out of a wide range of data where a sequence of decisions can be derived either directly from a given observed sequence or generated algorithmically (for example, in statistical software solutions such as R or as libraries for general programming languages such as the package DecisionTree for Python).

One interesting example of the former comes from professional sports. Players make decisions during gameplay, and a sequence of decisions can then be analyzed to see if there is some commonality. Offensive strategies require some degree of uncertainty to make it more difficult for the defending team to plan its response. As Major League Baseball pitcher C.J. Wilson has said, "Pitchers fall into traps. They get predictable with pitch sequences."

Sports data has become more widely available, and you can use this data to create a decision tree. For example, National Football League (NFL) fans collect and organize play-by-play data and also create programs to parse, extract, and summarize the data.

NOTE For an example of a collection of play-by-play data, see `archive .advancedfootballanalytics.com/2010/04/play-by-play-data.html`. For an example of a program used to parse, extract, and summarize the data, see `https://github.com/10flow/playbyplay`.

Based on this play data, you can construct a decision tree for each team to see the sequence of decisions on whether to pass the ball or run the ball for each down. Ideally, a team would not have a visible pattern (such as always passing on the first down and always running on the second down).

Using a simple Python script, you can count the number of plays in each sequence, as well as record the average number of yards gained. Each successive node records the data for that sequence. For example, a first-level node may indicate a first-down run, and a second-level node may indicate the previous decision followed by the current decision (for example, a first-down run followed by a second-down pass, and so on). The output is a tree that can then be visualized using Cytoscape, as shown in Figure 10-10.

In this example, each team has a decision tree summarizing pass versus run over the 2011 NFL season. Each level in the tree is a successive down. The first split indicates the decision at first down, the second split indicates the next decision at second down, and so on. For each split, there can be a pass (triangle) or run (circle), or neither (an octagon), which indicates a play that was something else (such as a kick, a sack, or data that was undetermined). The color indicates the average yards gained for that play type.

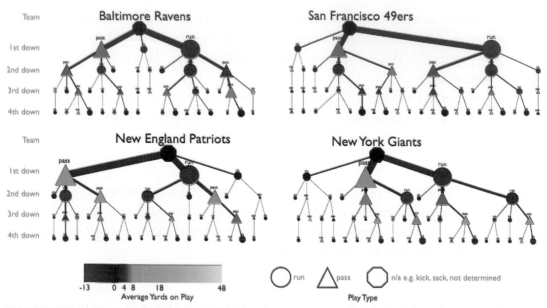

FIGURE 10-10: Pass or run decision trees for 2011 NFL conference final teams help users discern any patterns.

Looking only at the first down, you can see that Baltimore and San Francisco both tended to run a bit more than pass, whereas the opposite is true for New England and New York. Also, the first-down pass for New England and New York both tend to be a brighter cyan color than the passes for BAL and SF, indicating that the New England and New York teams gain more yards on average than do Baltimore and San Francisco for a first-down pass. At this first level, you can determine that New England and New York are strong passing teams.

Comparing the next level splits takes a bit more visual effort. Looking at San Francisco, for example, while first down is split with a slight bias toward runs, at the next level, the sizes of triangles and circles is fairly similar, again with a slight bias toward runs.

Looking at Baltimore, on the other hand, you can see a different pattern. On the first down, Baltimore tends to run. But on the second down, all the second-down triangles tend to be bigger than the corresponding run circles. This leads to the observation that Baltimore uses more runs for the first down and more passes for the second down.

You can also visually compare specific sequences. For example, you can see if a team does a first-down pass followed by a second-down pass or whether (for all teams) third down is more likely to feature a pass instead of a run.

This example is a naïve analysis of NFL plays because it does not take into account the game state (for example, how many yards to reach a first down or how many yards the team is away from scoring a touchdown). These other factors will also have an impact on decision-making. However, this example illustrates how you can use the approach to reveal patterns in decisions and, in the case of football, how teams might determine a defensive counter-strategy.

All the tree representations shown so far in this chapter depict only the tree. However, as shown in some of the examples, the trees may be extracted from more complex graphs. Tree representations can be helpful for analyzing these more complex graphs as well.

WEBSITE TREES AND EFFECTIVENESS

Websites are complex containers that mix together a wide variety of content and various interactions. Each click by the viewers on the website represents valuable information about what content is being viewed. More importantly, this information can also be used to understand what's working and what's not working—that is, portions of a site that are effective and how people are actually traversing the site.

Although a site may be made up of thousands or millions of pages, a site can often be thought of as a hierarchy, and most websites have a site map that is an explicit hierarchy showing the organization of the content of the site. All the pages on a website slot into a particular node within a site map. Thus, you can use a tree to represent all the content of the website as a hierarchy.

From a website analysis perspective, then, you can use this site map tree to collect and organize information about the site. For example, at a simple level, nodes can contain data such as the number of pages associated with them, the number of page views, or the average dwell time.

Figure 10-11 shows the website of an appliance manufacturer, organized following a site map. Nodes represent different portions of the site. Node color is the measure of effectiveness, ranging from light green (highly effective) to dark red (ineffective). Effectiveness can be measured in many different ways, such as explicit surveys (for example, "How would you rate your visit today?") or implicit surveys (for example, "How long did this visitor spend on the site?" or "How frequently was a particular page the exit page for a visit?"). This visit-oriented data can then be attributed back across all the pages that were part of a visit, giving a score per page. These page scores can then be rolled up per each site area, providing a sense of the effectiveness of various site sections.

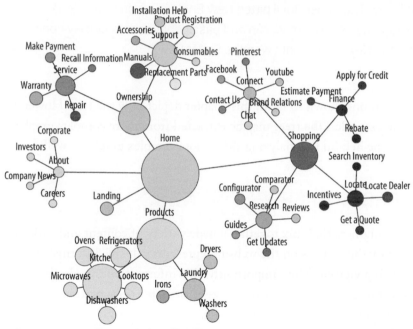

FIGURE 10-11: To show website effectiveness, nodes are sized by visits and colored by percent of effectiveness.

From the snapshot, it appears that the Products section (at the bottom) is ranked fairly effective, although Kitchen appliances are clearly more popular (more visits) and more effective (lighter, greener) than Laundry appliances. Some website sections (such as Finance) are universally red, while subsections of the Support website range from highly effective to poor. This tree diagram of the site can be very useful as shown here, and the same approach can be used to show more levels of a website.

A website tree can also be used to layer additional information on top of the tree. Because paths may move along the same branches as the tree, graph software that supports multiple simultaneous links is required (such as Cytoscape). First, all the links except for the web hierarchy must be filtered out so that the hierarchical layout can be applied. Then, you must restore and refilter all the links and then refilter them again, this time to leave only the hierarchy and specific path. To differentiate between the tree and the path, you must apply visual attributes such as color, line style, and line thickness.

Figure 10-12 shows a path for a single visitor depicted as tiny blue arrows on top of the tree. This is a visitor that starts at the landing page on the left, moves through the homepage into the Product section, and explores Refrigerators, Ovens, and Dishwashers. The visitor then proceeds to the Research section but backtracks to the Refrigerators and then proceeds onto the Dealer section and utilizes the Search Inventory section. This way of showing paths raises some interesting questions. For example, if the site was designed to facilitate forward progress from product overview to research, why did the viewer need to return from activities in the Research area back to the Products area?

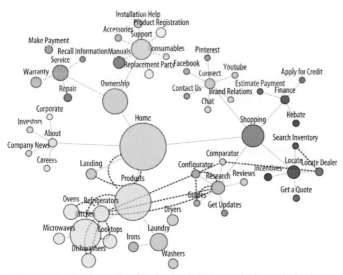

FIGURE 10-12: The path of a single visit through the website is shown in a line with blue arrows.

Rather than looking at paths of individual customers, you can aggregate path data. Some website analysis software may have visualizations of a *sales funnel*, which is a view of the number of customers at each step in a sales process (for example, shopping cart, address entry, credit card entry, and purchase confirmation). It is called a funnel because the number of customers at each stage of the process is typically fewer than the previous step, and when drawn as a bar chart, the successively smaller sizes may resemble a funnel.

A more holistic view of the customer is the *customer life cycle*. Over the course of the customer's experience with the company, the customer may have different objectives, such as learning about products, researching products, finding a store, getting help, or seeking service for the product. A customer life cycle can be thought of as a process proceeding through progressive stages of a relationship from initial courtship through to a loyal customer using ongoing services. In the tree shown in Figure 10-13, you can see the customer life cycle as an idealized counterclockwise flow.

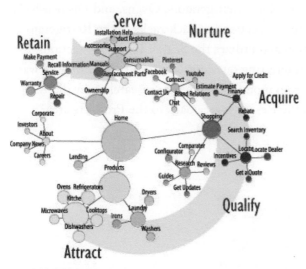

FIGURE 10-13: This website tree also shows a counterclockwise customer life cycle.

To analyze the life cycle, you can filter aggregate flows for specific regions of the site. In this case, the edge data has additional columns that indicate if a particular edge belongs to a particular step. You can also tag flows to differentiate forward flows from backward flows—the assumption being that building a relationship involves forward flows through the life cycle, while backward flows may indicate problems with the relationship or problems with the website that make it difficult for prospective customers to follow the planned sequence. Again, some effort is involved with creating filters to remove all the edges that are not of interest and to set up all the visual attributes.

Figure 10-14 shows the all the flows to the Research section of the site, with backward flows indicated by arrows.

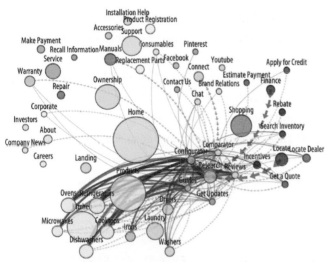

FIGURE 10-14: This shows all the flows to the Research portion of the website. Backward progress is shown as arrows.

Because Figure 10-14 is still complex with many overlapping links, you can apply additional filtering to remove forward flows and/or thin flows to result in an image similar to Figure 10-15. This image now shows the non-forward flows as arrows—for example, many flows from the research configurator step go backward to the product step. Perhaps this indicates some confusion regarding the configurator step resulting in people going backward.

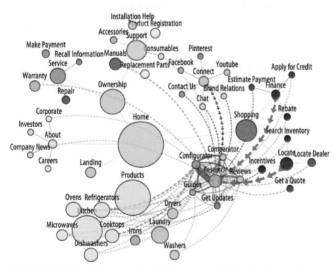

FIGURE 10-15: This uses arrows to show all the backward flows associated with the Research portion of the website.

Similarly, in Figure 10-15, there are many links not only back to Research from areas such as Finance, Locate, and Connect, but also from areas such as Replacement Parts and Warranty.

A much more complex flow-based analysis is discussed in Chapter 12, "Flows." Also, complex analyses that have some sense of hierarchy, some sense of flow, and a lot of filtering are not necessarily easy to create and analyze using freeware graph software. You should expect to expend some effort organizing data and adapting to the filtering and layout constraints of the software. Or, consider investigating specialized software solutions that exist for particular applications such as customer life cycle analysis.

SUMMARY

Tree drawing has been with us for a long time. Trees can clearly and unambiguously show a hierarchy of relationships, such as organizational charts, family trees, and decision trees. Or, a tree can be extracted from any graph—family trees are actually graphs where the authors have chosen to show only edges directly related to one immediate lineage.

Trees can be drawn with a minimum of overlap to create visually clear diagrams. Furthermore, the many different ways to draw a tree can be used to reveal different aspects of the hierarchy and the data.

You can use trees as an effective organizing device. A tree layout can be used to organize a complex graph and then used as a template for drawing other types of links on top of the tree.

However, for some types of analysis, such as understanding clusters that exist in graphs, other approaches are needed. Chapter 11 discusses techniques to identify and analyze clusters in graphs.

11

COMMUNITIES

One of the most valuable applications of graph visualization and analytics is to explore community structure in large data sets. As shown in Figure 11-1, by organizing individual nodes into communities, you can see who or what is related from the 10,000-foot level. Good visualization can express what communities exist, their relative sizes and key characteristics, as well as how they relate to each other. When needed, visualization can also reveal who or what members belong to each community, or to which communities a member belongs. Analytics can tell you how cohesive a community is or how representative certain members are.

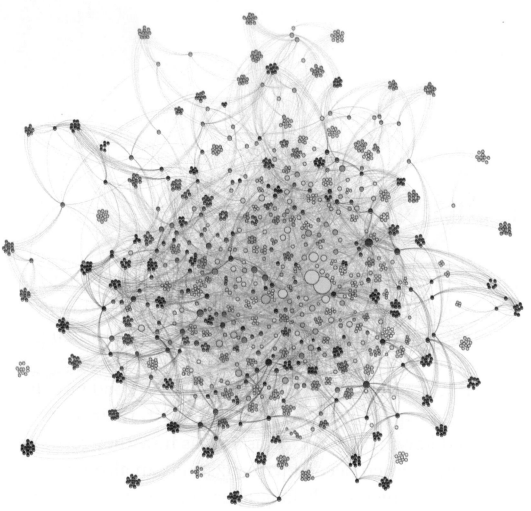

FIGURE 11-1: One of the primary uses for visualization of large graphs is to analyze community structure. Each cluster of nodes in this diagram reflects a community.

Knowledge of community characteristics and relationships is essential to any customer-driven business, especially when correlated with customer behavior. For example, when you can determine the defining qualities of your best and worst customers or discover purchasing patterns for different customer profiles, you can then optimize sales through better targeting strategies. And when you understand the way in which different types of clients tend to respond to promotions and experiences, you can better tailor services and improve performance, and ultimately increase revenues.

In the age of social media, understanding key social community influencers can be important to building and maintaining a positive company image and reputation for many businesses. Knowing which opinions matter most, and to which social groups, enables you to focus and tailor your marketing efforts and determine when rapid action is required in response to developing negative chatter.

You can also direct community analysis inward on your own performance to reveal patterns in the success or failure of business initiatives. Like a medical scientist who seeks to identify factors behind illnesses and to understand how they affect various communities of people, you can use insights into communities of company projects to identify key performance drivers and institute changes that will positively affect the health of the business.

This chapter begins with a definition of community, introduces graph clustering, and steps through an example social media application beginning with the ingestion of data. Layout, color, and filtering techniques for visualization are then described. Aspects of community detection algorithms are defined, and one is chosen for the exercise. The example continues with community topic analysis, followed by an introduction to cliques and use of convex hulls. By the end of this chapter, you should be familiar with basic use of NodeXL and Gephi, as well as key techniques for visualizing and analyzing community structure.

WHAT DEFINES A COMMUNITY?

In graph data, a *community* is a cluster of nodes with a relatively high density of internal connections, as shown in Figure 11-2. In technical terms, it is a set of nodes with high *modularity*. Communities may overlap each other. They may also be nested, such that higher-level communities are formed from more localized communities.

Visualization can be indispensable when trying to understand the nature of identified communities and their collective structure. Their makeup, their relative distance, and how they overlap (and to what degree) are all aspects that are difficult to describe in words, but that are naturally expressed visually.

Graph community visualization works similarly to many kinds of geospatial visualization in that the spatial coordinates of a node or data point are not important at the individual level, but rather in how they visually resolve into neighborhoods and geopolitical structures in the aggregate. It is, however, fundamentally different in that those neighborhoods and communities cannot be identified by their locations. Because spatial location in a graph is abstract, community characteristics must be visually expressed in a different way.

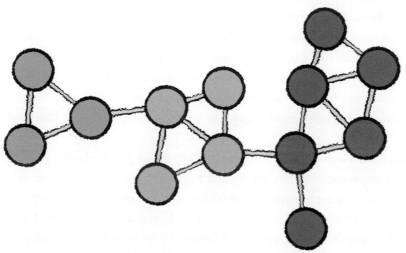

FIGURE 11-2: Graph communities are sets of densely connected nodes, illustrated here by color.

There is no one precise mathematical definition of a community, nor is there one single approach for detecting one. The suitability of a technique depends on the nature of the data and the problem you are trying solve, and algorithms must often be tuned in individual cases for best results. The following two sections illustrate two common ways to look at community, clusters, and cliques, using the same case study data set.

GRAPH CLUSTERING

The most common computational approach to community detection is to use graph clustering. *Clustering* is a goal-driven process by which sets of similar elements are grouped. Algorithms for achieving those goals vary, as do the goals themselves. One goal may be to organize data into a certain number of discrete clusters of similar elements. For example, it may be useful to organize customers into 10 to 12 profiles. A different goal may be to create clusters of a certain size. An online store, for example, may wish to find 10 books similar to the book a customer is interested in.

Graph clustering is a specialized form of clustering that uses graph structure to identify communities of nodes that are closely linked. Like all clustering, it is goal-driven. A goal may be to identify a limited number of connected subgraphs in a large data set to highlight top-level communities that are otherwise difficult to see. Or, it may be to make a graph easier to understand by simplifying areas that have dense connection internally but sparse connection externally. Fundamentally, clustering provides a higher-level reading of graph structure in large graphs in order to make higher level observations.

A Social Network Case Study

On November 3, 1995, the Toronto Raptors played their first basketball game in National Basketball Association (NBA) history, winning 94–79 over the New Jersey Nets. The Raptors, along with the Vancouver Grizzlies, represented the most recent NBA expansion teams and the first to cross the U.S. border into Canada. It marked the return of professional basketball to the province where its inventor, James Naismith, grew up and to the city where the first-ever NBA game was played. While the Grizzlies struggled to find success, eventually relocating to Memphis, the fortunes of the Raptors were to soon soar on the wings of popular star player Vince Carter, famous for his electrifying slam dunk prowess.

The following years saw the end of the Carter era and the dawn and sunset of the Chris Bosh era in Toronto. Bosh was a perennial All-Star player and the face of the franchise before he left to join an emerging championship team in Miami. With his departure in 2010, the team was left with the challenge of rebuilding an identity. Under new management, the 2013–2014 Raptors began the season banking on maturing young talent and the signing of high-scoring Rudy Gay from Memphis. A new marketing relationship was also announced. Internationally successful hometown rap artist Drake was introduced as team ambassador, bringing energy and star power to the building process.

After a slow start to the season, the team's general manager, Masai Ujiri, wasted little time in unloading Rudy Gay and his high salary to the Sacramento Kings, a move that was perceived by many as a plan to bail on the current year, finish low in the standings, and maximize the chances of signing prospect Andrew Wiggins. Wiggins was a marketer's dream, an exceptionally talented 18-year-old widely projected to be the first overall pick in the 2014 draft (a future he would soon fulfill) and a potential franchise NBA player. Wiggins was also a hometown boy, born and raised in Toronto.

A funny thing happened, though, when the Raptors traded Rudy Gay. They started winning. Through a combination of athleticism and renewed commitment to work ethic and team basketball, by the end of January 2014, Toronto had climbed from the bottom of the standings to third place in the Eastern Conference, winning twice as many games as they lost along the way. There was something else that they found along the way: their identity.

The fan community was buzzing with excitement. Team management may well have been motivated to find out what that buzz looked like. Who was talking about the team, and what were they saying? What personnel and marketing moves generated the most excitement? The NBA has more than 200 million followers on Facebook and Twitter across all of its league, team, and player pages. As the following examples show, graph visualization can be used to give visual form to social media data, providing opportunity for exactly this kind of analysis.

Social Media Using NodeXL and Gephi

The NodeXL plug-in extends Microsoft Excel with capabilities for ingesting and preparing graph data for display. Using the Social Network Importer extension for NodeXL, you can extract data easily from Twitter and Facebook for further processing and export it in common graph format for importing into graph visualization tools like Gephi.

> **NOTE** If you haven't yet installed the NodeXL and Social Network Importer, you can download them from `http://nodexl.codeplex.com` and `http://socialnetimporter.codeplex.com`. Version 1.0.1.251 of NodeXL and version 1.9.2 of Social Network Importer were used for this exercise.

From the Windows Start menu, find the NodeXL program folder and open `NodeXL Excel Template`. Select the NodeXL ribbon, and on the Data ribbon group click Import ⇨ From Facebook Fan Page Network.

A dialog box (Figure 11-3) appears. Before attempting to configure the options, click the Login button at the bottom and type in your Facebook credentials. In the Fan Page input box, type **Toronto Raptors**, and select the matching result. Click the option for "Based on co-comments," and limit the sample to a one-month time range from 12/15/2013 to 1/15/2014 and 15 comments or likes per post. Click Download to begin fetching the data.

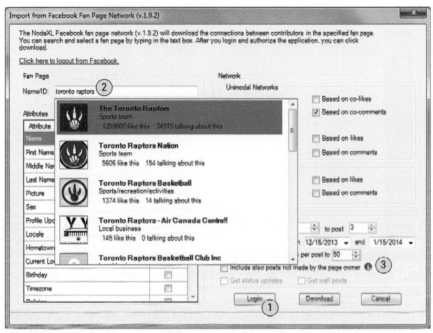

FIGURE 11-3: To import social media from a Facebook fan page, click to log in (1), type the name in the Fan Page box (2), and select it. Configure the network type, sample range, and limit count (3).

When it completes, you will end up with two worksheets populated with people who commented on the same posts. As shown in Figure 11-4, the Vertices worksheet will be populated with people who commented on the Raptors fan page (about 1,600), and the Edges worksheet will be populated with a list of every two people who commented on the same post (about 15,000).

For each fan, the Vertices worksheet will include a name and photo, as well as demographic attributes such as sex and locale. It will also include a concatenated collection of all comments made by each fan in the "Tweet" column. This will be an ideal place to do a little more analysis on the comments, but it's a good idea to get a visual look at the data first and see whether your sample is the right scale to give you some insights into community structure.

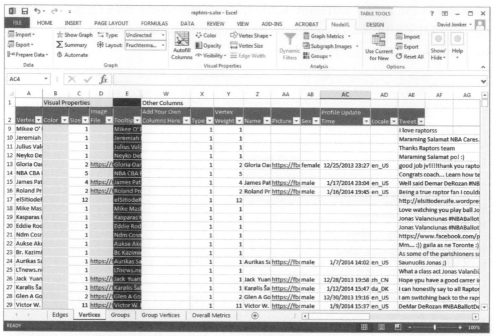

FIGURE 11-4: Importing Facebook data will populate the Edges and Vertices worksheets with people who commented on the same posts.

You might have already noticed that NodeXL includes some basic graph-plotting capabilities, which can sometimes be useful for validating any data processing and enhancements you are working on in the spreadsheet. However, to make any sense of a graph this size, you will probably want to import it into a visualization tool like Gephi. Under the NodeXL ribbon, click Export ⇨ To GraphML File… to save the file in a common graph file format.

Open the saved file in Gephi. A dialog box appears with options for interpreting the data. Choose Undirected as the link type, and proceed to finish the import and plot the resulting graph. If what you see looks like nothing you recognize (an indecipherable mess, as shown in Figure 11-5), congratulations, you have coughed up your first hairball. Because the graph file does not yet have coordinates assigned to the nodes, Gephi has distributed them randomly. Additional effort is required to make sense of the graph, starting with the application of layout.

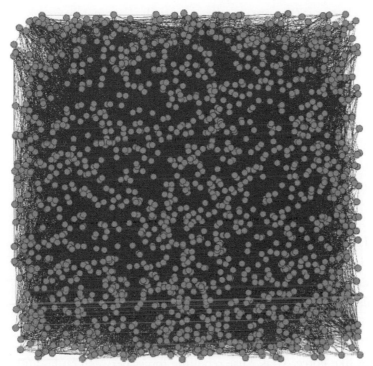

FIGURE 11-5: Without the application of community-oriented visualization techniques, large graphs tend to look like meaningless hairballs.

If your graph has a hairball problem, you will need to tease out clusters visually through the use of layout, color, and other techniques.

Layouts that Cluster

The term *cluster* by definition implies a spatial relationship. In common usage, the term is understood to mean a group of similar entities positioned (or occurring) closely together. Typically, in cluster algorithms as well the relative similarity of elements is represented mathematically as a distance. Like grapes on a vine, elements form a distinguishable cluster if collectively they are relatively near each other.

It is easiest to understand clusters if they are visualized spatially. Fortunately, graph layouts that are particularly good at isolating clusters are available. In a sense, all graph layouts cluster linked nodes together, because one of the primary goals is to provide optimal clarity by minimizing crossover and overlap. However, some layouts do a better job of detangling hairballs than others. One of these is OpenOrd.

Select OpenOrd in the Layout pane of the Overview task mode. As with other Gephi layouts, highly technical options for fine-tuning are available, but in most cases, the default settings are effective. Click Run to watch OpenOrd animate through several layout stages and complete. If the graph is now spread a little too thin relative the size of nodes, fine-tune it by running Force Atlas 2 for two or three seconds and then stop it.

Force-directed algorithms like Force Atlas 2 use repelling forces between nodes and attracting forces along links to iteratively propel nodes into optimal positions. While they are computationally expensive and often have trouble disentangling "knotted" graphs, they can be ideal for refining layouts once a faster, more aggressive algorithm like OpenOrd is used to unbind and isolate clusters.

Once a satisfactory layout is achieved, switch to Preview task mode, change the edge opacity to 20 percent, and click the Refresh button to update the visualization.

What you will see in the resulting graph is that the layout has pulled together discernible community clusters, some in the middle and some on the edge (Figure 11-6).

Clusters in the middle represent communities of people who often post together but who also post more regularly with others as well, whereas clusters on the periphery do not. The largest nodes represent people who participate in the most posts. They are social connectors in the Raptors fan base—those who are investing the most time and who are potentially among the most influential. From a business perspective, these are particularly interesting fans.

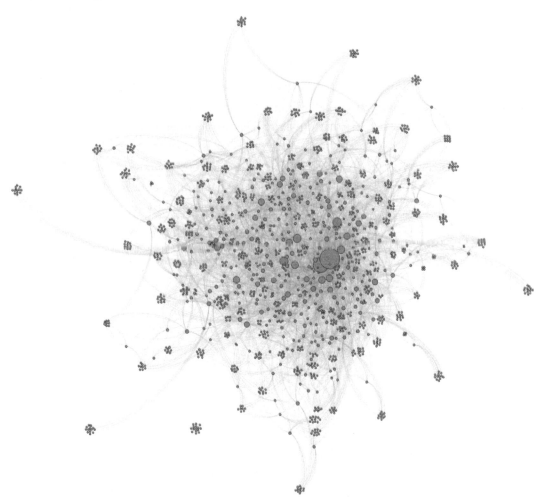

FIGURE 11-6: Layouts like OpenOrd pull clusters together spatially, revealing community structure.

Using Color to Characterize Clusters

One node in the middle is larger than all the others—a primary social connector. Using the Edit feature, you can click the node to see a list of any details known about that person.

One of the interesting details that may catch your eye in this case is that the "number one" fan is a woman. Suspecting that a significant percentage of basketball fans are men, you may wonder whether a pattern exists between gender and social connection in this data.

In the Overview task mode, select the Partition tab. As shown in Figure 11-7, the Partition tab provides controls to map a color from each unique data attribute value, whereas the Ranking tab provides controls to map a range of colors or sizes to a range of scalar values in the data.

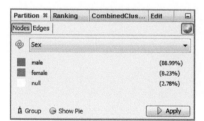

FIGURE 11-7: The Partition tab maps node and edge attributes from categorical data values.

Under Partition, select Nodes. Click the refresh button beside the drop-down menu, and select Sex. A list of unique values for gender appears, along with the frequency of occurrence, confirming your suspicion that more men are on the fan page than women. Choose culturally intuitive colors for gender (such as pink and blue), and a neutral recessive color (such as white or grey) for null (unspecified) values. Click Apply to see the results shown in Figure 11-8.

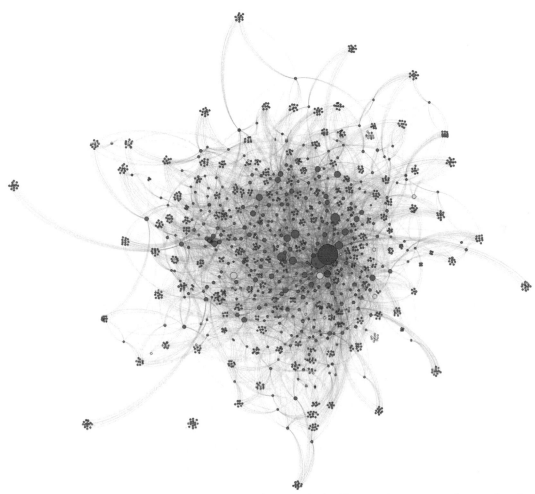

FIGURE 11-8: Mapping color to node attributes such as gender in this example expresses facets of each cluster.

TIP

The three most important considerations in choosing colors are cultural associations, discriminability, and relative salience (how much it "pops"). Chapter 16, "Design," includes more guidelines on color and other design choices.

The resulting visualization reveals the super-fan as a large pink node in the middle, with other female fans in pink spread throughout. Other pink nodes are social connectors, but if they are any more likely to be connectors than men, the difference is subtle. You can confirm this more precisely if desired by calculating graph statistics like average degree and centrality for both men and women. In NodeXL, you can calculate these statistics for each node in the workbook by running Graph Metrics and then subsequently analyze them using column filters and standard Excel statistical formulas.

Another observation you may note is that the pink nodes are evenly distributed across the graph. Women in this sample do not seem to be any more likely to comment together. In fact, the opposite seems to be true—or is it? Filtering may provide a clearer picture.

Find the Filters tab, and locate the Partition filters in the Attributes folder. Drag the Sex filter into the Queries pane below it. Check the "female" box and click the Filter button to hide the other nodes.

Now you can see which female fans are connected to other female fans. However, because the majority of nodes have been removed, you can no longer rely on spatial layout to see whether or not they belong to the same communities. To proceed with more advanced analysis, each node will need to be explicitly associated with a community.

Community Detection

Computational community detection is a fertile area of scientific research. Many algorithms have been written to identify communities, with various strengths and weaknesses and representing a wide variety of approaches. All of the following can be factors in choosing the most useful algorithm in any given situation:

- **Desired count**—This is the approximate number of communities that are informative and useful to display. In mathematics, this is often expressed as the variable k.

- **Minimum criteria**—While count is important, communities should still be held to a threshold of validity. If roughly seven is ideal for display but the fourth, fifth, sixth, and seventh are communities only by the loosest of definitions, it may be better in some cases to identify only three.

- **Factoring in link weight**—In most cases stronger links between nodes should be interpreted as tighter community bonds. This can be factored into computation. In technical terms, link strength in graphs is often referred to as *edge weight*. Links may, for example, be weighted by the number of transactions between two nodes or by the total value of all transactions if they vary in size.

- **Consideration of node similarity**—In some cases, it is useful to identify communities not only by how tightly they are linked but also by factoring in similarity of node attributes (such as demographic profile). For example, a cluster of closely associated, mostly middle-income Baby Boomers may be more actionable from a marketing perspective than simply a cluster of tightly linked customer accounts of all varieties.

- **Overlapping or discrete clusters**—In reality, communities often overlap. However, for the purposes of analysis and decision making, it can sometimes be more useful if each node is assigned to only one cluster. In such cases, it is often common practice to assign all remaining nodes to an additional cluster representing "other."

- **Compute time**—Some algorithms are inherently more time consuming to calculate than others. Depending on the size of the data set, a trade-off between time and quality may be required. Some algorithms are designed for this and work on a progressive refinement basis, which the user can monitor and stop when he or she achieves a satisfactory quality of result.

You can download many experimental community detection algorithms as plug-ins in graph tools like Gephi or Cytoscape. The Louvain modularity algorithm, however, provides one of the best balances of general utility and performance, making it a good choice as the core implementation of community detection in Gephi. Louvain strengths include relatively simple control over the number of communities, consideration of link weight, discrete classification of all nodes, and relatively fast computation.

In the Overview task mode, select the Statistics tab and click the Run button beside the Modularity statistic to execute the Louvain algorithm. Leave the option to use weights checked to consider strength of connection between members. You can use the resolution factor to control the number of communities into which the graph will be resolved. A setting of 1.0 is a good starting point, but return later to experiment with different values. Proceed to run the algorithm, assigning each node to a community.

Using Color to Distinguish Clusters

You can use color to characterize clusters that are visible spatially—by gender, for example, in this community of fans. You can also use it to more clearly distinguish clusters that are not easy to see spatially (like the ones in the middle of this graph), or when many of the nodes are filtered out.

To color clusters, you must first explicitly identify them. Now that each node belongs to a community, labeled a *Modularity Class* in Gephi, you can map it to color. In the Partition tab, assign Modularity Class to node color and apply the change. If the option isn't in the list, click the refresh button beside it.

The resulting plot shown in Figure 11-9 illustrates that color is an effective means of more easily distinguishing communities that do not have obvious spatial boundaries. Note, however, that this is relatively weak visualization thus far. Meaningful characterization of the communities being highlighted has been sacrificed, and far more colors are in use than can be deciphered by the partition legend. It is clear, however, where one community ends and another begins, which will be useful when filters are applied to hide nodes in the graph.

Find the Filters tab, and locate the Partition filters in the Attributes folder, as shown in Figure 11-10. Drag the Sex filter into the Queries pane below it. Check the "female" box and click the Filter button.

Return to the Preview pane to inspect the results. Now that fewer links are showing, increase the edge opacity to 80 percent and the thickness to 3.0. Take advantage of the additional whitespace to express more information by turning on node labels. Labeling can be a bit finicky in Gephi, so you may need to play with the settings a bit in both the Preview and Overview panes until you get something satisfactory.

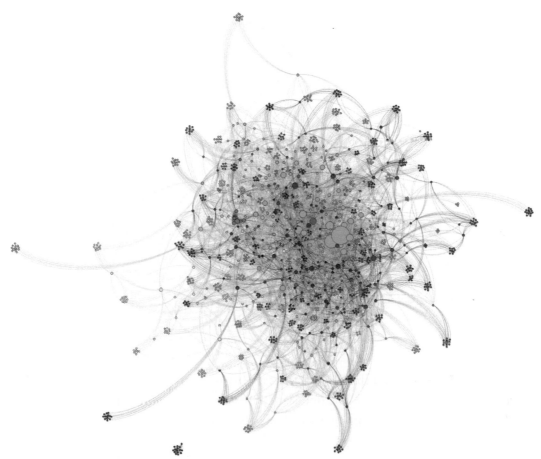

FIGURE 11-9: Coloring by cluster can complement spatial layout by more clearly distinguishing clusters but otherwise adds little insight.

The settings used here are Myriad Pro Condensed 8, proportional size, color by parent node, maximum characters 7, and an outline size of 4 in white at 80 percent opacity. Making the label size proportional to the node size maintains the mapping from original node weight (importance in the overall graph) but will require that you play with the node scale back in the Overview task mode to manipulate the range of label scales.

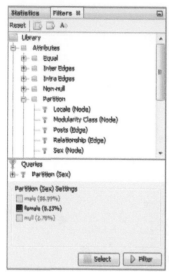

FIGURE 11-10: You can use filters to hide parts of the graph that are not relevant to immediate interests.

Return to the Preview task mode and refresh the view to see the results, as shown in Figure 11-11.

Hiding male nodes and their connections confirms that relatively few females seem to connect with other females. The implication may be that (at least in this sample) basketball is not a particularly common social topic between women, but a select few women may have a significant influence on the much larger community of male and female fans. From a business perspective, this is an observation that might help to shape marketing strategies.

In the process of mapping color to clusters, you may have noticed a cluster of medium-sized nodes with very thick links between them (in Figure 11-9, they are orange), which could easily have been overlooked before. Clear the gender filter by clicking the Filter button again to have another look. The thicker links indicate a higher degree of social media buzz. A stream of comments has been flying back and forth in that community. People seem excited about something. It would be very useful to know what.

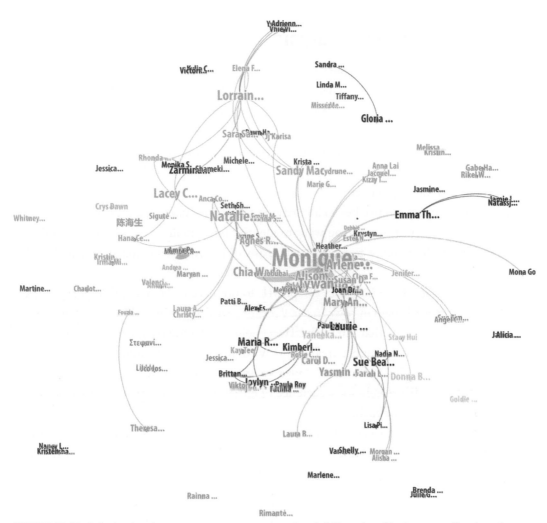

FIGURE 11-11: Coloring by cluster can preserve community visibility when filtering, revealing here how few female fans comment with other female fans, with the exception of a handful of social connectors from select communities.

Community Topic Analysis

Up until now, you have used layout, color, and algorithms to reveal community structure. You have identified key social connectors and made observations about the role of women in the Raptors fan base. But these are most likely confirmations of things that, to some degree, you already know. Looking back at the original objectives defined for this data set, what you really set out to visualize is how the fan community is responding to moves made by the organization. What player moves have been popular? What buzz has the involvement of Drake generated?

You can use many approaches to identifying topics in social media. Focus on what you want to know. In this case, you want to identify buzz about players and about Drake. A simple approach would be to identify when any of the comments made have included a mention of them.

Export the graph from Gephi in GraphML to preserve its layout and import it back into NodeXL. Recall that fan rows in the Vertices worksheet include a concatenation of all comments made by that fan in the Tweet column. To the right of the existing columns, outside of the data import area, add new columns for Drake and for each of the five starting players: Demar Derozan, Jonas Valanciunas, Kyle Lowry, Amir Johnson, and Terrence Ross. To search for occurrence of either first or last name, populate a row atop the new columns for each.

Create a formula in the cells of each new mention column that searches for the names above the column (Figure 11-12), recording a 0 if neither is found, and otherwise marking it with a 1:

```
=IF(AND(ISERROR(SEARCH(AL$2,Vertices[[#This Row],[Tweet]],1)),
        ISERROR(SEARCH(AL$1,Vertices[[#This Row],[Tweet]],1))),0,1)
```

AJ	AK	AL	AM	AN	AO	AP	AQ
		demar	jonas	kyle	amir	terrence	
Subject ▾	drake	derozan	valanciun:	lowry	johnson	ross	
other	0	0	0	0	0	0	other
Johnson	0	0	0	0	0	0	other
other	0	0	0	0	0	0	other
DeRozan	0	1	0	0	0	0	derozan
other	0	0	0	0	0	0	other
mixed	0	1	1	0	0	0	mixed
mixed	0	1	1	1	0	0	mixed

FIGURE 11-12: Search for references to names and record matches. Summarize subject by single match, no match ("other"), or multiple matches ("mixed").

Now, create a formula in a new column to the right of the mention columns that notes the single subject matched, "other" if none matched, or "mixed" if multiple subjects were matched:

```
=IF(SUM(AK3:AP3)>1,"mixed",IF(AK3=1,AK$2,IF(AL3=1,AL$2,IF(AM3=1,AM$2,
    IF(AN3=1,AN$2,IF(AO3=1,AO$2,IF(AP3=1,AP$2,"other")))))))
```

As a final step, copy the values of the new columns into the graph data area of the worksheet using the Paste Values option. You should see a header with a drop-down arrow appear above the new graph data column, similar to the others. Give the mention columns and the topic column meaningful names, and export the enhanced graph in GraphML format for import into Gephi. When you import, ensure that you uncheck the auto size option to preserve your original node sizes.

Map node color to topic using the Partition tab. Modify the random default color assignments to make them intuitive. The players are one family of topics, so choose colors from the same family. Blues and greens might be an appropriate choice for players, in which case, a distinctly different color like red might be a good choice for Drake. Neutral middle gray, a colorless color, is a logical choice for "other" topics, and "mixed" topics might naturally be represented by neutral-but-salient colors like white or black. Switch to Preview task mode, reapply edge opacity of 20 percent, and refresh the view.

> **TIP** Edge opacity is not preserved in a GraphML export and will need to be reapplied when importing back into Gephi.

In the resulting visualization shown in Figure 11-13, you can clearly see that the hot topic in the most "excited" community is Drake, shown in red. You can also see that comments about players (shown in blues and greens) are relatively evenly distributed, which may be reflective of the Raptors' identity as a team-oriented unit. There is no one player who particularly stands out.

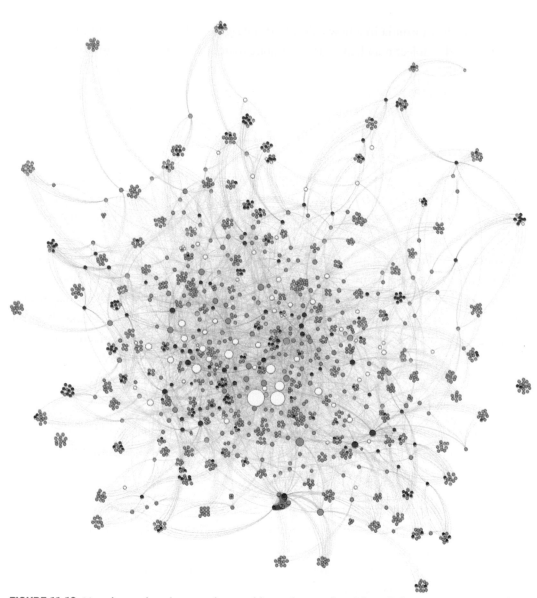

FIGURE 11-13: Mapping node color to topics provides a picture of social media buzz across communities. Drake, shown in red, is a hot topic spreading through communities on the periphery.

Looking more closely at the red clusters, you may also notice two things. One is that the communities where Drake is a hot topic are mostly on the periphery, whereas chatter about players is more likely to occur in the center of the fan community. Central members who are more involved across posts appear to be the hard-core fans with a higher basketball IQ, reflected by player knowledge. Another observation is that there is a density of communities near the nexus of Drake comments, which are also talking about Drake, a pattern that is not found with the player comments. Confirm that these communities tend to be linked by switching to the Overview task mode and hovering over the red nodes, as shown in Figure 11-14.

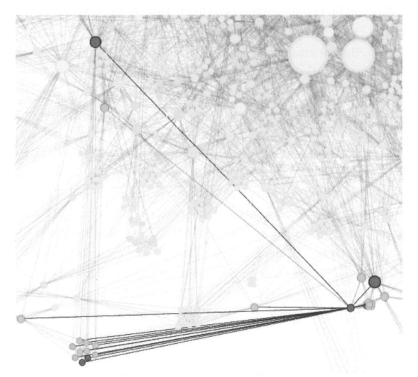

FIGURE 11-14: Hovering over a node in the Overview task mode highlights linked nodes, revealing here that chatter about Drake (shown in red) is spreading virally across communities.

These are exactly the kinds of phenomena that a marketing department would be hoping to see. The involvement of Drake is generating excitement outside of the hard-core fan base, where newbie fans are more likely to be drawn in, and the effect of that excitement seems to be viral.

Community Sentiment

Mapping color to topics has shown you what communities are talking about and revealed patterns among topics. But what if you want to know what they are *saying* about those topics? Are the fans in this data set raving about the players, trashing them, or something in between? Determining whether a text is likely positive, negative, or neutral is known as *sentiment classification*.

One way to perform sentiment classification is to use a computer process whereby an algorithm that has been previously "trained" by a person estimates the sentiment of a new text based on similarity to text on which it was trained. This approach is often ideal in that the algorithm is capable of learning by example without exhaustive semantic instruction from a human. But for results of reasonable quality, it requires that the algorithm be trained on similar data. For this data set, you want a classifier that has been trained specifically for social media.

For simplicity, this example uses a convenient online web service provided by Viral Heat to classify fan comments directly from Excel. If you don't already have a Viral Heat account, you will need to sign up for one at `https://app.viralheat.com/developer/` and request a developer API key online, or use an alternate service.

Reopen the Raptors fan spreadsheet you enhanced with player mentions, and start by adding a new row to the top of the `Vertices` worksheet, followed by four empty columns to the right of the Tweet column. Name the new columns "Mood," "Mood Probability," "Sentiment," and "Topic Symbols." To the far right, outside of the graph data area, add four new columns where the sentiment will be computed, and a fifth that will be reserved for visually expressing topics. Label these new columns "Classification," "Mood Calc," "Mood Probability Calc," "Sentiment Calc," and "Topic Symbols Calc."

In the Classification column, add the following formula to the vertex rows, replacing your_key_here with your own API key:

```
=WEBSERVICE("https://app.viralheat.com/social/api/sentiment?text=
    "&ENCODEURL(LEFT(Vertices[[#This Row],[Tweet]],
    360))&"&api_key=your_key_here&format=xml")
```

> **NOTE**
> If you have an earlier version of Excel than 2013, you will need to install an Excel PowerUp and prefix the WEBSERVICE, ENCODEURL, and FILTERXML functions with pwr.

The formula will send the lesser of all or the first 360 characters of each fan's comments to Viral Heat and populate cells with the results, which you will see appear in XML form. Note that any time the formula changes, the cells will resend requests, which is why you added the empty columns to the left beforehand to avoid that.

Now, add a formula to the Mood Calc column to extract mood from the classification result. The Classification column in these example formulas is AV, and the row is 4:

```
=IF(LEN(AV4)>0,FILTERXML(AV4,"hash/mood"),"")
```

Then add a second formula to the cells in the Mood Probability Calc column to extract the estimated probability that the classification is correct:

```
=IF(LEN(AV4)>0,FILTERXML(AV4,"hash/prob"),"")
```

Add a formula to the cells in the Sentiment Calc column that records the sentiment as positive, negative, or neutral using mood if the probability is beyond a threshold of 65 percent:

```
=IF(LEN(AW4)>0,IF(AX4>=0.65,AW4,"neutral"),"")
```

Finally, copy the cells from the mood and sentiment calculation columns and use Paste Values to write them into the corresponding graph data columns you created earlier.

You have enhanced the fan data with comment sentiment. Now you must decide how to represent it. Color is an ideal choice, but color is currently mapped to topic, and you want to see both topic and sentiment. Shape is not mapped to anything. So far, all the fan nodes have been represented as circles. If you map the shape of the nodes to topic, you can use color to express sentiment.

 TIP When choosing shapes for visualization, use intuitive symbols to make them easier to interpret.

Shapes are best if they are symbolic. If the information represented can be recognized in the form of the shape, it will be easier to interpret. For this data set, an intuitive symbol for players might be their initials or jersey number, and for Drake, something musical. Use the top row added earlier to insert a symbol above each player mention column. You can use the Symbol button on the Insert ribbon in Excel to insert font characters not found on your keyboard, like the musical note shown in Figure 11-15.

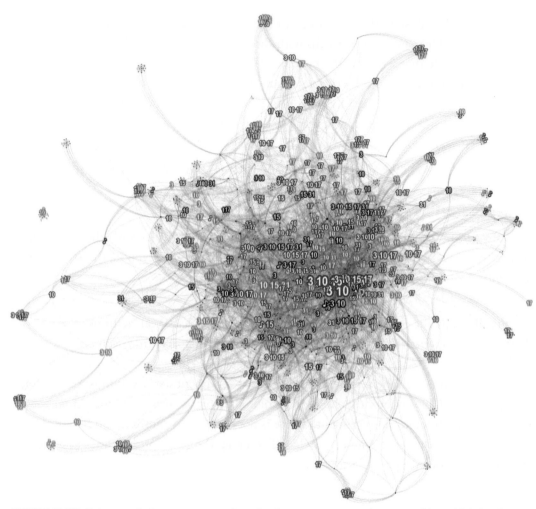

FIGURE 11-15: Using symbols to express topic and color to express sentiment provides a high-level picture of the subject and mood of community chatter. Here, red and black indicate estimated positive and negative comments about Raptor players, indicated by their jersey numbers, and team ambassador Drake, indicated with a musical note.

In the Topic Symbols Calc column, add a formula to the fan rows that concatenates the symbols of any topic mentioned, separated by spaces:

```
=CONCATENATE(IF(AP4,CONCATENATE(AP$1," "),""),IF(AQ4,CONCATENATE(AQ$1,"
    "),""),IF(AR4,CONCATENATE(AR$1," "),""),IF(AS4,CONCATENATE(AS$1,"
    "),""),IF(AT4,CONCATENATE(AT$1," "),""),IF(AU4,
    CONCATENATE(AU$1," "),""))
```

Copy the calculated symbol cells and use Paste Values to insert them into the Topic Symbols column you created earlier. Save the results, and export them in GraphML form.

Import the enhanced graph data into Gephi, and map the color to sentiment. Use a neutral color such as gray for neutral sentiment. Black is a natural choice for negative and will work well with any color you choose for positive. Click the expander at the bottom of the graph view. On the Labels tab, turn on node labels and switch their mapping from the Label data column to the new Topic Symbols column. In the Ranking tab, map the label size to degree.

In the Preview task mode, set the node outlines to zero width so they don't interfere visually with the labels. Choose a condensed font for the labels. Make them white and give them a thick outline of 8.0. Select the label outline color option, which inherits the parent node color. Reduce the edge opacity to a minimal number like 8.0 percent and refresh the view.

As you might expect, the fans in the middle of the graph who comment most often also talk about more of the players. Also notice that in the very tight clusters, the same symbols tend to repeat. They are relatively consistent in topic. The dominance of red across the graph indicates that the mood is more positive than negative, with a strong nucleus of positive sentiment around the most active fans. Interestingly, with the exception of some of the peripheral banter involving Drake, most of the negative sentiment in black is in the center of the fan community. Looking closely, however, you will notice that black is very often surrounded by red, implying heated exchanges.

Symbols and color together make for a powerful combination. This is the picture of social media buzz that this chapter's case study set out to see. Not only are patterns revealed, but enough individual character is expressed that you can spot community conversations that would be interesting to investigate further. What are those seemingly heated comments to the east about Drake about, or those clusters of red and black that did not mention the players or Drake?

Graph visualization and interactive exploration of social media topics and sentiment enables you to take the overall pulse of customer communities, and identify heated discussion around products and initiatives that are worthy of attention. The next section shows how you can use analytics, visualization, and interaction to identify and analyze social groups.

CLIQUES AND OTHER GROUPS

You may remember all too well what a clique is in common terms from your days on the school playground—a tight-knit social group that tends to speak and act as one, always together, and often to the exclusion of others. Perhaps not surprisingly, then, clique detection is often used in social network analysis. In the business world, for example, the presence of a clique may indicate a group with a strong collective perspective that is influenced by strategic direct marketing to key individuals in that group.

In graph terms, a *clique* is defined as a subgraph in which each node connects to each of the other nodes. However, this definition alone is not specific enough to identify a set of communities of interest. For example, technically, two linked nodes form a clique, and one of those nodes and another adjacent node form an overlapping clique. Clearly, identifying trivial relationships of this nature adds little to your understanding. Borrowing from the school playground example, describing each pairing of kids in a group of five as a clique, as well as each combination of three, four, and all five, is not a particularly helpful characterization.

A practical restriction for identifying cliques is that each be a *maximal clique*. A maximal clique is not a subgraph of any other clique, though it may overlap with others. This restriction limits identification to top-level cliques only. Other simple strategies of focusing clique identification may be to specify a minimum size as shown in Figure 11-16, or the neighborhood limits of a node of interest. No matter what the strategy, accurately computing maximal cliques is expensive, so keep in mind that most algorithms use some level of approximation.

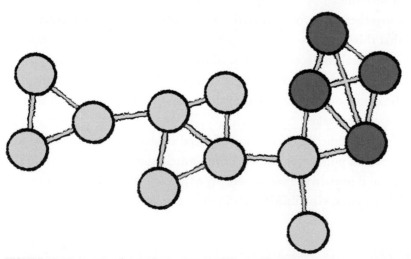

FIGURE 11-16: In a maximal clique, detected here with minimum size 4, every node is connected to every other node, and its entirety is not contained within any larger clique.

Cliques in Social Media

In the Raptors fan page data, all fans are linked to each other if they comment on the same post, so cliques are rampant. Isolating the largest cliques will be a useful constraint. NodeXL includes a method for identifying cliques and, provided they don't overlap, there is a way to bring them into Gephi for visualization. It isn't pretty, but it works.

Return to the NodeXL worksheet where you enhanced the data with topics. In the graph Analysis ribbon group, select Groups ⇨ Group by Motif. Motifs are not relevant here, but what will be relevant are the groups produced. In the options that appear, uncheck the fan and D-connector options, and specify a minimum size of 15 for cliques. The two Group worksheets will be populated with the results. Now comes the tricky part. To get the cliques into Gephi, you will need to transform them from their current form in the Group Vertices worksheet to a new form in the Vertices worksheet, which requires a bit of Excel wizardry.

Start by swapping the order of the Vertex and Group columns on the Group Vertices worksheet. Click the drop-down button on the Vertex column to sort it A to Z so that it can be used for lookup. Switch to the Vertices worksheet and add a column to the right of the graph data. Add a formula to the cells in the new column that will look for the Vertex in the Group worksheet, and populate each cell with the name of the clique group or an empty string if not found:

```
=IFERROR(VLOOKUP(Vertices[[#This Row],[Vertex]],
    GroupVertices[[Vertex]:[Group]],2,FALSE),"")
```

Create a new column in the graph data area of the worksheet and copy from the cells you added in the previous step. Use Paste Values to add a copy of the group references into the new column and label the column Clique.

It would be useful to explore the demographic characteristics of cliques. However, you already looked at gender in the data and determined that women do not often post together, so sex will not be a factor. What about locale? Facebook locale consists of ISO codes for language and country joined by an underscore. To explore language and country separately, extract a new column for each:

```
=IF(LEN(Vertices[[#This Row],[Locale]])>0,
    RIGHT(Vertices[[#This Row],[Locale]],2),"")
```

```
=IF(LEN(Vertices[[#This Row],[Locale]])>0,
    LEFT(Vertices[[#This Row],[Locale]],2),"")
```

Export the enhanced GraphML file and import it into Gephi. In the Partition tab, map the Node color to Clique. Map null (meaning a node that is not part of a clique) to white. Inspect the resulting visualization in the preview mode. As shown in Figure 11-17, the result is arguably beautiful, but is it useful? It's difficult to make sense of cliques in the middle where the nodes are densest. A clique has a very hard-edged definition. It would be ideal if the visual boundaries of the cliques were equally hard-edged.

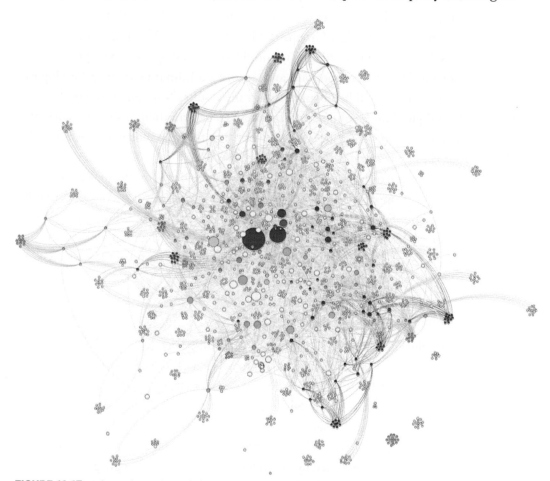

FIGURE 11-17: Using color to identify large cliques here wins points for artistic impression, but it is difficult to see their boundaries of inclusion or understand anything about them.

Community Groups with Convex Hulls

A *convex hull* draws a bounding shape around the edge of a set of nodes to depict it as a group. Gephi includes basic convex hull functionality for those who are up to mastering the finicky workflow.

The first step in generating hulls is to create groups. Back in the Partition tab, underneath the list of colored cliques, you will find a Group button. Before you click it, reset the color of the nodes in the view to gray. Groups will pick up the color of the nodes, and it will be useful in this case to reserve color for other purposes once the hulls are used to indicate cliques. Locate the reset buttons along the left border of the graph view and click to reset color. Then return to the clique partition list and proceed to group them.

Each node in the simplified graph will now represent a clique. Return to the reset buttons and reset size to see them all. Next, select them using the Rectangle Selection tool, and expand them using the context menu. Expanding will break up the groups into member nodes again, but this time with convex hulls drawn around each clique. Now that hulls are serving to cluster nodes, links are adding clutter. Toggle them off at the bottom of the graph pane.

The last thing that doesn't belong in this picture is the largest group, which is not actually a clique. Drag a Clique partition type attribute filter into the Queries pane, and use the context menu to select all groups. Then click to deselect the null group. Click the Filter button to hide everything but the true cliques.

Now that fewer elements are visible, you can use the extra space to further clarify the view. In the Layout tab, choose Force Atlas 2, and select the Prevent Overlap option before proceeding to run it. Even though links are not visible, linked nodes will still be drawn together, putting the most connected nodes in the middle. Use the Ranking tab to increase the size of nodes until they are touching by mapping degree to a range of 10 to 25. Expand the controls at the bottom of the graph pane. Map the labels from the new country column created earlier and make them white. Choose a condensed font and adjust the scale so that the labels fit snugly within their circles.

You will immediately note that the dominant country code is US. This is the Facebook locale that includes English-speaking Canadians, forming the most obvious group of local fans. Make it a relatively neutral color close to gray, appropriate for baseline normal, so that other countries are easier to see.

As shown in Figure 11-18, you can now see the 18 most significant cliques in the sample data. Two clusters of color immediately stand out. One mysterious cluster of dark gray nodes without country labels is found to the south, and to the far north a cluster of red nodes with the country code LT. Smaller clusters of LT exist throughout. LT is the code for Lithuania, home of starting center Jonas Valanciunas. The Lithuanian clique was one of two groups you may have noticed being placed most remotely from other cliques, implying that it is less connected to the others. Social media may be a virtual medium, but clearly there can be a strong ethnic identity to fan cliques.

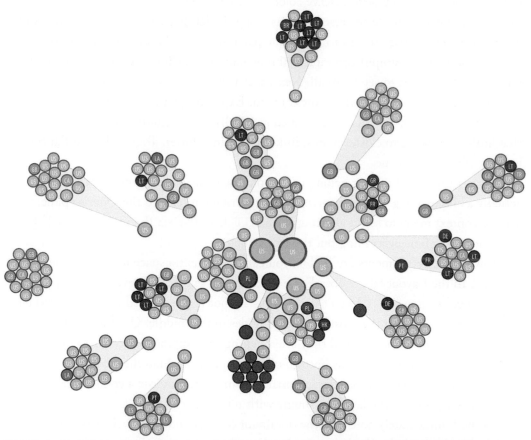

FIGURE 11-18: Using convex hulls to bound nodes and hiding links creates a clear view of groups and identifies key social connectors. Here cliques in Raptors fan data emerge with notable patterns in locale.

Another notable observation is that the orange British fans, coded as GB, are members of more than half of the cliques. Like the green French-Canadian fans marked with CA, they mix freely, but in larger numbers. In fact, in three of those cases, the Brits are primary social connectors linking the cliques to other communities, indicated by their attraction to the center of the graph.

Overall, there is a surprisingly large contingent of Europeans in these cliques, implying that the team has a sizeable following overseas. Cultivating international interest in the NBA has been a priority of the league over the past decade, and the effort has been largely successful. The number of foreign-born players in the league has grown dramatically, and international viewership has grown with it. Here you see a reflection of how social media can extend the reach of a fan base and how the involvement of players born abroad can help to grow strong communities of fans in other countries. Monitoring this over time would provide valuable feedback on the progress of these initiatives and may provide clues as to how to foster growth of those communities.

By applying clique detection and by using grouping with convex hulls and hiding links, a clear picture of social communities and involvement of key social connectors emerges. Hulls provide crisp group boundaries when not obscured by other geometry and leave color for expressing other facets of the data. An additional advantage of convex hulls is that they can indicate membership in more than one group, whereas a simple node color mapping cannot.

Convex hulls have a lot in common with *Venn diagrams*, which also depict overlapping groups. Venn diagrams are useful for summarizing community size and overlap in a simple-to-understand form for executive briefing but, unfortunately, do not scale well to more than three or four communities. The Cytoscape graph tool includes a plug-in for rendering groups in a graph as a Venn diagram for graphic export, but using the plug-in to illustrate topic mentions by fans in this sample data hints at the limitations of this approach. As shown in Figure 11-19, several overlaps are missing. It is interesting, though, to observe that, fittingly, point guard Kyle Lowry, whose job it is to distribute the ball, overlaps the most with other players.

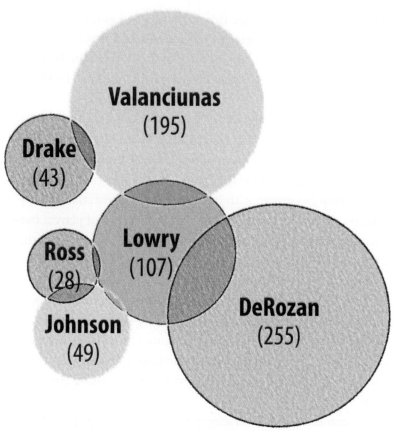

FIGURE 11-19: Venn diagrams provide an intuitive high-level expression of size and overlap for a small number of communities. Here, the Cytoscape Venn plug-in was used to organize fans by topic mentions.

SUMMARY

This chapter has looked at a relatively small sample of Toronto Raptors social media data containing about 1,600 people and 15,000 links. Exploring graph data visually is an ideal way to analyze community, identifying patterns and making observations that would otherwise be very difficult to detect and understand. Once potentially valuable observations are discovered and you now know what to look for, you can design targeted analytics and visualization to confirm those observations across all of the data.

Techniques for community visualization and analysis for much larger graphs is a challenge and has been an intense area of research. Approaches to this problem are covered in Chapter 14 on Big Data, including hierarchical community aggregation and summary visualization techniques.

In community analysis, like the examples in this chapter demonstrate, links very often serve the sole purpose of expressing collective connectedness in the aggregate. It is not important or even feasible using the techniques shown so far to understand the character or direction of links. However, in some data sets, direction is essential. Chapter 12 examines flows, illustrating how you can use graphs to reveal structures and patterns of flow through linked entities or events.

12

FLOWS

Flow visualization can be one of the most intuitive and compelling forms of visual representation of quantitative information. One of the most famous examples is Charles Joseph Minard's chart of Napoleon's disastrous 1812 campaign against Russia. Published in 1869, it showed loss of life as troops marched into battle and later retreated. As shown in Figure 12-1, route data like Minard's or like that used in typical traffic analysis is in most cases not a graph, but the same graphical techniques of line width and layout apply to graph data.

Flow is important in understanding systems and patterns of behavior. Flow visualization can be used to describe the structure and state of a system, such as a supply chain or an economy. It can also be used for displaying transactional events, such as information exchange between computers or money transfers between financial accounts. Flow visualization can also be used to depict "softer" systems such as behavioral models, showing the potential influence of various factors in a past, current, or future outcome, whether that be financial results or the latest sports scores.

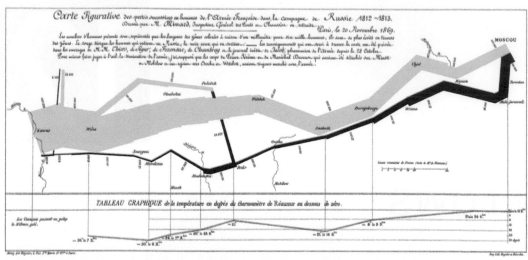

FIGURE 12-1: One of the most highly regarded visualizations of all time is Minard's depiction of Napoleon's ill-fated march on Russia in 1812. The use of route width to indicate volume (here, the size of army as it is decimated) can be applied with equal success to graph visualization.

This chapter describes how you can use graph visualization to reveal structures and patterns of flow between and through nodes using various techniques such as Sankey diagrams, traditional graph layouts with link weight, chord diagrams, and behavioral factor trees. Web-based examples and model code are provided for illustration.

SANKEY DIAGRAMS

Sankey diagrams are an effective way to see volume of flow through a multi-step process or system. In a Sankey diagram, the flows are conventionally laid out left to right, and the width of a link indicates the volume of flow. Incoming links always enter a node on the same side at right angles, and outgoing links exit in the same way on the opposite side. At each side of the node, links are stacked at their point of entry and exit to represent the total incoming and outgoing volume.

Transactional data is often ideally visualized in Sankey form. For example, money flow through various accounts can be represented in this way, showing sources of funding and where the money is going. For a financial crimes investigator, "following the money" is central to the task of identifying the perpetrators of fraud. Similarly, for an economist or business analyst, understanding structures of supply and demand and flow of goods and services can be essential to evaluating and managing financial health.

The flow of information can also be important in some industries, in addition to financial flow. For example, in cyber security, analyzing patterns of data flow can help to spot potentially nefarious activity by computer hackers. Or, in criminal investigations (such as the Enron scandal), the flow of e-mail and phone calls between employees can create a telling story.

Sometimes it's actually the flow of people that is of interest, rather than the flow *between* people. For example, in a sales process, the goal is to persuade people from one purchasing stage to another, with the final goal of sales conversion. Analyzing conversion rates through different sales channels and customer paths can provide valuable insights into which sales tactics are working and which are not. A website, for example, has the distinct advantage of being able to track movement of prospective customers through the site at a detailed level without any investment of effort.

Google Analytics provides a means to track visitors to a website and enables you to define related goals such as visiting a particular page or purchasing, in order to analyze success rates. As shown in Figure 12-2, one of the most useful visualizations available uses an interactive Sankey diagram to show paths that visitors took through the site. The height of each green block here reflects the number of visitors to that page. Gray links to left of each indicate how they arrived there, and links to the right indicate where they went next. Red exit arrows indicate visitors who left the site at that page.

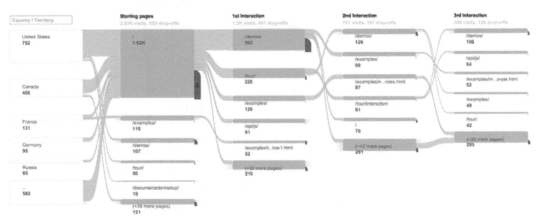

FIGURE 12-2: Google Analytics provides dashboard visualization of visitor flow through a website using an interactive Sankey diagram.

Google Analytics is currently free to use for anyone with a modestly sized website. After a simple setup process, Google Analytics requires only the addition of a few standard lines of JavaScript to each web page to track visits through the site.

> **TIP** Take advantage of free Google Analytics by signing up at www.google.com/ analytics/ to analyze traffic through your website.

One of the interactive features that the Google Analytics visualization includes is the capability to highlight the subset of flow through a particular node, which is one of the more generally useful techniques for any Sankey diagram. For example, as shown in Figure 12-3, clicking on Germany shows lines of flow from that country in a darker blue, while fading the other links.

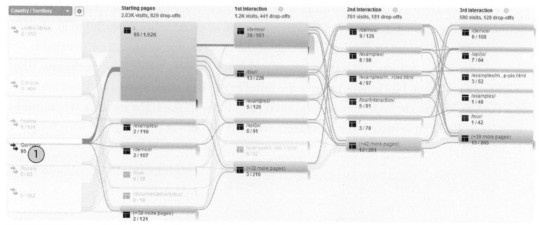

FIGURE 12-3: A useful interactive feature of Sankey diagrams is the capability to highlight the subset of flow through a node—in this case, visitors originating from Germany (1).

Another perfect use case for Sankey diagrams is supply chain management. For example, a manufacturing business must effectively manage the flow of supplies and associated costs to respond to demand and optimize the bottom line. Delays result in lost sales, and oversupply results in stock that does not move or that must be warehoused at a cost. Problems with a supplier may carry on down the chain. For example, delays in the supply of lithium from the Andes may delay battery production in Taiwan, which may lead to delays in meeting demand for the latest smartphone, causing lost sales because some would-be customers chose a more readily available phone.

As an example, Figure 12-4 shows a mock automotive supply chain where raw materials are supplied for parts production, which, in turn, are supplied for assembly. Vehicles are then supplied by the assembly plants to dealers. The width of each link indicates the value of goods being supplied as a measure of volume. The difference in width at each facility indicates value added. Color indicates a problem with the rate of production. Red links indicate a deficit of production against demand, and blue links indicate a surplus, making it easy to trace problems back to their source.

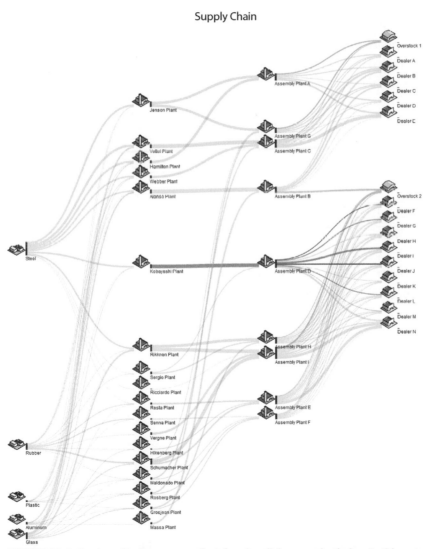

Supply Chain

FIGURE 12-4: Sankey diagrams are perfect for visualizing supply chains. In this automotive example, flow reflects value of goods supplied, and color represents variance from optimal rate of supply.

CONSTRUCTING A SANKEY DIAGRAM

This section steps through the process of coding the supply chain visualization shown in Figure 12-4. To try this yourself, download the example package for this chapter provided with the Supplementary Materials on this book's companion website.

Although it is always more rewarding to use real data when experimenting with visualization, supply chain data is often proprietary and difficult to find. In this case, the data has been handcrafted instead to illustrate how you might approach building a solution for this kind of problem. This example uses version 1.1 of the Aperture JS library, which, in addition to Sankey support, includes icon and layout services that will be useful in this case. As with most graph data, nodes and links are supplied as arrays. Here, JavaScript Object Notation (JSON) form is used:

```
{
    "nodes": [
        {
            "name": "Steel",
            "type": "rawmaterials",
            "id": 100
        },
        {
            "name": "Assembly Plant A",
            "type": "manufacturing",
            "id": 1
        }, ...
    ],
    "links": [
        {
            "sourceId": 100,
            "targetId": 2,
            "value": 145,
            "rate": 0.0
        }, ...
    ]
}
```

Online CSV-to-JSON converters in which you can paste your data and click a
button to transform it are easily found with a quick web search.

Create the Page Structure

Once you have your data file, you are ready to begin coding. If you don't already have
a place in mind to insert your visualization, start by creating the following simple web
page. The following HTML code creates an empty document with a title and some basic
styling, loads the JavaScript dependencies, and, after adding a graph container to the
body, loads the supplychain.js file, which you create next:

```html
<!DOCTYPE html>
<html>
<head>
    <meta charset="utf-8">
    <title>Supply Chain</title>
    <script src="jquery.js"></script>
    <script src="raphael.js"></script>
    <script src="aperture.js"></script>

    <!-- container styling -->
    <style>
        #graph {
            width: 1200px;
            height: 1400px;
            margin: 0 auto 0 auto;
        }
    </style>
</head>
<body>
    <div id="graph"></div>
    <script src="supplychain.js"></script>
</body>
</html>
```

Process and Model the Data

Create a supplychain.js file and open it for editing. Use jQuery to load the JSON file into a JavaScript object. When the callback completes, use Aperture utility functions to process the arrays of nodes and links, and model them for use in your Sankey diagram. The linkNodes function will link them based on their data IDs, and the weightNodes function will calculate and store total flow in and out of each node by summing the value field of each of its links. The layout API will assign a location to each node. Add a call to make the visualization when it completes, using a method that you will define next.

```javascript
jQuery.getJSON("supplychain.json", function(data) {


    // Link the nodes from raw data, and enhance with total flow
    // in and out.
    aperture.graph
        .linkNodes(data.nodes, data.links)
        .weightNodes(data.nodes, {
            flowIn: {linksIn: 'value'},  // record sum value of links in
            flowOut: {linksOut: 'value'} // ... and out, in each node.
        });


    // Use layout to assign nodes a location, and construct the graph.
    aperture.layout.flow(data, function() {
        makeMyGraph(data);
    });
});
```

Visualize the Data

Create the makeMyGraph function you invoked in the previous step after modeling the data. Begin by adding the base plot and a node layer.

```javascript
function makeMyGraph(data) {


    // CREATE THE NODE LINK PLOT
```

```
var graph = new aperture.NodeLink('#graph');

// map from extents of abstract x,y layout to graphical area
graph.map('node-x').from('x')
    .using(new aperture.Scalar('X').mappedTo([100, 1100]))
    .fromRange(data.nodes);
graph.map('node-y').from('y')
    .using(new aperture.Scalar('Y').mappedTo([100, 1300]))
    .fromRange(data.nodes);



// add a node layer
var nodeLayer = graph.addLayer(aperture.NodeLayer);
nodeLayer.all(data.nodes);



//...
```

Next, add the Sankey path layer to draw the links. Map the width from the flow key you created in the data processing stage. Map color and opacity from the rate of supply relative to demand to highlight deficits and surpluses.

```
//...

// CREATE THE LINK REPRESENTATION.
var linkLayer = graph.addLayer( aperture.SankeyPathLayer )
    .mapAll({
        'source-offset' : 5,
        'target-offset' : 43,
        'sankey-anchor' : 'bottom'
    });

// Create a key to map from flow values to link width
var flowKey = new aperture.Scalar('Flow Volume')
    .expand(data.nodes, 'flowIn')
```

```
        .expand(data.nodes, 'flowOut')
        .mappedTo([1,36]);


// map data-driven attributes from link data fields
linkLayer.map('stroke-width').from('value').using(flowKey);
linkLayer.map('source').from('source');
linkLayer.map('target').from('target');



// define range of supply rates to map link color and opacity from
var rates = new aperture.Scalar('Supply (+/-% of Demand)',
      [-20, 20]);


// map rate to red (deficit), grey (on target), blue (surplus) range
linkLayer.map('stroke').from('rate')
    .using(rates.mappedTo(['#e00', '#666', '#08a']));


// map rate data to a range of opacities (less opaque when
// on target).
linkLayer.map('opacity').from('rate')
    .using(rates.mappedTo([0.8, 0.2, 0.8]));



// finally, make a link for each data object
linkLayer.all(data.links, 'id');


//...
```

Now that you have added the links to show flow, create the representation for each facility in the supply chain. Each node will have an icon, a bar at the stem of outgoing flow, and a label. If you are using your own data and have performance information available for each facility, consider adding additional indicators here.

```
//...

// CREATE THE NODE REPRESENTATION.
var iconLayer = nodeLayer.addLayer( aperture.IconLayer )
    .mapAll({
        'x' : -4,
        'width' : 36,
        'height' : 36,
        'anchor-x' : 1,
        'anchor-y' : 1
    });

iconLayer.map('url').from(function() {
    return this.type + '.png';
});



var barLayer = nodeLayer.addLayer( aperture.BarLayer )
    .mapAll({
        'width' : 5,
        'orientation' : 'vertical',
        'fill' : '#666'
    });

barLayer.map('length').from('flowOut')
    .using(flowKey)
    .filter(function(v){return -v;}); // invert direction



var labelLayer = nodeLayer.addLayer(aperture.LabelLayer)
    .mapAll({
        'offset-y' : 8,
```

```
        'font-size' : 12,
        'text-anchor' : 'start'
    });


labelLayer.map('text').from('name');


//...
```

Highlight Flow through a Node

The final step in the construction of this example is to add the interactions for highlighting flow through a node. Create three sets for tracking highlight state: one for the focus node, one for its links, and one for linked nodes. Define mapping filters that apply to members of each set. Finally, add event handlers that add the node, its links, and linked nodes to the highlight sets when hovering over a node, and clear them when leaving. After modifying the sets, redraw the changed nodes and bring them to the front.

After adding the event callbacks, there is one last step to completing your supply chain visualization: call the redraw function to draw it all. You are now ready to try it.

```
    //...

// define sets to track highlight state.
var focusNodes = new aperture.Set('id');
var highlightedNodes = new aperture.Set('id');
var highlightedLinks = new aperture.Set('id');

// alter attributes when part of highlight sets
barLayer.map('fill').filter(focusNodes.constant('black'));
linkLayer.map('opacity').filter(highlightedLinks.constant(1.0));
labelLayer.map('font-weight').filter(focusNodes.constant('bold'));
labelLayer.map('font-outline').filter(focusNodes.constant
    ('#F0EFE7'));

// define three planes based on highlight state.
```

```
nodeLayer.map('plane').asValue('labeled')
    .filter(highlightedNodes.constant('highlight'))
    .filter(focusNodes.constant('focus'));

// highlight node, links and linked nodes when hovering over a node
nodeLayer.on('mouseover', function(event) {
    if (focusNodes.add(event.data.id)) {
        var changedNodes = [highlightedNodes.add(event.data.id)];
        var changedLinks= [];
        var links = event.data.linksIn.concat(event.data.linksOut);

        // Add to the highlight set.
        aperture.util.forEach(links, function(link) {
            changedNodes.push(highlightedNodes.add(link.other));
            changedLinks.push(highlightedLinks.add(link,id));
        },this);

        // redraw changed then bring the highlighted nodes to front.
        nodeLayer.all().where('id', changedNodes)
            .and(linkLayer.all().where('id', changedLinks))
            .redraw()
            .toFront(['labeled', 'highlight', 'focus']);
    }
});

// clear when leaving the node
nodeLayer.on('mouseout', function(event) {
    if (focusNodes.clear()) {
        nodeLayer.all().where('id', highlightedNodes.clear())
            .and(linkLayer.all().where('id',
                highlightedLinks.clear()))
            .redraw()
            .toFront('labeled');
```

```
        }
    });
```

```
    // finally, draw everything!
    graph.all().redraw();
```

```
}
```

As shown in Figure 12-5, hovering over a node should now highlight flow through that node.

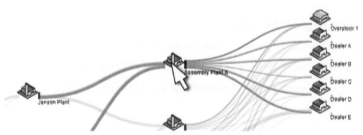

FIGURE 12-5: Hovering over a facility in the supply chain highlights flow through that node.

COMMUNITY LAYOUTS WITH FLOW

In certain cases, it may be desirable to lay out nodes in a more conventional fashion. If progression and clarity of flow is less important than seeing clusters of nodes with a general sense of volume around them, especially if the number of nodes is low, you can apply organic layouts. Figure 12-6 shows how the same supply chain example looks with an organic layout.

Supply Chain

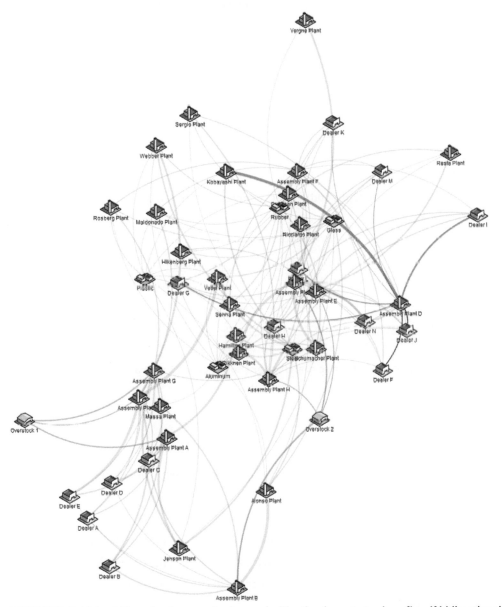

FIGURE 12-6: Link width and color can also be used with other layouts to show flow if bidirectional or the progression of flow is less important than node location.

You can make the following changes to the previous example to use an organic layout as shown in Figure 12-6. First, replace the Sankey layer with a link layer, but keep the same data mappings. Replace this:

```
var linkLayer = graph.addLayer( aperture.SankeyPathLayer )
    .mapAll({
        'source-offset' : 5,
        'target-offset' : 43,
        'sankey-anchor' : 'bottom'
    });
```

with the following:

```
var linkLayer = graph.addLayer( aperture.LinkLayer )
    .mapAll({
        'source-offset' : 24,
        'target-offset' : 24,
        'link-style' : 'arc'
    });
```

Next, remove the custom icon anchor settings, restoring them to the center of the node:

```
var iconLayer = nodeLayer.addLayer( aperture.IconLayer )
    .mapAll({
        'x' : -4,
        'width' : 36,
        'height' : 36,
        'anchor-x' : 1, // REMOVE THIS LINE AND THE NEXT!!
        'anchor-y' : 1
    });
```

Remove the BarLayer altogether. Then remove the anchor on the label so that it, too, is centered, but move it down further underneath the icon. Change these label mappings:

```
var labelLayer = nodeLayer.addLayer(aperture.LabelLayer)
    .mapAll({
        'offset-y' : 8,
        'font-size' : 12,
```

```
            'text-anchor' : 'start'
        });
```

to the following:

```
    var labelLayer = nodeLayer.addLayer(aperture.LabelLayer)
        .mapAll({
            'offset-y' : 24,
            'font-size' : 12
        });
```

Lastly, modify the layout call from flow:

```
    aperture.layout.flow(data, function() {
        makeMyGraph(data);
    });
```

To use the organic layout instead:

```
    aperture.layout.organic(data, function() {
        makeMyGraph(data);
    });
```

When the modified code is run, you should see the visualization shown in Figure 12-6. Note that organic layout has a degree of variability, so the node locations will not be exactly the same in yours.

CHORD DIAGRAMS

Chord diagrams are an effective method of visualizing reciprocal flow between entities. In a chord diagram, entities are arranged in a circle, and similar to a Sankey diagram, lines of flow linking entities are arranged side by side at their origin and destination with thickness indicating the volume of flow. What differs is that the lines are bidirectional, with varying widths on either end indicating the volume flowing in either direction. Chord diagrams are a good choice when flow is primarily bidirectional. You must be able to see flow between but not *through* entities.

One common use case for chord diagrams is to visualize exchange of goods. Figure 12-7 shows total trade between countries valued in U.S. dollars for the year 2010. The chord width as it touches each country represents outgoing flow of goods from country of origin, so the correct way to read direction of flow is inward from the perimeter rather than outward, like two arrows pointing at each other. The chord color is mapped to the country with greater exports of the two, indicating the dominant direction of flow of goods.

Global Trade Flow, 2010 ($USD)

FIGURE 12-7: Chord diagrams show reciprocal flow between entities. Here, all reported trade of goods between countries is represented by width of link at the exporting country. Color indicates the country with greater exports.

Data courtesy of DESA/UNSD, United Nations Comtrade database.

Countries in this example are arranged around the circle in order of geospatial orientation relative to the middle of the Atlantic Ocean, similar to the way you would view them on a map. Each country is then assigned a unique color, stepping through the full 360 degrees of the color wheel in equal increments going around the circle. The result is that countries that are physically closer to each other tend to have colors that are more similar. Because cost of transportation is a significant factor in trade, you would expect countries that are physically closer to exchange more goods. By arranging and coloring countries in this way, you can more clearly see patterns and anomalies in that regard.

Because the color of each chord indicates the dominant direction of flow, you can easily spot net exporters and net importers. Saudi Arabia, China, and the Netherlands, for example, have relatively uniformly colored chords, indicating they are net exporters, whereas the United States, Britain, and France are clearly net importers.

Patterns in the curvature of chords also tell a story. Germany is linked to many countries, but chords connecting them tend to bend more quickly, revealing how much of German trade is within Europe. No wonder, then, that Germany has such a vested interest in the economic health of the European Union (EU). By contrast, trade lines from the United States more often cross the circle to farther countries, implying higher transportation costs and, by extension, greater sensitivity to the price of oil, as well as the political and economic stability of oil-producing nations.

The relative distribution of chords within each exporter reveals patterns of economic dependency. Although Germany may be relatively dependent on export within the EU, look at how heavily the economies of Canada and Mexico rely on sales in the neighboring United States alone. Similarly, but to a lesser degree, notice how Australia relies on exports to nearby China, Japan, and South Korea, which are themselves net exporters, typically of manufactured goods. Interestingly, Canada, Mexico, and Australia have strong resource economies, implying that geographic proximity seems to be of greater advantage for sale of raw materials than it is for other goods and that, as a result, resource economies tend to be more exclusively reliant on the economic health of nearby importers.

CONSTRUCTING A CHORD DIAGRAM

Chord diagrams are a relatively specialized breed of chart. You will find most are built with the Scalable Vector Graphics (SVG) based JavaScript library d3.js. In this section, you find step-by-step instructions for coding the global trade visualization shown in Figure 12-7 using d3.js, which you can easily adapt to your own data and embed in your own web app.

Prepare the Data

Yearly import and export trade data is available for all reporting countries from the U.N., subject to availability and usage restrictions. Data available includes detailed statistics by classification of goods. This example uses the 2010 reported imports only for each of the 25 high gross domestic product (GDP) countries selected, which is recommended over the mirror statistics reported by the exporting country.

NOTE

Data for this example was obtained online from the DESA/UNSD, United Nations Comtrade database at `comtrade.un.org`, which makes data freely available for personal use or limited publications like this one. If you intend to use data from Comtrade, be sure you read its policy document first to understand usage and re-dissemination restrictions.

Locate the imports.csv data file in the example materials you downloaded from the Supplementary Materials provided on this book's companion website for this chapter. Each record in the data contains a reporting country and the partner country where the goods came from. The value column indicates the total value of goods in U.S. dollars.

```
Reporter,Partner,Value
36,36,872953626
36,56,1390394950
36,76,680796081
36,124,1561155248
...
```

Note that some countries report re-imports to themselves, which you will likely want to ignore. More obviously, countries in this data are represented by what looks like ISO 3166 numeric country codes. Because you want to not only label countries in the visualization but also arrange them according to location, you must merge in country detail data. That data is in the countries.csv file.

```
ISOCC2,ISOCC3,ISONo,CountryName,ContinentCode,Continent,Latitude,
    Longitude
AD,AND,20,Andorra,EU,Europe,42.5,1.6
```

```
AE,ARE,784,United Arab Emirates,AS,Asia,24,54
AF,AFG,4,Afghanistan,AS,Asia,33,65
AG,ATG,28,Antigua and Barbuda,NA,Americas,17.05,-61.8
AI,AIA,660,Anguilla,NA,Americas,18.25,-63.1667
...
```

Create the Page Structure

With the two data files and the d3.min.js library file, you are ready to begin coding. Start with a simple container page. The following index.html page creates an empty page with a title and some basic styling, loads d3.js, and loads a JavaScript file named worldtrade.js where you will put your code:

```html
<!DOCTYPE html>
<html>
<head>
    <meta charset="utf-8">
    <title>Global Trade Flow</title>
    <script src="d3.min.js"></script>

    <!-- container styling -->
    <style>
        body {
            margin: 1em auto 4em auto;
            position: relative;
            width: 720px;
        }
        h1 {
            font: 30px Myriad Pro;
```

```
                font-weight: normal;
                text-align: center;
            }
        </style>
    </head>

    <body>
        <h1>Global Trade Flow, 2010 ($USD)</h1>
        <script src="worldtrade.js"></script>
    </body>
</html>
```

You will come back to this page later to add styles for the visualization you are about to make. Create the worldtrade.js file and open it for editing. d3.js includes a basic utility function for reading from CSV files using asynchronous Ajax requests. A supplied callback is invoked on completion. When the first file completes, load the second, and when that completes, invoke your main processing function with both results.

```
// worldtrade.js
d3.csv('imports.csv', function(imports) {
    d3.csv('countries.csv', function(countries) {
        onLoad(imports, countries);
    });
});

function onLoad(imports, countries) {
    // [TO DO: process data here]
}
```

Process and Model the Data

The first processing step is to merge the country and import data and sort the countries geographically. Start by creating a function to reduce the list of countries to only those referenced in the import data:

```
function reportingCountries(imports, allCountries) {
```

```
        var i;
        var row;
        var country;
        var countryMap= {};
        var countries= [];

        // build a map of all countries by code
        for (i=0; i<allCountries.length; i++) {
            row = allCountries[i];
            countryMap[row.ISONo] = row;
        }

        // then form a list of only those countries in the data
        for (i=0; i<imports.length; i++) {
            row = imports[i];

            // (data is grouped by reporter so watch for a change)
            if (country !== row.Reporter) {
                country = row.Reporter;

                countries.push(countryMap[row.Reporter]);
            }
        }

        return countries;
}
```

Next, create a function to sort the countries by angle of direction from 40 degrees latitude and −40 degrees longitude, which is roughly in the middle of the Atlantic Ocean. Here, the country records are enhanced in place with an extra directional member property for sorting:

```
function sortCountries(countries) {

    var i;
    var row;

    // for each country...
    for (i=0; i<countries.length; i++) {
        row = countries[i];

        // store clockwise direction from middle of atlantic (40,-40)
        row.ClockwiseDirection = Math.PI*0.5 -
            Math.atan2(Number(row.Latitude)-40, Number(row.Longitude)
                +40);

        // make sure angles are positive
        if (row.ClockwiseDirection < 0) {
            row.ClockwiseDirection += Math.PI*2.0;
        }
    }

    // finally sort countries by clockwise direction from middle of ocean
    countries.sort(function(a,b) {
        return a.ClockwiseDirection - b.ClockwiseDirection;
    });

    return countries;
}
```

Now that you have functions to prepare the list of countries, it's time to add a function to process the import records and put them in the right form. d3.js requires that chord data be supplied in matrix form—a stripped-down array of arrays of numbers. The matrix cannot include anything but numbers, and no numbers can be missing. To ensure that the matrix will be valid, write a function to create the matrix and fill it first with zeros:

```
function initMatrix(size) {

    var i,j;
    var matrix= [];
    var row;

    matrix.length = size;

    for (i=0; i<size; i++) {
        row = matrix[i] = [];

        row.length = size;

        for (j=0; j<size; j++) {
            row[j] = 0;
        }
    }

    return matrix;
}
```

Next, define the function that will create the matrix by calling your initialization function and populating it with data. Remember to skip re-imports from the originating country to avoid extra noise in the data.

```
function createMatrix(imports, countries) {

    var matrix = initMatrix(countries.length);

    var i;
    var index= {};
```

```
    for (i=0; i<countries.length; i++) {
        index[countries[i].ISONo] = i;
    }

    var row;
    var irow, icol;

    // process the data
    for (i=0; i<imports.length; i++) {
        row = imports[i];

        icol = index[row.Reporter];
        irow = index[row.Partner];

        // skip re-imports
        if (irow != icol) {
            matrix[irow][icol]= Number(row.Value);
        }
    }

    return matrix;
}
```

Visualize the Data

Now that all of the data processing functions are defined, it's time to put them together
in the onLoad function you defined earlier and create a function to visualize the data.

```
function onLoad(imports, countries) {

    // pare down the countries to import reporters only
    // and sort them radially based on geography
    countries = sortCountries(reportingCountries(imports, countries));
```

```
    // reformat imports into a matrix of data
    imports = createMatrix(imports, countries);



    // build the visualization
    visualize(imports, countries);
}


function visualize(matrix, countries) {
    // [TO DO: construct the visualization!]
}
```

The first step in constructing the chord visualization is to add an SVG element to the DOM with a root group anchored at the center. In this simple web page example, the SVG element is appended directly to the body. The next step is to compute the chord layout. Layouts encapsulate much of the complex form-specific graphical construction. Sorting the exports for each country and layering chords in order of size will provide some additional clarity.

```
function visualize(imports, countries) {

    var width = 720,
        height = 720;

    // Construct an svg element with a root group anchored in the center
    var svg = d3.select('body').append('svg')
        .attr('width', width)
        .attr('height', height)
        .append('g')
            .attr('id', 'circle')
            .attr('transform', 'translate(' + width/2 + ',' + height/2
                + ')');



    // Compute the chord layout from the matrix
```

```
var layout = d3.layout.chord()
    .padding(.04)
    .sortSubgroups(d3.descending) // clockwise
    .sortChords(d3.ascending)     // layer-wise
    .matrix(imports);

// ....


}
```

NOTE

The grammar of graphical construction in `d3.js` is based on SVG. Creating new visualizations using `d3.js` requires a reasonably solid understanding of the SVG standard. SVG is a low-level graphics format that takes some time to learn. You will find that you can often get by with minor modifications to the plentiful examples provided at `d3js.org`, but if you are planning to use `d3.js` more extensively in the long run, it is worth the investment to learn SVG.

Now you are ready to begin creating the graphical elements. Start by creating the arcs for each country around the perimeter of the circle. Create an SVG group to parent them using the country groups produced by the layout data.

```
// ....

var chord;


// Add a group per country. On hover add the fade class to
// other chords
var group = svg.selectAll('.group').data(layout.groups).enter()
    .append('g').attr('class', 'group').on('mouseover',
        function mouseover(d, i) {
            chord.classed('fade', function(p) {
                return p.source.index != i && p.target.index != i;
            });
```

```
        });



        // Arcs will step through color spectrum...
        var startHue = 180,
            hueStep = 360 / countries.length;
        var radius = Math.min(width, height)/2 - 10,
            innerRadius = radius - 24;


        function countryColor(i, l) {
            return d3.hsl(startHue - i*hueStep,.7, l||.5).rgb().toString();
        }


        // Add the country arcs.
        var groupPath = group.append('path').attr('id', function(d, i) {
            return 'group' + i;
        }).attr('d', d3.svg.arc().innerRadius(innerRadius).outerRadius
              (radius))
            // Fill with unique hue.
            .style('fill', function(d, i) {
                return countryColor(i);
            })
            // Outline with darker version of fill.
            .style('stroke', function(d, i) {
                return countryColor(i, 0.33);
            });


    // ...
```

Assign a color to each country by circling a full 360 degrees around the color wheel in equal steps, as shown in Figure 12-8.

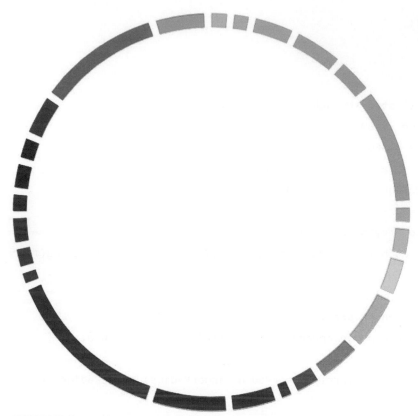

FIGURE 12-8: Arcs for each country step are assigned a hue by circling the color wheel.

Add a label for each country to follow the arc path. For countries with limited display space, use an ISO symbol instead of the full name:

```
// ...

// LABELS
var labelXOffset = 3,
    labelYOffset = 15;

// Add a label for each country...
var groupText = group.append('text')
    .attr('x', labelXOffset)
    .attr('dy', labelYOffset);
```

```
// ...tailoring arc of text to available space.
groupText.append('textPath').attr('xlink:href', function(d, i) {
    return '#group' + i;
}).text(function(d, i) {
    return d.value > 300e9? countries[i].CountryName :
        d.value > 100e9? countries[i].ISOCC3 :
        d.value > 50e9? countries[i].ISOCC2 : '';
});


// ...
```

Next, add the chords. Use the color of the source country and a darker version of the same for the outline color. The layout class will supply the complex path geometry.

```
// ...

// Add the chords, coloring by source country
chord = svg.selectAll('.chord').data(layout.chords).enter()
    .append('path').attr('class', 'chord')
        .attr('d', d3.svg.chord().radius(innerRadius))
        .style('fill', function(d) {
            return countryColor(d.source.index);
        })
        .style('stroke', function(d) {
            return countryColor(d.source.index, 0.25);
        });


// ...
```

Before displaying, add some CSS styling to index.html. Reduce the opacity of the country arcs and assign the font for the labels. Specify the fill and outline stroke for the chords just added.

```
<!-- D3 styling -->
<style>
    .group path {
        fill-opacity: .5;
```

```
  }
svg {
    font: 11px Myriad Pro;
}
.chord {
    fill-opacity: .9;
}
path.chord {
    stroke: #000;
    stroke-width: .25px;
}
```

Interactive Details on Demand

The resulting visualization should now look exactly like the trade diagram represented in Figure 12-7. As a final step, add a few basic interactions. Before returning to worldtrade.js, add a style to index.html for a circle that will not be visible but that, when hovered over, will hide any contained path with the fade CSS class applied.

```
#circle circle {
    fill: none;
    pointer-events: all;
}
#circle:hover path.fade {
    display: none;
}
</style>
```

Insert the circle underneath the chord diagram and add the titles to the arcs and chords to display quantitative values in a tooltip on hover, as shown in Figure 12-9.

```
function visualize(imports, countries) {


    // ...
```

```
// INTERACTIONS
var formatValue = d3.format('$,f')


// Add an invisible circle underneath for hover events to
// filter chords
svg.insert('circle', ':first-child').attr('r', radius);


// Add a mouseover title for each group.
group.append('title').text(
    function(d, i) {
        return countries[i].CountryName + ': ' +
            formatValue(d.value)
        + ' in imports';
    });


// Add a mouseover title for each chord.
chord.append('title').text(
    function(d) {
        return countries[d.source.index].CountryName + ' → '
            + countries[d.target.index].CountryName + ': '
            + formatValue(d.source.value) + '\n'
            + countries[d.target.index].CountryName + ' → '
            + countries[d.source.index].CountryName + ': '
            + formatValue(d.target.value);
    });
}
```

You now have an interactive chord diagram of flow between countries, easily integrated into any web page. An additional feature to consider would be an option to visualize change in flow from a previous point in time. An effective approach would be to map percentage change in export values for each country arc and percentage change in total flow for each chord to a new color ramp. An intuitive color ramp for change uses red for decrease, green for increase, and a neutral gray for no change.

Global Trade Flow, 2010 ($USD)

China → United States: $383,000,000,000
United States → China: $103,000,000,000

FIGURE 12-9: Hovering over a country filters out chords that do not involve that country. Moving the mouse to a single chord shows a tooltip summary of trade flowing in each direction.

BEHAVIORAL FACTOR TREE

Sankeys and chord diagrams are good at showing volumes of flow through or between nodes of a graph. But what if your data has a natural directional flow and observables at each node but does not have volume? In some cases, volume data might simply not be collected and available. In other cases, the issue might be inherent to the nature of the data. For example, a typical financial or economic model used for forecasting and risk management will include many factors that influence an outcome, but these relationships are about complex transitive effects, not simply quantified transactions.

When behaviors are involved and the relationship between nodes cannot be properly expressed with one or two simple measures, relationships can often be understood through correlation of linked behaviors if arranged in a factor tree and made visible through the use of time series.

You may remember factor trees from grade school math. As shown in Figure 12-10, a *factor tree* breaks down a number successively into constituent factors and links them with lines. A *behavioral factor tree* uses the same structural approach but describes complex relationships of influence instead of simple multiplications. This technique for showing linked visible behaviors is unique, specific, and useful enough to give it a name to refer to.

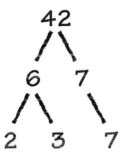

FIGURE 12-10: A traditional factor tree like the one shown here is used in teaching mathematics to show how factors combine hierarchically to produce a result.

Behavioral factor trees are particularly effective for understanding models that can otherwise suffer from lack of transparency. Models are used to explain and often project behavior. Models that are not transparent tend to suffer from the "black box" problem. Like the number 42, which is the answer to life, the universe, and everything in *Hitchhiker's Guide to the Galaxy* by Douglas Adams (New York: Del Rey, 1995), a simple summary often fails to offer enough explanation and requires an inordinate amount of trust on behalf of the analyst—which is not always warranted.

Figure 12-11 shows how a behavioral factor tree can be used to understand potential contributing factors in an economic model when drilling down on an indicator. Common points of inflection, patterns, and trends in the time series over multiple scenarios offer information as to the nature and degree of influence, as well as how they combine to effect an ultimate outcome.

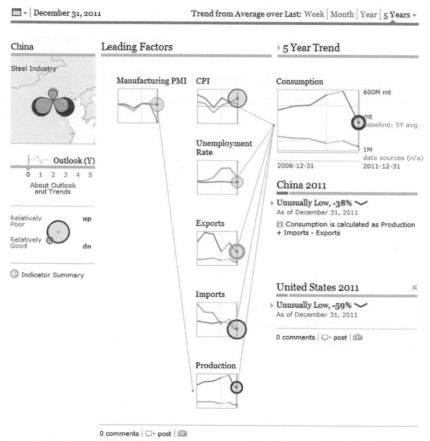

FIGURE 12-11: A behavioral factor tree shows the complex effects of influencing factors in an outcome through the use of links and correlation. Here, various factors driving consumption in an economic model are shown, revealing common inflection points and trends in associated behaviors.

SUMMARY

This chapter described how specific techniques like Sankey diagrams, chord diagrams, and traditional graph visualization can use links to communicate flow of goods, money, information, or other data. Model code examples were provided with detailed step-by-step instructions for use of each technique. Finally, behavioral factor trees were illustrated as a means of visualizing the complex flow of influence, as well as observed or projected effects in a model.

Chapter 13 looks at visualization of physical networks, some of which also involve flow. The importance of pre-existing, meaningful node locations in physical networks provides unique challenges for graph visualization.

13

SPATIAL NETWORKS

Spatial networks are a unique form of graph. Unlike in community analysis, where layout is instrumental in revealing how nodes are connected, nodes in a spatial network have pre-existing physical characteristics that are preserved, relying on link visualization alone to convey connections.

Spatial networks occur in nature, and graphs can be useful in understanding complex networks of this kind. Neuroscientists use graph visualization and analysis to learn more about how our brains are wired. In the business world, however, spatial networks are often equated with infrastructure. For example, supply chains have a spatial component that may be highly relevant to supply optimization. Oil pipelines, electrical power networks, transportation infrastructure, and computer networks are a few of the many other examples of spatial networks where graph visualization and analysis are of value.

Seeing how elements are connected physically and logically provides insight into the structure of a system. It also provides important context in understanding the health and performance of a system, the impact of failures, and how to plan for and mitigate them.

System routes and flows are often of central interest in spatial networks. One of the primary challenges of visualizing spatial networks is the limited number of links that can be successfully displayed at once. Links that cross each other or other nodes in their path introduce perceptual confusion. So, when node locations are fixed and cannot be arranged to mitigate this, connections can quickly become difficult to follow. This can be a significant issue, given that link visualization is critical to conveying a spatial network.

This chapter discusses strategies for effective visualization of spatial networks, including route aggregation, schematic representations, grouping of small worlds, and alternative representations for links.

SCHEMATIC LAYOUT

When Harry Beck began working for London Transport as a young draftsman in the 1920s, the London Underground was in a state of rapid evolution. Previously independently operated underground railway lines were in the process of integration, and lines were being extended further into the suburbs of the city.

It was only as recent as 1908 that the railway companies had coordinated the publication of a single integrated map of the London Underground. Ongoing integration and expansion meant that the map was subject to regular revision. As the system became more complex, creating an easily navigated map was becoming an increasing challenge. Not only was more information being continually added, but some downtown areas were also exceptionally dense where formerly competing railways overlapped, while the system extended ever further into the suburbs where stops were farther apart. Fitting everything into a legible pocket-sized map was becoming difficult.

It was not part of Beck's job description to make maps. He was an engineer working in the signals department, not a cartographer. However, as an engineer, he would have been familiar with schematic diagrams and the benefits of abstracting the representation of physical systems. He had an inspired idea about how to solve the map problem. He set about crafting it in his spare time and presenting it to his employer.

In 1933, with the still tentative support of the London Underground, Beck introduced a schematic variation of the "tube" map that would be quickly popularized into one of the most iconic symbols of London, and that would set the course for many future transit system maps to come.

Beck's map maintained a spatial layout, but constrained lines to cardinal and ordinal directions, and spaced train stops evenly so that station names were easily read. Lines were shortened to be just long enough to fit all of the stops comfortably. The River Thames was the only aboveground geographic landmark that remained, but it was wisely chosen, serving as a key reference point for the position and scale of the entire network.

Using the same principles, Figures 13-1 and 13-2 illustrate the difference between a geospatially accurate and schematic map for the fictional city of Lords. Both maps are printed at the same size, yet the schematic map is much easier to read. The introduction of this approach in the 1930s saw the same effect.

FIGURE 13-1: Prior to H. C. Beck's reinvention of the London Underground map, subway networks were drawn with geospatial accuracy. However, as the size of networks increased, it became difficult to provide all of the information in legible form, as illustrated in the fictional map shown here.

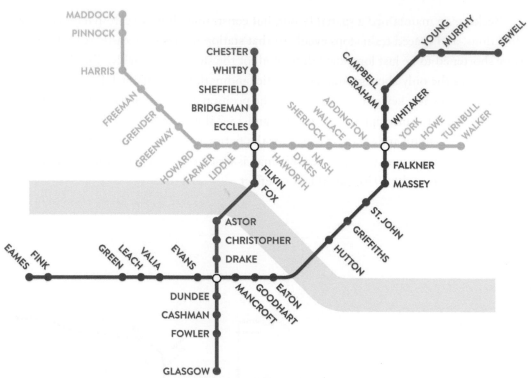

FIGURE 13-2: The same fictional network mapped in Figure 13-1 is shown here using a schematic approach. Geospatial accuracy is traded for clear communication of stops and logical physical relationships.

The lesson of Beck's map was that exact spatial locations in a network are often less important than spatial *relationships* and that some flexibility in the location of nodes and links can greatly improve legibility. The approach also serves to reinforce a universal principle of visualization, which is to make sure that every bit of ink is adding clarity to the essence of information being sought and to remove all else.

What Beck realized is that riders only need to know landmark station names, as well as the name and direction of the lines they are taking in order to navigate underground. Geographic context was useful for understanding where to get on and off but impractical for a pocket-sized map and not needed once traveling on the system. By removing all but one reference to what was above ground (other than what was communicated by station names), Beck was able to maximize the clarity of what was below ground.

The decision as to what adds clarity and what detracts from it is not always easy, however. Beck continued to battle against movements to revert key aspects of his design, some successful and some not, until parting ways with the department in 1959. Looking back from a twenty-first century perspective, with all the benefits of precise modern printing techniques, you might wonder whether Beck's design would benefit from a few additional aboveground landmarks as reference points. However, the fundamental principles behind the schematic approach to spatial layout remain timeless.

A Modern Application

Many of the best schematic spatial layouts are fixed and manually authored, like the London Underground. For a network of your own that is relatively static and that you want to revisit frequently, this is a practical approach. However, when you are working quickly to assemble a visualization of new data, you can apply techniques to achieve some of the same results. For example, the chord diagram of global trade flow in Chapter 12, "Flows," takes a schematic approach to country layout by arranging them around the circle by geographic orientation (see Figure 12-7). The following example uses a similar data set, this time with U.S. interstate transport of goods measured by value.

A chord diagram is an option you might consider here as well. However, there is one significant difference between the nodes in this network versus the previous one. In the global data, a ring is a reasonable approximation of spatial relationships between the countries involved, whereas here it is not. There is no way to keep neighboring interior states from ending up at opposite sides of the circle. Introducing confusion into spatial relationships (which have a natural correlation with transportation) will corrupt a clear view of patterns of transport flow across the country. Finding a means of maintaining approximate geographic location will give truer shape to the data.

The interstate transport data here was made available by the U.S. Department of Transportation's Bureau of Transportation Statistics (BTS). The BTS maintains statistics for all modes of transportation, much of which is updated continuously. This particular data set was obtained from the results of a detailed 1997 Commodity Flow Survey (CFS), and subsequently enhanced with state locations.

NOTE Raw data used for this example, along with a wide variety of other transportation-related data, is available for download from the Bureau of Transportation at http://transtats.bts.gov.

Flow of transport was aggregated across all commodities by value of shipments out, in, and within for each state, measured in millions of U.S. dollars. Note that state statistics include some zeros, indicating gaps in reporting, so caution should be taken in interpreting the results.

```
id,state,latitude,longitude,out($M),in($M),within($M)
AL,Alabama,32.799,-86.8073,0,29048,0
AK,Alaska,61.385,-152.2683,0,4644,0
AZ,Arizona,33.7712,-111.3877,63879,72882,37161
AR,Arkansas,34.9513,-92.3809,0,21455,0
CA,California,36.17,-119.7462,484287,307532,1930
...
```

States form the nodes in this graph, and links represent the value of shipments between states, in millions of dollars.

```
origin,destination,value
CA,AL,2633
CO,AL,277
CT,AL,124
FL,AL,1294
GA,AL,5380
IL,AL,1346
...
```

A relatively simple method of importing comma-separated value (CSV) node and link data into Gephi is to format it as a GDF file. A GDF file is a CSV file with some special formatting of the column headers and with node and link data sections within the same file.

Copy the node data into a new file, and start by inserting the nodedef> tag and changing the name of the state id column to name so that Gephi recognizes it as the node identity column. Next, assign a type to each column: VARCHAR for text and DOUBLE for numbers. Append the link data below the node data and repeat a similar process, beginning with an edgedef> tag. Change the name of the value column to weight so that Gephi will know to map it to link width. Save it as a file with a GDF extension, like interstate-transport-1997.gdf. The following snippet shows how to do this:

```
nodedef>name VARCHAR,state VARCHAR,latitude DOUBLE,longitude DOUBLE,out
```

```
        DOUBLE,in DOUBLE,within DOUBLE
AL,Alabama,32.799,-86.8073,0,29048,0
AK,Alaska,61.385,-152.2683,0,4644,0
AZ,Arizona,33.7712,-111.3877,63879,72882,37161
AR,Arkansas,34.9513,-92.3809,0,21455,0
CA,California,36.17,-119.7462,484287,307532,1930
...
edgedef>origin VARCHAR,destination VARCHAR,weight DOUBLE
CA,AL,2633
CO,AL,277
CT,AL,124
FL,AL,1294
GA,AL,5380
IL,AL,1346
...
```

Open the new file in Gephi, being sure to flag it as a directed graph. Once the graph data file is opened, the first step is to arrange the states according to location. Choose the Geo Layout and, using the default options, click Run to arrange the nodes geographically. Next, use the Ranking tab to map the value of incoming shipments to node size, and do the same for links. Make the nodes large enough to comfortably accommodate labels. Then, using the label editing pane at the bottom of the graph pane, turn on the two-letter state code labels, and bind their size to the size of the node.

NOTE

GeoLayout is a Gephi plug-in. If you have not already installed the plug-in, you will need to save your work and do so now.

In the Preview task mode, hide nodes by setting their opacity to zero, and turn on node labels, giving them a white outline. Bump up the maximum width of links to 20.0, and change their color to be universally gray, rather than mixing the colors of the nodes. Make them semi-transparent and refresh the view. You will now be looking at a view of transport volume between states. The fact that each state is connected to almost every other state, however, is making it difficult to understand much about the flow, especially for midsize to small states. An analytic would be useful here.

Return to the Overview task mode and, in the Statistics pane, run the Modularity algorithm to group states into clusters where there is more localized flow. Experiment with the settings until you get four to six clusters. Any more than that will be too localized to be interesting, and any less will be too global. Using the Partition tab, assign the modularity class of each node to color. Return to the Preview task mode to view the result, as shown in Figure 13-3.

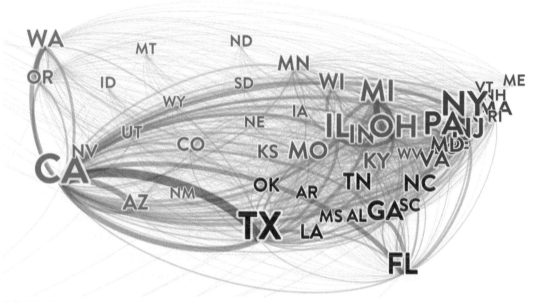

FIGURE 13-3: Mapping size to value of shipments and using a modularity analytic identifies regions of flow and a few broad patterns. However, overlapping nodes make it difficult to see links.

Notice that the modularity clusters (which are computed based solely on the topology of flow between nodes) map nicely into geospatial regions. In fact, not only do the clusters have pure spatial boundaries, they are almost exactly the same as the four official national regions defined by the United States Census Bureau. Given that census regions are defined primarily for statistical purposes, it seems very likely that the states within have additional statistical attributes that unite them outside of this data set.

Though the modularity analytic tells you there are more cycles of flow within the four state groups, it is difficult to see it. It's particularly difficult to see much of anything in areas like the Northeast, where there is a lot of overlap. This is where Beck's lesson comes into play. To see relationships more clearly, a schematic geographic layout would be ideal.

Use the Label Adjust layout to shift the nodes for legibility. Return to the Preview task mode, turn off the curve option on links, and give edge arrows a relative size of 2.0.

By separating nodes, the links between them have become visible, revealing characteristics that were previously obscured, as shown in Figure 13-4. For example, it is apparent now that New Jersey is a net producer of goods, and many of those goods flow to New York and Pennsylvania. It is also clear that Florida is a net consumer. By adjusting spatial position to better space nodes while preserving spatial *relationships*, more information can be shown.

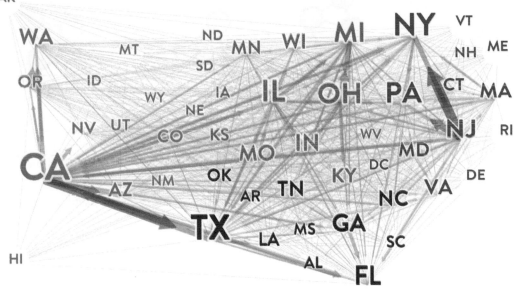

FIGURE 13-4: Using post-geospatial layout adjustments to give each node uncontested space provides room for more expressive links. Here, New Jersey is revealed as a net producer of goods, and Florida as a net consumer.

SMALL WORLD GROUPING

Another technique that can be useful in structuring a spatial network representation for legibility is to *group small worlds*. This technique can be appropriate if the links between physical nodes are abstract relationships rather than routes, as in this case here. The small world phenomenon in graphs is closely associated with strong clusters and cliques or near-cliques in that it describes a set of nodes that are highly interconnected and significantly less connected to those outside the world. They can be predefined by logical business divisions, or they can be computed.

Small worlds lend themselves well to grouping and hierarchical nesting to produce a network view where links do not cross other nodes or links. In this technique, small worlds are organized into larger bounding group nodes, and, while their internal links are visually preserved, links to nodes outside the world are instead aggregated and drawn between groups, as shown in Figure 13-5.

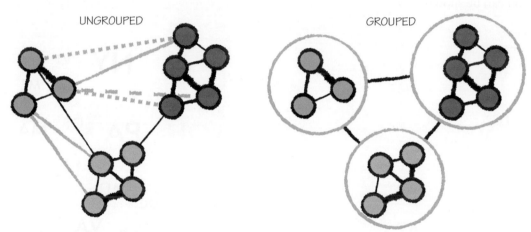

FIGURE 13-5: Grouping small worlds and aggregating links between them is another useful technique for being able to see flow clearly.

In the transport data set used for this exercise, every state is connected to almost every other state. The whole country is a small world, making it unsuitable for this technique.

LINK ROSE SUMMARIES

Links are the essence of a spatial network visualization. But when nodes are highly connected, and the center of the network is densely populated, drawing lines between each of the nodes creates visual interference.

Looking again at the Gephi interstate transport visualization in Figure 13-4, restrained use of color and opacity has revealed a few broad-stroke characteristics of large states like Florida, California, and New Jersey, but it is difficult to see much else. What are the characteristics of transport to and from Montana? How do Massachusetts and

Virginia compare? You can see approximately where major transport corridors must lie, but this is somewhat misleading because the data does not contain route information. Are there any other interesting patterns that can be observed?

When traditional approaches are not working to solve a particular problem, it is useful to step back and re-evaluate what information is truly essential. What's of interest in this data is not the flow of goods *through* states, but the flow of goods *in* and *out* of a state from each other state. The few insights you were able to take away in the previous exercise were most likely spotted by looking at the direction and thickness of incoming and outgoing lines directly around a node.

Those patterns are easiest to see, especially if the node lies on the perimeter where it is less likely that interfering lines will cross it. If the interfering lines are removed, leaving only the ink that describes incoming and outgoing flow at each node, it would reveal key characteristics more clearly, no matter where the nodes lie. That is precisely what a *link rose* is useful for.

In a link rose, the volume of link flow associated with each node is summarized by subdividing the space around the node into radial sectors and aggregating the flow of links for each sector. Flow in and out can be represented separately, which is useful for a directed graph like this one, or as a single sum flow.

Figure 13-6 shows the same interstate transport graph using link rose summaries. The faded inside sectors represent goods entering state borders from various directions, and the outside sectors represent goods leaving. Large net goods producers like California, Michigan, and New Jersey are clearly visible here, as are net consumers like Florida. However, unlike in the graph representation produced with Gephi, so are smaller net producers like Minnesota (MN), Oregon (OR), and Massachusetts (MA), as well as net consumers such as Virginia (VA).

The link rose visualization provides a clearer view of flow of goods to and from interior and coastal states alike. One limitation, however, is that for states that have flow pointed in the direction of many other states (such as California or Massachusetts), it is difficult to tell how far the goods travel. For example, how much of the flow out the bottom of California heads to Texas versus Florida? You can get a sense of the relative proportion in that case by looking at the matching incoming sector in the other two states. But what about Massachusetts? Interactions could be added to show links when hovering over a state. However, there is a way to add more information to the overview as well.

Figure 13-7 shows how subdividing each sector into a series representing linked groups and sorting by distance can help to articulate relationships in more detail. For example, the largest sector heading out of Massachusetts bypasses the nearby states to destinations in the

Midwest and West in equal measure. The following example illustrates how to make this diagram in Aperture JS using graph data from the previous example.

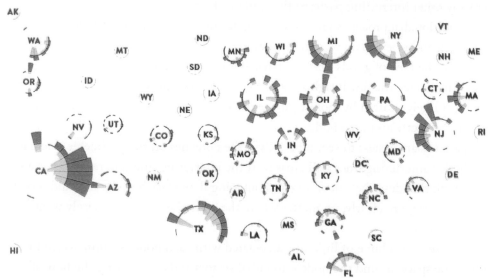

FIGURE 13-6: A link rose summarizes volume of incoming and outgoing links by direction, pointing back at the other end of the relationship. Here, the value of goods shipped into each state is shown by the interior part of the rose, and shipments out are shown by the exterior. By removing links, smaller state relationships are no longer obscured.

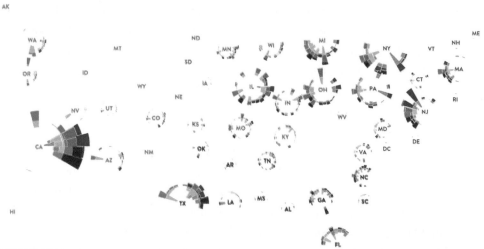

FIGURE 13-7: A link rose can be subdivided into a series to better indicate the characteristics of linked nodes, and the series can be sorted by distance to communicate near and far in the direction being summarized.

Building a Link Rose Diagram

To try this yourself, download the example package for this chapter from the Supplementary Materials provided on this book's companion website. To begin creating the link rose diagram, export the previous graph from Gephi in GraphML format. Following a model similar to those in earlier chapters, create a basic HTML page to host the visualization, as shown here:

```
<!DOCTYPE html>
<html>
<head>
    <meta charset="utf-8">
    <title>Inter-State Transport</title>
    <script src="jquery.js"></script>
    <script src="raphael.js"></script>
    <script src="aperture.js"></script>

    <!-- container styling -->
    <style>
        body {
            margin: 0;
            position: absolute;
            width: 100%;
            height: 100%;
        }
    </style>
</head>
<body>
    <script src="transport.js"></script>
</body>
</html>
```

Next, create the transport.js JavaScript file referenced previously. Your first statements will load the GraphML file and parse it into object form. In the process, node positions will be transformed to fit the screen and flip the y-axis from bottom-up to top-down. Subsequent steps will be to compute the rose summaries for each of the nodes in preparation for visualization.

```
jQuery.get("transport.graphml", function(data) {

    // parse the graph ml file
    var graphData = aperture.graph.fromGraphML(data, {
        left: 50,
        top: 10,
        width: 1500,
        height: 750
    });



    var numSectors = 24;

    // enhance nodes with link rose data
    aperture.graph.linkRose(graphData.nodes, {
        value: 'value',
        group: 'group',
        numSectors : numSectors
    });



    // construct the graph
    construct(graphData.nodes, numSectors);
});
```

Now create the construct function that you just called, passing it the data. Create the root visual elements, mapping node locations from the x and y of each data object, and then adding the nodes to a new layer. The next step is to add the rose layers. Before doing that, find the upper range of the sum of values in and out of each state. This will be used to scale the visuals.

```
function construct(nodes, numSectors) {

    // Create the root element for nodes and links
    var usa = new aperture.NodeLink(jQuery('body').get(0));
    usa.map('node-x').from('x');
    usa.map('node-y').from('y');

    // Create and populate the node layer
    var nodeLayer = usa.addLayer(aperture.NodeLayer);
    nodeLayer.all(nodes);



    // Find the data range
    var valueRange = new aperture.Scalar('Transported Value ($M)', [0]);

    nodes.forEach(function (node) {
        valueRange.expand(
            node.rose.linksIn.totals.sectorMax
            + node.rose.linksOut.totals.sectorMax);
    });

    //...
```

Next, define the rose for links out of each state. The base radius from which the sectors will grow should be configured to leave enough space for both the state label and the sectors for inflowing links. The scale for both needs to be the same.

```
    //...

    // Define the visual range which the data range will be mapped to
    var roseStart = 18;
    var roseWidth = 145;
    var roseOutKey = valueRange.mappedTo([0, roseWidth]);
    var roseBaseKey = valueRange.mappedTo([roseStart,
        roseStart+roseWidth]);
```

```
// Assign colors to each group, which is a number 0-4 in the data.
var roseColorKey = new aperture.Ordinal('Groups',
    [0,1,2,3]).mappedTo(['rgb(0,138,138)', 'rgb(139,69,19)',
    'rgb(189,74,0)', 'rgb(120,114,97)'
]);


// Add the layer
var outRose = nodeLayer.addLayer( aperture.RadialLayer );
outRose.map('opacity').asValue(0.9);
outRose.map('sector-count').asValue(numSectors);
outRose.map('series-count')
    .from('rose.linksOut.series.length');
outRose.map('base-radius')
    .from('rose.linksIn.totals.sectorMax').using(roseBaseKey);
outRose.map('radius')
    .from('rose.linksOut.series[].sectors[]').using(roseOutKey);
outRose.map('fill')
    .from('rose.linksOut.series[].group').using(roseColorKey);


//...
```

Add a second layer for the links coming into each state, but with its scale inverted and its base offset by one to leave a gap representing the anchor line.

```
    //...


// The inward rose inverts the scale and shifts the base one pixel
var roseInKey = valueRange.mappedTo([0, -roseWidth]);
var roseInBaseKey = valueRange.mappedTo(
    [roseStart-1, roseStart + roseWidth - 1]);


// Add the layer
var inRose = nodeLayer.addLayer( aperture.RadialLayer );
inRose.map('opacity').asValue(0.35);
inRose.map('sector-count').asValue(numSectors);
```

```
inRose.map('series-count')
    .from('rose.linksIn.series.length');
inRose.map('base-radius')
    .from('rose.linksIn.totals.sectorMax').using(roseInBaseKey);
inRose.map('radius')
    .from('rose.linksIn.series[].sectors[]').using(roseInKey);
inRose.map('fill')
    .from('rose.linksIn.series[].group').using(roseColorKey);


// Grow the labels a bit by state totals
var labelKey = valueRange.mappedTo([18, 48]);


// Add label layer
var label = nodeLayer.addLayer( aperture.LabelLayer );
label.map('font-weight').asValue('bold');
label.map('font-outline').asValue('white');
label.map('font-outline-width').asValue(3);
label.map('text').from('id');
label.map('fill').from('group').using(roseColorKey);
label.map('font-size')
    .from('rose.linksIn.totals.sectorMax').using(labelKey);


// Draw it all
usa.all().redraw();


}
```

Execute the code and you will see the rose diagram shown in Figure 13-7. To create the diagram shown in Figure 13-6 (which represents only the sum total of flow using a single color), remove the mapping of series-count in the radial layers, and replace references to series value data with totals. If you want to focus more exclusively on the proportion of regional transport to the whole, a middle-ground option is to show one colored series only from the second example for flow local to the group, and another for the remainder in the gray tone used in the first example.

Now that you have a visual summary of transport between states, it would be useful to have a method of getting detail for a single focused one. It is clear to which states many of the sectors point, but not all. One option would be to show the subset from each of the other nodes that involves the focused node and fade out the rest. A simpler approach would be to show links for the focused node.

One advantage of using links is that the scale can be made relative to the focused state, which will ensure that details are easy to see for smaller nodes as well. At the bottom of your `construct` function add an empty link layer, as shown here:

```
// ...

var linkLayer = usa.addLayer( aperture.LinkLayer );
linkLayer.map('link-style').asValue('arc');
linkLayer.map('source')
    .from('source');
linkLayer.map('source-offset')
    .from('rose.linksIn.totals.sectorMax').using(labelKey);
linkLayer.map('target')
    .from('target');
linkLayer.map('target-offset')
    .from('rose.linksIn.totals.sectorMax').using(roseBaseKey);
linkLayer.map('stroke')
    .from('other.group').using(roseColorKey);
linkLayer.map('stroke-width')
    .from('weight').using(new aperture.Scalar('weight',[0,1])
        .mappedTo([0,20]));
linkLayer.map('opacity').from(function() {
    return this.other === this.target? 0.9 : 0.35;
});

// ...
```

Next, add the interaction functions. On click, hide the rose representations, add the links for that node, and then redraw. When the viewer clicks off, restore the original state.

```
// ...

var selected = null;

inRose.map('visible').filter(function() {return !selected;});
outRose.map('visible').filter(function() {return !selected;});

nodeLayer.on('click', function(event) {
    if (selected !== event.data) {
        selected = event.data;

        linkLayer.all(event.data.links);
        usa.all().redraw();
    }
    return true;

});
jQuery('body').click(function(event) {
    if (selected) {
        selected = null;

        linkLayer.all([]);
        usa.all().redraw();
    }
});

// ...
```

Figure 13-8 shows an example result of clicking on Texas. Curved links always flow in a clockwise direction, so here it is clear that Louisiana receives far more goods from Texas than it sends. This more general trend between Texas and other Southern states can be seen in the link rose visualization as well, but interactions reveal variance in the pattern across specific states.

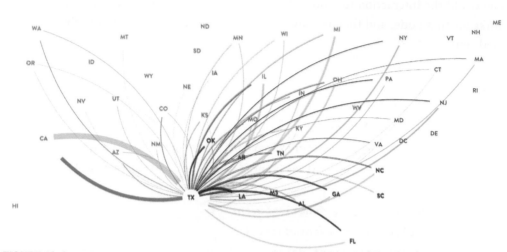

FIGURE 13-8: Adding interactions enables the viewing of details for a single state. Here, shipments in and out of Texas by value of goods are shown, revealing a relative imbalance of flow with other Southern states. Use of curved links reduces overlap and expresses flow in a clockwise direction.

ROUTE PATTERNS

Routes can be an important dimension of spatial networks. Sometimes you may simply want to find the optimal path between two nodes, as in the subway map example shown earlier in Figure 13-2. Other times you may be looking for meaningful patterns in paths traveled across the entire network. In some cases, those paths may have a spatial dimension in the data.

For example, transportation vehicles for a postal delivery service may use a global positioning system (GPS) to record tracks followed over time and upload them to a central database, contributing to information about frequency of routes traveled and efficiency of routes at various times of day. Other times, just an origin and destination may be available for each trip. For example, the same postal delivery service may record the time and location of pickup and delivery of each item, including every distribution center along the way. This would contribute to statistics on the number and type of items transported between each location, and time taken to reach each stop. Analyzing patterns in route data can provide valuable insights into delivery optimization, where increased efficiency can have a significant impact on profitability.

Passenger airlines form one of the most universally relevant transportation networks for businesses that operate nationally or internationally. If you fly frequently for work, you probably have travel efficiency down to a science, minimizing time wasted waiting for departures, connections, security, luggage, and ground transportation. Contending with delays, missed connections, and canceled flights is not only extremely frustrating, but it is exceedingly costly. A 2010 study led by researchers at the University of California, Berkeley, put the estimated annual cost of flight delays to U.S. passengers at more than $16 billion, with an additional $4 billion impact on the GDP. For the business traveler, "time is money," and for a high-level company executive, that time can be worth a lot.

As a frequent traveler, you will likely have formed opinions about the reliability of certain airlines and flights based on personal experience, which have since informed your flight preferences. Typically, little other consideration is given to the likelihood of travel delays when planning flights. In reality, however, these delays tend to form patterns, and factoring patterns into the choice of a flight route (the same way you would for your drive to work) can further maximize the chances of a smooth flight.

This example takes you through the exercise of examining patterns in flight delays across the United States using another data set from the Bureau of Transportation Statistics (BTS). A single month of BTS on-time performance data was combined with aviation support tables and subsequently aggregated in Excel using pivot tables.

The data collected and combined includes the number of flights between each origin and destination and the average delay in arrival. These will form links in the graph between each airport node.

```
Origin,Destination,Flights,Avg Arrival Delay (min)
BOI,SUN,1,0
SFO,SUN,20,14
SLC,SUN,137,19
ATL,SAT,332,9
BNA,SAT,57,15

...
```

For each airport the number of arrivals and departures was computed, along with average arrival and departure delays. Since location is central to understanding routes and patterns, latitude and longitude was also included for each airport:

```
Airport,Arrivals,Departures,Flights,Avg Arrival Delay (min),Avg
     Departure Delay (min),Airport Name,Latitude,Longitude
ATL,31894,31887,63781,15,14,Hartsfield-Jackson Atlanta International,...
DFW,23763,23752,47515,17,19,Dallas/Fort Worth International,
     32.89694444,...
```

```
LAX,19060,19052,38112,14,14,Los Angeles International,
    33.9425,-118.4080556
DEN,19028,19006,38034,21,25,Denver International,
    39.86166667,-104.6730556
...
```

Visualizing Route Segments

For a data set of this scale, Gephi is a good option for rapid analysis. Use GDF again to import your data. Copy the node data into a new file, and insert the nodedef> tag, labeling the airport code column as name. Next, assign a type to each column—VARCHAR for text and DOUBLE or FLOAT for numbers. Append the link data to the node data and repeat a similar process, beginning with an edgedef> tag. Change the name of the Flights column to weight so that Gephi will recognize it, and save it as usflightdata-dec-2013.gdf.

```
nodedef>name VARCHAR,Arrivals DOUBLE,Departures DOUBLE,Flights
    DOUBLE,Avg Arrival Delay (min) DOUBLE,Avg Departure Delay (min)
    DOUBLE,Airport Name VARCHAR,Latitude FLOAT,Longitude FLOAT
ATL,31894,31887,63781,15,14,Hartsfield-Jackson Atlanta International,...
DFW,23763,23752,47515,17,19,Dallas/Fort Worth International,
    32.89694444,...
LAX,19060,19052,38112,14,14,Los Angeles International,
    33.9425,-118.4080556
DEN,19028,19006,38034,21,25,Denver International,39.86166667,
    -104.6730556
...

edgedef>Origin VARCHAR,Destination VARCHAR,weight DOUBLE,Avg
    Arrival Delay (min) DOUBLE
BOI,SUN,1,0
SFO,SUN,20,14
SLC,SUN,137,19
ATL,SAT,332,9
BNA,SAT,57,15
...
```

Open the GDF file in Gephi, choosing the default directed graph option and letting Gephi rescale the weighted links to reasonable widths. Once the graph data file is opened, the first step is to arrange the airport nodes according to location.

Choose the Geo Layout and review the options a little more closely this time. For this data, geography will be preserved with more accuracy. The layout should discover the latitude and longitude columns and select them automatically. The projection determines how coordinates on the spherical earth are flattened into a two dimensional representation. The default Mercator projection will work fine for the U.S. data here, as will the other defaults. If you were instead mapping global data, consider an alternate projection that has less spatial distortion at the poles.

Click Run to arrange the nodes geographically. Next, use the drag tool with a relatively large-diameter drag dot to pull in states and territories outside of the mainland United States (such as Alaska and Hawaii) for more efficient use of space, as shown in Figure 13-9. Move Guam from the far right of the map to the Pacific Ocean on the west, near Hawaii.

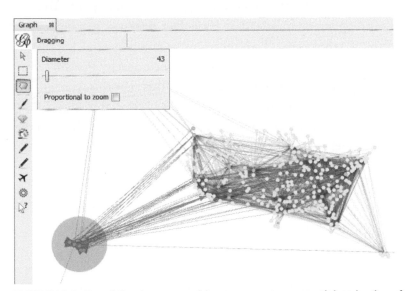

FIGURE 13-9: Use of Geo Layout provides an accurate geospatial projection of nodes in Gephi. Some of the states and territories in this case are spread out too far to see without zooming out. Use the drag tool with a large diameter to move Alaska and the islands closer to the mainland.

You now have a basic map of airports to work with. However, very large and very small airports are represented by the same basic circle representation. It would be truer to the data if the size of each node reflected the size of the airport, and because the data conveniently contains familiar three-letter airport codes, it would be intuitive to use these instead of circles.

Using the Ranking tab and the Label controls at the bottom of the window, make the nodes small. Then, turn on labels and map them to the number of flights through each airport, adjusting the size until you achieve a reasonable range. Some labels will overlap, especially if they are from the same city. To spread them apart you will use the Label Adjust layout again, but before you do, save your work in case you need to return to the previous layout and try again until you are happy with the result. Once the graph is saved, apply the Label Adjust layout for a second or two to push apart overlapping labels a bit for better readability.

If you switch to the Preview task mode, you should see a basic view of flight patterns across the country. The size of the labels indicates the size of airport by number of domestic flights, and thickness of links indicates the number of flights between airports. You may need to select the rescaled option on links and increase their thickness to a higher value (such as 4 or 6) to better see the results. Turn the arrow heads off by reducing their sizes to zero. Similarly, remove nodes from the view by setting their opacity to zero.

It's finally time to map flight delay visually to the representation. For this, you will be using color. Return to the Overview task mode and, using the Ranking tab, assign average flight delay to the default color scheme. Do this for both nodes and links. Back in the Preview task mode, select the label color option, which inherits the original node color, and give the labels a thick border of five black pixels. Refresh the preview to see the finished result, as shown in Figure 13-10.

Viewing the visualization, you can immediately see best and worst performers, as well as some overall geographic patterns. Among the worst are the two main Chicago area airports, O'Hare (ORD) and Midway (MDW), along with Denver (DEN) and Newark (EWR). A seasoned traveler might recognize these as airports that experience flight delays with more regularity. Areas around Chicago and Denver seem to be similarly susceptible to slowdowns, implying perhaps overcrowded airspace, or weather-related delays. These are December statistics after all. However, Newark, seemingly an area anomaly, is not so easily explained. Interestingly, though, one of the worst-performing East Coast airports in this data appears to be Trenton-Mercer (TTN), a small airport also located in New Jersey.

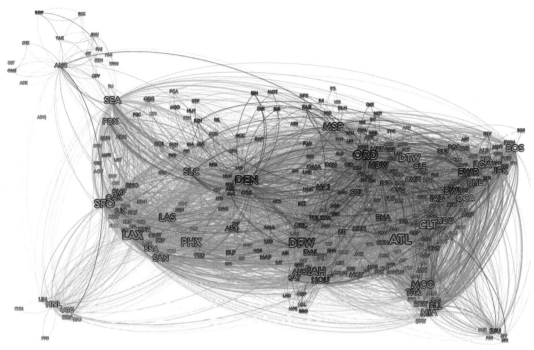

FIGURE 13-10: Visualizing average flight delays geospatially across all airports reveals interesting patterns. Here, label size indicates the size of airport, and red indicates greater average delay for December 2013.

> **NOTE** As of this writing, Gephi did not yet have controls for sorting nodes or links back to front, nor was it controlled by the data. To draw airports and routes with higher delays over the top of those with less, the authors wrote a quick Gephi plug-in in Java. The popularity of Gephi among researchers (along with the somewhat organic, unplanned feel of the user interface) can be attributed in no small part to its extensive plug-in architecture.

Examining some of the best-performing airports closely like Seattle (SEA), Portland (PDX), and Salt Lake City (SLC), you may notice that the few incoming flights that do tend to be delayed involve airports where the issue is much more prevalent. Overall, several broad trends also emerge.

One is that the middle of the country, north to south, is delayed more frequently than either the East Coast or West Coast. This is a more prevalent trend even than the general pattern of improving performance as you move southward, which you might imagine could be attributed to weather.

Another trend that seems apparent is that larger airports seem a bit more likely to be delayed than smaller airports. This is particularly evident on the West Coast and the area around Florida. One explanation might be that larger volumes of air traffic tend to be more susceptible to congestion. However, given that this phenomenon seems fairly exclusive to areas where flights are often on time, a more likely reason might be that the smaller airports in these areas do not have as many flight connections to airports that tend to incur delays.

Track Aggregation

So far, you have analyzed flight delays as a consumer. You may have concluded that you are best off by booking connections along coastal routes and avoiding particular airports. Taking it further, you might gather additional data to analyze time of day and seasonal differences, and correlate with weather patterns, or compare patterns between particular airlines or aircraft types. Given the observations made, you could develop algorithms to forecast the best flight options when booking and use visualization to help explain why certain routes are better than others.

However, as a consumer, you only need to optimize your choice of flight segments, similar to how you might choose roads to take to work, but with fewer options. From the perspective of an airline or airport air traffic controllers, routing decisions are decidedly more complex. An optimal path through airspace can, in theory, be different for each flight, each day.

When route data is not bound to path segments but rather is tracking freely across a spatial field, it is often more feasible to aggregate the data in the form of a two-dimensional (2D) or three-dimensional (3D) field. Aircraft and ship tracks are good examples of this kind of data.

Figure 13-11 shows a visualization of ship tracks by frequency over a little more than a year. This aggregation technique lends itself well to a tiled, multi-resolution visualization approach with zooming and panning, similar to what you would expect of an online map.

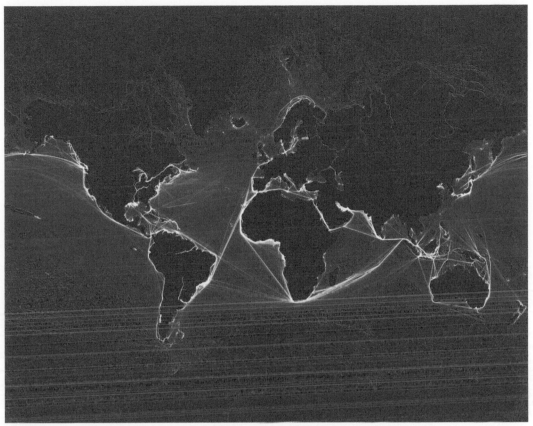

FIGURE 13-11: Aggregation in the form of a 2D or 3D spatial field is a useful technique for track data and scales well for large data sets. Here, ship position reports are plotted using a luminance scale, revealing the relative frequency of routes.

SUMMARY

This chapter covered various strategies for effective visualization of spatial networks, including schematic layout, link rose summaries, grouping of small worlds, and track aggregation. Each of these techniques is useful for a certain type of data and not appropriate for others. For example, small world grouping is appropriate for a graph that includes clear small world phenomenon, and a link rose diagram is appropriate for a graph with flow across many internal links.

The last section of this chapter on track aggregation touched briefly on the challenge of large-scale data. Chapter 14 covers this subject in detail. Big Data presents scalability challenges, not only with respect to computing at speeds that support human interaction but also with respect to the limits of human perception. As with the problems presented in this chapter and with all graph problems, solutions for Big Data vary with the nature of the data and the questions being asked of it.

## PART 4

Advanced Techniques

The chapters in this book have thus far dealt with the application of fundamental graph techniques, with an emphasis on venturing outside the boxed confines of classic approaches to find the most effective solution to a particular problem. This chapter covers issues on the frontier of research and development of graph technologies and tools, as well as core principles to consider when executing graph design. These are also areas of particularly keen interest to the authors. Table P3-1 provides a summary of topics covered in the following chapters.

TABLE P3-1: Advanced Graph Techniques

TOPIC	EXAMPLE	DESCRIPTION
Big Data (Chapter 14)		Standard in-memory graph approaches quickly break down with Big Data. Unique technologies and techniques are required, guided by a clear vision of what the goals are. Chapter 14, "Big Data," describes how graph databases and query languages can be used to dynamically retrieve and analyze specific subgraphs of interest. Equally important techniques for exploring massive graphs visually are also discussed.
Dynamic Graphs (Chapter 15)		Understanding graph change is a difficult problem for which graph tools often provide little support. Use of animation to evolve a graph from one state to another can be viscerally compelling but difficult to extract sensible information from. Chapter 15, "Dynamic Graphs," offers several helpful techniques for seeing how a graph evolves over time. It also looks at relational patterns between entities. Examples show how transactional aspects (which are relatively common in graph data) can be expressed in ways that reveal patterns of behavior.
Design (Chapter 16)		Graph design is both an art and a science. Much of this book is dedicated to the choice of forms and approaches based on the nature of the data and the questions being asked of it. Detailed design decisions, however, are also extremely important to the success of a graph analysis application. Chapter 16, "Design," focuses on core design principles that apply across all forms of graphs.

## 14

BIG DATA

Big Data has been at the center of much of the innovative research and development in the field of graph analytics and visualization. With so many of our social, consumer, and other exchanges occurring online, the amount of data being collected every day, as well as opportunities to link across data sets, stretches the limits of our ability to take full advantage of it. For businesses, the central problem is no longer getting better data, but *getting better information out of data.*

The term "Big Data" can mean different things to different people, but defining issues are generally agreed to include the four V's—volume, velocity, variety, and veracity. Simply put, challenges exist with the size of data, how rapidly it is streaming in, how extremely multi-faceted it has become, and how uncertain some of the source or derived data can be. Big Data is not strictly defined by how big it is, but by the fact that it is large and complex enough that it defies management and analysis using traditional systems and approaches.

Traditional systems often store structured data in table form on a server. Queries are then used to slice and dice along dimensions for subsequent analysis. Analysis is done in the memory of a single machine, typically with facets displayed independently in separate views. In some of the more advanced tools, filtering and interactive cross-view highlighting provide the capability to explore relationships one at a time with dimensions that are outside the view of a single facet.

By contrast, Big Data is often rightly associated with alternative data structures and distributed systems, where processing and management tasks are spread across a cluster of computers. In reality, however, an extremely wide variety of technologies are involved that may, at times, include traditional systems such as relational databases. Because the data is often complex, so are the back-end processes and systems for exploiting it.

Big, complex data also tends to defy traditional approaches to visualization and analysis. Slice-and-dice approaches, though often useful for understanding overall characteristics of data and discovering broad patterns across one or two dimensions, provide a view of only one facet at a time. Interactively discovering correlations across additional dimensions can require painstaking exploration time, not to mention a bit of good luck. Moreover, not being able to see what is often a much richer picture in the whole makes it difficult to understand the broader narrative.

The nature of the approach itself also tends not to lend itself well to certain kinds of analysis. If you are looking for proverbial needles in the haystack, there is a limit to clues that can be gleaned from high-level views of facets of the haystack. As shown in Figure 14-1, inventive approaches to displaying and navigating Big Data, coupled with analytics, are needed for analysts to more easily access essential information.

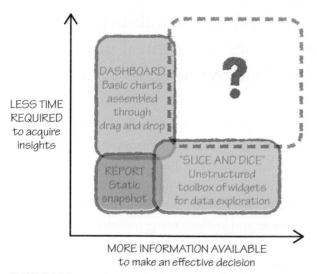

FIGURE 14-1: Creative approaches are needed to make insights in Big Data more accessible to analysts, with less effort.

Graph approaches to structuring, analyzing, and visualizing data have been a significant area of interest for application to Big Data. Graphs are well-suited to expressing complex interconnections and clusters of highly related entities.

This chapter begins with an overview of back-end graph systems for Big Data using a practical example and then examines visualization techniques and technologies.

GRAPH DATABASES

A system for dynamic interactive analysis of graphs begins with a data storage and access solution. Relational databases like Oracle or SQL Server have many points of strength but, contrary to the term itself, are not particularly efficient for exploring the complex relations or relatively noisy heterogeneous data typical of large graphs. Data within a table must conform to rigid pre-defined schemas, and linking data across many tables requires complex and expensive joins that limit query speed.

A significant amount of research has been invested in providing relational database functionality on distributed systems. For example, Google Big Query provides cloud-based data storage and query using a core subset of SQL. Cloudera Impala is similarly a SQL query engine for Hadoop that has progressed to the point where it may no longer be necessary to copy subsets of data from the Hadoop Distributed File System (HDFS) to local relational databases in order to achieve interactive performance for analysis. The benefit of carrying SQL forward with these solutions is a well-known, time-tested interface language that provides relatively straightforward migration from traditional databases.

In parallel, work has been ongoing for alternatives to tabular storage and SQL, known broadly as *NoSQL* or "Not only SQL." Architectural approaches include column-based, document-based, and key-value stores. In addition, a number of graph databases such as Neo4J and Titan have emerged, which represent data in a fundamentally different way. Instead of storing and representing data as a regular set of dimensioned structures, data is represented as a property graph where elements are nodes, and relations between elements are represented as links.

Figure 14-2 shows a notional example of product data for two Blu-ray discs. The products are associated by a single common categorization, but also share reviewers. Both nodes and links in a property graph can include properties. In this example, each review relation includes a rating from one to five stars.

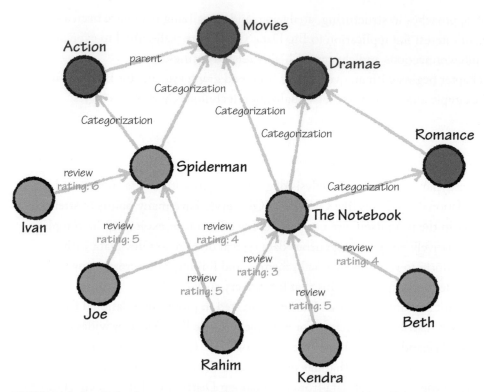

FIGURE 14-2: Graph databases represent data using property graphs, where links are used to express relations between entities. In this case, movies are categorized at varying levels for sale and have been reviewed by customers.

One of the fundamental differences when working with large graph databases as opposed to many of the graphs shown previously in this book is that frequently the goal is to display graph properties of only a relatively small subgraph of interest. In that respect, graph databases provide a critical function, which is a method of efficiently querying for the information of interest when the graph is too large to fit in memory.

A Product Marketing Example

Online product and customer data provides the basis for an excellent case study illustrating how a graph database can be used to explore associated interests for the purposes of product marketing. In a conventional retail setting, an experienced salesperson may observe and use any number of demographic, social, and behavioral cues to instinctually guide consumers to products they might be interested in buying.

Contrastingly, in online retail, what is known about customers is often limited to behaviors that amount to expressions of interest, like clicking links to view products or authoring reviews. Although this can sometimes be like the experience of the proverbial blind men and the elephant, observed interest in even one product can be used to inform the choice of associated products to highlight to a consumer in the hopes of maximizing sales. One of the luxuries of online product marketing is that the choice of products to try to cross-sell or up-sell can be made dynamically in response to observed interests. In business, the science of product interests is called *affinity analysis*.

This example uses public Amazon product data collected in 2003 by Jure Leskovec and published by the Stanford Network Analysis Project (SNAP) for scientific research. The data includes product data such as title, group classification, and sales rank, as well as various ways in which the product is hierarchically categorized for browsing. Also included is a reference to the five most "similar" products and reviews by customers. Similar products are defined as those most often purchased at the same time: "Customers who bought this item also bought…"

```
Id:    6
ASIN: 0486220125
   title: How the Other Half Lives: Studies Among the Tenements of
       New York
   group: Book
   salesrank: 188784
   similar: 5  0486401960  0452283612  0486229076  0714840343  0374528993
   categories: 5
    |Books[283155]|Subjects[1000]|Arts & Photography[1]
        |Photography[2020]|Photo Essays[2082]
    |Books[283155]|Subjects[1000]|History[9]|Americas[4808]
        |United States[4853]|General[4870]
    |Books[283155]|Subjects[1000]|History[9]|Jewish[4992]|General[4993]
    |Books[283155]|Subjects[1000]|Nonfiction[53]
        |Social Sciences[11232]|Sociology[11288]|Urban[11296]
    |[172282]|Categories[493964]|Camera & Photo[502394]|Photography
        Books[733540]|Photo Essays[733676]
```

```
reviews: total: 17   downloaded: 17   avg rating: 4
  1997-7-4  cutomer:  ATVPDKIKX0DER  rating: 5  votes:  12
      helpful:  11
  1998-10-11  cutomer:  AUEZ7NVOEHYRY  rating: 5  votes:  13
      helpful:  12
  1999-4-15  cutomer:  ATVPDKIKX0DER  rating: 5  votes:  18
      helpful:  7
  2000-1-4  cutomer:  AJYG6ZJUQPZ9M  rating: 4  votes:  14  helpful:
      10

  ...
```

> **NOTE**
>
> Data was made available at http://snap.stanford.edu/data/ by the SNAP project and is published with the following source citation: J. Leskovec, L. Adamic and B. Huberman. *The Dynamics of Viral Marketing*. ACM Transactions on the Web (ACM TWEB), 1(1), 2007.

Prior to analysis for use in this book, the data was imported into a Titan database. Titan is a leading open source graph database that can be distributed across a multi-machine cluster to achieve claims of scalability on the order of hundreds of billions of nodes and links. It can also easily be installed and run locally on a single machine for comparatively small graphs like this one on the order of tens of millions.

> **TIP**
>
> Titan is documented and made available for download on GitHub at https://github.com/thinkaurelius/titan/wiki.

Creating and Populating a Graph Database

The original source data used in this example was formatted for easy reading by humans rather than computers, so the authors have done the time-consuming parsing for you and exported the result in GraphML format. Before proceeding, download the compressed data file from this book's companion website and extract it for importing into Titan. It's a large data set, so expect that it will take more time to download than other files in this book. If you haven't already done so, you will also need to download and install Titan. The examples in this chapter were used with version 0.4.4.

Once you have the data, you are ready to create the database. The first step in making a new Titan database is to configure its storage. To take advantage of advanced text search on select properties, it is also important to configure an index for Lucene or Elastic Search. Create a `productdb.properties` file with content similar to the following, altering the two directory paths as appropriate. You will use this to initially create the database and to reopen it each time after.

```
storage.backend=local
storage.directory= storage
storage.index.search.backend=lucene
storage.index.search.directory= storage/lucene
```

The next step is to define schemas for the data. In Titan this is simply a matter of defining any properties of nodes and links that will be used, indicating which should be indexed for fast lookup. The quickest way to do this is to use a script. Create the following `makeproductdb.groovy` file, entering the first line listed to open the database. File paths in the script should be modified to reflect actual locations. Relative paths will typically be evaluated relative to the Titan bin directory.

```
graph = TitanFactory.open('productdb.properties')
```

Next begin to define the schema for product nodes. Make a key that will be used to distinguish all nodes by type, followed by keys for the specific properties of products. When defining the `productno` key, add an index for fast lookup by product number. Add an index to `title` as well, but this time use the Lucene index declared earlier in the properties file.

```
graph.makeKey('type').dataType(String.class).make()

graph.makeKey('productno').dataType(String.class)
     .indexed(Vertex.class).unique().make()
graph.makeKey('title').dataType(String.class)
     .indexed('search', Vertex.class).make()
graph.makeKey('salesrank').dataType(Integer.class).make()
graph.makeKey('group').dataType(String.class).make()
```

```
graph.makeKey('status').dataType(String.class).make()
graph.makeKey('reviews').dataType(Integer.class).make()
graph.makeKey('avgrating').dataType(Float.class).make()
```

Now that the keys for products are defined, specify the keys for customer and category nodes. Index all three for fast lookup by exact match.

```
graph.makeKey('customerno').dataType(String.class)
     .indexed(Vertex.class).unique().make()


graph.makeKey('categoryno').dataType(Integer.class)
     .indexed(Vertex.class).unique().make()
graph.makeKey('categoryname').dataType(String.class)
     .indexed(Vertex.class).make()
```

Next, define the property keys for links, starting with reviews and categorizations. Reviews link customers to products, and categorizations link products to categories. The specificity key is a value from 0 to 1 that reflects how specific the categorization was relative to others in the category hierarchy for that product.

```
date = graph.makeKey('date').dataType(Long.class).make()
votes = graph.makeKey('votes').dataType(Integer.class).make()
rating = graph.makeKey('rating').dataType(Integer.class).make()
helpful = graph.makeKey('helpful').dataType(Integer.class).make()


specificity = graph.makeKey('specificity').dataType(Float.class).make()
```

Finally, declare the links themselves as labels, associating them with the keys you just made. Products are linked if they are similar, and linked to customers through review. Categories are linked to parent categories, and from products by categorization. Commit the graph when all the keys and labels have been defined.

```
graph.makeLabel('similar').make()
graph.makeLabel('review').sortKey(date).sortOrder(Order.DESC)
     .signature(votes, rating, helpful).make()
graph.makeLabel('parent').manyToOne().make()
graph.makeLabel('categorization').sortKey(specificity).make()


graph.commit()
```

Now that you have defined properties of nodes and links, the database can be populated from the GraphML file. Add the following final lines to the script, save it, and exit.

```
reader = new GraphMLReader(graph)

reader.inputGraph('productdb.graphml')
```

The script is now ready to be executed in a command-line shell from the directory where you installed Titan. If you have a 64-bit operating system and the memory available, it's a good idea to make use of the JAVA_OPTIONS environment variable to grant more to the import process you're about to run. Setting the options and running the script will look something like this, depending on your operating system and location of the files. Be prepared for it to take some time.

```
> export JAVA_OPTIONS=-Xmx4096m

> cd titan-all-0.4.4/bin

> gremlin.sh ../../productdb/makeproductdb.groovy
```

GRAPH QUERY LANGUAGES

Once the graph database has been populated, you are ready to start querying it for information. There is a good chance that you are familiar with SQL. SQL is the standard query language for pretty much anything that resembles a relational database. Graph databases, however, have unique structures that require unique query languages, so, unfortunately, SQL will not get you very far here. You will need to spend some amount of time learning a new language. Luckily, a little basic knowledge will go a long way.

Two of those most universal standards are SPARQL and Gremlin. Titan supports both.

SPARQL Protocol and RDF Query Language (SPARQL) is supported by many graph databases for querying Resource Description Framework (RDF). RDF is a formal standard for knowledge representation that was born out of the "Semantic Web" movement, the goal of which is to provide structured representations of the vastly unstructured data available on the Internet. SPARQL is a standard query language for RDF-encoded information and bears some resemblance to SQL in both name and syntax. The following is an example of a query that you might use to retrieve all categorizations of product 44:

```
SELECT ?category WHERE

   tg:44 tg:categorization ?category

}
```

TIP

To try out SPARQL on a massive RDF collection of knowledge statements extracted from Wikipedia, visit DBpedia at http://wiki.dbpedia.org/.

Gremlin is a distinctly different and elegant graph-traversal–oriented language for query, analysis, and manipulation of graphs. Gremlin can be a little cleaner and more intuitive in some cases, and less so in others. For example, the same query for data on product 44 would look like this in Gremlin:

```
g.v(44).out('categorization');
```

Because SPARQL looks more like SQL and Gremlin is closer to a programming-style grammar, you may find one more natural than the other, depending on your previous experience. Personally, the authors find Gremlin a little more intuitive for interactive querying, especially if link traversal is involved. Gremlin is used for the examples in this chapter.

Gremlin for Graph Queries

The best way to learn Gremlin is to try it out. Launch a Gremlin shell from the bin directory of your Titan folder again, and issue a command to reopen the database, assigning the result to a variable that you will use to reference the graph.

```
> bin/gremlin.sh


          \,,,/
          (o o)
-----o000-(_)-o000-----
gremlin> g = TitanFactory.open('../productdb/productdb.properties')
```

Next, try a query. If you are reading this book, you (hopefully) have an interest in graphs, so look for any books in the product catalog that contain the word "graph" in their titles. Type the following command, where g is the reference to the graph stored in the last statement, and V is shorthand for vertices:

```
gremlin> g.V.has('title',CONTAINS,'Graph')
==>v[871604]
==>v[1449164]
==>v[1894568]
==>v[1974620]
==>v[2621360]
...
```

Gremlin will return a long list of vertices represented by their internal IDs enclosed in square brackets, with a v to indicate that they are vertices. Unless you have a brilliant memory for numbers, it's difficult to tell which products have been selected. Repeat the same query, but ask for the title property of each result to be shown instead, as shown here:

```
gremlin> g.V.has('title',CONTAINS,'Graph').title
==>Algorithmic Graph Theory
==>Algebraic Graph Theory
==>Schaum's Outline of Graph Theory: Including Hundreds of Solved
      Problems
==>Introductory Graph Theory
==>Graph Theory
==>Math Skills Made Fun: Great Graph Art Multiplication & Division
      (Grades 3-4)
==>Graph-Theoretic Concepts in Computer Science: 21st International
      Workshop, Wg '95 Aachen, Germany, June 20-22, 1995 : Proceedings
      (Lecture Notes in Computer Science)
==>Introduction to Graph Theory (2nd Edition)
==>LightWave 3D 7 : Motion Graph Modifiers & Expressions - Class on
      Demand Video Training Tutorial DVD
...
```

The first eight books are mathematical books on graph theory, which may or may not be your cup of tea. But notice that the ninth product down is a DVD. You were looking for graph books, but you did not restrict the query to the book group. Most Gremlin commands are pipelines of input, and output filters can be chained together. Type the following to select only book vertices, and *then* search them for the titles of interest:

```
gremlin> g.V('group','Book').has('title',CONTAINS,'Graph').title
```

Review the list again, and notice that the DVD is no longer included. So, how many books are left in the list? You could count them yourself, or just ask Gremlin to do it, as shown here:

```
gremlin> g.V('group','Book').has('title',CONTAINS,'Graph').count()
==>39
```

So far, the queries have focused on narrowing down a list of books, which are represented in the graph as vertices. The list now has 39 books in it, many of which seem to be mathematical in nature. To narrow down the list even further, you can add another criterion to look for "Visualization" in the title. However, you may also want to see what the reviews are like for those books. Reviews, if you recall, are represented as edges pointing from the reviewer to the product. The following query looks for books on graph visualization and outputs the rating of incoming review edges:

```
gremlin> g.V('group','Book').has('title',CONTAINS,'Graph').has('title',
    CONTAINS,'Visualization').inE('review').rating
==>1
==>4
==>3
==>5
```

The output of the query is a list of review ratings. A list of titles with reviews would be more useful. You can use the `transform` step to output multiple fields for each result, and before doing so, you can use an `order` step to sort them in order of most helpful to least helpful. Note that you must call `next()` on `inV`, the vertex with the link incoming, because any traversable property will return a pipeline rather than the object itself.

```
gremlin> g.V('group','Book').has('title',CONTAINS,'Graph').has('title',
    CONTAINS,'Visualization').inE('review').order{it.b.helpful <=>
    it.a.helpful}.transform{[it.inV.next().title, it.rating,
        it.helpful]}
```

```
==>[Graph Drawing: Algorithms for the Visualization of Graphs, 3, 36]
==>[Graph Drawing: Algorithms for the Visualization of Graphs, 1, 5]
==>[Graph Drawing: Algorithms for the Visualization of Graphs, 4, 4]
==>[Graph Drawing: Algorithms for the Visualization of Graphs, 5, 0]
```

The queries have so far found nodes and output incoming edges. One of the more central and powerful design features of Gremlin, however, is a grammar for traversing links to other nodes. For example, the following query will find books that are linked by similarity to the graph-drawing algorithms book. The term both() here selects both outgoing and incoming edges, accounting for cases when the book is either the subject or object of similarity.

```
gremlin> g.V('group','Book').has('title',CONTAINS,'Graph').has('title',
        CONTAINS,'Visualization').both('similar').title
==>Algorithms on Strings, Trees, and Sequences: Computer Science and
        Computational Biology
==>Computational Analysis of Biochemical Systems : A Practical Guide
        for Biochemists and Molecular Biologists
==>Drawing Graphs : Methods and Models (Lecture Notes in Computer
        Science)
==>Computational Modeling of Genetic and Biochemical Networks
        (Computational Molecular Biology)
==>Introduction to Graph Theory (Dover Books on Advanced Mathematics)
==>Drawing Graphs : Methods and Models (Lecture Notes in Computer
        Science)
```

Finally, notice that, because you gathered nodes linked in both directions, there is a duplicate reference to the *Drawing Graphs* book, indicating that each book is listed as being similar to the other. If the title is any indication, they are also the most similar in subject. You can use the dedup() step to eliminate duplicates, as shown here:

```
gremlin> g.V('group','Book').has('title',CONTAINS,'Graph').has('title',
        CONTAINS,'Visualization').both('similar').dedup().title
```

Alternatively, you can use the groupCount() step to count instances of each. Processing the results of grouping requires more advanced Gremlin and shows how Gremlin tends to become more complex when the output of a step is not easily expressed as a simple list of single elements. To output a list of counts by book, the cap statement used in the following code moves back one step in the pipeline output (which is otherwise a list of counts) to the map produced as a side effect. The scatter() step then unrolls the map into a list of key/value entries, and transform is used to output each entry with its title.

```
gremlin> g.V('group','Book').has('title',CONTAINS,'Graph').has('title',
    CONTAINS,'Visualization').both('similar').groupCount().
    cap.scatter().transform(){[it.value, it.key.title]}
==>[1, Computational Modeling of Genetic and Biochemical Networks
    (Computational Molecular Biology)]
==>[2, Drawing Graphs : Methods and Models (Lecture Notes in
    Computer Science)]
==>[1, Introduction to Graph Theory (Dover Books on Advanced
    Mathematics)]
==>[1, Computational Analysis of Biochemical Systems : A Practical
    Guide for Biochemists and Molecular Biologists]
==>[1, Algorithms on Strings, Trees, and Sequences: Computer Science and
    Computational Biology]
```

Using Graph Queries to Extract Neighborhoods

Now that you know a few of the basics of Gremlin syntax and you've explored the structure of the data a little, it's time to put it to use. The goal of this exercise is to analyze product associations represented by co-purchasing and reviews to gain insights that will be useful for marketing and advertising around a particular book. A subgraph of products representing the neighborhood of interest will be output for visualization and analysis.

Customers link products through reviews, and, unlike co-purchasing, similarity links for the list are not limited to five. You'll start with a single product, extract related products and edges between them, and export the resulting subgraph for visualization and further analysis. For this exercise, you focus on associated interests for one of Edward Tufte's seminal visualization books, *Envisioning Information* (Cheshire, CT:1990, Graphics Press).

Begin by finding the book and storing a reference to it. Note that one of the limitations of using the Lucene index in Titan is that each term is indexed separately, making it necessary here in common syntax to query separately for "Envisioning" and "Information." Because the output of Gremlin steps are lists, add a call to next() to store a reference to the book itself, the first item in the list.

```
gremlin> tufteBook = g.V.has('title',CONTAINS,'Envisioning').has
        ('title', CONTAINS,'Information').next()
==>v[4745708]
```

Before collecting related nodes, it's a good idea to do a quick sanity check on the counts of products that are linked through co-purchasing or co-review, being careful not to count the same nodes twice.

```
gremlin> tufteBook.both('similar').dedup().count()
==>25
gremlin> tufteBook.in('review').dedup().out().dedup().count()
==>124365
```

Clearly, something unusual is going on here. The count of products linked through reviews is more than 100,000, a fifth of the entire product catalog. Use the transform function to stop the pipeline earlier, and write out the number of reviews that each customer has made.

```
gremlin> tufteBook.in('review').dedup().transform
        {it.outE.count()}
==>164
==>2
==>86
==>1
==>176
==>203
==>327
==>9
==>1
==>140
==>22
==>1
==>15
==>6
```

```
==>10
==>42
==>13
==>1
==>945065
==>1
==>21
==>5
==>2
==>1
==>51
==>185
==>1
```

One customer has been responsible for almost a million reviews, which is impossibly high. It seems someone has found a way to artificially submit reviews. Those edges will need to be excluded.

The final step is to create a new subgraph, adding copies of the neighboring nodes and any edges that connect them (but no others), and then write the result to file. Begin by creating an in-memory TinkerGraph and declare two helper functions that will copy nodes and links, as shown here:

```
gremlin> sg = new TinkerGraph()
==>tinkergraph[vertices:0 edges:0]

gremlin> def addNode(v, sg){
   sg.addVertex(v.id, ElementHelper.getProperties(v))
}
==>true

gremlin> def addLink(e, sg) {
  outv = sg.getVertex(e.outV.next().id);
  if (outv != null) {
    inv = sg.getVertex(e.inV.next().id);
    if (inv != null) {
```

```
        sg.addEdge(e.id, outv, inv, e.label, ElementHelper.getProperties
        (e))
}}}
==>true
```

Add linked customers and products, being sure to filter out the false customer, and eliminate any duplicate nodes. Use `store` to cache the list of products for the next step, which will be to add the edges.

```
gremlin> products = []
gremlin> tufteBook.in('review').filter{it.outE.count() < 5000}.dedup
        ( ).sideEffect{addNode(it,sg)}.out().or(tufteBook.both('similar')).
        dedup( ).sideEffect{addNode(it,sg)}.store(products)
```

Use the products list to add a copy of all incoming edges. The vertex check in the `addLink` function you defined earlier ensures that only edges with both ends in the graph will be added. The populated subgraph will have a little more than 1,000 nodes and 2,000 links. Write it out somewhere as a GraphML file.

```
gremlin> products._().inE.sideEffect{addLink(it,sg)}
==>...


gremlin> GraphMLWriter.outputGraph(sg, new FileOutputStream
        ('tufte.graphml'))
```

ANALYZING NEIGHBORHOODS

Import the `tufte.graphml` file into Gephi for visualization and analysis. As a first step, plot the graph and highlight different types of products to get a sense of what the data looks like. Apply the ForceAtlas2 layout and use the Partition tab to color the nodes. Recall that this example has only two types of nodes—products and customers—and that nodes of different types have different properties. Products have a `group` property. The group value will be `null` for customers, so assign the color black to `null` to distinguish the relatively few customers from types of products, and view the result in the Preview tab. Map link color to the target of the link.

As shown in Figure 14-3, displaying the result reveals distinct clusters of associated products, often surrounding a single customer. Looking more closely, you can see many products within those clusters are linked to each other, indicating that products reviewed by the same people are also often purchased together. This seems to confirm that reviews are an effective complement to purchasing in reflecting customer interest.

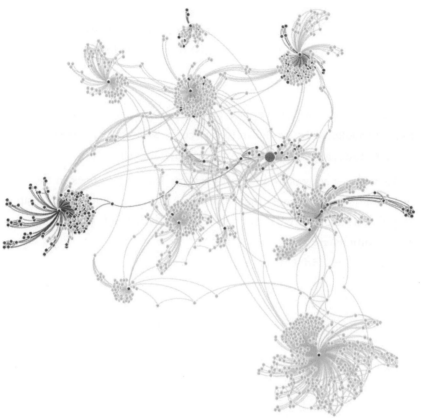

FIGURE 14-3: Associated products of interest are shown by co-purchase and co-review. Customers here are shown in black. Green products are books, red are music, blue and purple are movies. The large node is the root product, Tufte's *Envisioning Information*.

Another clear pattern that emerges is that product type is correlated with interests. Both music and movies tend to be clustered together. This is not only true in the global sense, but also at the subcluster level. Also interesting is that music tends to be more interesting to purchasers of this book than movies and that, in several cases, music products link clusters of interest.

It may also be useful to see if any patterns exist in customer rating of products with respect to interests. Using the Ranking tab, map node color to avgrating. Use a spectrum where green is a good rating, red is a bad rating, and gray is a neutral rating.

As shown in Figure 14-4, when you view the result, you see that there is no strong correlation between product interest and rating, other than the products with the worst reviews tend to be clustered together, and the very worst of them are clustered around Tufte's book where the least prolific reviewers are. Those customers were seemingly passionate enough about Tufte's book to review it, but also compelled to rate the poorly reviewed books as well. In contrast, the most prolific reviewers don't seem to take the time to review unpopular books.

FIGURE 14-4: Mapping color from customer ratings here reveals little correlation with clusters of interest, except that products with exceptionally poor reviews at the red end of the spectrum tend to be clustered together.

Color alone is enough to observe some overall patterns in the data, but it is difficult to get a sense of the character of clusters of interest.

Turn on node labels and map them from product titles. More than 1,000 titles makes for a lot of words, so a little work is required for them to be useful. Ideally, the most important titles would be featured in various clusters, and the others would be small enough not to obscure the structure of the graph. Run the Eigenvector Centrality statistic on the nodes in the graph, and map it to node size as well as intensity of color to highlight the most central nodes. Use a brief application of LabelLayout to reduce occlusion so that more of the labels are readable. Use the Preview tab to ensure that labels are turned on and proportional to node size before viewing the result.

Visualizing the graph with labels creates something akin to a word cloud for each cluster, as shown in Figure 14-5. Though it is not possible to read many of the labels, enough of the larger ones are visible to lend a sense of the characteristics of each cluster.

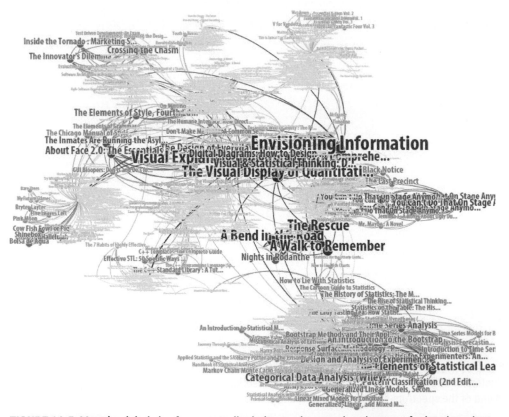

FIGURE 14-5: Mapping label size from centrality helps to characterize clusters of related products.

To begin with, the most highly related and central books by co-purchasing and co-review appear to also be highly related by subject. In fact, several of Tufte's other books are clustered around the central book of interest. The video cluster in the upper right seems to favor superhero movies. The cluster on the upper left is dominated by both marketing and higher-level software development process books, whereas the small cluster on the middle bottom left features programming books. The cluster to the left of Tufte central is dominated by design books, and below it the music cluster seems to be mostly alternative. Finally, the biggest and most spatially distant cluster, separated strangely enough by a number of romantic drama novels, is dominated by books on statistics, data analysis, and computational modeling.

Putting all of that together, you might conclude that buyers of this book are also interested in design, computer science, data science, the software business, alternative music and sci-fi action movies. If you are a fan of the book, judge for yourself, but you might find that conclusion to be surprisingly accurate.

The observations thus far about product relationships are purely based on co-interest. It would be interesting to see to what degree the categorizations applied to this book reflect the same associations.

Back in a Gremlin console, query for all of the category names, as shown here:

```
gremlin> tufteBook.out('categorization').categoryname.dedup().order
==>
==>Amazon.com Stores
==>Art & Music
==>Arts & Photography
==>Books
==>Business & Finance
==>Business & Investing
==>Business & Investing Books
==>Business Life
==>Communication
==>Communications
==>Computer & Internet Books
==>Computer Science & Information Systems
```

```
==>Computers & Internet
==>Design
==>Digital Business & Culture
==>General
==>Graphic Arts
==>Graphic Design
==>Graphics & Illustration
==>Graphics & Visualization
==>HTML, Graphics, & Design
==>Home & Office
==>Humanities
==>Internet
==>Mathematics
==>New & Used Textbooks
==>Nonfiction
==>Project Management
==>Reference
==>Sciences
==>Social Sciences
==>Specialty Stores
==>Statistical Computing
==>Statistics
==>Studio Art
==>Subjects
==>Web Development
==>Web Graphics
==>Words & Language
```

The categories seem to be a pretty close match to interests. Even categorizations such as business and project management (which are otherwise inexplicable) are reflective of interest, implying that this may be exactly the kind of data that is used to inform categorizations.

Topic Word Clouds

Categorizations were not included in the subgraph used for neighborhood analysis, but they provide a promising alternative for summarizing associated interests. Showing categories by count of products in the neighborhood of Tufte's book will provide a weighted summary of topics.

The following Gremlin queries reuse variables and functions declared earlier. The count of products for each category is calculated and stored in a map. In the next step, the categories and parentage edges are added to the new subgraph. Then, the Tufte categorizations are marked. In the last step, a root node is added to parent the top-level categories before writing out the graph.

```
gremlin> cg = new TinkerGraph()


gremlin> cmap=[:]
gremlin> products._().out('categorization').sideEffect{nv=cmap.get(it);
    cmap.put(it,nv==null?1:1+nv)}.count()


gremlin> cmap.each{k,v-> nv=cg.addVertex(k.id, ElementHelper.
    getProperties(k)); nv.setProperty('productcount',v)}
gremlin> cmap.keySet()._().outE('parent').sideEffect{addLink(it, cg)}


gremlin> tufteBook.out('categorization').dedup().sideEffect{
    cg.getVertex(it.id).setProperty('own',true)}


gremlin> root = cg.addVertex(0, [categoryname:'all', productcount: 0])
gremlin> cg.V.filter{it.outE.count() == 0 && it != root}.sideEffect
    { cg.addEdge(null,it,root,'parent'); root.productcount+= it.
    productcount}


gremlin> GraphMLWriter.outputGraph(sg, new FileOutputStream
    ('topics.graphml'))
```

Import the topics graph into Gephi and size the nodes based on productcount. Apply the OpenOrd layout to cluster, and then use ForceAtlas2 with the option to prevent overlap to fine-tune. Use filtering to reduce the graph to categories to which Tufte's book belongs, and apply a green range of colors to those nodes. Then, reverse the filtering and apply blue to the others.

Figure 14-6 shows what the data looks like. Category size is relatively uniform, and there are a lot of them. The book's own categories represent a small portion of the total, but the counts in those categories are higher than average.

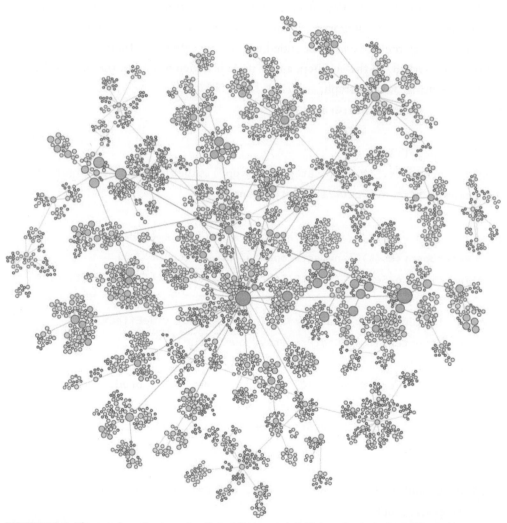

FIGURE 14-6: The number of categories linked by interest is high and relatively uniformly structured. The categorizations of Tufte's own book shown in green represent a small percentage but contain more products than most.

Showing labels for so many categories will make this difficult to read. Because they are hierarchical, with each parent summarizing its children, this is a good opportunity to use filters to remove smaller categories until the graph is easy to read but still detailed enough to describe the distribution of topics. Map labels to category names, and then use dynamic filtering on product count until you find a good threshold for displaying the right level of categorization.

Figure 14-7 shows how a display of most-significant product categories in the neighborhood of Tufte's book can be used to form a word cloud reflecting topic interest. The somewhat surprising categorization under business management is validated here because interest in those products is strong. However, one of the revelations here is that although there is some representation of statistics in the categorization of the book, it is not cataloged in the dominant categories of that nature, suggesting a missed sales opportunity.

Using node-link representations of products and customer interests, this example has shown how graph databases and queries are used to extract valuable, focused business insights from Big Data. The next section examines methods for analyzing all of the data and the situations in which that has value.

FIGURE 14-7: Filtering categories and mapping size to the number of products in each forms a topic word cloud reflective of related consumer interests surrounding *Envisioning Information*. Categorizations of the book itself are highlighted in green, highlighting the fact that although it is surprisingly filed under business management categories, it is not filed under the statistics-related categories that many related books are.

PLOTTING NETWORK ACTIVITY

The dominant type of analysis in very large graphs is to branch outward from focus nodes of interest and to analyze properties of the resulting subgraph. However, sometimes you may find it useful to analyze the graph as a whole. Physical networks are one such case. Chapter 13, "Spatial Networks," provided an example of ship routes, where plotting all of the data reveals an informative picture of all traffic. This approach can be useful for simple graph structures as well.

Figure 14-8 shows how plotting a very large graph of brain data using Aperture Tiles reveals hot paths of activity. A multi-level tiled approach achieves exploratory scalability in a similar way to Google Maps. Aperture Tiles provides a framework for computing tile-based analytics using the Apache Spark engine for large-scale data processing and, similar to Titan, can be run locally on a Hadoop cluster to scale.

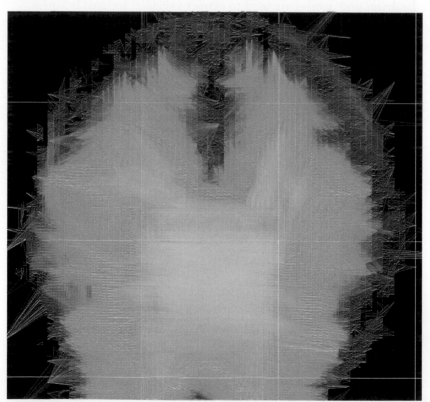

FIGURE 14-8: Multi-scale plots of network data with Aperture Tiles provides interactive pan and zoom exploration of very large graphs like the brain data shown here. A tiled approach similar to Google Maps is used to achieve massive scalability.

The same multi-level pan-and-zoom approach can be applied to visualizing geospatial networks, such as the one shown in Figure 14-9. Here, consecutive tweets by the same user are linked by location to represent travel. Millions of Twitter users sending hundreds of millions of tweets in this data set form a picture of travel patterns layered on a map. The binned batch aggregation approach is a natural fit for cloud computing platforms, providing scalability to much larger data sets. Tiles are rendered dynamically to provide runtime filtering and color scale control and can be layered, as in the case here where nodes and links are controlled and rendered as separate tile sets.

The tiled examples show how spatial plotting of all network data can be used to show hot spots and paths, overall patterns that portray the big picture. Aperture Tiles also supports annotation layers, so, for example, the most important nodes identified by page rank can be layered on the view.

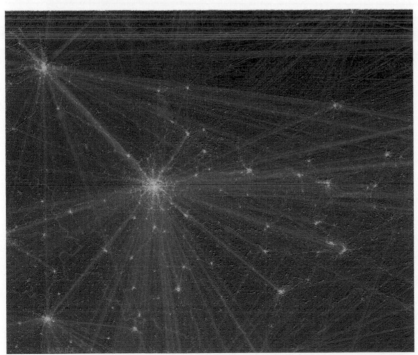

FIGURE 14-9: Tiled geospatial network plots are a seamless fit with map systems. Here, Twitter activity of millions of users is overlaid on a map, where graph links represent user travel to different locations.

COMMUNITY VISUALIZATION

Another case when depicting all of the data in a very large graph is useful is for understanding communities. This is, in fact, a primary use case for graphs on the scale of thousands of nodes as well, as reflected in many of the examples in this book. Community visualization is a significant challenge at large scales. It is difficult see communities even at a basic level without extensive interaction.

An effective approach for community visualization is to use community detection algorithms to aggregate nodes hierarchically by community. Figure 14-10 shows how the use of sized rings that represent the distribution of community members can portray more about the nature of a community and its relationships than would a traditional plot of all nodes. In this Aperture JS example, anonymous communities of donors shown in green represent those who contribute to communities of charities shown in purple. Each community is subdivided by the proportion of members in each level of "wealth" (how much they send or receive). More intensity in the color indicates greater wealth.

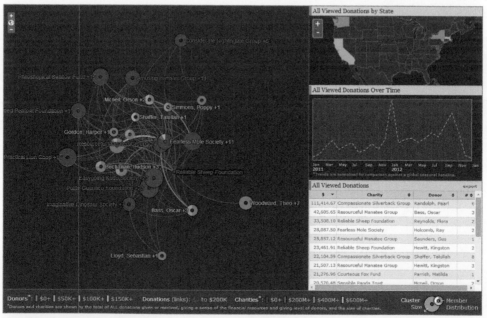

FIGURE 14-10: Community rings visually express characteristic distribution of their members. Here, anonymous donor and charity communities reflect size and makeup with links expressing flow of funds between them. When you click communities, you see additional information about their geographic makeup and financial activity in linked panes on the right.

Preserving the representation of the distribution of members provides a clear view of communities and their boundaries. It also makes it easier to interact with them and see characteristics of the links between them. In Figure 14-10, the links represent flow of money. You can click a community to explore more information—in this case, showing its geographic makeup on a map and flow of money over time. Effective visualization techniques can overcome the hairball problem common to large graphs that causes breakdown of traditional approaches as scale increases.

Versions of the modularity-based community detection algorithm used in earlier Gephi-based examples are available in distributed form for cloud platforms, providing the same functionality for larger graphs. Figure 14-11 shows community detection applied to the full product affinity graph analyzed earlier in this chapter, containing millions of nodes and links. The analytic approach here is to use Aperture Tiles to draw *all* nodes and links while still providing highlighting and drill-down interactions at the community level.

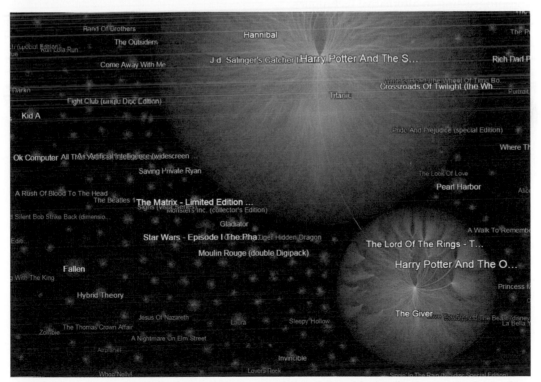

FIGURE 14-11: Community detection analytics can work in concert with visualization at massive scale. Here, Aperture Tiles is used to provide interactive exploration of a product affinity graph with millions of nodes and links. Zooming into communities reveals subcommunities of products at 14 levels of detail.

SUMMARY

This chapter introduced the challenges of Big Data and described strategies for common types of analysis. Graph databases and query languages provide a powerful and scalable interface for selecting nodes of interest and exploring characteristics of the surrounding neighborhood.

You can extract subgraphs for visualization and further analysis. You can use tiled approaches for situations in which there is benefit in seeing all of the data (for example, to analyze paths in network data). Finally, you can use community-detection algorithms coupled with expressive visualization to provide scalable views of communities in large-scale graphs, along with capabilities for exploratory analysis.

Chapter 15 examines the aspect of time and change in graph data. Dynamic graphs are a unique Big Data problem, requiring unique solutions. Several approaches are discussed, beginning with animation (which is the most common response to the problem) and progressing to alternative techniques.

15

DYNAMIC GRAPHS

Dynamic graphs represent data where nodes and links are created or removed from one point to another. Some such graphs are only concerned with viewing a snapshot of the graph at a single point, or collapse time to include all nodes and links from start to end. This time focuses on the other cases, when change in time or scenario is an important dimension of the story being portrayed.

Representing a time dimension can be particularly challenging with graphs. In scientific circles it is generally accepted that simultaneous representations of states over time are more informative than sequential representations. For example, a time series bar chart is much better at communicating behavior over time than animating changes to a single bar. In the latter case, scrolling the animation back and forth through time repeatedly would be a means of getting the gist of change but would not be as instantly accessible as a time series, as accurate for comparison, or as easy to spot correlations in behavior. Being able to see values over time at the same time is more effective. However, it may not be immediately obvious how to apply that principle to graphs.

In a graph, like a map, the horizontal and vertical dimensions are reserved for the fundamental representation itself, so they cannot be used to portray time. This presents a challenge when using both types of representations. However, things get even more challenging when using graphs. The spatial location of nodes on a map has meaning in relation to a fixed geographic frame of reference across time, whereas the spatial location of nodes in a graph has meaning only in a dynamic frame of reference, which is their relation to other linked nodes. Having no constant frame of reference when comparing graph states makes it difficult to understand the pattern of change.

This chapter looks at the problem of representing change and behaviors in graphs and walks you through approaches to best serve particular kinds of analyses.

GRAPH CHANGES

One of the most common goals in analyzing dynamic graphs is to be able to understand how network members and connections change over time or between different scenarios. For example, looking at the product affinity data from Chapter 14, "Big Data," it might be interesting to see the evolution of interest in associated products over time.

You may recall that, in the affinity example of the *Envisioning Information* book (Cheshire, CT:1990, Graphics Press) from Chapter 14, most associated products are linked through co-review and that each review has a date, ranging from Christmas 1998 to the summer of 2001. Narrowing the window of time and including only those reviews and co-reviewed products that fall within it will reveal what the neighborhood of associated products looked like at that time. Scrolling the window of time will lend a taste of how the market has evolved over the years.

This section examines several methods of visualizing changes between windows of time in the affinity data set, giving a sense of the relative strengths of each technique.

Organic Animation

In many ways, *organic animation* (where the beginning and end states look exactly as they would if treated independently, and the organic evolution between states is animated) is the most obvious technique for portraying change in graphs.

Gephi includes a dedicated capability for dynamic graphs where each graph state in a series of states is specified in full and associated with a time. A time slider is then provided to view the graph state over time. If the end goal is to produce a finished animation of evolution over time, this capability would be the first step in doing so. However, for the purposes of the exercises in this chapter, time is better spent exploring simpler and more flexible approaches to achieve a similar effect.

Return to the subgraph of product interest associated with Tufte's *Envisioning Information* book extracted in Chapter 14. Open it in Gephi, and select the Filters pane to the right. Filters provide a means of constraining the set of visible items to those that fulfill specific criteria. Filters in Gephi can be chained together by assembling them hierarchically. When assembled in this way, the filter at the lowest level of the hierarchy is evaluated first. The items that fulfill the criteria are then passed upward for evaluation to the next filter in the hierarchy, until the root filter is reached.

In this case, the root filter (to be evaluated last) should constrain the visible graph to those items that are linked in two degrees to Tufte's book. Because *all* product nodes in the subgraph are within two degrees of Tufte's book, the root filter will have no immediate effect, but once links begin to be removed by date, it will serve to hide nodes that are no longer connected.

Find Ego Network under the topology filter grouping and drag it to the Queries pane below it. The Ego Network filter constrains the set of visible nodes to those connected to the specified focus node within a specified number of hops. Enter the ID of *Envisioning Information*, and choose two as the depth of the ego network, indicating a constraint of two degrees. You can find the ID of the book by clicking it with the edit selection tool to view its properties or by selecting it in the Data Laboratory pane.

NOTE

You will often see the term *queries* or *dynamic queries* used interchangeably with filters in academic visualization literature and products. *Dynamic queries* is an old-school term that abstractly describes an interactive, on-the-fly subselection of currently viewed data based on criteria, in contrast to normal queries that select and retrieve data from a data store based on the same. In practice, this is more easily understood as *filtering*.

Expand the Ego Network filter so that its subfilter drop target is showing. Locate the Range filters under Attributes, and drag a date constraint into the Queries pane, adding it as a child of the Ego Network constraint. Turn on the filter using the button below the pane to hide those linked nodes that do not fall within the time range, as shown in Figure 15-1.

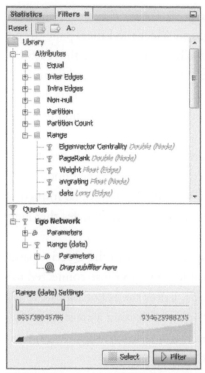

FIGURE 15-1: You can use filters to constrain the visible graph to a specific time window. Here, a Gephi Range filter is combined with an Ego Network filter to constrain the set of visible products to only those that are linked roughly within the first 8 of 32 months. Note that dates here are being represented as milliseconds since the epoch, a common standard for computers.

Activate the Force Atlas 2 layout and let it run. Use the Range (date) filter slider to adjust the start and length of the time window, and observe how the graph organically animates from one state to the other like a living thing. Playing with the slider should give you a taste of how mesmerizing graph animation can be and how well it can sometimes communicate the gist of change. It should also give you a sense of how difficult it can be to follow what is happening in any great detail.

Once you have a sense of how the slider works, constrain the date range to the first quarter of the time period. Let the layout settle a bit, and then expand the range to the first half of the time period, about 16 months. Figure 15-2 shows how the graph compares from the 8-month mark to the 16-month mark. Additional filters were applied to constrain labels to the more significant nodes. At the 4-month point, two larger clusters are visible, one at the bottom that contains a book about interpreting numbers, and one at the top near another of Tufte's books, *Visual Explanations* (Cheshire, CT: Graphics Press, 1997). At the 8-month mark, it is clear that the lower cluster has grown. However, the cluster at the top has dispersed, and it is not clear exactly how.

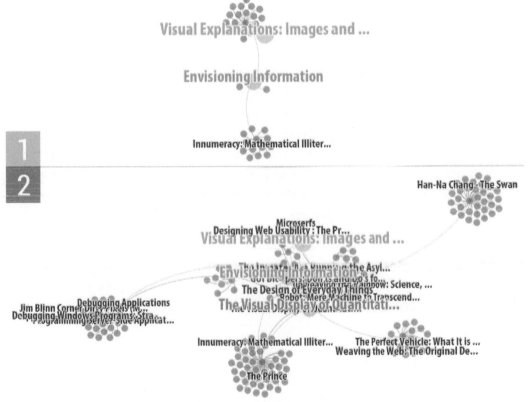

FIGURE 15-2: Applying time range filters shows the evolution of the co-interest neighborhood of the book *Envisioning Information* from the 8-month (1) to the 16-month (2) mark. The cluster at the top has clearly dispersed, but it is difficult to get a handle on the nature of the change.

The difficulty of following what happens to the upper cluster in this relatively small example illustrates the challenge of organic animation. As a graph gets bigger, it becomes increasingly impossible to maintain a sufficient number of markers in the graph (such as labels) to track and fully grasp the meaning of the movement of nodes. Although the live morphing of the graph is undeniably mesmerizing, to be truly informative, a fixed frame of reference is needed.

Full Time Span Layout

One of the most effective strategies for visualizing graph change is to apply layout to the sum of all nodes and edges across the full time span and maintain the layout through time. Fixing the layout provides a consistent frame of reference, making it easier to spot change. Applying the layout to all of the nodes ensures that space is reserved for each node to appear.

The product affinity data example already spans the full date range, making it easy to apply layout across time. When data instead describes the graph separately at each point in time, you must compute an aggregated graph that includes all nodes and links. Assign nodes their maximum size over time to reserve space for them to reach their full scale.

Returning to the graph in Gephi, turn off the date range filtering, and apply the Force Atlas 2 layout with overlap prevention on until the graph resolves itself, and then turn it off. Re-apply the date range filtering to restrict the visible graph to the first quarter of the time range. Export the resulting image for comparison, and then repeat the same process for the other three quarters.

> **NOTE** As of this writing, Gephi does not have a good method for viewing multiple graph snapshots at once. To experiment with viewing snapshots side by side, paste the images into a presentation tool like PowerPoint.

Figure 15-3 illustrates the result of viewing multiple snapshots in time using a fixed layout. The three Tufte books that appear in each of the four views provide consistent markers that anchor each view, and clearly when nodes do not move, changes are more easily understood. Unlike the previous example, here it is apparent that the cluster that seemed to disperse in fact disappeared, while new nodes appeared nearby.

To be able to see change at the node level more clearly, even more labels have been filtered out, leaving only those that are referenced most often. At a high level, the story told here (albeit with a very small sample of data) is of interest first by the design community appearing in the second time interval, then by statisticians in the third interval, and by software architects in the final interval.

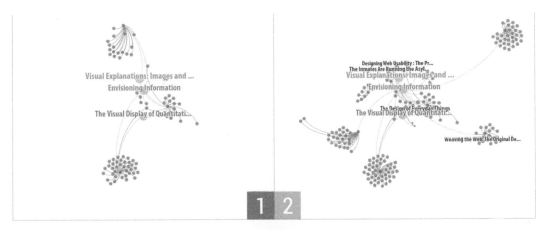

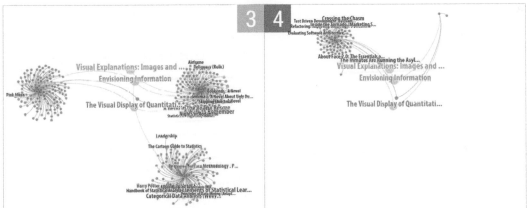

FIGURE 15-3: Snapshots of the graph over four successive periods show how communities appear over time in this sample, starting with designers (2) and followed by statisticians (3) and software architects (4). Fixed layout provides a consistent frame of reference for understanding change.

Ghosting

Although the four snapshots provide a crisp picture of each time period, the degree of change from frame to frame requires back and forth comparative inspection in some cases to figure out whether a node or cluster of nodes has disappeared in the subsequent frame. Without the constant central markers anchoring each view, it would be even more difficult to compare. The strength of the frame of reference varies depending on how many nodes carry over from the previous frame.

A second strategy for graph comparison is to carry over nodes that no longer exist and represent them in ghost form in the subsequent view. *Ghosting* is a faint or translucent "barely there" rendering. In Gephi, you can do this by using operation filters to identify the set of nodes that exists before the current time span, but are *not* in the current time span, and resetting their colors to something close to the background color. This is a bit of a tricky one-off process in Gephi, but the results indicate the value of this graphical technique.

The four frames of Figure 15-4 show the current graph in full color at successive times, with the nodes and links that are no longer part of the graph shown in light gray. Ghosting a previous state provides the perfect frame of reference for understanding change. The added advantage of this approach in a live context is that you can interact with the still-present ghosted nodes to make sense of the changes.

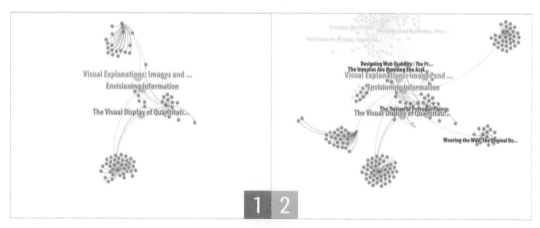

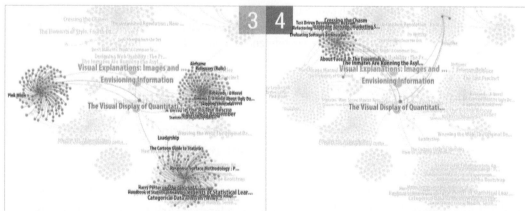

FIGURE 15-4: Ghosting past nodes clearly shows the state of the current graph in relation to previous states.

Fading

Ghosting past nodes enables you to continue to use color in the graph to express other characteristics. However, the visualization of time using this technique is limited to two states: before and after. When you need a richer understanding of evolution over time, you can use fading.

Fading uses transparency or color to progressively ghost representations of past nodes based on the length of time since they dropped out of the graph. Though it is theoretically possible to apply fading using transparency while color continues to express other properties, in practice this works only with a very limited number of colors. Age can be expressed more clearly if color is reserved for that purpose.

Figure 15-5 shows the same graph, where black nodes and links represent the current graph, and past nodes and links are shown in a fading metallic color.

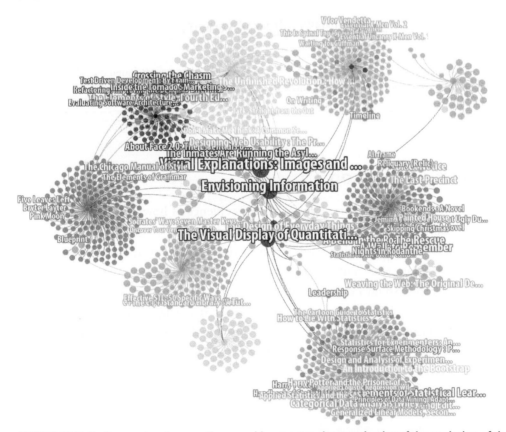

FIGURE 15-5: Fading past nodes over time provides greater characterization of the evolution of the graph and is a good choice if color is dedicated to this purpose. Here, linked black products are current and past nodes, and links shown in metallic color fade over time.

Using this technique, you can summarize the evolution of the graph over time in a single view. You can also use color to emphasize new nodes in the same context, as shown in Figure 15-6, where green nodes are new, and black nodes carry over from the previous frame.

FIGURE 15-6: Using color, you can also highlight new nodes, while old nodes are faded out. Here, new co-referenced products predominantly about software are shown in green, and carry-over products are shown in black.

Community Evolution

So far, the examples in this chapter have provided evidence of how fixed layouts are ideal for understanding graph change. You can use color to understand how communities change by gaining and losing members over time. But what if, instead of seeing change to communities, you want to see change *of* communities? Communities in this chapter's examples so far take form through layout, which is computed across all time. In some data sets, however, community structure may change dramatically in that span. New communities may form, and old ones break apart. In certain cases, it is valuable to compare communities in the current state of the graph to communities from another state.

Comparing community structures requires a different visual approach. Often, you can use layout alone (if the graph does not resolve into a hairball) or layout reinforced with color to visualize communities. To compare community structure, however, one of layout and color should depict the same structure in both views, while the other is applied independently to each. Fixing layout and coloring independently for computed communities in each view is one of the options. But a more effective choice is to compute communities for one of the views, map it to color in both views, and let both views lay out naturally to express community structure in each.

Returning to the Gephi product affinity graph, turn off filtering to see communities across all time. Run the modularity statistic to compute them, and use the partition pane to assign color to each community. Export a snapshot of the result in the Preview tab. This image will represent the final state of product communities, taking into account the full history of reviews. Return to the Overview tab, toggle filtering back on, and restrict the date range to the first part of the time period. Run the force-directed layout again. Export a second image, representing the initial state of product communities, and compare the results, as shown in Figure 15-7.

Comparing the images clearly reveals the nodes in the initial community at top, which eventually migrate to neighboring communities. In this data set, communities do not tend to change dramatically over time, but the example demonstrates how you can use the technique to see changes in community structure, however big or small.

FIGURE 15-7: Computing communities and assigning them colors that carry over to previous views shows how they evolved from previous communities. Here, members of the top-most product community split into neighboring clusters, and, surprisingly, the pink community computed in the later view is actually more cohesive in previous views.

TRANSACTION GRAPHS

In the product affinity data set used in the examples thus far, a link represents a customer product interest, the nodes of interest are products, and the goal with respect to time is to understand how associated product interests change over time. Change in product interest is manifested visually by the appearance and disappearance of product nodes. An understanding of related product interests is a valuable source of information for marketing decisions. Knowing that customers interested in visualization design books are also interested in software development is an indication that cross-advertising should help improve sales.

Similarly valuable would be an understanding of customer purchasing patterns over time by customer and customer profile. For example, knowing that customer experience with certain books triggered increased follow-on sales would be reason to put more marketing emphasis on those books. Patterns like purchasing, which involve a series of transactions over time, would not be readily visible using the approach taken thus far.

Links in a graph indicate relationships between entities. A series of graphs portrays the overall pattern of relationships at each point in time and can be compared using the techniques described earlier in this chapter. *Transaction graphs* go one step deeper and articulate the series of events within each relationship in the graph for the purposes of understanding patterns of behavior. Unique approaches to visualization and interaction are required to support transaction graph analysis.

Clustered Transaction Analysis

The immediate challenge presented by transaction graphs is one of scale. Many dynamic graphs already represent a Big Data problem, but given that transaction graphs involve the addition of a whole new dimension, they virtually *always* do. Effective visualization and navigation of transaction graphs requires strategies to deal with scale. Hierarchical clustering and aggregation of linked nodes is one such strategy. Chapter 14, "Big Data," introduced these concepts. This chapter will illustrate how they can also be applied with a time dimension, using Influent.

Influent is an open source tool for transaction analysis designed for enterprise data system integration. Influent is web-based, and, conveniently, a number of live demonstrations are available for exploration online using public transaction data sets. This example uses the small microloan demo available for download on the Influent website. The demo uses an anonymized sample of data published by Kiva, and subsequently curated for research use.

NOTE

You can find Influent documentation, demos, and download online at `http://influent.org`. To find out more about the Kiva organization, including how you can participate, visit `http://kiva.org`.

Kiva is a leading non-government organization that facilitates the international crowd-sourcing of microloans, primarily to individuals in second- and third-world countries. Participants fall into three classes:

- *Borrowers* who apply for a loan

- *Partners*, which are the financial institutions that administer the loan locally, dispensing and collecting payments

- *Lenders* who contribute to loans

Each loan has a single partner, acting as a local broker. Loans almost always have many lenders collectively contributing the funding. Lenders typically give small amounts of money to each of many loans.

To protect the system from abuse and encourage the trust of lenders, Kiva's policy is that all financial transaction activity of borrowers and partners be an open book. In addition to transaction activity, detailed descriptive information is published about both borrowers and partners. Lenders also self-publish information about themselves and the loans they support as endorsement and encouragement for others to do the same.

The Kiva data set is typical of many financial transaction data sets in nature and scale. Kiva has millions of participants and hundreds of millions of transactions, making for an ideal test case for approaches to understanding patterns of behavior.

NOTE

Although the loans that each lender in the demo contributes to are based on real data, the individual transactions of lenders are simulations only, and participants have been anonymized.

The workflow in Influent starts similarly to that of the graph database example in Chapter 14, with one or more focal nodes of interest. Like Titan, Influent supports Lucene-backed free text or criteria-based search, in this case using Solr. A graph node in Influent is an account, represented by a card. In the example shown in Figure 15-8, Farrah Sorenson is the initial node of interest, found by a search.

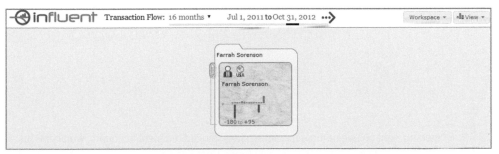

FIGURE 15-8: In Influent, a card represents an account showing key attributes using icons, and activity over the selected time period using a time series chart. Bars above and below indicate incoming and outgoing transactions.

The card for Farrah Sorenson's account shows that she is a lender (indicated by the icon of a person in a business suit), and that she lives in the United States (indicated by the geographic icon). Icons in Influent are selected for each application or data set to represent the most important summary attributes of an account holder.

Farrah's account activity from July 1, 2011, to October 31, 2012, is represented by a time series chart. Bars above the middle line indicate the pattern of deposits into her account each month, and bars below indicate withdrawals. As you might expect, the money loaned by Farrah exits her account in lump sums (indicated by the two longer bars on the bottom), and repayments enter her account in smaller increments at regular monthly intervals. Cards visually communicate chosen account attributes and activity in an efficient compact form.

Like many of the examples in Chapter 12, "Flows," transaction flow in Influent is left to right. Clicking the branch button on the right of Farrah's card retrieves all linked accounts that receive money from Farrah, as shown in Figure 15-9. The stacked card representation with the number 5 in the corner indicates a cluster of five such accounts. Clusters are aggregated for scalability, and aggregate volume of transaction flow for the selected period is reflected by a Sankey representation. The icons on the stack depict the strongest characteristics of those accounts, where the bar underneath the icon indicates what proportion of the cluster shares those characteristics. In this case, all five accounts are held by partners (indicated by the multi-person business icon), are in Indonesia, and were flagged with a configured annotation. Hovering over an icon produces a tooltip with more information.

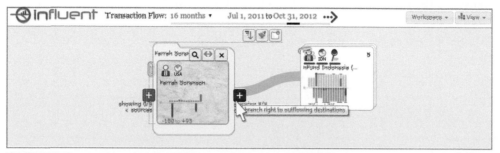

FIGURE 15-9: Branching right on one or more accounts shows linked recipient accounts, which, in this case, are five partner financial institutions that receive funds from Farrah.

The stack of partner accounts has a paper clip in the upper-left corner. Clicking the paper clip expands the cluster, revealing its member accounts, where the amount of money flowing to each account is indicated by the width of the link, as shown in Figure 15-10.

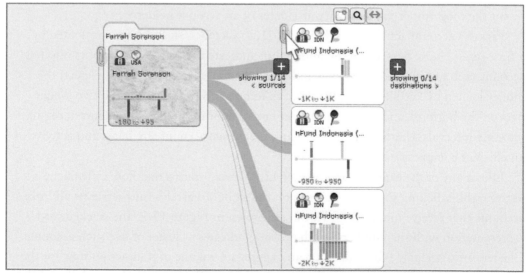

FIGURE 15-10: Expanding a stack reveals members of the cluster, which, in this case, are five loan accounts administered by the same partner. Width of line indicates how much Farrah lends to each.

In this case, each of the accounts belongs to the same partner. Because partners act as brokers, where all fund transfers are associated with one particular loan, there is an account for each loan. In this case, all five loans that Farrah gives to are apparently managed locally by the same partner. Because Farrah is the highlighted account (outlined in orange), the subset of transactions that involve her in the linked accounts to the right are also highlighted in orange. Highlighting is a way of seeing the pattern of activity across links, in the context of all of the activity for that account.

The pattern of activity for partners should look symmetrical. Partners simply broker payments between lenders and borrowers, so asymmetry would suggest something unusual. It's difficult to tell, however, if this is the case, because bars are being clipped, indicated by the black caps.

Clicking the highlight flow button on the top partner card makes it the focus, as shown in Figure 15-11. In addition to highlighting flow to adjacent accounts, highlighting an account scales all activity charts to it. Now that they have been rescaled, the charts reveal that the pattern of transactions is indeed symmetrical, albeit sometimes with a minor delay in processing repayments. Flow lines and cards provide a rapid means of understanding transaction activity between entities, as well as scanning for abnormal patterns.

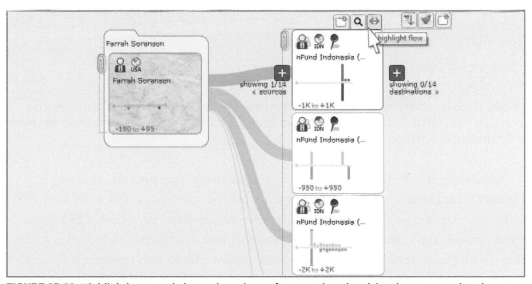

FIGURE 15-11: Highlighting a card shows the subset of transactions involving that account in other accounts and scales other charts to it.

Collapsing the partner stack using the paper clip and highlighting it scales the charts to the sum of all transactions for that cluster. Clicking the branch button on the right side of it retrieves all accounts that receive money from it, as shown in Figure 15-12. There are two stacks to the right. A stack of five loans is represented by the plain person icon. Because lenders receive repayments that partners pass along, all contributing lenders to the five loans appear here as well, including Farrah. Now that members of the cluster come from different countries, it is clear how the bars underneath each icon work to indicate the proportion of members that share that attribute. In this case, almost half of the lenders live in the United States.

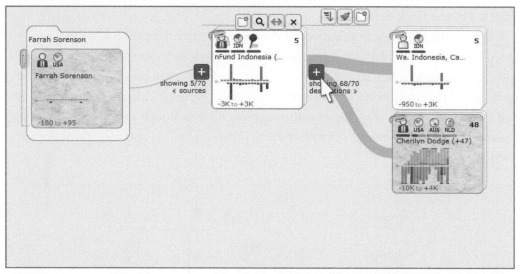

FIGURE 15-12: Branching right on partner accounts here shows all loans and lenders that receive payments. For each cluster of accounts, bars beneath the icons show the proportion of members that share that defining characteristic.

Expanding the cluster of five loans reveals their transaction patterns, as shown in Figure 15-13. Different types of accounts have different patterns of normal activity. For loans, you might expect "normal" to be a lump-sum loan dispersal, followed by repayments on a regular schedule. Looking at the charts here, that pattern holds for most of them, with the exception of one, which seems to show a lump-sum repayment. One of the accounts also shows no activity for the current time period, indicating that the loan was taken out earlier or later.

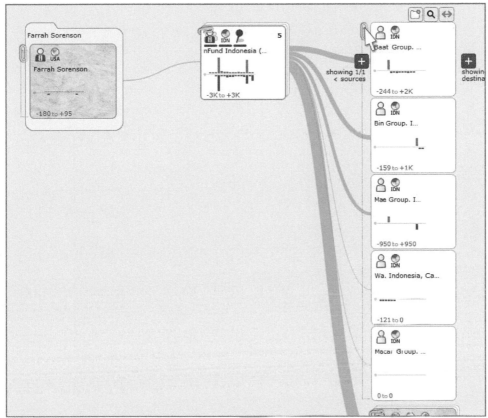

FIGURE 15-13: Expanding a cluster of loans reveals the pattern of activity for each. Most receive a lump sum and follow a monthly repayment schedule, with the exception of one, which seems to pay the money back in a lump sum. Making activity visible makes it easy to spot anomalies.

If you expand the larger cluster of lenders as shown in Figure 15-14, you see that clustering is hierarchical. When the number of accounts exceeds a manageable number for viewing, it is clustered again. The attributes on which an account is clustered are configurable. Here, you can see that after type of account, they are clustered geographically. The first set of lenders is from the Americas, mostly from the United States, and the next set is from Europe. The width of the links leading to each indicates the amount of money flowing to each cluster.

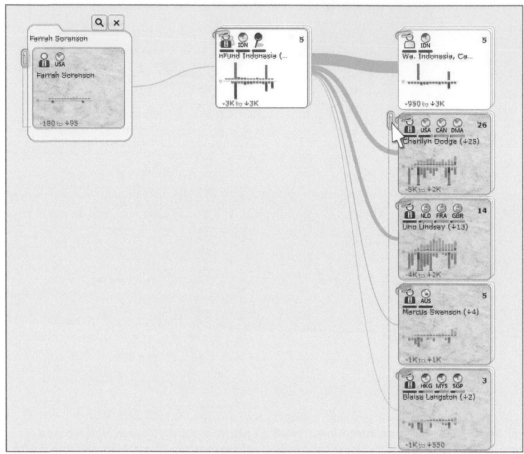

FIGURE 15-14: Clustering is hierarchical. Unstacking using the paper clip reveals the next level down in the hierarchy. In this case, accounts are clustered by type, then by geography at several levels, and eventually by name. Clustering occurs on each level of expansion until a manageable number of accounts exist for viewing.

Time series charts and selective use of icons chosen to suit a particular data set provide compact summary visualization of key account characteristics. Tailored ensemble clustering provides scalability and allows for a much richer representation of nodes in large numbers than a single-colored dot per node. Aggregating nodes and links, as well as using a left-to-right layout, ensures that the visualization does not turn into an indecipherable hairball. Rich representations and drill-down capabilities ensure that valuable details are not lost through aggregation.

Spatial Transaction Analysis

Dynamic spatial networks present a unique challenge. When spatial location is an important part of the story, options for expressing time visually are limited. Not only do transactions occur between entities in the network over time, entities themselves move. For example, courier services may track their vehicles by GPS to manage routing and delivery, and opportunities for package transfer may occur if routes cross at the same time.

When nodes are in motion over the course of a time span being analyzed, the most natural way to visualize it is to draw a line through their path, forming a trail. Figure 15-15 shows a simple example of the route of two taxis in the San Francisco Bay Area using this technique. One of the limitations of this approach, however, is that time is not actually a visible dimension. Sequences are visible, but not *when* things happen or the rate at which they happen. For example, you cannot see here when the taxis started and ended their routes, how fast they were driving, or how long they stopped in any one place.

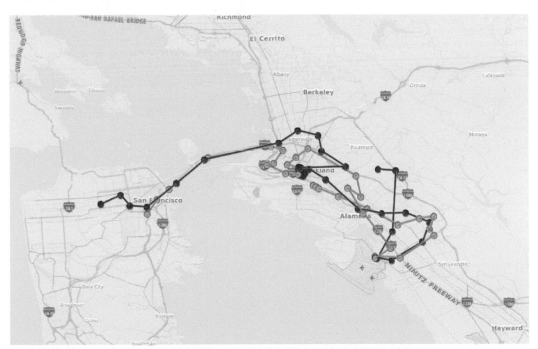

FIGURE 15-15: Trails are a natural method of expressing a path through space and a sequence, but lack a time dimension. Although this visualization of taxi routes could potentially be improved by varying saturation by age, it wouldn't be enough to see if and when a meeting occurred.

The lack of a time dimension also limits the expression of transactions between entities. Viewing the taxi example in this case would not answer the question of whether the two taxis met to exchange an item, and, if so, where and when. As was the case in the financial transaction data set, you need a time dimension to be able to see behaviors. In this case, the solution is to escape flatland.

Figure 15-16 shows the same data in 3-D using GeoTime. The third dimension in this case is time, where things that happened most recently are closest to the ground. Interactively rotating the view around helps you to see where the lines are steep, indicating speed of travel, and when they are flatter. More importantly, whereas the 2-D view indicated that they crossed paths many times, only in the 3-D view is it clear that they may have met in the Oakland area. A time dimension makes it possible to see when events occur and provides a way to see an entire series of events, enabling an analyst to understand the whole story.

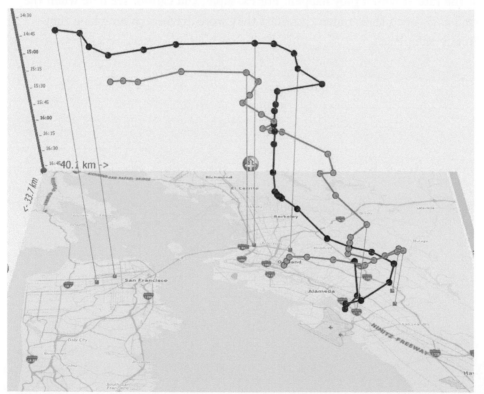

FIGURE 15-16: Using a third dimension allows movements and events to be expressed in time, telling the whole story. Unlike in the previous 2-D example, visualizing taxi routes here in 3-D using GeoTime shows a meeting could not have occurred anywhere but in Oakland.

You can find information about GeoTime and additional examples at
http://geotime.com.

Visualization of behaviors may be complemented by computational pattern finding. Both Influent and GeoTime include capabilities for matching patterns of activity. Figure 15-17 shows a simple example of how you can use an algorithm to find close proximity intersections of routes in space and time and highlight them visually.

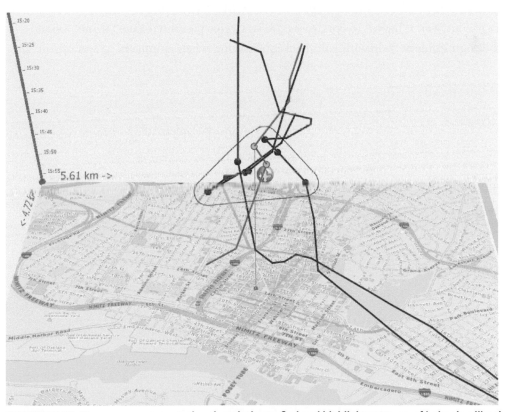

FIGURE 15-17: You can use computational analytics to find and highlight patterns of behavior, like the GeoTime meeting finder here, which looks for close proximity encounters in space and time.

SUMMARY

Dynamic graphs represent a unique and challenging aspect of the Big Data problem. The addition of time adds an order of magnitude to the data needing representation. This chapter covered strategies for seeing and making sense of the evolution of the world of entities and relationships represented by graph structure. It also covered strategies and tools for visualization and analysis of transaction patterns between entities that share a relationship, in both abstract and spatial contexts.

Two of the lessons of this chapter and of this book as a whole are that a graph can take many forms and that the best approach is highly dependent on the questions you are seeking to answer. Chapter 16 condenses the strategies presented thus far into a structured design guide to help with your decision-making when approaching a new problem.

16

DESIGN

Great visualization requires design. The use of standard forms and visual mappings can deliver reasonable results, but you can achieve greater effectiveness by tailoring visual representations to the data and the information sought.

Many people make the mistake of thinking that design is simply the cosmetic process of taking something and making it pretty. Great visualization design is about maximizing human performance. Effectiveness of visualization is about communicating the best possible information more fully, more clearly, and more quickly. Different forms are ideal for different problems. Choosing visual representations and interactions for data elements can make a significant difference in how accurately, easily, and quickly the viewer can perceive information. Information visualization design is the art of making those choices.

Design is both an art and a science. For example, many of the decisions made in designing an opera house involve a great deal of science about how humans interact with and in a built environment. Yet, no two opera houses look the same, and it would be inconceivable to think of fully automating the design of one. That's where the art of design comes in.

Visualization design is guided by principles of human perception and cognition, the specific information-seeking goals and experience of a user community, and the characteristics of data. Synthesis of a system that satisfies all of these complex factors is an art.

Many of the tools for graph visualization and analysis in this book offer very little in the way of design support. They tend to offer a lot in the way of low-level customization, but very little in the way of higher-level patterns and structures. Choosing graph type and layout were covered earlier in this book. This chapter consolidates principles and techniques used in previous chapters and assembles them in a concise, structured form as a reference that you can use to help you design a graph.

NODES

Nodes are the most important elements of a graph. They are the subjects between which you are looking to find relationships. No facet of information is complete without them. A rich and informative graph visualization begins with expressive nodes. The world of possibilities is much bigger than with colored circles. Application of even the least bit of creative thinking about node expression can increase graph effectiveness immensely.

Because nodes are more important than links, they should be drawn in a layer above them. The one exception is if a subgraph is highlighted in the context of a larger graph, in which case links in the subgraph should be drawn above nodes that are not. For example, Figure 16-1 shows how flights in and out of William P. Hobby airport in Houston (HOU) might be highlighted in the context of larger graphs to look for flight routes with high average delays.

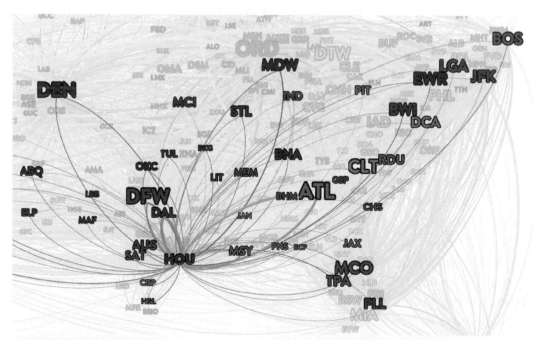

FIGURE 16-1: Draw links over the top of nodes only when the links belong to a highlighted subgraph, and the nodes do not. In this flight delays example, routes in and out of Houston are highlighted in the context of the full network of airports.

Links should be drawn in a layer under nodes, except when they are part of a highlighted subgraph, in which case they should be drawn above nodes that are not highlighted.

Node Shape

Virtually all graph visualization tools support some choice of shape. Circles are used far more than any other option. Of the abstract shapes, circles centered on the node coordinate are the perfect choice. Knowing the radius of each node, links drawn to that same distance from each coordinate can be guaranteed to end at the edge of the node at perfect right angles.

Circles form an ideal relationship with their links, which helps when visually deciphering which links and nodes are connected. This is especially helpful in a more densely connected graph where links cross nodes in their path.

Circles easily outperform other shapes like squares and triangles as shown in Figure 16-2. However, the airline network visualization shown in Figure 16-1 serves as an illustration of the value of using symbols over abstract shapes altogether. Using airport codes in this case makes each of them immediately identifiable while maintaining a relatively compact shape.

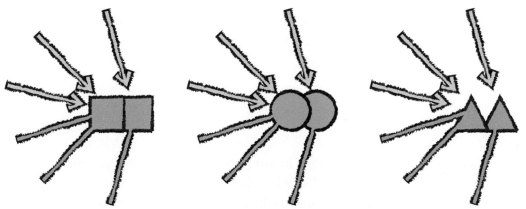

FIGURE 16-2: Circles centered on the node coordinate outperform all other abstract shapes. They are easily perceived as discrete shapes, unlike the squares here, and their clear centroid and equidistance from it forms a perfect graphic relationship with links, making it clear what connects to what.

Symbols

Striving for "recognition rather than recall" (as phrased by usability expert Jakob Nielson in 1995) is a fundamental strategy for improving visualization. It is also one that is often overlooked. For example, the use of arbitrary colors and abstract shapes is common practice but requires an analyst to learn and recall the unrelated mapping between visual and real-world elements to decode a visualization. This can be a significant source of friction in comprehension. Legends are useful and important, but they are not a cure-all for poor design.

The use of symbols increases the chance that an analyst will immediately recognize what's being presented, improving the analyst's ability to perceive information. Even in cases when recognition is not immediate, symbols provide a mnemonic for more easily remembering the mapping. For example, in Figure 16-1, you might not immediately recognize the airport symbol MCO, but once informed, it is easier to remember that MCO represents the Orlando International Airport than it would be by location alone.

Use of all caps for a letter-based symbol helps to ensure that each symbol fills a more consistent block of pixels and is equally weighted left to right, making for better spatial harmony in the visualization. A condensed font where letters are not as wide can help to keep the symbol more square in shape, which tends to work better in a typical graph layout.

> **TIP**
>
> Avoid the use of abstract shapes like squares and triangles to communicate information. Use simple circles if the graph is large enough that nodes are extremely small or dense. Otherwise, use symbols that can leverage recognition or aid recall.

Icons

Letter-based symbols are a great choice in many cases, but if nodes are too small or densely grouped, it becomes difficult to read them. Sometimes icons are a better option. Icons can often be recognized more universally across languages, which is why they are often heavily used in applications like airport signage. They also can be more compact than letters, allowing for greater density of use.

Icons can also work in combination with colors to better tell types apart when the number of unique colors required is high enough that there is potential for confusion. They can also be used inside of circles if the nodes are large enough (and, by implication, if the graph is small enough). Figure 16-3 shows a portion of the same graph of National Basketball Association (NBA) fan communities by gender previously shown in Chapter 11, "Communities" (Figure 11-8), this time with iconic shapes instead of circles. By using standard icons, you make it immediately clear what the nodes represent, without the need to refer to a legend.

FIGURE 16-3: Icons provide a compact shape that can help to tell a story more clearly. Universally recognizable standards like the ones used here are best, but relatively rare.

One thing to be careful about when using icons or any other shape is not to rely solely on shape as a means for the analyst to spot patterns. In the gender icon example, it is really still color that is crucial to seeing trends. Shape adds clarity to the representation by color, but it does not replace it.

When you use icons as the primary shape as shown in Figure 16-3, they can be deciphered at relatively small scales. However, they do not have the ideal relationship with links that circles do, and they include small variations in area that make indication by size a little less precise. If the graph is small enough that nodes can be drawn at a larger scale, you could embed the icon in a circle as an enhancement to it, gaining some of the best of both worlds. Figure 16-4 shows a small portion of the graph using this approach. This technique can work when both icon and color are encoding the same thing as shown here, but it can also work if mapped to different properties like age and gender.

Icons like the one you see when you want to save a file have become universally recognizable standards—so recognizable that they can outlive the object or concept that they model (like the floppy disk icon that indicates Save functionality). Other icons become standards in a particular industry. Standards serve as a useful shared lexicon to leverage for recognition.

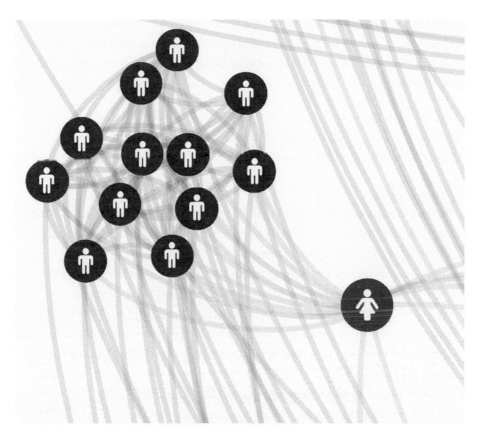

FIGURE 16-4: If the graph is small enough and nodes are large enough, icons can be embedded inside of circles, enhancing or complementing what is being shown by color.

Standard iconic symbols are an ideal choice but seldom available for the types in the data being represented. Fortunately, to be useful, symbols do not need to be immediately recognized by everyone. The reality is that the representation of only a small percentage of icons is instantly clear, such as the gender icons used here. Most icons require some degree of interpretation. Interpretation of an icon typically involves basic knowledge of the nature of the data, as well as inference as to what the symbol might map to in that context.

Interpretation of an icon also depends on being able to see other icons in the same context. Icons do not work in isolation. They operate as a family. Even in the gender icon case here (where the symbolic mapping seems obvious), the clarity of interpretation depends heavily on the presence of both icons. As a pair, the symbols have become a standard for signifying female and male, but the symbol used for male works only in contrast to female. On its own, it is likely to simply signify a person. For that reason, it is important to consider whether an icon will appear in isolation, and, if so, an accompanying label will be important.

> **TIP** Symbols work together as a family to facilitate interpretation. Consider that icons used in isolation are more ambiguous.

Icons can also serve as mnemonic tokens to help cognition, even when there is little hope that they will be recognized immediately by a new viewer. The game Monopoly serves as a simple illustration of this phenomenon.

Monopoly is a game for up to eight players, an unusually high number for a board game. Most board games are designed for four or six players, and, in the majority of those, each player is represented by a distinct color that distinguishes his or her piece on the board. Monopoly instead uses physical tokens like a wheelbarrow, a hat, a car, and an iron. A token is replaced every so often, but what does not change is that the tokens have nothing to do with the theme of the game—real estate.

In fact, there is no theme at all to the tokens used. The pieces chosen have only two common traits. Each represents a simple, easily recognized and memorable concept, and that concept is distinctly different from every other. Contrast that with the use of color (the choice of many games with four to six players), which becomes more difficult to distinguish in higher numbers.

Distinct icons can be more easily recognized than distinct colors if more than seven or so types are represented. Icons can also have a stronger character or identity on the whole, making it easier to remember what they represent.

For example, the Monopoly pieces have no thematic relation to the game, but they have a strong conceptual identity. Players don't generally rationalize their choice of token, but if Mom chooses the wheelbarrow, you might remember that by associating the piece with her love of gardening, or if Tim chooses the top hat, you might associate it with his passion for acting. There is no right or wrong interpretation of a choice of representation. It simply serves as a device for remembering which tokens represent whom. In the same way, icons serve a useful function even when the mapping to data is not immediately self-evident.

A conceptually strong and distinct icon serves as a mnemonic device, even when the data it represents is not immediately self-evident.

So, if icons don't always need to be immediately self-evident to be useful, where can you go wrong when using them? Icons can destroy a perfectly good visualization in a number of ways. The first and most obvious one is through confusion. Icons need to not only be conceptually and visually distinct from each other, but they also need to be distinct from types (or expected types) in the data that they do *not* represent. If an analyst is regularly confusing the mapping of an icon with a different data type, it will continually be a source of frustration.

More common pitfalls have to do with the visual design execution of an icon. The first is an icon that is too intricate and overly complicated. An icon should have a clear and recognizable dominant shape. It should not look like a series of chicken scratches. Related to that, it should have a fill area of reasonable size, and that fill area should be relatively consistent across the family of icons. The amount of "ink" that an icon is given to show meaning (that is, its *perceptual budget*) should be the same as other icons drawn at the same scale. Icons should generally also be designed to be relatively square—that is, their width and height should be similar.

Design icons with a recognizable dominant shape that is relatively close in width and height. Use a relatively uniform fill density across icons.

Misuse of color is also a common issue. You should not use color for icons except to represent data. You should not use color to communicate the construct used as the symbol. Use of color creates too much visual "noise," interfering with display of other more important information. Some of the best icons often use only one color for fill. If there is a chance that the background will include the same color as the fill, a contrasting outline is also important.

Avoid icons with color except when communicating properties of the data. Use of complex colored icons is a common way to wreck visualization.

Icon Libraries

Icon design is a time-consuming task that requires both skills and software programs that many people don't have. So, what are the best sources for icons, and how can they be integrated into a visualization? In keeping with the theme of this book, here are a number of open source options that highlight the different approaches.

Unicode is the standard map of character codes to font glyphs, which enables the same text to appear correctly in any font. As shown in Figure 16-5, Unicode includes many code blocks for symbols. The musical symbol used in some of the visualizations in Chapter 11 is an example of a Unicode symbol.

FIGURE 16-5: Unicode includes code blocks for thousands of icons, such as the weather and transportation icons shown here in the Segoe UI Symbol font. Few fonts, however, include these characters.

The great thing about Unicode is that it can take advantage of symbols that are already present on your computer system and are coded consistently across fonts. The drawback, however, is that Unicode is far too big for any one font to support in entirety, so relatively few fonts include these characters, and the quality of those that do can vary widely. The other limitation is that the set of defined Unicode symbols is finite and not particularly well-curated.

The second option is to use a specially crafted font that contains only symbols, where the symbols are inserted in place of normal character codes in the font, like the letter "a" or "q." This is a longstanding trick that came back into fashion in web design with the introduction of browser support for dynamically supplied web fonts, enabling them to be reliably supplied as a component of the page that uses them, rather than depending on them being already resident on a user's computer.

An example of a symbol font is Font Awesome, which was used for the gender icons in the previous examples. The potential disadvantage of using a symbol font stems from it being a bit of a hack of a system designed for something else. The character-to-symbol mapping is unique to the font used, so if the characters appear in any other font, the result will be incomprehensible.

Use of web fonts ensures that the right font will be used in a browser. However, problems can still occur in desktop visualizations with regularity if, for example, graph files are opened on another computer. If the tool does not support embedding fonts in the file and the font is missing from the system (which is very often the case), the intended symbols will not be displayed.

It can also be a bit tricky to get the characters into the visualization. With a graph visualization tool like Gephi, the typical method would be to code the icon text values directly into the source data, which works but is essentially a blind process. The values will not be intelligible in any view of the source data. If the visualization tool supports it, the best solution is instead to specify the icon abstractly through the use of a type name and have the tool map that to the appropriate character code. As shown in Figure 16-6, this is essentially the approach that Font Awesome provides for web-based visualization through use of CSS class names.

FIGURE 16-6: Specialized symbol fonts like Font Awesome as shown here provide custom icon libraries in a relatively convenient and efficient form.

Common advantages of font-based icons in a web browser include simple potential for efficiency of loading. Downloading one font file is much more efficient than downloading a similar number of symbols individually. Another advantage universal to both web and desktop includes support for mapping fill or outline to data-driven colors to visualize properties of the data.

Disadvantages include alignment headaches when you are trying to center symbols at different scales, and wasted bandwidth and load time if only a few icons are used. Fonts also do not support more than one fill color per character, which can present a challenge when it comes to achieving clarity at small sizes. Sometimes that constraint can be a good forcing function for better design, but, in reality, plenty of poor results still happen.

The third icon library option is the most obvious one, which is to supply the icons as images. In addition to traditional image formats like JPEG or PNG, which define the image as a grid of pixels, modern web browsers support images in Scalable Vector Graphics (SVG) format, which, similarly to fonts, describes shapes in vector form. SVG images perfectly scale to any size but differ from fonts in that they can include more than one color and transparency, which can help to disambiguate similar shapes.

The Aperture JS icons used in Chapter 12, "Flows," and shown in Figure 16-7 are examples of SVG format icons. Like fonts, any image-based set of icons can also be provided as one file for efficient loading in a web environment, using Cascading Style Sheets (CSS) to draw from the correct area of the image. They can also be embedded directly in the source for a web page. The downside of image-based icons is difficulty in mapping color dynamically from data. If required, it is easier and more optimal to do that with font-based icons.

FIGURE 16-7: SVG image icons like the Aperture JS icons shown here provide support for subtle use of color to complement differentiation by shape but can still scale to any size. Colors can be styled through CSS.

> **TIP** Symbol fonts provide a fast and efficient source of icon shapes for coloring dynamically from data. SVG icons provide a source for icons that use shading or color to enhance the use of shapes in clearly distinguishing types.

Node Size

Node shape is only one dimension of graph expression, but clearly it is an important and highly nuanced one. Node size is another, and comparatively, it is dead simple. You should generally use node size in any reasonably large graph. Node size emphasizes what's most important in a graph when there is a lot to take in.

The first rule of node size is hopefully a rather obvious one, which is that size should only be mapped from magnitudes, with larger sizes indicating greater magnitude. Often, node size is mapped from a derivate graph data value like degree, which is the number of links attached to it, or a more sophisticated (but computationally expensive) measure of significance (like betweenness centrality). The minimum node size in a large graph is typically related to the number of pixels required to display the node shape with sufficient clarity. A node should also be a little bigger than its widest link. The maximum node size is typically related to the number of nodes in the graph.

A smaller graph can afford a greater range in node size, whereas, in a very large graph, the range of size must be minimal. Even a size difference of a few pixels in each direction, however, can make for a perceptible, informative difference.

Technically, to be perceptually correct, the area and not the radius or height and width of a node should be linearly proportional to the value it represents. However, in graph visualization, very often this is less useful than a rule of thumb about the overall distribution of node size.

Because the function of node size in a graph is to communicate relative significance of nodes and significance is a fuzzy measure, it is more important to be able to see size relative to others than it is to be able to visually decode it precisely to a value. A reasonable rule of thumb is that the number of first-class nodes that can be easily perceived to be most important is 25 or less, and the number of perceptible second-class nodes is not much more than 100. The goal is to be able to make out the key nodes individually in the general mass context of communities. To achieve the target distribution, you can use non-linear scales.

> **TIP**
>
> Use node size to emphasize nodes that are most significant in the graph. You can use non-linear scales to create several visible levels of significance, starting with a small number of nodes that are most important.

Node Labels

Labels are a critical part of virtually all forms of graphs. Geographic maps are an example of a highly evolved form of visualization that uses sophisticated systems of labeling. Compare that to a graph, where, unlike in a map, location of elements cannot be learned over time. Yet, labeling is notoriously poor in graph tools. Labeling everything in a medium- to large-sized graph quickly becomes too cluttered. In those cases, use graph analytics to identify the most important nodes and label those.

You should draw labels over the top of nodes, and, in most cases, you should give them an outline so that they can draw on top of each other on occasion without rendering the topmost label unreadable. Try to keep labels short. If the data contains long names, add a shortened version for display, and make the full version accessible through selection or hover.

LINKS

Links are what makes a graph a graph. But what they tell us, they tell us about nodes. Nodes are the principal subject of a graph visualization, and so, accordingly, node perception is more important than link perception.

To use an audio analogy, if links begin to interfere with the ability to read nodes, they should be dialed down to be visually quieter so that the nodes can be heard. For example, you should draw links behind nodes and not use fully saturated, attention-grabbing colors. Often, transparency is useful in displaying links because they will naturally then blend with the background color, making them less visually noisy. As an added bonus, transparency allows the overlapping of links to be more easily seen. In most cases, you should either draw links in neutral colors or interpolate between colors of the nodes at either end.

Link Shape

Links are almost always represented as lines but, like nodes, can also vary in form. One common variation is that you can draw them as either curved or straight lines.

Straight lines point directly from one node to the other, which makes it a little easier to see where they are headed when focused on or zoomed into one of the nodes. In a geographic layout, for example, this can imply a destination, even when the destination cannot be seen. Straight lines can also be drawn more quickly, so in a graph with a lot of links, straight lines will perform better.

Curved lines, on the other hand, are less likely to completely obscure each other. A short line and long line in the same path will be easier to see because their arcs will follow a different path. Curved lines also communicate directionality, if the links have a direction. Typically, you use a clockwise arc, so clockwise swoops indicate the direction of flow. A link from A to B and one from B to A will also disentangle nicely when they are curved, providing the capability for you to express different weights in each direction.

Try curved links unless the number of them is so high that drawing them all is too slow. Unless the graph is geospatial, this will almost always produce clearer results, and the curved links can be used to communicate directionality.

Directional Indication

Clockwise arcs are a great base-level indication of direction. You can also add arrowheads for clearer self-expression, but only when you have few links to display. Otherwise, they will create too much visual clutter. A third option is to use tapered links, which resemble arrowheads that span the complete distance from source to destination node. Tapered links can indicate direction along their whole length.

However, it's good to keep in mind that if directionality is important in a graph and the graph is big enough that arrows are no longer easily perceived, you should consider techniques other than link representation, like those documented in Chapter 12. More often, directionality is present in large graph data but is not as important to see as communities are. In these cases, typically curved links are sufficient.

Offsets

When links become dense, it can be difficult to see whether a link passes through a node or terminates at it. A small link offset of a few pixels around the node in a small- or medium-sized graph can help to clarify where the link begins or ends. Offsets are particularly important if arrows are used. Offsets give arrowheads enough space to display comfortably next to each other. The lower graph image in Figure 16-8 demonstrates the use of offsets on the target end of the link for exactly this purpose.

Line Styles

Line styles can sometimes be used to indicate different types of links, if differentiation by type is important. Geographic maps have a longstanding tradition of using line style for features such as rail lines and borders. However, several principles are at play in making these successful, and these principles apply to graphs as well.

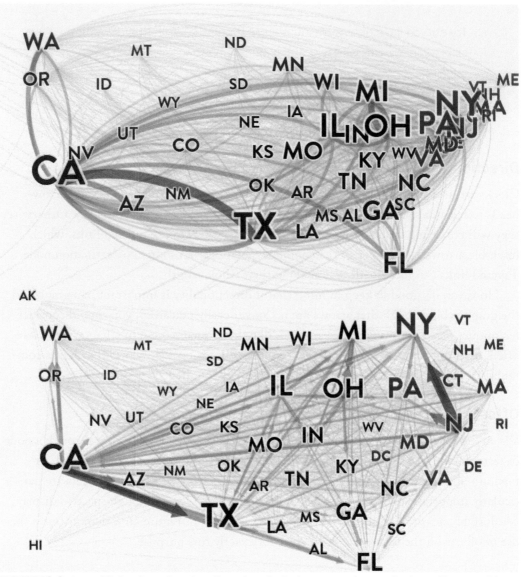

FIGURE 16-8: Curved links show directionality using clockwise arcs and naturally deconflict, as evident here with incoming flow of goods to California, which are obscured in the straight-line version below it. Extra spacing and offsets are used in the straight-line version to make room for arrowheads.

The first is that the style used, in most cases, refers to a physical property of the feature. A rail line has regular ticks along a solid line (which refer to railway ties at regular intervals along rails), and borders are dashed (indicating an intangible feature). To an extent, like icons, these are learned vocabularies, but their form reminds the analyst physically of what they represent.

The second principle is that application of line style is rarely combined with application of color. Railway lines and borders are drawn in gray, operating as a second order to the principle order of roads, which use color to differentiate levels of hierarchy within the network.

The exception to the rule of not combining line style and color (and the third principle) is that dotted lines virtually always refer to an insubstantial version of the same class of item shown in solid, whether that is because they are planned but not yet made or because they are highly uncertain or unreliable.

> **TIP**
>
> You can use line styles in gray that use symbolic reference to hint at what is being represented as a complement to the use of color in differentiating link types. You can use dotted lines to indicate uncertain or otherwise insubstantial links.

Line Width

Line width is an obvious choice for indicating strength of relation or volume of flow, depending on the data being represented. Similar to node size, line width should only be mapped to magnitude values.

> **NOTE**
>
> Line width figures significantly in the visualization of flows. Chapter 12 is devoted to flow-focused graphs, including Sankey diagrams.

Unless a Sankey diagram is the form of choice, the variation in line width will need to be relatively small. With only a few pixels to work with, if it is informative to do so, line widths can be quantized to represent ranges of data. For example, if links represent cash flow from $1 to $100,000, rather than simply scaling line width linearly based on amount, you can choose line widths categorically based on the range that values fall into—$1 to $25,000; $25,000 to $50,000; or $50,000 to $100,000.

Whereas scaled lines portray a fuzzy impression of magnitude, quantized line choices enable the viewer to know immediately whether a link value falls above or below meaningful thresholds.

Relational Nodes

In most cases, a relation between two nodes (where nodes are the subject of interest) is expressed as a single link. In certain cases, however, it can be useful to break out relation types into their own nodes.

For example, if your goal is to identify communities in a social network, a view of three people who are related as real-life neighbors can benefit from having links loop through an address relation node of "20-27 Harper Lane," or a view of three nodes that share a phone number might be improved by looping through a common node, "1-800-899-2121."

Breaking down shared relations into relational nodes enables a single label to express the relation and helps nodes that share that relation to be drawn together in layout. This approach is often referred to as a *shared attribute graph*. Figure 16-9 shows an example.

When nodes are used to express relations, it is important to visually express them differently from subject nodes. Relational nodes should be perceptually recessive relative to primary nodes and should blend seamlessly with the links they are articulating. You can think of relational nodes as stepping stones in links, and they should be expressed accordingly.

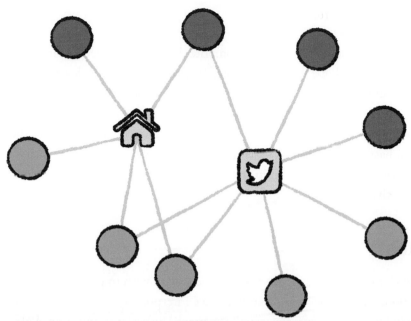

FIGURE 16-9: A shared attribute graph extracts commonalities as relational nodes to reveal associations between entities. Here, a common neighborhood and shared Twitter feed imply a community. Relational nodes should use a different representational vocabulary, making it clear that their function is to join primary nodes.

Link Labels

Link labels are seldom advisable. Use them only in small graphs and in cases when they can independently and fully express a concept.

For example, a link from the nodes "Wardrobe" to "Forest" that is labeled "Lucy enters Narnia" is self-expressive. A link from "Lucy" to "Edmund" labeled "sister of" may have use in other disciplines but is a poor communication device. Do not require the viewer to piece together fragmented concepts across links. Consider using a system of relational nodes instead, where the link representation simply indicates a shared attribute. For example, in this case, Lucy and Edmund might be linked to a secondary node labeled "Pevensie Child," where all links of this type are represented the same way and understood to be attributes.

COLOR

Color is an important dimension of any visualization. The difference between a visualization with good color choices and one with poor choices is enormous. Poor color palettes can render a visualization incomprehensible. Color choice is undoubtedly an art, but there is a great deal of science behind it that has to do with how we see and perceive.

The principles involved provide a framework for approaching color choices and, at the very least, should be a basis for recognizing when poor choices are being made. Principles are by no means prescriptive, however. Within the guidelines presented here, there is still plenty of room for creative artistry.

Color Palettes

One primary principle of color choice is that colors come loaded with import. Colors have both cultural and natural associations that influence interpretation. If you choose a palette that intuitively fits expectations, the visualization will be easier to interpret. Palettes that go against the grain of expectation will cause endless frustration.

Color associations are firstly cultural and, as such, are subject to a certain amount of variation in cultural expectations. For example, in most business cultures (not least of which, finance), red signifies loss or bad, and green signifies gain or good. In military circles, red signifies enemies (also bad), but green signifies neutral parties, and blue indicates the good guys.

Table 16-1 lists a number of broad color associations to consider when mapping to data. Notice that one of the themes evident in this list is that although colors have cultural import, meanings are often rooted in natural associations.

Two important and related principles of color were alluded to in reference to red in Table 16-1. Firstly, colors have certain optical properties that make them more or less noticeable than others, and secondly, this depends a great deal on the color field surrounding it. Red is the most salient color on light-colored backgrounds, but the heat map of shipping traffic shown in Figure 16-10 shows how this changes on a black background. No legend is needed to know that green, yellow, and white are all clearly representing higher volumes. Your eye is naturally drawn to areas that are brightest.

TABLE 16-1: Common Mappings of Color

COLOR	MAPPINGS	COMMENT
Red	Loss, negative, alert, trouble, enemy, heat, volatility	Red has one of the most consistent set of expectations for meaning of any color in Western culture. It holds the status of being the most alarming and action-inducing of colors. Red is the color of blood, which is plenty alarming, but another likely explanation for the association has to do with how we see. Red is the most salient of colors on a common white background, making it the most likely to gain immediate attention. Fire and heat, as well as volatile and powerful forces, are also associated with red.
Orange, yellow	Highlight, warning	Orange and yellow are one and two steps down the heat scale from red and, as such, are most often used to indicate things that warrant attention once immediate fires, if any, are put out.
Light green	Gain, growth, health, impartiality	Green indicates growth and health, as well as impartiality in conflict. These are all things you might naturally associate with plant life, also green.
Cyan, blue	Positive action or force, selection, cold	Like green (or any cool color, for that matter), blue generally indicates reason for confidence. Unlike green, however, which suggests organic change, blue communicates controlled action. Blue is the color of uniformed officers. In computer interfaces, it is also the standard color of selection. Ice and cold are also associated with blue, and expressions like "ice in his veins" and "keeping her cool" would suggest a further connection with controlled action.

The shipping traffic visualization uses a spectrum of five hues spaced at perception-derived intervals and ordered by luminance, based on a concept from visualization and perception expert Colin Ware. This is actually a much truer representation of heat than a standard heat map would use. However, as you might imagine, white hot on a white background doesn't have quite the same effect as it does on black. In fact, clearly the effect is entirely opposite. Use of white or off-white backgrounds (the color of traditional paper) has had a great deal of influence over traditional palette choices.

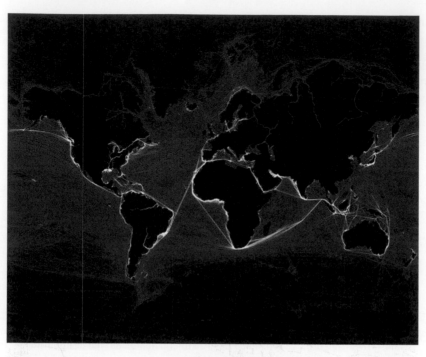

FIGURE 16-10: On a black background, this ship traffic map uses a luminance spectrum because brightness naturally demands attention, whereas on white, red stands out most.

Another principle closely related to optical properties making colors more noticeable is that different backgrounds (light or dark) perform better or worse in different mediums. White backgrounds are a better choice for paper, where pigments are applied for foreground elements. Dark backgrounds tend to perform a little better on computer screens, where light is invoked for foreground elements.

However, this is highly dependent on the quality of the display device. Dark backgrounds tend to perform poorly on a digital projector because the maximum luminance is so much lower that it becomes difficult to see small or thin objects below a certain level of brightness. There simply isn't enough strength in the light being pushed through such a small window. White backgrounds have a different issue with projectors in that the amount of bright white tends to wash out color depth, but the result is not a total loss. Because white backgrounds print better and have less catastrophic issues with display projection, it is often wiser to base a palette on a white or light background.

TIP

Start all palettes by first choosing a background color. Dark backgrounds work well on a computer screen. Visualizations with white backgrounds print better and do not suffer as badly from loss of small items when digitally projected, though color depth will be lost.

The last set of principles is about neutral colors, saturation, and brightness. *Color neutrality* is a spectrum, where grays are the most neutral of all. Gray plays an important role in visualization. Color in visualization is loaded with meaning, so unless a color is coded to information, it should generally be a shade of gray. Sometimes the meaning being encoded is neutral, in which case it should also be a shade of gray (for example, an unchanged value in the spectrum of loss and gain).

An important quality of neutral grays is that they are also visually recessive. They need to be quiet enough to let the important information sing. This need also applies to the use of colors to represent the information itself. The intensity of color needs to be applied judiciously based on the size of area that will be occupied by the color. Large swathes of full-intensity colors are like a room full of shouting people. Sensory overload makes it very difficult to perceive anything at all. Full-intensity colors should be used only in very small doses, if at all. Another aspect to keep in mind is that intensity maps intuitively to magnitude, so when color gradients are used, diminishing values should approach neutrality.

The *Hue, Saturation, Brightness (HSB)* model for color definition, also known as HSV (where V stands for Value), is the most useful of common color models. *Hue* is what we typically think of as color, the spectrum of the rainbow. *Saturation* is the degree of color, where a saturation of zero defines the grayscale spectrum. The *brightness* of a color is a range from black to full color.

Saturation of zero and brightness of one is white. A simple rule of thumb for a visualization with a white background is to lower saturation to approach neutrality, and for a dark background to lower brightness. This has the effect of blending more with the background color in each case. Decreasing opacity has exactly the same effect, except when translucent items also blend with other items that they overlap. Sometimes varying opacity is a better choice. But oftentimes, using saturation or brightness to achieve the same effect produces less confusion from color mixing that occurs from overlapping elements of different hues.

Brightness can be varied a bit on a white background, and saturation can be varied on a black background. But in either case, these should be close to full value when you encode information. Stay away from dark color sets on white, or pastels on black.

SUMMARY

Design is essential to getting the most relevant information out of data. The art of designing an effective graph, however, can seem like a mystical process with an overwhelming number of options. An understanding of core underlying principles of visualization design can go a long way toward demystifying the process and developing a framework for making design decisions.

Nodes are the most critical elements of a graph. Choosing the right shapes and size mappings are important factors in success. Symbols help significantly in bringing information to life. Links need to tell a story about nodes, not compete with them for attention. Principled choices of form and color will ensure that the visualization operates effectively.

Hopefully you have found inspiration in this chapter and the rest of this book as to how graph analysis can be applied in your business and to think creatively about graph forms when choosing the right solution. Applying the principles and approaches used in this book will help you make effective choices.

Graph analysis is a rapidly rising and evolving area of technology development for business. Many of the world's biggest and most innovative companies are invested in exploring the potential of this field. Enjoy experimenting with the current state of the art in open source graph tools, and look forward to exciting advances in product development to come.

GLOSSARY

Acyclic Graph

A graph that contains no cycles if links are followed from any node through any others.

Adjacency Matrix

A table where all nodes are assigned both a row and column, and a non-zero value in a cell represents a link between the row node and column node.

Adjacent Nodes

Two nodes that are directly linked.

Betweenness Centrality

A measure of the importance of a node reflecting the number of times it is involved in the shortest path between each of the nodes in a graph.

Bipartite Graph

A graph where one class of nodes only ever links to a second class of nodes, and vice versa. For example, in consumer purchase data, customers may connect only through common products, never directly to each other, and the same may apply for products.

Breadth-First Search (BFS)

An algorithm that starts with a node and traverses each adjacent node in turn before descending another degree out, until the target node or nodes are reached.

Centrality

The importance of a node in the graph based on its connections.

Chord Diagram

A graph visualization technique for data with asymmetric bidirectional flow where nodes are arranged in a circle and joined by bands of varying thickness at each end.

Clique

A subgraph where each node is connected to every other node in the subgraph.

Closeness Centrality

A specific computational measure of the importance of a node in a graph based on shortness of path distance to all other nodes. In this form of centrality, a node is most important if it can reach all other nodes in the shortest number of steps.

Clustering

Grouping by relative relatedness. Graph clustering is a specific class of clustering that evaluates links when computing relatedness.

Community

A cluster of closely connected nodes in a graph.

Decision Tree

A tree in which each node represents a decision, starting with the root node, and branches reflect criteria for following one path or another.

Degree

When used in the singular form, degree commonly refers to node degree, the count of link connections for a node. In plural form the term refers to path degree, meaning the number of steps out from a node to other nodes when following links.

Degree Centrality

A simple measure of the importance of a node in a graph based on the number of links it has.

Depth-First Search (DFS)

An algorithm that starts with a node and traverses each branch in turn as far as possible before backtracking and descending down to the next branch, until the target node or nodes are reached.

Directed Acyclic Graph (DAG)

A directed graph that contains no cycles (paths that link back to a node already on the path).

Directed Graph

A graph where links have direction (in other words, a start and end that would mean something different if reversed).

Disconnected Graph

A graph with two or more subgraphs that are not connected.

Edge

A relationship between nodes, typically represented with a line. An edge is more commonly known as a link.

Ego Network

The subgraph around a node consisting of its linked nodes and any links between them. An ego network can also be called a neighborhood. Ego networks may be defined by degrees.

Eigenvector Centrality

A specific computational measure of the importance of a node in a graph based on transitive influence. In this form of centrality, a node is most important if other important nodes link to it.

Force-Directed Layout

A class of graph layout that uses repelling forces between nodes and attracting forces along links to spatially cluster related nodes.

Incident Links

A link is incident to a node if it connects to it.

Isolated Node

A node with no links.

Leaf Node
A node with incoming links, but no outgoing links.

Link
A relationship between nodes, typically represented as a line. In graph theory, a link is more often referred to as an edge.

Loop
A link in which both the start and end are connected to the same node. Also known as self-loop.

Modularity
A measure of community strength, or, more often, a reference to the community-detection algorithm based on computation of that measure.

Network
Another name for a graph, where each node typically represents a physical entity, rather than something more abstract or conceptual.

Page Rank
A variant of Eigenvector Centrality that formed the foundation of Google's first search algorithm. Page Rank was used to weigh the relevance of a web page by the aggregate weight of other relevant web pages that linked to it. Despite the implication of the name, the algorithm can be used for any type of graph data to estimate the importance of nodes.

Path
A series of links traversed to reach one node from another.

Planar Graph
A graph that can be drawn without links crossing.

Neighborhood
The subgraph around a node consisting of its linked nodes and any links between them. In social networks, an ego network is a neighborhood. Neighborhoods may be defined by degrees.

Node
An entity (or "thing") linked to other entities (or things). In graph theory, a node is typically referred to as a vertex.

Sankey Diagram
A visualization technique where nodes are arranged in columns, and links of varying size flow in one side and out the other.

Self-Loop
A link in which both the start and end are connected to the same node.

Shortest Path
The minimal path or distance between two nodes.

Spanning Tree
A subgraph that includes all connected nodes but only the minimal set of links needed to connect them, thus forming a tree.

Spatial Network

A graph in which node locations reflect intrinsic spatial attributes of the elements represented, rather than relationships to other nodes.

Subgraph

A subset of nodes and links in a graph.

Tree

A graph that contains no circular paths and has only one path between any two nodes. A hierarchy is an example of a tree.

Undirected Graph

A graph in which link direction is not meaningful (such as links that represent mutual relationships like friendships).

Vertex

An entity (or "thing") linked to other entities (or things). A vertex is more commonly known as a node.

Weight

Weight refers abstractly to the strength or importance of a link or node relative to other links or nodes. Link weight typically maps directly from an underlying property of the relationship it represents, whereas node weight often maps from a derived measure like centrality. In both cases, weight is often normalized and is most often reflected visually by size.

INDEX

Printed and bound by CPI Group (UK) Ltd, Croydon, CR0 4YY
07/01/2022
03102768-0001